Investigating Difference

Investigating Difference

Human and Cultural Relations in Criminal Justice

The Criminal Justice Collective of Northern Arizona University

Allyn and Bacon

Boston ■ London ■ Toronto ■ Sydney ■ Tokyo ■ Singapore

0178783

Editor-in-Chief, Social Sciences: *Karen Hanson*
Series Editorial Assistant: *Karen Corday*
Marketing Manager: *Brooke Stoner*
Composition Buyer: *Linda Cox*
Manufacturing Buyer: *Megan Cochran*
Cover Administrator: *Jenny Hart*
Production Administrator: *Rosalie Briand*
Editorial-Production Service: *Spectrum Publisher Services*
Electronic Composition: *Cabot Computer Services*

Copyright © 2000 by Allyn and Bacon
A Pearson Education Company
160 Gould Street
Needham Heights, Massachusetts 02494

Internet: www.abacon.com

All rights reserved. No part of the material protected by this copyright notice
may be reproduced or utilized in any form or by any means, electronic or
mechanical, including photocopying, recording, or by any information storage
and retrieval system, without the written permission of the copyright owner.

ISBN 0-205-30205-X

Printed in the United States of America

10 9 8 7 6 5 4 3 2   04 03 02

Cover Illustration: The cover is a composite of symbols from a variety of cultural and
religious traditions: the four-direction symbol from a Navajo petroglyph; the Zen circle
(enso); the gay and lesbian triangle; the cross (from a number of cultures); and the pre-
revolutionary Chinese ideogram for sun and community.

For our Criminal Justice students,
past, present, and future.

CONTENTS

FOREWORD

Northern Arizona University (NAU) celebrates its centennial in 1999. This milestone marks a century of commitment to excellence in instruction and innovation in curriculum. Throughout its history, NAU has defined itself as a community that embraces equity, dignity, respect, and civility for everyone. President Clara Lovett states that, "valuing diversity involves accepting and appreciating individual differences and understanding that this diversity is a societal and organizational advantage." This value and expectation is a cornerstone of the Liberal Studies curriculum required of all students and appears as a central theme throughout curricula as diverse as the social sciences, forestry, education, business, and hotel and restaurant management.

There can be no more fitting tribute to this century-long tradition of respecting difference than the creation of *Investigating Difference: Human and Cultural Relations in Criminal Justice*. The authors, most of whom are faculty within Criminal Justice at NAU, have synthesized diverse perspectives on categories of difference and have elevated those definitions to a framework for political and social action. Consistent with their collective commitment to making a difference, all proceeds from the sale of this book will benefit educational and student projects within the department, and not the individual authors.

As a dean, I am proud to be a part of a college where investigating the impact of difference is not just an intellectual concept discussed in the classroom, but is also a value and behavior demonstrated every day by students and faculty. I watch students struggle with their desire to be alike and their wish to believe that difference is superficial and physical. I see them shed stereotypical beliefs about "the other" as their discussions encompass an ever-widening diversity of ideas, people, and experiences. And I see them confront the history and the present that may be part of the experience of people different from them.

Recently, a student came to me with tears in her eyes after a visit to a county jail. "I had been to jails before but for the first time I really saw the injustice. Most of the staff and managers were white males and the detainees were mostly ethnic minorities. What's this about?" she asked more than rhetorically.

Exploring difference in their classrooms and writing may be the first time some students really confront the consequences of difference, and the fact that someone else may have defined both the "difference" and the "consequence." They realize some categories may carry privilege, some responsibility, some burden, and some rejection. And they learn such consequences are not predetermined because perception of difference interacts with every individual's cognitive and emotional framework.

I see this struggle as they try to reconcile perception, physical evidence, and social construction. And often they cannot; yet they commit to the struggle. If students learn to appreciate difference as the experience of others, not just the appearance of others, they have taken important steps toward understanding injustice in a time of striving for justice.

Susanna Maxwell
Dean, College of Social and Behavioral Sciences
Northern Arizona University

ACKNOWLEDGMENTS

The development and writing of this book has been a remarkable exercise in collaboration and cooperation. It is a rare collective of faculty who can work together so well, and often so seamlessly. The creative energy that lies behind this endeavor is a hallmark of the Department of Criminal Justice at Northern Arizona University (NAU). Thus, our first offering of gratitude is to the department, including all those who contributed directly to this volume and all those who contributed indirectly through their support of our efforts. We would also like to acknowledge the contributions of Carole Mandino (NAU Institute for Gerontology), Cynthia Baroody Hart (University of San José, Administration of Justice Department), and Brian Smith (formerly of NAU Department of Criminal Justice, now at MSU–Bozeman, Department of Sociology and Anthropology). Without the support of Ray Michalowski and Marilyn McShane, successive chairs and contributors to the book, this project would not have developed as successfully as it did—Thank you! We also thank Susanna Maxwell, the Dean of the College of Social and Behavioral Sciences, for her support and encouragement of the book. This is reflective of her commitment to diversity initiatives throughout the College.

An integral part of every academic unit is, of course, its students. It was our students who first inspired this project. It is for them we developed it. In addition, many students played an active role in the production of the book. We are grateful to the many graduate student assistants who assisted with research, critiques, proofreading, and copy editing: Angela Ahrendt, Varvara Harvey, Kristin Jensen, Michael Muñoz, and Holly Vargas. We were delighted to discover that one of our students had remarkable artistic talent. Kathleen West, who was one of our undergraduate students when the project was conceived and is now entering our graduate program, created the cover art for the book. We were proud when Allyn & Bacon chose her design to represent our work.

In addition, a number of our undergraduate students supplied us with feedback. This was an important mechanism for ensuring that we were reaching our intended audience effectively. Many thanks to: Sara Aerne, Amy Barnes, Brandon Barr, Anthony Butch, Bridget Demosky, Heather Ferrall, Michael Fidone, Bryan Folger, Diane Fuluvaka, Roleio Grijalva, Dino Haley, Spencer Kerr, Daniel Latham, Julie Martin, Robert Mayhew, Ernie Montana, James Palmeri Jr., Jennifer Partin, Christina Pittman, Brianna Salley, Emily Schubert, Stephen Soli Jr., Jennifer Steele, Gregory Tully, and Amy Wilson. We also received helpful suggestions and comments from the manuscript reviewers: Sheryl J. Grana, University of Minnesota, Duluth; Bill Kelly, Auburn University; and Gregory Talley, Broome Community College.

We would have been slowed down considerably had it not been for our office staff: Jan Perez, Helena DeFina, Pamela Steen-Kurtz, and our student workers. We are especially grateful for the many pages of photocopying they did as we circulated successive drafts of all chapters. Thank you for making this so convenient for us!

Finally, we wish to thank Karen Hanson from Allyn & Bacon, whose enthusiasm for the book convinced us that Allyn and Bacon was the publisher for us and whose unfailing support and patience has made the project less arduous and more enjoyable.

We are pleased to tell you that all royalties from this book will go into a general fund for student scholarships and educational development.

PART ONE

Framing Difference

1 Introduction

Investigating Difference

MARIANNE O. NIELSEN

BARBARA PERRY

Let us look at one year as a microcosm of how the United States responds to difference. In this one year, difference was used as a valuable resource: John Glenn returned to space at the age of 77; Democrat Tammy Baldwin, who is openly lesbian, was elected to represent Wisconsin's Second District; and Daniel C. Tsui from Princeton won the Nobel Prize for Physics.

The United States is one of the most diverse countries in an increasingly diverse world. Improved transportation and communication systems have led to increased interaction, both temporary and permanent, with people seen as "Others." Immigrants, refugees, visiting students and business people, tourists—all have brought their differences to our country. We are also becoming more conscious of our long resident groups that are nonetheless considered different: Native Americans, Latino/as, African Americans, religious groups, the disabled, gays and lesbians, women, the elderly, the young. It is a relatively rare individual who cannot claim membership in one or more categories of difference.

Difference has been one of the great strengths of the United States in the past, and in our increasingly small world, has the potential to be our greatest strength in the future. Not that long ago in historical terms, the United States entered World World II to stop the mass killing of millions of people who were considered different—Jews, Gypsies, gays, and others who were not deemed sufficiently "Aryan" by the Nazi party. It is one of the great paradoxes of human nature that perceptions of difference can lead to fear and hate, terror and bloodshed, but perceptions of difference can also lead to strength and hope, discoveries and innovation, as different groups come together to stop the slaughter. Integral to ending that war were the Navajo Code Talkers, the (African American) Tuskegee Airmen, the 442nd Battalion of Japanese Americans who suffered 9,486 casualties (Takaki, 1989), and the women working, perhaps for the first time outside the home, in munitions factories and flying transport planes.

This strength based in difference is available to us not only in times of disaster and conflict, but every day: in scientific accomplishments by individuals as diverse as Albert Einstein (German American), Stephen Hawkins (disabled), Carolyn Shoemaker (female), Steven Chu (Asian American); in leadership by President John F. Kennedy (Catholic), President Franklin Delano Roosevelt (disabled), Justice Sandra Day O'Connor (female), Major Colin Powell (African American), César Chávez (Latino), Malcolm X (African American), and Nobel Peace Prize winner Elie Wiesel (Jewish); in economic development by such business leaders as Jerry Yang (Asian American), co-owner of Yahoo; Oprah Winfrey (African American), owner of one of the country's largest entertainment businesses; and William B. Fitzgerald, African American bank founder; and in the arts, with performers such as Denzel Washington and Spike Lee (African American), Celine Dion and Alanis Morrisette (French Canadian [and female]), Burning Sky and Carlos Nakai (Native American), Jimmy Smits and Gloria Estefan (Latino/a), k.d. lang and Anne Heche (lesbian), Christopher Reeve and Ray Charles (disabled), and so many others that all the pages of this book could be used just to list them. These people, of course, have many other identities than those by which they are identified here, and certainly, many of them are the rarest members of our society, the famous and the rich. We see them on the covers of magazines and profiled on television shows, but it is important to remember that these individuals had to work hard, often against great social odds, to win such honors. Most importantly, the knowledge, skills, experience, and talent they have provided to this country are representative of the human resources that are plentiful among the "ordinary" people perceived as different. As a society, we need the wisdom to see these groups as the resource they are, and ensure that they have equitable opportunities to participate and contribute for the benefit of us all.

We must recognize that we are united in our diversity. It is one of the traits that makes this country a relatively peaceful, healthy, and safe place to live. Arthur Solomon (1994:127), an Anishnabe Elder, teacher, and poet, states it elegantly in a passage from a poem about healing in Native communities:

Our strength is in our togetherness.
Our weakness is in our aloneness.
As long as we don't care about each other and for each other
we will all be alone and we will be destroyed one by one.

One of the objectives of this book is to present diversity as a resource to the criminal justice system, not as a problem to be solved, or a situation to be managed, or an inconvenience to be tolerated. It should be recognized and celebrated. This approach to dealing with diversity should be reinforced throughout our educational system. It can and should begin with our classrooms, which are as diverse as our society.

Support for diversity education is growing rapidly within the criminal justice field. Significant changes in student demographics, shifts in cultural values, and pressures from university administration and criminal justice agencies have led to criminal justice and criminology programs reviewing and revising their curricula. As a result, universities and colleges around the country are adding courses on topics such as gender, race and ethnicity, cultural diversity, and social inequalities (Nielsen and Stambaugh, 1998).

Northern Arizona University (NAU), we would like to think, is a leader in this movement. Even though criminal justice is a field still dominated by men, the number of women in the student body here at NAU is increasing. Also, our student body is 9% Latino/a, 6% Native American, 1.5% Asian American, and 1.4% African American (Nielsen and Stambaugh, 1998). This student body is a fairly good representation of the general population of the northern part of the state of Arizona. No doubt our student body is quite different from the student body at any other university. At NAU, we use this diversity as a resource. We have special events that celebrate films about and by women, we have an Institute for Native Americans, we have a Latin American Studies minor—just to name a very few of the programs, resources, and educational opportunities that are available to our students, faculty, and to the wider community(ies) that surround us. Our students in criminal justice use these resources to prepare themselves to be more effective criminal justice personnel. They learn Spanish or Navajo if they want to be police officers or lawyers in the Southwest, they take classes about women's issues to provide better services in domestic violence situations, they intern with Native Americans for Community Action (a social services organization) or any number of other community service groups to learn more about issues from the community's point of view.

In turn, we use the students' experiences and ideas about difference as teaching resources. Their family background, life experiences, and occasional resistance to valuing difference can all become part of our teaching tools when used with respect and sensitivity by their instructors (see Nielsen and Stambaugh, 1998). In a similar vein, difference can also be a resource for training academies, community colleges, and organizational training departments.

Difference is not just an educational resource; however, it is also a service resource. Personnel from diverse backgrounds bring knowledge and skills into an organization, to the job, that are becoming essential for effective service provision and good community–criminal justice system relations. Individuals with knowledge of cultural differences in attitudes toward authority, family structure, and communication styles; community leadership structures; and community issues are more likely to gain not only the cooperation of community members, but are also more likely to be able to protect the public and themselves.

In this one year, difference led to fear and death: Matt Shepherd, an openly gay student, was beaten and hung on a fence to die in Montana; Dr. Barnett Slepian was killed by a sniper in his home because he performed legal abortions in order to provide women with their legal reproductive rights; that James Byrd, Jr., an African American, was beaten, tied behind a car, and dragged to death by three members of a White Supremacist group.

There is a dark side to difference, in that it is feared and rejected by many groups and individuals. Their negative responses can vary from prejudice and avoidance to hate crimes such as lynchings, homicide, and other attempts at the physical extermination of the group.

The United States is a country that has reached a crossroads. We can accept, celebrate, and use difference as a resource as we have done so ably in the past, or we can use power, coercion, and hate to try to eradicate diversity from our country as many fundamentalist, militant, and radically conservative groups and individuals advocate—as happened this year in the examples listed previously. Unfortunately, the criminal justice system has often contributed to attacks on difference. In the past, for example, laws were used to exclude immigrant groups such as Jews and Japanese; they restricted the rights and justified the exploitation of African Americans and Native Americans; and they put women, gays and lesbians, and children "in their place"—that is, ensured they did not have the rights and protections granted to males, heterosexuals, or adults. Legislators cannot be given the whole blame, of course; police and courts enforced these laws, and the correctional system punished the transgressors. The criminal justice system is a powerful arm of the status quo. Its function is to ensure conformity to the laws. Sometimes, as members of groups perceived as different are well aware, the laws were unjust, and sometimes the criminal justice system went beyond enforcing conformity to the law to enforcing conformity to values and norms not regulated by law.

Legal changes began to gather momentum with the civil rights era and the criminal justice system began to change, too, although many would argue that the changes came with reluctance and resistance. It could be argued that a second change began within the criminal justice system in the late 1980s and early 1990s. Racism in the criminal justice system hit the 6 o'clock news with the videotaping of the beating of Rodney King. On the witness stand and again in prime time, Officer Mark Fuhrman of the Los Angeles Police Department proved racism was thriving within the ranks of the police force. The trial of O.J. Simpson split the country's view of criminal justice along black/white lines. The criminal justice system's historical role in the oppression of diverse groups once again became part of the public consciousness.

The criminal justice system is responsible for protecting and serving the public, yet justice professionals are sometimes not aware that this public has many different views on crime and the criminal justice system itself, based on history and their own life experiences. Rather than try unsuccessfully and with futility to coerce groups to conform and assimilate, a more effective and less traumatic alternative is to "coopt" difference, to use difference, to incorporate difference as a normal part of criminal justice.

In this one year, governments, organizations, and courts acted to protect differ-ence: New Orleans passed an ordinance that protected cross-dressers from harass-ment and intimidation; the American Civil Liberties Union filed suit against the Maryland State Troopers for using race-based profiling in stopping motorists ("Driving while Black"); the U.S. federal government mandated that hospital emergency rooms treat patients regardless of insurance status; and Arizona's former governor, Fife Symington, resigned because he was found guilty of six charges of bank and wire fraud totaling $23 million.

If we wish to celebrate and use our differences, then we must protect and defend them. To live up to this ideal of criminal justice service provision, differ-ence must become part of criminal justice educational and training curricula—not in token 2-hour modules, but woven into the tapestry of the whole curriculum. As Gould states later in this book (Chapter 17), diversity education and training must be required early and often throughout criminal justice careers. Diversity must become part of hiring and promotional criteria. It must become part of organiza-tional culture, leadership style, and management practices. It must become so all-encompassing that it becomes invisible.

Most of all, difference must be respected—in our families, in our work-places, and in our day-to-day interactions any place we find ourselves. As the centuries-old knowledge of Indigenous peoples tells us:

> Receive strangers and outsiders with a loving heart and as members of the human family. . . . All the races and tribes in the world are like the different coloured flowers of one meadow. All are beautiful. As chil-dren of the Creator they must all be respected. (Bopp *et al.*, 1988:82)

This book is our contribution to this essential effort.

This Book

In designing the book, we decided there would be three main "through-lines" that all the chapters would share. The first of these is that all issues are presented in historical context. This kind of historical approach is necessary because the present can only be understood as the product of the past. History teaches us that the social world is "two-sided"; we create it and we are created by it (Abrams, 1982). Both individual actions and the structures within which they occur must be investigated. We cannot understand current events in the criminal justice system, for example, without recognizing that they are the results of processes that hap-pen over time, and that these processes are shaped by the social and cultural con-texts within which they occur (Skocpol, 1984).

A second through-line is that the authors use a paradigm of power and powerlessness. As Wonders explains in Chapter 2, difference is a social construc-tion, and some groups within society have more power than others in defining who is different and who is not. Power, or lack of power, is one of the most important factors in defining how various groups will be treated by the criminal justice system. Based on their race, gender, age, or sexual orientation, will they face positive or negative discrimination, or no discrimination at all? Will they have the resources to "buy justice"? Or will they even understand the workings of the wheels of justice in motion?

The third through-line is that a balanced view must be taken of each diverse group so that each is discussed not only as offenders and victims, but that their contributions as service-providers, policy makers, and innovators are also recognized and discussed. The disciplines of Criminology and Criminal Justice have been guilty in the past of perpetuating stereotypes of dangerous minority offenders; passive female or elderly victims; tough, male police officers who form the "thin blue line." These are stereotypes because they are simplistic, inaccurate generalizations. A more realistic portrait is one of rich complexity as the criminal justice system interacts with all the diverse groups that comprise its environment and its internal human subsystems.

In keeping with the emphasis of the book on maintaining a balance in how we perceive the relationship between the criminal justice system and diverse groups, a final through-line is that the book identifies trends in how these various issues are being handled in innovative ways (see Part Three).

This book is divided into three main parts. Part One, Framing Difference, provides a theoretical and empirical framework for the discussions of the categories of difference that make up the majority of the book. This section begins with an overview of how difference is conceptualized within our society and more specifically within the criminal justice system in Chapter 2 by Wonders. Chapter 3, by Gould, describes the two main standards of "normal" within our society and within the justice system: being white and being male. Part Two describes the experiences of 12 diverse groups with the criminal justice system. It contains chapters on Native Americans (Nielsen, Chapter 4), immigrants (Perry, Chapter 5), African Americans (Smith, Chapter 6), Latino/as (Alvarez, Chapter 7), Asian Americans (Perry, Chapter 8), class (Michalowski, Chapter 9), women (Hackstaff, Chapter 10), gays and lesbians (Perry, Chapter 11), the elderly (Mandino, Chapter 12), youth (Ferrell, Chapter 13), special needs populations (Baroody Hart, Chapter 14), and religious groups (Perry, Chapter 15).

Part Three presents four chapters on important strategic trends in dealing with difference. There are chapters on diversity in criminal justice employment (McShane, Chapter 16), cultural diversity training (Gould, Chapter 17), intercultural and interpersonal communication (Nielsen, Chapter 18), and the relationship between crime workers and crime victims (Morgan and Perry, Chapter 19). In the concluding chapter, the many strategies presented throughout the book of social and political action that various diverse groups have developed to further their equality within the criminal justice system, are woven together (Perry and Nielsen, Chapter 20).

This outline hints at two of the important strengths of this book. The first is that this book presents a perspective on the relationship between difference and the criminal justice system that is "outside the box" usually presented in criminal justice and criminology courses. Although groups based on race, ethnicity, and gender are important parts of the discussion, so are groups such as the disabled, religious minorities, and the elderly, who are often mentioned only in passing in more traditional courses on diversity and criminal justice. Second, the authors of these chapters, in the majority of cases, are scholars active in carrying out research agendas on the groups they write about, or are teachers of courses on difference and criminal justice. At NAU, this book will be used in a required senior under-graduate course called "Human and Cultural Relations in the Criminal Justice System" (CJ 345) taught at this point by Wonders, Nielsen, and Perry.

Related to this is another important strength. Many of the first drafts of these chapters were reviewed and commented upon by students in CJ 345, meaning that this book is very likely to be responsive to the needs of our students. In addition, we have also had discussions with various criminal justice agencies throughout Arizona about the kinds of resources they would like to see available to their personnel. Their needs are also reflected in the content of this book.

References

Abrams, P. (1982). *Historical sociology*. West Compton House: Open Books.

Bopp, J., Bopp, M., Brown, L., and Lane, P. (1988). *The sacred tree, special edition*. Lethbridge, AB: Four Worlds Development.

Nielsen, M. O. and Stambaugh, P. M. (1998). Multiculturalism in the classroom: Discovering difference from within. *Journal of Criminal Justice Education*, 9/2, 281–291.

Skocpol, T. (1984). Sociology's historical imagination. In T. Skocpol (ed.), *Vision and method in historical sociology*, pp. 1–2. Cambridge: Cambridge University Press.

Solomon, A. (1994). *Eating bitterness: A vision beyond the prison walls*. Toronto: NC Press.

Takaki, R. (1989). *Strangers from a different shore: A history of Asian Americans*. New York: Penguin.

2 Conceptualizing Difference

NANCY A. WONDERS

Despite the critical role that difference plays within the criminal justice system, it is rare for either practitioners or scholars to spend time investigating difference. It is often taken for granted that the differences between people are natural and obvious and, therefore, uncontroversial. Yet, little about difference is actually either natural or obvious. And difference is far from uncontroversial. Since the late 1980s, there has been an explosion of work on difference and identity. This scholarly work has highlighted the complex nature of difference; it also contains lessons that are invaluable for those seeking to understand the place of difference within the criminal justice system.

In this chapter, I outline some of the important insights about difference that have emerged from the contemporary literature on difference and identity. My objectives are to explore the complexity of "difference" as a topic of study, to forge conceptual links between the concept of difference and justice issues, and to introduce some of the common themes regarding difference that are contained in the chapters that follow. The subsections that follow offer answers to these questions: What is difference, and where does it come from? Why do some differences matter while others do not? What is the relationship between law and difference? Why study difference within the field of criminal justice?

Difference Is Socially Constructed

Most people think that the most important differences between individuals are fundamentally biologically based. Race, ethnicity, sexual orientation, gender, age, and even social class are frequently viewed as inherited traits—what sociologists call "ascribed characteristics." In this view, people are "black" because they were born with dark skin; "white" because their skin is lighter in color. People are designated "female" or "male" because they are born with female or male genitalia. What is most interesting about biology, however, is not how different we all are from each other, but rather how remarkably similar most people are in both design and function.

Indeed, the biological differences that do exist between people rarely matter in themselves; instead, they are made to matter through the process of social interaction. To say that difference is socially constructed, then, is to say that the meaning attached to difference, including biological difference, is created by people in interaction with each other. From this perspective, difference is a social process that can only be understood historically, contextually, and culturally. To reiterate an earlier point, "difference" is the term used to describe the social and cultural *meanings* attached to human variation.

Of course, there are biological differences between us. Some people have larger noses, smaller feet, larger breasts, or lighter skin. However, biological differences do not come with instructions telling us how to deal with or respond to them. In fact, if biology were destiny, we probably would not spend so much time and money dressing our boys in blue and our girls in pink, because boys would be "naturally" masculine and girls "naturally" feminine, regardless of the color of their clothes or other markers used to signify their sex to the rest of the world. Nor would Jews have been made to wear yellow stars during World War II so that they could be identified easily. Nor would we emphasize the importance of eating certain kinds of traditional foods or engaging in particular cultural celebrations. Instead, we put enormous energy into constructing and enforcing gender, ethnic, sexual orientation, race, and other differences as a kind of insurance against "nature." Race, ethnicity, social class, sexual orientation, even age reflect the *meaning* we give them rather than natural facts about our biology. Some additional examples may help to illustrate this point.

Today, it is frequently assumed that women are naturally more interested than men in fashion and beauty, and that these interests are associated with femininity and femaleness. It is important to remember, however, that in Victorian England, it was men who wore wigs, high heels, stockings, and frilly blouses. Instead of exhibiting femininity, this set of differences was strongly associated with masculinity and power. Only "real men" wore wigs! Biology is clearly not destiny. In fact, some scholars (Caulfield and Wonders, 1993; Belknap, 1996) find it useful to make a distinction between biological "sex" and "gender": "sex" refers to human variations in genitalia and reproductive abilities (which have relatively limited consequences because reproduction directly affects only a small portion of the human life cycle), whereas "gender" refers to the social characteristics that have come to be loosely associated with sex (e.g., femininity and masculinity). Sexual variation exists, but it is the meaning that is made out of that variation through the construction of gender that has the greatest consequence for individual life chances. Thus, children must be taught how to act in gender-appropriate ways. The behaviors associated with each gender, however, have changed over time as society has changed, and are not determined by biological differences. History reveals that:

> Sex categorization involves no well-defined set of criteria that must be satisfied to identify someone; rather, it involves treating appearances (e.g., deportment, dress, and bearing) as if they were indicative of an

underlying state of affairs (e.g., anatomical, hormonal, and chromosomal arrangements). The point worth stressing here is that, while sex category serves as an "indicator" of sex, it does not depend on it. Societal members will "see" a world populated by two and only two sexes, even in public situations that preclude inspection of the physiological "facts." Gender, we argue, is a situated accomplishment of societal members, the local management of conduct in relation to normative conceptions of appropriate attitudes and activities for particular sex categories. From this perspective, gender is not merely an individual attribute but something that is accomplished in interaction with others. (West and Fenstermaker, 1995:20–21)

In other words, we are all constantly "doing gender" (West and Zimmerman, 1987) by acting in ways that signal to others how we ought be categorized and by reacting to others in ways that define them as "male" or "female." We "do" gender everyday by dressing, sitting, talking, and acting in ways that create and reinforce gendered patterns of behavior. In fact, we are often confused and bothered by individuals who do not act consistently with our own expectations of appropriate "female" or "male" behavior. We may also be troubled by individuals whose dress or physical features seem inconsistent with their gendered behavior; for example, women who are unusually tall or men who are unusually petite. Indeed, such inconsistencies have often led to prejudice and discrimination against individuals in the justice system and in the larger society for their failure to communicate their sex and gender "appropriately" and consistently with dominant expectations (Kruttschnitt, 1984).

Similarly, it was often assumed historically that "race" reflected biological differences between people. Yet the anthropological evidence is clear that race is not a biological difference; there are no genetic markers that clearly differentiate where "white" or "black" begins. Instead, race is a social construction, given meaning by people in the context of social interaction (Brown, 1998; Kendall, 1997; Omi and Winant, 1994). Pieter-Dirk Uys (1988), a satirist from South Africa, illustrates this well in the following remarks, which appeared in the *New York Times:*

Let me quote from one of our few remaining daily newspapers, the Government Gazette: "Nearly 800 South Africans became officially members of a different race group last year, according to figures quoted in Parliament and based on the Population Registration Act. They included 518 colored who were officially reclassified as white, 14 whites who became colored, 7 Chinese who became white, 2 whites who became Chinese, 3 Malays who became white, 1 white who became an Indian, 50 Indians who became colored, 54 coloreds who became Indian, 17 Indians who became Malay, 4 coloreds who became Chinese, 1 Malay who became Chinese, 89 blacks who became colored, 5 coloreds who became black." I couldn't make it up if I tried.

This clip illustrates the flexible nature of race, depending on who is doing the defining. Stuart Hall (as cited in Scott, 1995:6) personalizes this in the following:

> The fact is "black" has never been just there either. It has always been an unstable identity, psychically, culturally, and politically. It, too, is a narrative, a story, a history. Something constructed, told, spoken, not simply found. People now speak of the society I come from in totally unrecognizable ways. Of course Jamaica is a black society, they say. In reality, it is a society of black and brown people who lived for three or four hundred years without ever being able to speak of themselves as "black." Black is an identity which had to be learned and could only be learned in a certain moment. In Jamaica that moment is the 1970s.

Race as a category of meaning can be changed to fit changing circumstances. Like gender, the meaning of race is constructed through human interaction. Ethnicity is similar in this regard, as evidenced by the historical process by which immigrants to the United States, particularly non-Hispanic whites, were able to transform themselves from Italian, Irish, or Japanese ethnic groups into "Americans" (Alba, 1990), and more specifically into "white" Americans (Frankenberg, 1993). That racial and ethnic identities reflect a long process of historical construction is further evidenced by the fact that our own sense of identity often does not correspond to our appearance. Thus, "a National Center for Health Statistics study found that 5.8 percent of the people who called themselves 'Black' were seen as 'White' by a census interviewer. Nearly a third of the people identifying themselves as 'Asian' were classified as 'White' or 'Black' by independent observers. That was also true of 70 percent of people who identified themselves as 'American Indians'" (Wright, 1998).

Even social class differences cannot be explained merely by external variation in wealth or income. Social class is also a social construction that must be learned in interaction with others, and is evidenced through barometers such as material success and social location in the economic system, but also by the presence or absence of particular styles of speech, behaviors, and attitudes. Donna Langston (1995:112) argues that "class is also culture":

> Class is how you think, feel, act, look, dress, talk, move, walk; class is what stores you shop at, restaurants you eat in; class is the schools you attend, the education you attain; class is the very jobs you will work at throughout your adult life. We experience class at every level of our lives; class is who our friends are, where we live and work even what kind of car we drive, if we own one, and what kind of health care we receive, if any. Have I left anything out? In other words, class is socially constructed and all encompassing. When we experience classism, it will be because of our lack of money (i.e., choices and

power in this society) and because of the way we talk, think, act, move—because of our culture.

Because class is cultural, individuals who are poor have a difficult time becoming middle class even when they obtain more money. Being middle class means learning how to "act" middle class—to "walk the walk" and "talk the talk." Growing up poor creates a distinct cultural disadvantage given that "proper" behavior, dress, and linguistic style in much of the world of work and within the criminal justice system is determined by those from higher social classes. Research has found that individuals who violate expectations of "proper" behavior during encounters with the police are much more likely to be arrested (Wordon and Shepard, 1996). Indeed, there is a well-documented history of discrimination against lower-class individuals within the criminal justice system, beginning with the creation of laws specifically designed to control the "dangerous classes" (Gordon, 1994; Michalowski, 1985) and affecting virtually every stage of the criminal justice system (Parenti, 1995). As Michalowski illustrates later in this volume, the price for class differences can be high.

As these examples illustrate, the construction of difference reflects a historical process of human interaction and negotiation. All differences have a cultural component that carries enormous weight in shaping attitudes and behavior. In this sense, it may matter more who others "think" we are than who we "really" are. This is a particularly important point for justice workers. Police officers may think of themselves as caring citizens trying to help others, but this matters little if citizens "think" police officers are "pigs" and, therefore, act toward them with hostility. A young man wearing baggy pants and a bandanna may think of himself as a hardworking student, loving son, or good friend, whereas others consider him to be only a gangbanger. Being regarded as "black" or "white," "gay" or "straight," or "female or male" carries the weight of the culture behind it. For this reason, it is important to realize that saying that difference is socially constructed is not the same thing as saying that individuals construct their own identities. We each have some control over how we are viewed in the world, but the identity choices available to us are limited by our culture, the historical time period we are born into, and where in the society we are located. You might think of yourself as without a race or gender, for example, but try getting everyone else to treat you that way and see how far you get!

Understanding that difference is socially constructed is a critical first step toward ensuring justice in a democratic society. We all bear some responsibility for the differences between us and for the real consequences those differences have for human lives. It is especially important for those who work in the justice system to understand the role they play in giving differences meaning and making some differences matter. It is crucial that those who use differences as the basis of discretionary decision making do so responsibly and with an appreciation of the way that they are helping to create and maintain differences at the same time that they are reacting to them.

Difference Assumes a Norm or Standard That Reflects Power Relations within the Culture

Because differences are socially constructed through a process of human interaction, power plays an important role in determining how differences are defined and which differences matter. Not surprisingly, some people have more power to define differences than do others. In general, history evidences a process whereby those with greater power become the standard of comparison against whom everyone else is measured. It is through this process that difference comes to have meaning.

> The characteristics and attributes of those who are privileged group members are described as societal norms—as the way things are and as what is normal in society. This normalization of privilege means that members of society are judged, and succeed or fail, measured against the characteristics that are held by those privileged. The privileged characteristic is the norm; those who stand outside are the aberrant or "alternative." (Wildman, 1996:14)

Indeed, difference can only exist where there is a norm or standard against which everyone else is compared. Difference always implies a contrast, and frequently it depends on the construction of a dichotomy. Therefore, we can only understand the concept "man" by understanding the concept "woman." We can only understand "black" because we can conceptualize "white." As Cornell West writes (1995:162):

> Social theory is what is needed to examine and *explain* the historically specific ways in which "Whiteness" is a politically constructed category parasitic on "Blackness," and thereby conceive of the profoundly hybrid character of what we mean by "race," "ethnicity" and "nationality." For instance, European immigrants arrived on American shores perceiving themselves as "Irish," "Sicilian," "Lithuanian" and so on. They had to learn that they were "White" principally by adopting an American discourse of positively valued Whiteness and negatively charged Blackness. This process by which people define themselves physically, socially, sexually and even politically in terms of Whiteness or Blackness has much bearing not only on constructed notions of race and ethnicity but also on how we understand the changing character of US nationalities.

West goes on to articulate the ways that other differences are similarly constructed via the development of binary opposites, such as male/female and heterosexual/homosexual. Over time, these dichotomies come to take on a life of their own—to seem "natural," even biologically based. Yet social scientists have provided compelling evidence that virtually all human variations fall along a continuum rather than into two (or more) discrete boxes. People are not "black" or "white," but instead exhibit a huge range of skin colors, making racial designations based on skin color exceedingly arbitrary (Brown, 1998). People are not just "heterosexual" or "homosexual," because a large number of individuals have same-gender sexual experiences at some point during their lives without ever considering themselves gay or lesbian (Duberman, 1986). Similarly, biological genitalia and body function provide a relatively weak basis for dichotomizing gender, because physical variation, even on such narrow criteria as breast size, the capacity for menstruation, and the size of one's external genitalia, vary widely among humans and over the life course (Orobio de Castro, 1993).

Dividing social reality into dichotomies is not just inaccurate, it can have very harmful consequences. This is especially true when one half of the dichotomy is valued while the other half is devalued, a tendency that is all too common. The destructive impact of this devaluation has been well documented in research, such as that conducted by Thomas and Hughes (1986:839), which found that being black was associated with a lowered sense of psychological well-being and quality of life—in their words, being black implies "a less positive life experience than being white." Another example of this devaluation can be found in research on girls (Miedzian, 1991). The internalization of these negative values also has adverse consequences for justice in the United States. Some scholars, for example, argue that citizen perceptions that justice workers regard women and people of color as second-class citizens may reduce reliance on the police by the very groups most likely to experience certain kinds of personal victimization (Russell, 1998; Buchwald, Fletcher, and Roth, 1993).

Dichotomizing differences into two parts or groups, then, does not mean that each part is viewed as equal. Not only is one group often devalued, but the other, more privileged group typically comes to be viewed as somehow more "normal" and, therefore, less worthy of study. In general, we have a tendency to focus on only one portion of the dichotomy when discussing difference. The more powerful and privileged group often remains invisible. When we discuss "race," most people assume we are only talking about people of color. When the issue of "gender" is raised, people assume it is a women's issue. However, to the extent that a society divides people into categories, then *everyone* is subject to the impact of categorization. Some people benefit, some do not, but everyone is affected.

In this volume, the authors have chosen to devote relatively more time to description and analysis of groups within the United States that have historically been disadvantaged and marginalized within our culture and within the justice system. The enlarged attention to these groups is regarded as a needed anecdote to the lack of attention to these groups within the criminal justice literature. However, the chapters that follow also investigate and problematize the behavior of those groups who have historically been privileged by justice practices in the United States. We believe that issues of difference do not belong to only one group; they are human issues that ought to concern us all.

Difference Matters

Although the meanings attached to differences are socially constructed (rather than natural or biological), once differences are created they have real consequences for human lives and for the justice system. Because difference construction is a historical process, the place and time period into which we are born will have a lot to do with defining which characteristics will matter to the larger society. To be born with dark skin in the United States means something different today than it did during most of the 1800s, when slavery was commonplace. Those born without eyesight earlier in the twentieth century had significantly different life chances than those born without eyesight today. Yet in every case, once society has decided that a particular characteristic or set of characteristics warrants differential treatment, those viewed as having those characteristics have a difficult time escaping categorization, prejudice, and discrimination.

Categorization is the process by which society decides which individuals fit into the boxes used to create difference (Wildman, 1996). Once categories are created and given significant societal consequence, it becomes extremely important to decide who fits into which category. That is why so many individuals in South Africa had their race changed—different racial categories are linked to different privileges and opportunities in South African society. It is also why we work so hard to be sure that "boys will be boys" (Miedzian, 1991). Research has evidenced that males experience greater privilege in our society in numerous areas, including in employment, education, and economic opportunity.

Part of what should be clear by now is that we do not simply "choose" to be female or male, Hispanic or Asian, and so on. Once society has created categories, enormous effort goes into forcing people into one category or another. This process of categorization helps to ensure that differences will continue to matter from generation to generation. As shown later in this chapter, the criminal justice system has played an active role in defining and maintaining differences in our society, especially by way of the law.

Two other processes that help to ensure the continuation of difference are prejudice and discrimination. Prejudice and discrimination are different although related phenomena. Prejudice is set of beliefs and attitudes about people based on their group membership. Stereotyping is closely linked to prejudice and helps reinforce it. Stereotypes are based on the assumption that all individuals who belong to a particular group share the same characteristics. It is important to point out that stereotypes and prejudices can be "good" or "bad" in intent, but they are much more often bad than good in their consequences. For example, it may be that Asian Americans are stereotyped as being especially good at academics (presumably a "good" trait), but this assumption can be devastating for the Asian American youth who does not fit the stereotype, even though it is an apparently positive stereotype. While prejudice is a set of attitudes about individuals and the groups they belong to, discrimination is a *behavior* whereby individuals are treated adversely because of their group membership. Discrimination serves to privilege some characteristics over others by linking particular characteristics with either positive or negative consequences. Prejudice ensures that those on one side of the dichotomies we create—male/female, dark/light, straight/gay—are viewed as "less than" those on the other end. Discrimination is the behavioral component of prejudice. When people discriminate, they act toward others in positive or negative ways based on real or imagined group membership.

Although some people argue that people are discriminated against because they are different, it is more plausible to argue that people come to be viewed as "different" because they are discriminated against. As Scott (1995:6) writes: "difference and the salience of different identities are produced by discrimination, a process that establishes the superiority or atypicality or particularity of others." Because privilege and opportunity often result in greater power in the society, it is in the interests of those who are privileged by the construction of difference to perpetuate differences so that they, their children, and others like them can continue to receive disproportionate benefit. Said differently, while we all want to avoid the negative consequences attached to prejudice and discrimination, at the same time we desire the advantages offered to us by our privileged statuses; thus, there is a built-in incentive to try to maintain categories that privilege some rather than others. In Wildman's (1996:12–13) words: "When we discuss race, sex, and sexual orientation, each needs to be described as a power system that creates privilege in some people as well as disadvantages in others. Most of the literature has focused on disadvantage or discrimination, ignoring the element of privilege. To really talk about these issues, privilege must be made visible." The implication of this is that the power attached to difference can be reduced by eliminating the discriminatory and/or privileging effects attached to difference. Merely having blue eyes rather than brown eyes is a difference that does not "matter" because neither privilege nor negative consequences accrue to those with different eye colors. Other differences might matter less if we could successfully alter the dichotomous nature of the rewards attached to them.

In the chapters that follow, the authors explore the ways that difference matters within the criminal justice system, for offenders, victims, and for justice professionals. The impact of power, privilege, prejudice, stereotyping, and discrimination on the administration of justice is explored for a wide range of social groups. Importantly, strategies for reducing the adverse consequences associated with difference are also discussed.

Law Plays a Critical Role in Creating and Maintaining Difference; It Can Also Be Used to Ameliorate the Negative Consequences of Difference

Historically and contemporarily, law has played a central role in the construction and maintenance of difference. In some cases it is obvious that law works to categorize people in ways that artificially construct difference. One good example is age. Everyone is one age or another, but the social meaning attached to age has varied over time and from culture to culture (Cunningham, 1995; Archard, 1993). Less than 100 years ago in the United States, children were expected to take on the responsibilities of adulthood as soon as they were able. Until relatively recently, people of all ages worked in factories or farms, performing the work of society. This is still true in many cultures and indeed in some neighborhoods in the United States.

Childhood as a separate category does not exist "naturally." The meaning of childhood must be created, and this is often accomplished through legal mechanisms, such as the creation of laws regarding the age of majority. In the United States, the age of majority has fluctuated over time, ranging since the early 1970s between the age of 18 and 21; those younger than this age were considered to be "children" under the law, with limited rights and responsibilities. The arbitrary nature of this boundary is highlighted by the contradictions it creates, such as the fact that individuals 18 years old cannot drink alcohol but can be tried as an adult in a court of law or drafted into military service. The definition of childhood and the rights and responsibilities attached to that definition also vary cross-culturally (Archard, 1993). For example, in the United States, a 17-year-old can drive but not drink alcohol (although this is changing in some states such as Michigan, which has raised the driving age to 18), whereas in many European countries, such as the Netherlands, the opposite is true—young people are able to drink well before they gain the privilege of driving.

The meaning attached to race and ethnicity has also been shaped by the law. During the period of slavery, the United States developed a law saying that individuals with even one drop of black blood were to be considered black (Doob, 1999; Davis, 1996). Similarly, laws passed to define who constituted an American Indian rested on "blood quantum" or "degree of Indian blood," a measure that became useful in reducing the official number of Native Americans. At the turn of the twentieth century, this standard facilitated the federal government's strategy of forced assimilation for American Indians via land seizure and acceptance of the ideology of private property (versus collectively held property). Land seized was reallocated to individuals; "each Indian identified as being those documentably of *one-half or more Indian blood*, was entitled to receive title in fee of such a parcel; all others were simply disenfranchised altogether" (Jaimes, 1992). Today, federal laws continue to set standards that define who may be considered a member of a particular Native American tribe. The consequences of this definitional and legal power are captured in the following remarks by Limerick (1987:338): "Set the blood quantum at one-quarter, hold it to a rigid definition of Indians, let intermarriage proceed as it had for centuries, and eventually Indians will be defined out of existence. When that happens, the federal government will be freed of its persistent 'Indian problem.'" As these examples illustrate, law plays a critical role in defining difference.

Law also plays an important role in maintaining differences once they are created and helps to ensure that differences will "matter." For example, when one man hits another man, this behavior may be prosecuted as assault in every state. However, if a husband hits his wife, in most states this behavior is defined as "domestic violence." Not only does the phrase "domestic" make the violence sound less serious, but extensive research has evidenced that the designation of violence between intimates as a "disturbance" rather than an "assault" slows police response, reduces the likelihood of arrest, and reduces penalties if the perpetrator is convicted (see Belknap, 1996, for a review of this literature). This differential treatment of women's harms reinforces the differences between men and women and helps to ensure that the category "woman" will be less valued than the category "man." Historically, legal restrictions on voting rights, marriage rights and property rights for women, certain racial and ethnic groups, children, the differently abled, and for individuals with particular sexual preferences have helped to ensure that socially constructed differences privilege some and disadvantage others.

A great deal of scholarly work has explored the link between law and difference. This work has evidenced the way that law has been used to maintain and perpetuate ageism (Ferrell, 1993), racism (Russell, 1998), ethnic discrimination (Alvarez, 1997), gender discrimination (Caulfied and Wonders, 1993), classism (Michalowski, 1985), homophobia (Herek and Berrill, 1992), and other differences between people as well. Some of this work is drawn on in the chapters that follow.

It is important to point out that law is not just a vehicle for creating and maintaining difference; it can also be used to ameliorate the negative consequences associated with difference in our society. It is evident that law served to restrict the rights of huge segments of the U.S. population when the country was founded. For example, when the Constitution was written, those who did not own property, women, and people of color were all precluded from voting in the newly created "democracy" (Parenti, 1995). However, the law has also been used to extend rights to groups formerly disenfranchised. Although some would argue that law is a limited method for creating social change, because it may not change deeply held attitudes and beliefs, it can provide important protections to those who experience inequality (Minow, 1997). As Martin Luther King, Jr. (as cited in Ayers, 1993:135) said: "The law cannot make an employer love an employee, but it can prevent him from refusing to hire me because of the color of my skin. The habits, if not the hearts of people, have been and are being altered by legislative acts, judicial decisions, and executive orders."

Although efforts to use the law as an instrument of social change are often controversial, it is clear that laws and policies like affirmative action, busing, and hate crime legislation will continue to have an important impact on the meanings and consequences attached to difference in our society. For this reason, throughout the book substantial attention is devoted to the role of law in promoting social changes and ensuring greater justice.

Differences Overlap One Another

For the most part, the chapters in this book address difference by describing the historical and contemporary experiences of particular social groups in our society: African Americans, religious minorities, women, lesbians and gays, and so forth. Yet, identity is a complex construct for most people. Although it is possible to talk generically about "women" or "Hispanics" or "heterosexuals," most people would deny that their membership in a single group defines who they are as individuals. People differ from one another in many ways and they belong to many groups simultaneously. Too little work within the field of criminal justice has considered the importance of this social reality. Most of the work that has been done to understand difference within the justice system analyzes only one difference at a time, focusing on race *or* gender *or* social class. Only recently has research been conducted that tries to analyze more complex relationships between differences. A sample of this research highlights the complex way that differences intersect with one another to shape our experience of justice.

For example, it is often believed that women are treated more leniently within the criminal justice system than are men. However, work by Daly (1989a,b) has suggested that their lenient treatment at the time of sentencing may be due to the fact that women are more often caretakers of small children than are men. In fact, in Daly's research, men who cared for small children were also treated more leniently by judges who realized that imprisoning parents with dependent children would ultimately cost the state more (because children would have to be cared for by the state) and would punish the children as well. This research is just one example of a new wave of research trying to explore difference in more complex ways.

It is important to appreciate that differences cannot just be added together to yield individual identities. Understanding the experience of "blacks" in the justice system and then analyzing the experience of "women," is not the same thing as understanding the experience of "black women." Similarly, men are never just "men" or "children" just "children"—they always occupy other categories simultaneously.

Still, most of the research and practice of criminal justice separates groups into distinct categories. The organization of this book uses these groupings as a heuristic device for exploring differences. However, to the extent that it is possible, each chapter touches on some of the ways that differences overlap to affect justice experiences and outcomes as a way to remind readers that lived experiences are always a product of unique intersections between individual biographies and the larger social world.

Differences and Their Consequences Can Be Changed

Perhaps the most hopeful aspect of studying difference is realizing that because differences are constructed by people, they can be changed by people. However, this is often more easily said than done. Even if we choose to live as though our race, or sex, or ethnicity are irrelevant to who we are, these characteristics will still

be important in our lives if the rest of the world links arrest decisions, employment decisions, educational opportunities, and so on, to our membership in certain groups. In other words, attitudinal change toward difference is often very
difficult to achieve in the short run; constructing difference differently often requires a great deal of patience. However, changing behavior is often easier to accomplish. We may not be able to easily change how others will perceive us, but
we can restrict their ability to use differences as a basis for discrimination. Those
who work in the justice system have a special obligation to ensure that their behavior promotes justice rather than injustice.

Some people today claim that focusing on differences is actually part of the
problem because dividing the world into separate groups—even for analytic purposes—reinforces the differences further. This is a serious danger. When we
study "race" or "ethnicity" we make them "real" for the purpose of our study.
When we divide people into "Hispanic" or "female" or "white" groups, we give
the meaning attached to group membership greater weight. However, an even
more serious risk occurs when differences that have real consequences are ignored. This is a risk criminal justice professionals cannot afford to take. For instance, claiming that race does not "really" exist in nature does little to help us
explain why the majority of those incarcerated in U.S. jails and prisons are people
of color (Donziger, 1996). For those who work daily in justice occupations, misunderstanding or ignoring difference can be a matter of life and death. Assuming
that the only danger in our society comes from people who look a certain way
may make us vulnerable to those who do not fit the stereotype. Much research,
for example, has shown that the crime engaged in by white-collar and corporate
offenders is far more harmful to the public than the crime committed by traditional street offenders (see Reiman, 1996, for a review of this literature). Partly because white-collar offenders do not fit our stereotypic image of the "criminal," we
have failed to respond effectively to a wide range of extremely harmful behavior,
including environmental pollution, consumer fraud, and occupational injury.
This is a mistake that can only be remedied by careful attention to the construction of difference and the consequences of privileging some groups over others
within a democratic society.

Part of what makes talking about difference so difficult to do is that there is
a tendency to assume that creating differences must be a bad thing. Yet it is too
simplistic to say, "Let's just do away with difference!" Indeed, if we could do
away with difference, the world would be an extremely boring place. The problem is not with difference *per se*; the difficulty arises in the meaning we make out
of difference. It is not a problem that some people have lighter skin and some
darker, or that some people hold one set of religious beliefs but not another. The
problem is that some societies treat those with one set of characteristics or beliefs
as valuable and one set as less worthwhile. It is this process of giving meaning to
and placing value on differences that requires our attention. This is especially
critical within the criminal justice system.

Ultimately, the goal of studying difference within the criminal justice system is to ensure that, as a democratic society, we do not penalize people for the

0178783

differences they exhibit and that we create a justice system that does more to foster human diversity rather than to constrain it. Indeed, it is our job to protect the rich diversity of groups that live in the United States and to guarantee that justice is available to all. The authors of this book recognize that this can be difficult to accomplish on a practical level. The goals of the justice system are often contradictory, and there is no clear standard of "fairness" with which we all agree. Too often, justice practitioners lack the knowledge and skills needed to ensure that justice prevails in an increasingly multicultural society. Surely, one book cannot analyze, let alone overcome, all of the problems associated with "difference" in the criminal justice system. However, we do hope that this book, by investigating how identity and difference affects the justice process, will provide a useful starting point for those committed to creating a just society. Minow's (1997:157) words eloquently summarize our intent:

> Identity politics ties us in knots. Yet even without unity in the sense of a single, shared American identity, the peoples of this nation can recognize and deepen ties, sufficient to enhance self-governance. Those ties are enlivened by the paradoxes of our shared experiences as unique individuals with varieties of affiliations. We have all made differences matter; we all must sense freedoms for self-invention would help. Promoting daily contact across lines of differences in schools, jobs, and communities would strengthen the kind of ties that permit a solidarity sufficient for sustaining debates over the future. The important question is not just what to do, but when.

References

Alba, R. D. (1990). *Ethnic identity: The transformation of white America.* New Haven, CT: Yale University Press.

Alvarez, A. (1997). Adjusting to genocide: The techniques of neutralization and the Holocaust. *Social Science History, 21(2),* 139–178.

Archard, D. (1993). *Children: Rights and childhood.* New York: Routledge.

Ayers, A. (1993). *The wisdom of Martin Luther King, Jr.* New York: Meridian.

Belknap, J. (1996). *The invisible woman: Gender, crime and justice.* New York: Wadsworth.

Brown, P., Jr. (1998). Biology and the social construction of the "race" concept. In J. Ferrante and P. Brown, Jr. (Eds.), *The social construction of race and ethnicity in the United States,* pp. 131–138. New York: Longman.

Buchwald, E., Fletcher, P., and Roth, M. (1993). *Transforming a rape culture.* Minneapolis: Milkweed Editions.

Caulfield, S. and Wonders, N. A. (1993). Gender and justice: Feminist contributions to criminology. In G. Barak (Ed.), *Varieties of criminology: Readings from a dynamic discipline,* pp. 213–239. Westport, CT: Praeger.

———. (1993). Personal AND political: Violence against women and the role of the state. In K. Tunnell (Ed.), *Political crime in contemporary America: A critical approach,* pp. 79–100. New York: Garland.

Cunningham, H. (1995). *Children and childhood in Western society since 1500*. New York: Longman.

Daly, K. (1989a). Neither conflict nor labeling nor paternalism will suffice: Intersections of race, ethnicity, gender and family in criminal court decisions. *Crime and Delinquency, 35,* 136–168.

——— (1989b). Rethinking judicial paternalism: Gender, work-family relations, and sentencing. *Gender and Society, 3,* 9–36.

Davis, J. F. (1996). Who is black? One nation's definition. In K. E. Rosenblum and T.-M. C. Travis (Eds.), *The meaning of difference: American constructions of race, sex, and gender, social class and sexual orientation*, pp. 35–42. New York: McGraw-Hill.

Donziger, S. (1996). *The real war on crime: The report of the National Criminal Justice Commission*. New York: Harper.

Doob, C. B. (1999). *Racism: An American cauldron*. New York: Longman.

Duberman, M. (1986). *About time: Exploring the gay past*. New York: Gay Presses of New York.

Ferrell, J. (1993). *Crimes of style: Urban graffiti and the politics of criminality*. New York: Garland.

Frankenberg, R. (1993). *The Social construction of whiteness: White women, race matters*. Minneapolis: University of Minnesota Press.

Gordon, D. R. (1994). *The return of the dangerous classes: Drug prohibition and policy politics*. New York: W. W. Norton & Company.

Herek, G. and Berrill, K. (1992). *Hate crimes: Confronting violence against lesbians and gay men*. Newbury Park, CA: Sage.

Jaimes, M. A. (1992). Federal Indian identification policy: A usurpation of indigenous sovereignty in North America. In *The state of Native America: Genocide, colonization, and resistance*, pp. 123–138. Boston: South End Press.

Kendall, D. (1997). *Race, class and gender in a diverse society*. Boston: Allyn & Bacon.

Kruttschnitt, C. (1984). Sex and criminal court dispositions: The unresolved controversy. *Journal of Research in Crime and Delinquency, 21(2),* 13–32.

Langston, D. (1995). Tired of playing Monopoly? In M. L. Anderson and P. H. Collins (Eds.), *Race, class and gender: An anthology*, pp. 100–110. New York: Wadsworth.

Limerick, P. N. (1987). *The legacy of conquest: The unbroken past of the American West*. New York: W. W. Norton.

Michalowski, R. J. (1985). *Order, law and crime*. New York: Random House.

Miedzian, M. (1991). *Boys will be boys: Breaking the link between masculinity and violence*. New York: Doubleday.

Minow, M. (1997). *Not only for myself: Identity, politics and the law*. New York: The New Press.

Omi, H. and Winant, H. (1994). *Racial formation in the United States: From the 1960s to the 1980s*. New York: Routledge.

Orobio de Castro, I. (1993). *Made to order: Sex/gender in a transsexual perspective*. The Hague, The Netherlands: Het Spinhuis.

Parenti, M. (1995). *Democracy for the few*. New York: St. Martin's Press.

Reiman, J. H. (1996). *The rich get richer and the poor get prison: Ideology, class and criminal justice*. Boston: Allyn & Bacon.

Russell, K. K. (1998). *The color of crime: Racial hoaxes, white fear, black protectionism, police harassment, and other macroaggressions*. New York: New York University Press.

Scott, J. W. (1995). Multiculturalism and the politics of identity. In J. Rajchman (Ed.), *The identity in question*, pp. 3–12. New York: Routledge.

Thomas, M. E. and Hughes, M. (1986). The continuing significance of race: A study of race, class, and quality of life in America, 1972–1985. *American Sociological Review, 51,* 830–841.

Uys, P.-D. (1988). Chameleons thrive under apartheid. *New York Times*, September 23.

West, C. and Fenstermaker, S. (1995). Doing difference. *Gender and Society, 9(1),* 8–37.

West, C. and Zimmerman, D. H. (1987). Doing gender. *Gender and Society, 1,* 125–51.

West, C. (1995). The new cultural politics of difference. In J. Rajchman (Ed.), *The identity in question*, pp. 147–171. New York: Routledge.

Wildman, S. M. (1996). *Privilege revealed: How invisible preference undermines America*. New York: New York University Press.

Wordon, R. and Shepard, R. (1994). Demeanor, crime and police behavior: A reexamination of the police services study data. *Criminology, 34,* 83–105.

Wright, L. (1998). One drop of blood. In J. Ferrante and P. Brown, Jr. (Eds.), *The social construction of race and ethnicity in the United States*, pp. 422–426. New York: Longman.

3 White Male Privilege and the Construction of Crime

LARRY A. GOULD

What if we took the position that racial inequities were not primarily attributable to individual acts of discrimination targeted against persons of color, but increasingly to acts of cumulative privileging quietly loaded up on whites? That is, what if by keeping our eyes on those who gather disadvantage, we have not noticed white folks, varied by class and gender, nevertheless stuffing their academic and social pickup trucks with goodies otherwise not as readily available to people of color?

—Michelle Fine, 1997

Popular history has often suggested that the first Europeans to settle in the United States were egalitarian groups seeking a place to practice their religious, political, and economic ways without the interference of dominant and oppressive groups from their home country. For the most part, nothing could be further from the truth. Then, as now, race, class, and gender were used as a means of assigning the "real" value of people, particularly in how these characteristics were and are used to either include or exclude individuals as service providers, offenders, and victims in the criminal justice system.

Then, as now, white males occupied the most powerful and privileged positions in our society. White males dominate our corporate structure, public bureaucracies, and other organizations; thus, they are in a position to make the decisions that have major consequences for American society (Murray and Smith, 1995). Historically, much of the power of white males was achieved by basing voting rights on property ownership. This meant that minorities and women were systematically excluded from the power base (Murray and Smith, 1995). One of the effects of the dominant position that white males hold in our society is that they have become the baseline against which they themselves measure all other groups.

In Chapter 2, Wonders discussed how concepts of race, class, and gender are basic to the principles of social organization and to the human interaction process (Chow, 1996). The construction of race, class, and gender are also central to the development of oppressive ideologies (Lieberson and Waters, 1988; Winant, 1997;

Rubin, 1998). Making use of difference (real or constructed) is an essential step in the racist and sexist process, which leads to the devaluation of groups typified as being "different" by the dominant group (Rubin, 1998; Walker, Spohn, and Delone, 1996; Yinger, 1994). Differences attributed to moral sensibilities have alternately been treated as either innate or acquired, as have cultural/value differences. It is common for a dominant group to use these categories in combination to devalue members of the less dominant group(s). White, male, middle-class, Protestant, heterosexuals of European descent (most likely Northern European) usually set the "standard" against which others have and continue to be judged (Foner, 1998; Sacks, 1998).

Although Wonders (Chapter 2) is correct in her views of how characteristics can have an impact on the way in which individuals or groups are viewed, there is an additional ingredient that needs to be added to the process of inclusion or exclusion. There is a pattern running through the matrix of white male privilege, a pattern of assumptions that are passed on to white males at birth. As noted by McIntosh (1998), the cultural turf is theirs by fact of their skin color and genitalia. These attributes serve as assets in terms of access to education, career opportunities, and making the social systems work to their advantage. McIntosh refers to this form of privilege as *unearned advantage*. Power from unearned privilege can look like strength when it is, in fact, permission to escape or to dominate.

The white privilege that results from *unearned entitlements* can lead to *unearned advantages* (McIntosh, 1998). These unearned advantages can privilege an individual in their interactions with the justice system in ways that are sometimes difficult to understand, particularly if one is white. Thus, being a white male privileges an individual by providing an invisible set of assets that can be used to their advantage every day. McIntosh (1998) notes that for whites, particularly white males, "privilege is like an invisible weightless knapsack of special provisions, maps, passports, codebooks, visas, clothes, tools and blank checks." The irony is that white males are all-too-often unaware that they occupy privileged positions (Murray and Smith, 1995; Rubin, 1998; Sacks, 1998).

The outcome of these privileges can be measured in many ways both related to and outside of the justice system. Statistically, white males constitute 39.3% of the populations in the United States, but account for 82.5% of the *Forbes* 400 (individuals with a net worth of at least $265 million), 77% of members of Congress, 92% of state governors, 70% of tenured college faculty, almost 90% of daily newspaper editors, and 77% of television news directors. The effect of this is to place white males in a particularly powerful position so that they can make the rules by which others must play the game. As the reader reviews the information in this chapter, another set of statistics that is equally impressive includes the following: 94% of serial killers have been white males; 96% of those individually accused of environmental crimes have been white males; and the vast majority of those accused and/or arrested for sexual abuse are white males. Most whites in the United States think that racism does not affect them because they are not people of color; they do not see "whiteness" as a racial identity (McIntosh, 1998)

One factor that seems clear about all of the interlocking forms of oppressions: they take both active forms that we can see and embedded forms that, as a member of the dominant group, one is taught not to see. That is, whites, as an ethnic group, do not see themselves as racist because they are taught to recognize racism only as individual acts by members of white society, never in the form of the invisible system that confers unsought racial or sexual dominance on the group at birth (McIntosh, 1998)

The criminal justice system, a white-male controlled group of organizations, has played an important role in maintaining the status quo of the dominant group(s), by using the law to maintain, among other things, social differentiation. Martin and Jurik (1996) suggest that social differentiation, or the practice of distinguishing categories based on some attribute or set of attributes, is a fundamental social process and the basis for differential evaluations and unequal rewards. Given the mission of the criminal justice system, to control conduct that violates the criminal laws of the state (Martin and Jurik, 1996), and the vast discretion accorded to the members of the system (police, courts, and corrections), it has become a powerful gatekeeper in determining which groups and individuals are going to have their visibility raised as the result of some action or inaction on the part of the system. For instance, the "Jim Crow" laws (1867–1965), which were designed to maintain the separation of blacks from whites and to control the behavior of blacks in the South, are an example of the type of law used to subordinate groups. Another example of laws use to subordinate groups are those that prohibited Irish and Italian Catholics from teaching in public schools or even entering certain trades. Finally, Websdale (1991) provides several examples of how the police have been used to control the behavior of subordinate groups and suppress the development of unions.

There are many myths and misperceptions concerning the involvement of the majority population as offenders, victims, and service providers in the criminal justice system. These myths have often been perpetuated by the majority population to either create the image that they were the protectors of the moral fiber of the country or hide the fact that they were responsible for a much greater proportion of the crime problem than they wished to acknowledge. This chapter focuses on the involvement of majority population members in the criminal justice system, but first we discuss how the "majority population" (Franklin and Moss, 1994; Wirth, 1945) is defined and how "image of whiteness" or "visibility" (i.e., being different from the majority population) (McIntosh, 1998; Stanko, 1990) either increases or decreases the chance that an individual will become an offender, victim, or service provider. This chapter also reviews the majority population(s) in terms of both their efforts to protect their status and the perceptions that these efforts have created.

Continuum of Discrimination or Disparate Treatment

Discrimination or disparate treatment exists on a scale, the polar ends of which are systematic discrimination and pure justice (Walker, Spohn, and DeLone,

1996). *Systematic discrimination* refers to the type of discrimination that occurs at all level of a social system including the criminal justice system. It is evident at all times and all places within the system, including arrest, prosecution and sentencing. *Institutionalized discrimination* involves racial disparities in outcomes that result from established (institutionalized) policies. It is often the case that such policies are not directly related to race or gender, but involve *de facto* practices that become codified, and thus sanctioned, by *de jure* mechanisms. Two examples of this type of treatment are the "poll" or voting tax and the height/weight limitations to be considered for employment as a police officer. Until the 1960s in many parts of the South, one of the requirements to vote included the payment of a poll tax. If the individual was unable to pay the tax, that person could not vote. Blacks, even though they might have been registered to vote, were often unable to vote because they could not afford the poll tax. Second, women and some members of minority groups were frequently excluded from joining police forces because they did not meet the minimum height and weight requirements to be police officers. The height and weight requirements were usually based on the average height and weight of Northern European white males.

Contextual discrimination involves discrimination in certain situations or contexts. One of the most common examples is the victim–offender relationship and its outcome in death penalty cases. Controlling for other causal factors, the likelihood of a black receiving the death penalty for murdering a white is much greater than the likelihood of a white receiving the death penalty for murdering a black. *Individual discrimination* results from discriminate treatment of disadvantaged or minority group members by an individual most frequently acting alone. The acts of this individual do not represent the general patterns of the rest of the criminal justice agency. For example, a police officer, parole officer, prosecutor, or judge may single out a minority group member for harsher treatment. *Pure justice* refers to a system in which there is no discrimination at any time or place in the criminal justice system.

Majority Population Defined

A full explanation of the term "Anglo-Saxon" is beyond the limited scope and space of this chapter (see Aguirre and Turner, 1998); however, a short description is useful. For our purposes, the term *Anglo-Saxon* or *WASP* (white Anglo-Saxon Protestant) refers to a person of northern European cultural and social institutional heritage. This category, although a mix of ethnic backgrounds, is usually dominated by the English and, to some extent, other northern Europeans. It should be noted that the term *English*, as opposed to *British*, has been deliberately used here. *British* is a term most often used to refer to the Commonwealth, including parts of Ireland, Scotland, and Wales, whereas *English* is a term used to refer to a specific subdivision of that Commonwealth. More specifically, the term *WASP* refers to an ethnic complex consisting of northern European ethnic stock with light skin; most often Protestant religious beliefs; Protestant-inspired values based on individualism, hard work, savings, and secular material success; and

English cultural traditions (language, laws, and beliefs) and institutional structures (politics, economics, and education) (Aguirre and Turner, 1998).

It is, of course, interesting to note that many of the Anglo-Saxons who arrived in the United States in the various waves of immigration were themselves members of a subordinate group and, thus, the victims of disparate treatment in the countries from which they came. Examples include the Puritans, the Quakers, many debtors, and landless workers. The Anglo-Saxons established themselves in what is now the eastern United States, putting into place the cultural and institutional structures by which all later groups would be compared and evaluated and would have to compete within. The elite members of this group tend to be overrepresented by the descendants of those who arrived prior to the American Revolution. This observation is contextually important because it was the elite members of this group that came to have the power to influence beliefs and, thus, the development of policy that has led directly to how people are either rewarded or punished for violating the rules and standards set by the dominant group (Aguirre and Turner, 1998). The dominance of white ethnic groups, especially those in the Anglo-Saxon core as well as others who have adopted this core culture, is reflected in not only their economic well-being (Aguirre and Turner, 1998), but in the laws, mores, and cultural means by which the effect of differences are emphasized in the United States. The core group is generally considered to be composed of groups from England and Germany, but includes those of Scottish (Protestant), Irish (Protestant), Dutch, and Scandinavian descent. An example of those groups that have been assimilated, for the most part, into the core includes Irish (Catholic), Italians, and Jews. Most research suggests that the members of the original core and later immigrants who were absorbed into this core do much better politically, economically, and educationally than do other groups, particularly those groups that can be singled out based on skin color or facial configurations.

White Ethnic Groups

Biological differences, as noted by Wonders in Chapter 2, are superficial, often inaccurate, and mostly difficult to use as markers of boundaries between peoples; nevertheless, they are important sociologically. It is interesting to note that current genetic research suggests that there is only eight-tenths of 1% (0.8%) difference in the genetic makeup between individuals and, of that small amount, only sixth-tenths (.48) accounts for racial differences. It is unfortunate that many people continue to believe that members of other racial or ethnic groups are biologically distinctive; thus, they tend to respond to them as being different, and most often as being inferior. It is quite common that people associate superficial biological differences with variations in psychological, intellectual, and behavioral makeup, and in cultural and/or ethnic difference. Because of this, they all too often feel justified in using discriminatory behavior (Aguirre and Turner, 1998). For example, a high forehead in many cultures is considered a sign of intelligence; whereas in other cultures blue eyes are considered evil; and in yet other cultures certain, and very different, body shapes signify anything from fertility to virility to criminality. The important thing to note is that manner of dress, body type, and facial configuration, as they all relate to either positive or negative attributes, are social constructions *defined by the dominant group based own their on physical appearance.* It is the mark of the dominant group that they have the power to define not only what constitutes difference, but also the intensity and methods of discrimination. Given the present levels of discrimination, whether systematic, institutional, contextual, or the result of individual acts perpetrated on currently disenfranchised groups (African Americans, Hispanics, Asians, Native Americans), it is often forgotten that similar discrimination was faced by the newly arrived Irish (Catholic), Italians, and Jews, who are now members of the core, of just a century ago. One of the reasons, among many, that the former groups are less assimilated results from their visibility, that is, their outward appearance is sufficiently different from the latter group that they do not fit the "image of white."

The dominant group uses several methods by which it can either establish or rationalize its superiority over other groups, one of which is reliance on the belief in a natural hierarchy. This was the method most often used by the "core" group in earlier American history. It should be noted at this point that this is also the method used by white supremacist groups today. Historically, and contemporaneously, dominant and "wannabe" dominant groups often absolve themselves of the racist or sexist connotations in the way difference is defined. Belief in, and use of, the nature/biology paradigm performs a critical function in the role of absolution. Absolution in this case is gained through one or more of the following means, all of which avoid any condemnation of the majority group for the problems of the disadvantaged group(s). First, it implicitly and explicitly defines a hierarchical order as natural. That order is, of course, represented as the natural order of things, with the dominant group at the top. It is suggested here that other groups are atavistic throwbacks to earlier forms of human evolution. Second, it holds the victim(s) responsible for their own condition, thus absolving the dominant group from any responsibility for the conditions of the inferior group. The dominant group suggests that no better can be expected of the subordinate classes because they do not know any better, and even if they did, it would not matter because they could not act any better any way. Third, it forestalls efforts to change the ranking of the groups, whether racial, ethnic, religious, or gender related, by portraying the differences as one of kind, not degree (Miller and Levin, 1998). Again, the argument of the dominant class is that other groups are most likely genetically different, thus they are different species rather than simply people with different cultural values.

Visibility

Each of us also has "ascribed characteristics," such as race, gender, age, and outer appearance of social class. These ascribed characteristics often affect the way in which others react to us and, in turn, how we react to others. In general, the less an individual's appearance mimics the characteristics associated with the appearance of northern Europeans the more visible that individual becomes. Conversely, the more closely an individual "fits" the profile of northern European in terms of ascribed status, and the more "standard" is that individual's appearance in terms of dress, skin color, and so on, the more invisible they become.

Research on crime, deviance, and living on the fringe tends to focus on acts or behavior committed by groups other than the "invisible white." Moreover, when crimes in which Euro-Americans (typically northern Europeans and now Irish, Italians, and Jews) are the most likely to be the offender (e.g., white-collar crimes, arson, driving under the influence, burglary, and serial murders), race is usually not mentioned as a factor in the crime (Miller and Levin, 1998; Kunen, 1990; Podolsky, Balfour, Eftimiades, and McFarland, 1990; Ellis, 1988; Hackett, McKillop, and Wang, 1988; Van Biema, 1995). However, it is quite typical for researchers to mention, either as a means of comparison or as an example, the race of either the individual offender or the group of offenders when talking about street crimes, drugs, violent crimes, and crimes of passion (Ellis, 1988; Hackett, McKillop, and Wang, 1988; Van Biema, 1995; Walker, Spohn, and DeLone, 1996). This typification of offenders has created a widely shared stereotype of what the potential offender might look like. Although typification is also based on ethnicity, gender, manner of dress, styling of hair, or body ornamentation, the most common characteristic on which it is based is race. For example, even though African Americans are more likely to be the victims of crime, whites express higher levels of fear of crime. Crime, for whites, tends to be a code word for fear of social change (Walker, Spohn, and Delone, 1996; Rosenbaum, Lewis, and Grant, 1986).

Miller and Levin (1998) suggest that the imagery of crime that has been created by the media and ourselves is that the only true victims of crime are innocent whites caught in the crossfire or preyed on by others. This further suggests that the "imagery also implies that whites who do commit violent crimes are somehow unique—they don't reflect white culture and society more generally" (Miller and Levin, 1998). The media focus on street crime typically does not pay attention to the participation of whites in those activities, even though the evidence suggests that the majority of participants are white (Miller and Levin, 1998; Walker, Spohn, and DeLone, 1996). Researchers, the media, politicians, and the police have helped create, for the rest of us, an image of a potential offender that is non-white, young, and male (Walker *et al.*, 1996; Rosenbaum *et al.*, 1986).

It might be interesting at this point to provide an example from this writer's experience as to how this works. I am a white male of northern European extraction. Except for my size (just under 6 feet and about 250 pounds), there is little about me that is different from many others of my genetic heritage. As do most people, I have several roles that I play during a week. One of my recent roles was as chair of the Faculty Senate at my current university. Another of the roles that I play is that of motorcycle rider. The experience that I recently had went as follows:

I recently made two visits to a local national chain discount store. On the first trip, I was standing in line behind a Native American man. I had just been in my role as Chair of the Faculty Senate and was dressed in a sports coat, tie, and slacks, all western cut. The Native American gentleman was nicely dressed, in blue jeans and a western type shirt. When he paid for his purchases, he used a credit card. The cashier ran his credit card through the card verification machine and then asked to see some identification, which the man produced. When the cashier asked for the identification, she said, without being asked, that it was company policy for the protection of the card user.

When I checked out, I also used a credit card to pay for my purchases. When I started to produce my identification the same cashier said, "That won't be necessary."

A couple of days later I was at the same store and was being checked out by the same cashier. This time I was in my motorcycle rider garb: black leather jacket, bandana covering my hair, and dark sunglasses. I was in a line behind two women, both of whom were nicely dressed and white. Both paid for their purchases with credit cards. Neither was asked for identification. When I paid for my purchases—with the same credit card that I had used a couple of days previously—I was asked for identification. Now I was very curious, so I decided to stand around the checkout area for a few minutes and watch a few transactions.

In short order, it became apparent that those people who were more visibly different—that is, who appeared to be of minority status—were much more likely to be asked for identification when paying with a credit card than were whites. In addition, those people who were dressed in somewhat unconventional ways— ragged, dirty, cultish—were slightly more likely to be asked for identification than were those dressed in more conventional ways.

Although my "study" lacks most of the necessary elements of scientific research, it does provide a pointed example of how visibility and distance from the "standard" affect treatment and, to some extent, how white privilege works.

As previously noted, "difference is socially constructed"; that is, race, ethnicity, sexual orientation, gender, age, and social class take on social content that is out of context with their real meaning. The perception of difference and how it is constructed either increases or decreases the visibility of an individual or a group. In the example given previously, I would suggest that I was invisible to the cashier on my first visit to the store, but on my second visit I stood out—that is, I was visible to the cashier and, therefore, seemed less trustworthy. The apparent lack of trust probably resulted from her feeling of discomfort with me, which was related to her perception of the distance that I was from her view of the norm. In other words, my whiteness could not overcome the other aspects of the image that I was portraying that day. In sum, it appeared that there was one set of rules for middle-class whites and another for minority members and for whites who did not sufficiently fit the image of white. It is, however, important to note that there are many varieties of "whiteness" (Winant, 1997) and that, over time, many but not all newly arrived groups have been assimilated into the core (Curtis, 1971). Among the groups that have been mostly assimilated are the Irish, Jews, and the southern and southeastern Europeans, predominately composed of Italians.

The Catholic Irish, Italians, and Jews

When the Catholic Irish, Italians, and Jews began to arrive in large numbers in the United States in the nineteenth century, the dominant Anglo-Saxon population undertook to portray the new immigrants as distinct and biologically different races. Members of these groups became the targets of discrimination as the result of their religions, their poverty, and their willingness to work for lower wages than earlier immigrants. Much of the stereotyping of the Irish that occurred in America resulted from the British construction of the image of the Irish in Ireland. The Irish, often for their own self-protection, formed groups, some of which became a part of the criminal class. This served as evidence to the dominant classes that the Irish could never be anything more than a bunch of thugs. They were stereotyped as being apelike, drunken, hostile, and immoral (Curtis, 1971), and were viewed as the "missing link" between apes, Africans, and the English (Aguirre and Turner, 1998). Catholic Irish were excluded by Protestant employers from anything but unskilled work as a result of the belief (or rather, misbelief) in their racial inferiority, low intelligence, pugnaciousness, and unreliability (Aguirre and Turner, 1998; Lieberson and Waters, 1988). One of the stereotypes about the Irish that seems to endure is their involvement in graft, corruption, and other forms of criminal activity associated with big-city or local politics (Aguirre and Turner, 1998). It is noted, however, that success at the local political level did not translate into success at higher levels, where the Catholic Irish were excluded from judiciary and executive branches of government until the 1930s. One of the arguments (or rather, excuses) for excluding Irish from higher positions was that they owed their allegiance to the Pope in Rome, not to the United States.

The experience of the Italian immigrants was similar to that of the Catholic Irish. There was some immigration of the more highly educated Italians from northern Italy in the early part of the nineteenth century. The northern Italians assimilated more easily than the later-arriving Italians from southern Italy, who were less educated, less skilled, and of generally darker complexion. Southern Italians were often portrayed as a distinct "race," with lower intelligence, a different set of cultural values, and criminal tendencies, as well as being oversexed and Catholic (Kamin, 1974; Gambino, 1974; Tomasi and Engel, 1970; Lopreato, 1970). Italians were also viewed as being ingratiating, jealous, racist, and physically tough (Gambino, 1974). Italians are often credited in the movies with having invented organized crime in America, but it should be noted that up to the time of prohibition, Irish and Jewish Americans controlled most of the organized syndicates. Although organized crime was a means for upward mobility in a hostile society, the crime rates for Italians were actually quite low (Lopreato, 1970).

As was the case with the Irish and the Italians, but for a much longer period, Jews have been considered a separate "race." The basis for this is, of course, social and cultural, not biological. Most often, Jews are identified by religious beliefs with a foundation in the Torah, or the first five books of the Bible (Aguirre and Turner, 1998). An additional source of Jewish identity is the awareness of a shared history of persecution and the sense that they constitute a community with traditions that are very different from those of Protestants or Catholics (Aguirre and Turner, 1998). As shown later in this chapter, it is the very organizations, networks, and shared beliefs that have allowed them to survive extremes in discrimination.

Some of the negative perceptions that have been used to stereotype Jews include beliefs that they are money-grubbing, materialistic, sly, involved in a "Jewish conspiracy" to control all governments, and that they control all of the banks. Despite a record of economic and academic success, Jews have been underrepresented in many occupations, professions, and high-level positions due to discriminatory practices that result from the negative perceptions listed here (Zweigenhaft and Domhoff, 1982; Alba and Moore, 1982).

The Irish, Italians, and Jews began to make strides economically, educationally, and socially by the turn of the twentieth century; however, they came into serious conflict with the African Americans, who were migrating north. African Americans were viewed as a threat to the Irish-developed unions because they were used as strikebreakers and would work for lower wages. African Americans still suffer from the legacy of this hostility (Bonacich, 1976), as noted by the school-bussing riots in Boston and the attacks on blacks in predominantly Irish neighborhoods (Bensonhurst). In addition, blacks are still excluded, or only included in limited numbers, from certain Irish-controlled labor unions and trades. The Catholic Irish have more easily assimilated into the mainstream of American society and are today virtually indistinguishable from the descendants of the Anglo-Saxon core in terms of their place in the American socioeconomic hierarchy (Aguirre and Turner, 1998; Lieberson and Waters, 1988). This is in a large part due to their ability to become invisible or blend in with the Anglo-Saxon core—that is, the fact that they are white.

The Typical Offender, Victim, and Service Provider: Gate Keeping

Gate keeping of one sort or another is common within virtually any society. By *gate keeping* we mean that access to or exclusion from the resources or rewards in the society are often closely guarded. The various organizations in the criminal justice system often participate in the gate-keeping process by determining who becomes a police officer, lawyer, correctional officer, or a member of many of the other professions working in the system. Criminal justice organizations also determine who is accorded the official status of victim and offender.

Members of criminal justice organizations, either consciously or unconsciously, use many standards, including visibility, as measures of who gets to be a member. Many ascribed statuses such as height, weight, physical ability not related to job expectations, gender, and race have at one time or another been used to either include or exclude a person as an offender, victim, or service provider. What this means is that, as an individual's ascribed status approximates or resembles that of those people already in the criminal justice organization, there is an increased likelihood of that individual being accepted as a new member. Conversely, the greater the difference of the individual's ascribed status from that of the majority of the members of the criminal justice organization, the less likely that individual is to be included as a member of the organization. Gould (1997) found that black female police officers had the greatest difficulty in entering the police force and, if they were hired, they had an increased likelihood of leaving the force within a few years. Other examples of exclusion and inclusion based on ascribed status include the following: women have been excluded from policing as the result of the perception that an officer must be physically strong; blacks have been arrested out of proportion to their representation in the population due to their race; Hispanic women have been accorded less status in the justice system as compared to white women; and blacks have been excluded from law schools.

Irish, Italians, and Jews (males) have been more successful in moving into criminal justice organizations as service providers than have blacks, Hispanics, Native Americans, and Asians. Blacks, Hispanics, Native Americans, and certain groups of Asians have had a greater likelihood of being included as offenders, and these same groups have often not been accorded an equal status as victims when compared to whites. In part, these differences can be attributed to the visibility of blacks, Hispanics, Native Americans, and Asians as compared to Irish, Italians, and Jews.

White America has been successful in creating the image of the black man and, to a lesser extent, the black woman as the universal bogeyman (Fishman, 1998), whereas whites, males in particular, have been imaged (falsely) as the universal "good guy" (Hamm, 1998). Whites, particularly white women, are most often portrayed as the victims of crime (Harjo, 1998; Castro, 1998), whereas minorities are most often portrayed as the offenders (Castro, 1998; Harjo, 1998; Hamm, 1998; Laidler, 1998). Whites, particularly white males, have been advantaged in terms of their employment as service providers (Martin and Jurik, 1996). The next three subsections of this chapter review some of the descriptive statistics associated with the gate-keeping practices of criminal justice organizations.

The Typical Offender?

The crimes that receive the most attention, particularly from the media, politicians, and criminal justice policy makers, are the so-called street crimes, such as murder, robbery, and rape (Walker, Spohn, and Delone, 1996). For all too many people, particularly those of European heritage, the image of the criminal is a young African American (in some areas of the country, a young Hispanic) male armed with a gun who commits a robbery, rape, or murder. In other words, the term *crime* is synonymous with *minority crime* (Walker, Spohn, and DeLone, 1996). It thus comes as something of a surprise to many to learn that the majority of

violent crimes are committed by young white males (Hamm, 1998). It is somewhat uncomfortable for many, particularly whites, to learn that they account for
54% of the yearly arrests for murder, rape, robbery, and aggravated assault
(Donziger, 1996; Miller 1996) and 66.9% of all crime is committed by whites (U.S.
Department of Justice, 1997). Although much of the other violent crime is committed by young black males from urban areas (Fagan, 1992; Boyum and Kleiman,
1995), it is interesting to note that much of that violence is related to trade in crack
cocaine and heroin, a market largely supported by middle-class white males
(Chambliss, 1994).

It is very easy for the majority group to blame those people who look and act
different for crime problems while ignoring the fact that white males are responsible for the vast majority of white-collar crime. The vast majority of bank frauds,
insider trading, junk-bond deals, environmental crime, and savings and loan
frauds have been committed by white males. The Charles Keating (Lincoln Saving
and Loan) scandal in Arizona cost investors more money than was stolen in all
bank robberies since the late 1970s. In 1986, Michael Milkin was indicted for insider trading, racketeering, market manipulation, price fixing, and other criminal
stock market activities. The results of his activities led to large-scale layoffs, loss
of savings for thousands of individuals, and the firing of many people. The damage done to the ordinary citizen by white-collar crime committed by white males
has a much greater impact than all other crimes put together. The difficulty of the
majority white community in accepting the image of offenders as being white,
whether it be for violent crimes or for white-collar crimes, results in a misplaced
fear and certainly a prejudicial response to white crime. When former Governor
of Arizona Fyfe Symington was on trial for fraudulent schemes, his biggest defenders in the community were older white retirees, many of whom were demanding that the government go after real criminals such as drug users and
burglars. What this means is that if television and movies, along with the news
media, were to portray offenders in proportion to their actual numbers, they
would have to give more play to white crime. In addition, many middle-class
whites would have to rethink the image of the criminal most likely to be of threat
to them. In short, the image of the stereotypical criminal would have to be ad-
justed.

The Typical Victim?

The white majority, when it thinks of the victims of crime, is more likely to imagine a person very much like themselves. As already noted here, our perception of
crime and the criminal is, to a large extent, shaped by the media, whether it is the
nightly news, news documentaries, films, and/or television. Often, the assumption of too many of the dominant-group members of our society is that the typical
crime is a violent crime, that the typical victim is white, and that the typical offender is African American, Hispanic, or some other nonwhite. There is compelling evidence to suggest that this picture is inaccurate on all counts. A review of
the *Sourcebook* (1995) provides the following picture.

The homicide (victim) rate for African Americans (34.0 per 100,000 persons) was seven times greater than was the rate for whites (4.9 per 100,000 persons). For males between the ages of 14 and 17 the difference was even greater (65.9 for African Americans and 8.5 for whites).

African American–headed households have higher victimization rates for burglary (69.3 per 1,000 for blacks and 44.3 per 1,000 for whites), household larceny (218.5 per 1,000 for blacks and 203.5 per 1,000 for whites), and motor vehicle theft (22.2 per 1,000 for blacks and 12.1 per 1,000 for whites).

Victimization rates for crimes of violence were 88.7, 100.1, and 110.8 per 1,000 persons age 12 and older for whites, Hispanics, and African Americans, respectively. The victimization rate for African Americans for robbery was 15.6 and for whites was 4.7. African Americans were about three times more likely to be the victims of robbery than were whites.

The stereotypical victim is often portrayed as either a white female or an elderly white person. Although this does hold true for certain crime types, it does not hold true for those crimes listed here. The image of the "victim" has led to an inordinate fear of being the victim of those crimes listed here, by both the elderly and females; thus, it has played a significant role in how these people conduct their lives.

Minority victims of crime are often discounted by the criminal justice system and the dominant members of the our society. It is sometimes hard for whites to develop sympathy for members of other racial groups who have been victimized. In this sense, minority victimization tends to be invisible to whites. Because the vast majority of police officers are white, the insensitivity to minority needs as crime victims tends to be very broad and runs very deep. The dominant members of the society find it difficult to be sympathetic to the problems of members of the minority community. This can be demonstrated by the number of police officers and amount of resources and attention paid to the needs of middle- and upper-class neighborhoods as compared to minority neighborhoods. White communities have greater political power to demand police protection and get results than do minority communities, even though minority communities suffer greater rates of crime.

The Typical Service Provider?

Each of the criminal justice professions (police, corrections, and those associated with the legal profession) are currently dominated by whites (males) of European extraction, including the Irish, Italians, and Jews. As the "controllers" within the justice system, whites, particularly white males, have variously excluded females and members of the less-dominant ethnic groups from entry into these professions. Currently, white males constitute 75.2% of all full-time police officers in local police departments (*Sourcebook*, 1996), 60% of all full-time correctional employees (Martin and Jurik, 1996), and 60% of enrollees at American Bar Association–approved U.S. law schools (Abel, 1989). Although the number of black police officers in the 50 largest cities has increased since 1983, in some cases by as much as 128%, they are still underrepresented. Even when blacks do become police officers, they suffer from double marginality (Alex, 1969). Black officers must deal with the expectation that they will give other blacks a break while they often experience overt racism from white police officers. Another problem is the difficulty that black officers have in attaining command positions despite the growing numbers of black officers on most police forces.

Hispanics have also made some gains in terms of their representation on police forces, although these gains are generally not as dramatic as those made by blacks. In addition, the changes for Hispanics have been very uneven nationwide, with some cities showing gains while others have shown losses in the number of Hispanic officers employed.

Although courts have repeatedly supported the addition of women to the ranks of policing by striking down entrance requirements that were intended to keep all but a few women from qualifying as successful candidates, their numbers have only grown to about 9% of all sworn officers (Martin, 1988; Daum and Johns, 1994). Women also continue to be underrepresented in the senior administrative ranks, and they are often assigned duties that underutilize their skills (Martin and Jurik, 1996; Garrison, Grant, and McCormick, 1988). Surveys of male officers indicate that only one-third accept women on patrol, and that less than half of the male officers believe that women can handle the physical requirements of the job as well as men (Brown, 1994).

Employment in the criminal justice system has, for the Irish, Italians, and Jews, proved to be a stepping stone to employment in other professions and the business sector. Historically, the denial of employment to blacks, Hispanics, Native Americans, and Asians in the criminal justice systems meant that they either had to wait for a change in the policies that led to the denial or they had to find different routes to employment in other sectors.

For the Anglo-Saxon core and for the later arriving Irish, Italians, and Jews, employment in the justice system, particularly in policing, has been either a means of controlling local neighborhood politics or a means to move up the ladder of success in America. This means that it has been important to control entry into the justice system so as to, either knowingly or unknowingly, maintain the privileges that are attached to being white. Along with control of entry into the justice system comes the means to control who gets arrested and for which crimes. Again, we can see that control of the arrest process privileges those ethnic groups who play a dominant role in the justice system.

Conclusions

The core of the dominant group have long since ceased to be in the numerical majority; however, they and those who have been assimilated into that core still tend to be in the political and economic majority. By the year 2035, whites will be in the numerical minority in the United States and white males will be less than 25% of the population, but will still control 70 to 80% of the wealth.

If the criminal justice system continues to not represent the minorities—that is, the peoples who are currently in the category of more visible—what will this mean for the effectiveness and reputation of the criminal justice system? It is not only necessary that the deliberate disadvantaging of groups cease, but also that the more insidious advantaging of one group over another cease. For the system to continue to function and, better yet, to improve the delivery of its services, it will be necessary for the "visible" to become "invisible" in terms of how victims are treated, how service providers are hired, and how offenders are treated.

For the institutional discrimination to end, for unfair economic competition to assume some sense of fairness, and for Social Darwinist ideologies to be relegated to the dustbin, the barriers that have to this point either prohibited or reduced the likelihood of nonwhite minorities from entering the justice system on a level playing field with whites must be removed.

References

Alba, R. and Moore, G. (1982). Ethnicity in the American elite. *American Sociological Review, 47,* 373–383.

Abel, R. L. (1989). *American lawyers.* New York: Oxford.

Alex, N. (1969). *Black in blue: A study of the Negro policeman.* New York: Appleton-Century-Crofts.

Aguirre, A. and Turner, J. (1998). *American ethnicity: The dynamics and consequences of discrimination,* 2nd ed. Boston: McGraw-Hill.

Bonacich, E. (1976). Advanced capitalism and black–white race relations in the United States: A split labor market interpretation. *American Sociological Review, 41,* 34–51.

Boyum, D. and Kleiman, M. (1995). Alcohol and other drugs. In J. Q. Wilson and J. Petersilia (Eds.), *Crime,* pp. 47–94. San Francisco: Institute for Contemporary Studies.

Brown, M. (1994). The plight of female police: A survey of NW patrolmen. *Police Chief, 61,* 50–53.

Castro, D. (1998). Hot blood and easy virtue: Mass media and the making of racist latino stereotypes. In C. R. Mann and M. S. Zatz (Eds.), *Images of color: Images of crime,* pp. 134–144. New York: Roxbury Publishing.

Chambliss, W. J. (1994). Why the U.S. government is not contributing to the resolution of the nation's drug problem. *International Journal of Health Services, 24,* 675–690.

Chow, E. N. (1996). Transforming knowledge: Race, class and gender. In E. Ngan-Ling Chow, D. Wilkinson, and M. B. Zinn, *Race, class & gender: Common bonds, different voices,* pp. 5–18. Thousand Oaks, CA: Sage.

Curtis, L. P. (1971). *Apes and angels: The Irish Victorian caricature.* Washington, DC: Smithsonian Institution Press.

Daum, J. and Johns, C. (1994). Police work from a woman's perspective, *Police Chief, 61,* 46–49.

Donziger, S. R. (1996). *The real war on crime: The report of the National Criminal Justice Commission.* New York: Harper Perennial.

Ellis, D. (1988). Hedda's hellish tale. *Time,* December 12:32.

Fagan, J. (1992). Drug selling and licit income in distressed neighborhoods: The economic life of street-level drug users and dealers. In A. V. Harrell and G. E. Peterson (Eds.), *Drugs, crime and social isolation,* pp. 78–101. Washington, DC: Urban Institute Press.

Fine, M. (1997). Witnessing whiteness. In M. Fine, L. Weis, L. C. Powell, and L. M. Wong (Eds.), *Off white: Readings on race, power, and society,* pp. 57–65. New York: Routledge.

Fishman, L. (1998). Images of crime and punishment: The black bogeyman and white self-righteousness. In C. R. Mann and M. S. Zatz (Eds.), *Images of color: Images of crime*, pp. 109–126. New York: Roxbury Publishing.

Foner, E. (1998). Who is an American? In P. S. Rothenberg (Ed.), *Race, class, and gender in the United States: An integrated study*, 4th ed., pp. 84–91. New York: St. Martin's Press.

Franklin, J. H. and Moss, A. A., Jr. (1994). *From slavery to freedom: A history of African Americans*, 7th ed. New York: Knopf.

Gambino, R. (1974). *Blood of my blood: The dilemma of Italian-Americans*. Garden City, NY: Doubleday.

Garrison, C., Grant, N., and McCormick, K. (1988). Utilization of police Women. *Police Chief, 55*, 32–33.

Glazer, N. (1957). *American Judaism*. Chicago: University of Chicago Press.

Gordon, M. (1964). *Assimilation in American life: The role of race, religion, and national origins*. New York: Oxford Press.

Gould, L. (1997). Can old dogs be taught new tricks? Teaching cultural diversity to police officers. *Policing, 20*, 339–357.

Hackett, G., with McKillop, P., and Wang, D. (1988). A tale of abuse. *Newsweek*, December 12:56.

Hamm, M. S. (1998). The laundering of white collar crime. In C. R. Mann and M. S. Zatz (Eds.), *Images of color: Images of crime*, pp. 244–256. New York: Roxbury Publishing.

Harjo, S. S. (1998). Redskins, savages and other enemies: A historical overview of American media coverage of native people. In C. R. Mann and M. S. Zatz (Eds.), *Images of color: Images of crime*, pp. 30–46. New York: Roxbury Publishing.

Kamin, L. J. (1974). *The science and politics of I.Q.* New York: Wiley.

Kunen, J. S. (1990). Risen from near death, the Central Park Jogger makes her day in court one to remember. *People*, July 30:32.

Laidler, K. J. (1998). Immigrant bashing and nativist political movements. In C. R. Mann and M. S. Zatz (Eds.), *Images of color: Images of crime*, pp. 169–178. New York: Roxbury Publishing.

Lieberson, S. and Waters, M. C. (1988). *From many strands: Racial and ethnic groups in contemporary America*. New York: Russell Sage.

Lopreato, J. (1970). *Italian Americans*. New York: Random House.

Martin, S. (1988). Female officers on the move? A status report on women in policing. In B. Dunham and J. Alpert (Eds.), *Critical issues in policing*, pp. 23–45. Grove Park, IL: Waveland Press.

Martin, S. and Jurik, N. (1996). *Doing justice, doing gender*. Thousand Oaks, CA: Sage.

McIntosh, P. (1998). White privilege, color, and crime: A personal account. In C. R. Mann and M. S. Zatz (Eds.), *Images of color: Images of crime*, pp. 207–216. New York: Roxbury Publishing.

Miller, J. G. (1996). *Search and destroy: African-American males in the criminal justice system*. New York: Cambridge University Press.

Miller, J. and Levin, P. (1998). The Caucasian evasion: Victims, exceptions, and defenders of the faith. In C. R. Mann and M. S. Zatz (Eds.), *Images of color: Images of crime*, pp. 217–233. New York: Roxbury Publishing.

Murray, C. B. and Smith, J. O. (1995). White privilege: The rhetoric and the facts. In D. A. Harris (Ed.), *Multiculturalism from the margins*, pp. 139–154. Westport, CT: Bergin & Garvey.

Podolsky, J. D., Balfour, V., Eftimiades, M., and McFarland, S. (1990). As the Central Park Jogger struggles to heal, three attackers hear the bell toll for them. *People*, September 30:47.

Rosenbaum, D., Lewis, D. A., and Grant, J. (1986). Neighborhood-based crime prevention: Assessing the efficacy of community organizing in Chicago. In D. Rosenbaum (Ed.), *Community crime prevention: Does it work?*, pp. 103–134. Newbury Park, CA: Sage.

Rothenberg, P. S. (Ed.) (1998). *Race, class, and gender in the United States: An integrated study*, 4th ed. New York: St. Martin's Press.

Rubin, L. (1998). Is this a white country, or what? In P. S. Rothenberg (Ed.), *Race, class, and gender in the United States: An integrated study*, 4th ed., pp. 92–99. New York: St. Martin's Press.

Sacks, K. B. (1998). How Jews became white. In P. S. Rothenberg (Ed.), *Race, class, and gender in the United States: An integrated study*, 4th ed., pp. 100–115. New York: St. Martin's Press.

Stanko, E. (1990). *Everyday violence: How women and men experience sexual and physical danger*. London, UK: Pandora.

Tomasi, S. and Engel, M. (Eds.) (1970). *The Italian experience in the United States*. New York: Center for Migration Studies.

Van Biema, D. (1995). Abandoned to her fate. *Time*, December 11:50.

U.S. Government, Bureau of Justice Statistics (1995). *Sourcebook of Criminal Justice Statistics, 1994*. Washington, DC: Department of Justice.

U.S. Government, Bureau of Justice Statistics (1997). *Sourcebook of Criminal Justice Statistics, 1996*. Washington, DC: Department of Justice.

Walker, S., Spohn, C., and DeLone, M. (1996). *The color of justice: Race, ethnicity, and crime in America*. New York: Wadsworth Publishing.

Websdale, N. (1991). Disciplining the non-disciplinary spaces: The rise of policy as an aspect of governmentality in nineteenth century Eugene, Oregon. *Policing and Society, 2*, 89–115.

Winant, H. (1997). Behind blue eyes: Whiteness and contemporary U.S. racial politics. In M. Fine, L. Weis, L. C. Powell, and L. M. Wong (Eds.), *Off white: Readings on race, power, and society*, pp. 40–56. New York: Routledge.

Wirth, L. (1945). The problem of minority groups. In R. Linton (Ed.), *The science of man in the world crisis*, pp. 23–54. New York: Columbia University Press.

Yinger, J. M. (1994). *Ethnicity: Source of strength? Source of conflict?* Albany, NY: SUNY Press.

Zweigenhaft, R. and Domhoff, B. W. (1982). *Jews in the Protestant establishment*. New York: Praeger.

PART TWO

Categories of Difference

4

Stolen Lands, Stolen Lives

Native Americans and Criminal Justice

MARIANNE O. NIELSEN

Native Americans are the original inhabitants of the United States, and include American Indians, Inuit, Aleutian Islanders, and Native Hawaiians—that is, they are "peoples who trace their ancestry in these lands to time immemorial" (Morse, 1985:1). They make up about 0.9% of the American population, with much higher percentages in states such as Alaska (15.6%), New Mexico (8.9%), Oklahoma (8.0%), South Dakota (7.3%), Montana (6.0%), and Arizona (5.6%) (U.S. Government, 1999; Utter, 1993:17–19). There are more than 500 federally recognized Native American Nations in the United States and more than 200 tribal entities that do not have federal recognition for reasons that include not having signed a treaty and having been unilaterally terminated as an Indian Nation by Congress (Utter, 1993).

It should be noted that many Native American Nations are called by names that are not their own—that is, the name they have now may be based on an inaccurate description (like the word "Indian" itself) or on a name that European explorers learned from unfriendly neighboring Native American Nations (the Navajo, for example, call themselves "Dine"). In general, the most respectful name to use is the name that the Native American people in question call themselves.

Native Americans are of great importance as a "category of difference" within the criminal justice system for a number of reasons (Snipp, 1989). As the original inhabitants of this land, Native Americans have a unique legal status and have contributed to the development of American law, politics, and justice. Another reason is that the United States has highly held values of equal opportunity and justice, yet the history and living conditions of many Native Americans are in direct contradiction to these values. Also, Native Americans and the dominant European-based society have basic cultural beliefs about justice that are in conflict, and cause misunderstandings and injustice when they interact in the courtroom and elsewhere (Dumont, 1993). Another very important reason is that the myths and stereotypes that exist in our culture about Native Americans (see Harjo, 1998; Mihesuah, 1996; Trigger, 1985) have led and continue to lead to discriminatory actions by people in positions of authority. Also very important is that Native Americans are overrepresented as offenders and victims in the criminal justice system, especially in some states and in some offense categories. Last, Native Americans are underrepresented as service providers and policy makers in the criminal justice system, meaning that Native Americans have little input into the justice policies and decisions that affect their lives and communities. For these important reasons, no textbook on categories of difference within the criminal justice system is complete without a section on Native Americans.

Historical Context

In discussing how the current situations of discrimination, overrepresentation, and underrepresentation came about, it is necessary to examine four important aspects of Native American history: colonialism, urbanization, cultural revitalization, and self-determination.

Colonialism is the invasion and takeover of political authority of a geographic area and its inhabitants by outsiders. North America was invaded and eventually controlled by Europeans, as were Australia and much of Africa and Asia. There were three general "ages" of European/Native American relations in North America (Miller, 1989). In the first age, which lasted from Native American/European contact until shortly after the Revolutionary War, Native Americans and colonists lived together more or less cooperatively, with Native Americans being the dominant group during this period. The Europeans were dependent on the Native American Nations for food, shelter, trade, knowledge of the land and its resources, and military aid.

The second age, which was one of coercion against Native Americans by the colonists, lasted until about World War II. Military campaigns and massacres by colonists, along with massive epidemics of foreign diseases such as smallpox and tuberculosis and the resulting social disorganization took their toll, so that the Native American Nations, despite their active efforts, were unable to resist the colonial invasion. It is estimated that the precontact Native North American population was somewhere between 2 to 12 million (Snipp, 1989; Stiffarm and Lane, 1992); however, by 1900 the Native American population of North America was at its lowest, having shrunk to around 250,000 (Utter, 1993).

During this era, missionaries, Indian Agents, and well-meaning reformers tried to impose on American Indians what they assumed to be vastly superior European cultures, languages, religions, economies, and social structures. Alcohol and usurious credit were introduced by traders to exploit them. The reservation system relocated them onto small lots of unproductive land. Their children were stolen and put into boarding schools. The schools physically punished the children for speaking their language, trying to see their families, or refusing to learn

European culture. Indian Agents had the right to determine who married, who could work, who got farming tools and medicines, and were not above using starvation and violence to make them obey. Even so, not all Native American Nations were treated the same by the colonists; it depended on each Nation's usefulness, annoyance, or irrelevance to the increasingly dominant European-based society.

An important part of the colonization process was the development of first a religious-based ideology, then later a racist ideology of "biologically inferior" Native Americans. At first, Native Americans were seen as pagan, heathen, savages, dirty, drunken, and violent. The colonizers felt justified in denying them basic human rights and, in general, treating them as less than human. The colonial ideology also had a paternalistic theme, labeling Native Americans as naive children incapable of controlling their own lives, and in need of protection and the civilizing influence of Europeans. By the nineteenth century, the ideology of Social Darwinism, which stated that some biological "species" of human were more highly evolved than others, gave "scientific" credence to colonial prejudices and, in their minds, justified discriminatory acts (Trigger, 1985).

The third age, which continues today, was one of confrontation between Native Americans and the dominant society. Religious, educational, economic, and political rights are part of Native American/dominant society negotiations. Public awareness of Native American issues is growing. Yet now more than ever, thanks to the long-term impact of colonial processes, Native Americans are engaged in a struggle to survive as culturally distinct indigenous peoples (Boldt, 1993).[1]

The main impact of the colonial processes was that many Native American peoples became marginalized from what is now the dominant society in the United States. Suffering from social disorganization and without control over their own lives and resources, many Native American communities became immersed in a subculture of poverty. According to the 1990 Census (U.S. Government, Bureau of the Census, 1992), more Native Americans in general (50.7%) lived in poverty than other Americans; they left school earlier (46.2% did not finish high school); and they worked in lower skilled and income jobs (about 44% are engaged in service, laboring, and other blue-collar occupations). High rates of suicide, family violence, and alcohol abuse are also characteristic of some Native American communities (Bachman, 1992). Also, Native Americans still suffer from discrimination in employment, housing, and in their general contact with the dominant society (French, 1994). These are criminogenic living conditions; that is, they put the inhabitants of these communities at higher risk of getting involved with the criminal justice system.

The impact of these social conditions is complicated by urbanization. More than 60% of Native Americans live outside of the mainly rural areas officially designated "Indian" (Utter, 1993:20). Many cities have significant numbers of Ameri-

---

[1] This section on colonialism is, of necessity, extremely generalized and short. For excellent overviews of North American colonization, see Nies (1996), Jennings (1993), Wright (1992), and Deloria and Lytle (1983).

can Indian residents: Los Angeles has the largest population (about 86,000 in 1990), followed by Tulsa, New York, Oklahoma City, San Francisco/Oakland, and Phoenix (Utter, 1993:22). Many Native Americans live in the marginalized areas of the city, although they may also be quite successful and be members of the middle and upper classes. Moving to an urban area also has a number of other possible consequences for Native Americans that could increase the likelihood of criminal justice involvement, including lack of the family, clan, and friend support network found back home; lack of understanding of urban behavioral expectations; lack of knowledge about what special services, if any, are available to Native Americans; lack of contact with Nation-based spiritual and cultural life; and increased visibility to the police.

Another element that must be taken into account is cultural revitalization. Although many Native American cultural practices were repressed by laws and a great deal of knowledge was lost as the result of population decimation, a great deal of cultural knowledge also remains. Native American individuals, communities, and Nations resisted the imposition of foreign laws, religion, and government. Native American societies have been and are still extremely flexible, adaptive, and dynamic. They had to be in order to survive the active oppression they have suffered since colonialism began. Cultural revitalization is a movement, actually a series of movements as diverse as the communities in which they originate, with the objective of regaining (sometimes rediscovering) and reinstitutionalizing the cultural traditions, ceremonies, languages, and social structures that were damaged by colonialism.

There are also movements towards self-determination; that is, movements to regain the right of Native American Nations to control their own social institutions, including education, social services, health services, leadership, and criminal justice. American Indian Nations have the status of "domestic dependent nations," meaning that they have limited legal rights to control their own society (Pommersheim, 1995). Some of these rights have been unilaterally legislated away since the time of the Treaties, including the right to handle major crimes on the reservations. Many of these rights, such as hunting and fishing rights and the right to establish new industries (e.g., casinos), are under ongoing attack. Many Native Americans believe that increased self-determination will enable them to implement culturally based social processes that will more effectively deal with the social ills brought about by colonialism.

In summary, the current involvement of Native Americans in the criminal justice system can only be understood in historical context. Colonialism, urbanization, cultural revitalization, and self-determination must all be taken into account when considering Native Americans, crime, and justice.

Native American Offenders

Crime rates for Native Americans are extremely suspect. As Silverman (1996) points out, the FBI's Uniform Crime Reports (UCRs) sometimes miss rural areas including American Indian Nations, where a significant number of Native Americans live. Also, "race" on the forms is usually based on the police officers' best guess. Statisticians estimate that up to 50% of Native American arrests are missing from the UCRs. There are also problems of missing information in the Census, which is used to calculate the "per 100,000" part of the crime rate. Almost 10% of the respondents did not specify race in the last Census. There is also the issue of how to classify yourself if you are of mixed race, as are a significant (although unknown) proportion of Native Americans. Taking these factors into account, it can safely be said that past calculations of Native American crime rates have been very inaccurate (see also U.S. Government, 1999).

Keeping these issues in mind, Silverman (1996) reports that from 1987 to 1992, the Native American general crime rate pattern (between 5,400 and 6,330 per 100,000) was about 25% higher than that of whites, but much lower than that of African Americans. Similarly, Native American arrest rates for violent crime were just below the rates for the total U.S. population for the same time period. For property crime, the Native American arrest rates were above the rates for the white population, but far below those of the African American population. It was only in the area of alcohol-related offenses (drunkenness, driving while intoxicated, and liquor violations) that Native Americans had the highest rates over whites and African Americans. In the area of drug-abuse offenses, Native Americans had the lowest rates. The most recent statistics, although still problematic, confirm these patterns of Native American arrests. Native Americans comprise 1.1% of arrests while comprising only 0.9% of the total U.S. population; they are overrepresented in alcohol-related crimes (2.4% of both liquor law and drunkenness arrests); and they are underrepresented in drug abuse violations with only 0.5% of arrests (U.S. Government, 1997a). American Indians account for 0.9% of all arrests for violent crimes (U.S. Government, 1999). The total arrest rate for Native Americans in rural counties (2.7%) is much higher than in urban areas (1.1%) and suburban areas (0.4%), reflecting residence patterns to some extent (Reddy, 1995).

The stereotypes discussed earlier may inform the decisions of members of the dominant society, including criminal justice personnel; however, no studies were found that directly investigated the role of discrimination in the arrest of Native Americans, although the issue was raised by Lujan (1998) in her discussion of the effects of stereotyping on Native Americans. It could be, for example, that if police officers expect Native Americans to have drinking problems that they will be more likely to watch individuals who "look Indian." This is decision making based on a stereotype because the percentage of Native Americans having a drinking problem varies from Nation to Nation and, in fact, more young white people than Native Americans use alcohol (Mail and Johnson, 1993).

Discrimination may also play a role in the sentencing of Native Americans. The evidence is contradictory. For example, in a sample of five states, Bachman *et al.* (1996) found a pattern of discrimination in the lengths of sentence and percentage of sentence served for Native Americans in some offense categories. Yet Hutton *et al.* (1996) found no evidence of judges discriminating on the basis of race in the sentencing of Native American women. A more complex pattern was found by Bynum and Paternoster (1996), who report that Native Americans in their sample were sentenced to shorter sentences but served a greater proportion of their sentences than did white offenders.

Native Americans were overrepresented as inmates, comprising 1.1% of the total correctional population, which breaks down to 1.5% of federal inmates, and 1.0% of state inmates and 2.9% of local jail inmates (U.S. Government, 1999). They are represented in proportion to their general population numbers in probation (0.9%; U.S. Government, 1999). According to Grobsmith (1994), the overrepresentation is even higher in a number of state correctional facilities, including those in Alaska (31.9% of prison population), South Dakota (25.4%), North Dakota (22.2%), and Montana (18.3%). Despite laws to the contrary and despite the documented effectiveness of Native American spirituality programs as a rehabilitative mechanism (Nechi, 1994), Native American inmates in some correctional institutions are still being denied access to spiritual counseling and ceremonies and to culturally sensitive drug- and alcohol-abuse treatment programs (Waldram, 1996). Native Americans are also somewhat less likely to get parole, with just 0.6% of the adults on parole being Native American (U.S. Government, 1999).

Of the 6,139 inmates sentenced to death between 1973 and 1997, 52 or 0.8% were Native American (U.S. Government, 1999). Since the death penalty was reinstituted in 1976, two Native Americans have been executed (1% of the total), compared to 108 whites, 77 blacks, and 12 Latinos (Reddy, 1995). In 1999 this number increased to three with the execution of a Native American inmate in Arizona (U.S. Government, 1999; Ettenborough, 1999).

Native American women are overrepresented as offenders, being 1.3% of federal inmates and 1.2% of state inmates (U.S. Government, 1997b). Like Native American male inmates, Native American female inmates suffer from lack of culturally appropriate rehabilitation and treatment programming, and lack of access to spiritual guides and ceremonies.

Native Americans are also overrepresented as juvenile offenders, with about 1.2% of juveniles arrested being Native American. Juveniles were most heavily overrepresented, like adults, in alcohol-related crimes. In addition, they were overrepresented in property crime arrests (1.3%) and proportionately represented in violent crime arrests (0.8%) (U.S. Government, 1997a). Even so, it as been suggested that the rate of violent juvenile crimes against persons is three times higher in Indian country than in the general U.S. population (Armstrong *et al.*, 1996). Young Native Americans are more likely to be arrested in rural counties (3.1%) than in urban areas (1.0%) and suburban areas (0.5%), again, partly reflecting residence patterns (Reddy, 1995). Armstrong *et al.* (1996) report that substance abuse is usually associated with Native American juvenile crime, as are negative socioeconomic conditions and child abuse. Thirty-nine percent of Native American children under the age of 18 live in poverty, compared to 12% of whites and 40% of blacks (Snyder and Sickmund, 1995). There also has been an 18% increase in the rate of child abuse and neglect of Native American children under the age of 15 (U.S. Government, 1999).

Native American juveniles are also overrepresented in custody, with 1% of juveniles in public long-term facilities being Native American, and 3% of those in open facilities (Snyder and Sickmund, 1995).

Cultural revitalization is an issue particularly relevant to juvenile crime because many community-level justice initiatives are aimed at preventing juvenile offenses. These programs are often based in traditional justice processes such as counseling by Elders, and the learning of traditional language, and ceremonial and economic skills in the belief that by learning these, young persons will feel more pride in their community and themselves. An important problem with this strategy is that many young Native Americans live in urban areas or feel no connection to tradition because they come from families that are significantly acculturated into the dominant society.

In summary, Native American men, women, and young people are overrepresented in the criminal justice system for some offenses and in some facilities. In addition, more culturally sensitive and appropriate rehabilitation, treatment, and spiritual programming is needed for Native American offenders throughout the criminal justice system.

Native American Victims of Crime

Native Americans have been victims of crime as Nations and as individuals. As Nations, Native Americans had their own laws and justice systems. These were not recognized as such by the invading colonists, because to do so would have consequences for the "legality" of their exploitation of the new resource-rich continent. Colonial powers consciously broke international law by staking claims and declaring ownership over land occupied by indigenous peoples. The colonial powers justified their actions by the "right of first discovery," which stated that "a Christian nation was divinely mandated to exercise dominion over non-Christian 'primitives' and to assert proprietary title to any 'unoccupied' land" (Boldt, 1993:3).

Second, the Treaties, legal documents signed between the colonial government and Native American Nations, were broken by the colonial government when it no longer remained in its political or economic interest to honor them. This trend continues today, as the American federal and state governments chip away at remaining Treaty rights. Third, laws were used to define Native American identity so that they were seen as less capable and rational than adults. In the *Cherokee Nation* case (1831), the federal government placed itself in "guardianship" over American Indians, ostensibly to protect them from unscrupulous whites; however, this relationship made it possible for the federal government to facilitate the theft of their lands and resources. Laws such as the *Indian Removal Act* of 1830 forced the majority of American Indian Nations in the eastern part of the country to leave their lands and move west of the Mississippi River (Deloria and Lytle, 1983). Native Americans in some states were forbidden the vote unless they could prove that they had "become civilized" by severing all ties with their Indian identity (Deloria and Lytle, 1983).

Native American individuals have also been the victims of crime, both historically and currently. Unfortunately, until recently little research has been done on Native American crime victimization, and in the existing research, many of the same methodological problems that plague offender statistics affect statistics about victims. Bureau of Justice Statistics research investigated Native American (not including Native Hawaiian) victimization from 1992 to 1996, and found that "the rate of violent victimization estimated from responses by American Indians is well above that of other U.S. racial or ethnic subgroups and is more than twice as high as the national average. This disparity in the rates of violent victimization affecting American Indians occurs across age groups, housing locations, income groups, and sexes." (U.S. Government, 1999:iii). Their annual rate of violent victimization was 124 per 1,000 persons age 12 or older, compared to 50 per 1,000 for all races (49 for whites, 61 for blacks, and 29 for Asians). This pattern of violent victimization applied to both males (153 per 1,000) and females (96 per 1,000), and held true for rape/sexual assault, aggravated assault, and simple assault, but not for armed robbery where the rate was about the same as the rate for African Americans (U.S. Government, 1999).

American Indian victimization was more likely to occur in an urban area (207 per 1,000) rather than a rural area (89 per 1,000), at the hands of someone from another race (70%), mainly whites (60%), and the offender was more likely to have used alcohol or drugs or both (55%). Just over 50% (52%) of the victims were between the ages of 12 and 24 (U.S. Government, 1999).

Bachman (1992) found that the rate of family violence was higher for Native American populations than for whites, meaning that there are proportionally more Native American victims of family violence. In 1992, 0.4% of all reported hate crimes were against Native Americans, which is an increase from 0.2% of the year before (Reddy, 1995).

About 45% of American Indians reported their violent victimization to the police, a rate which did not vary a great deal from that of whites (41%) or African Americans (50%). The reasons given for not reporting were about the same as those for the other groups—the matter was private or too minor to bother the police (U.S. Government, 1999).

American Indians were about 0.7% of murder victims from 1976–1996, but the rate has been declining since 1991, as has the murder rate for all groups. The only exception to this decline is the murder rates among American Indians age 40–49, which has had a 2.8% increase, and age 50 or older, which has had a 12.7% increase (U.S. Government, 1999). The murderer of an American Indian was most likely to be a non-American Indian (40%), in fact to be white (33%). Where the "typical" murder victim was killed by a handgun, American Indian victims are most likely to be killed by a rifle, shotgun, or stabbing (U.S. Government, 1999).

The reasons for the relative lack of academic research on Native American individual victims of crime are only speculative. It is likely that the overwhelming predominance in numbers of Latino/a and African American victims of crime diverts scholarly and public attention away from Native Americans. It is also possible that not investigating Native Americans as present-day victims is a form of "guilt management" (Boldt, 1993:18). Members of the dominant society may be repressing or denying the past treatment of Native Americans in order to prevent acknowledging that these wrongs were so severe that Native Americans still suffer from them—directly and indirectly—today. Finally, despite their high rates of victimization, Native Americans may perceive today's criminal justice system as hostile or indifferent, because of historical patterns of discrimination and hostility by the colonial criminal justice system, and therefore not report their victimization as readily. The long distances from some Nations to police, schools, hospitals, and other services may not only prevent prompt assistance to victims, but may also hinder reporting. Language barriers and cultural prohibitions about involving outsiders may also be factors in relatively low rates of reporting (U.S. Government, Office for Victims of Crime, 1992).

Victim assistance services are just beginning to be established in and around Native American Nations. The federal Office for Victims of Crime (OVC) began an initiative in 1987 to provide funding, training, and technical support to Native American Nations. Programs included Assistance to Victims of Federal Crime in Indian Country and the Children's Justice Act Program for Native Americans. Funding was also mandated under the Indian Child Protection and Family Violence Prevention Act of 1990. OVC funding has been used, so far, for setting up emergency funds for U.S. Attorney's Offices to assist Native American special needs victims, setting up a grant program to develop victims assistance programs on Native American Nations, and initiating an outreach program to inform Native Americans about state crime compensation programs (U.S. Government, OVC, 1992).

In summary, Native Americans have been the victims of past and present crimes, but little academic research has been done to document this, and victim services programs are only in the early stages of development in and around Native American Nations.

Native American Service Providers

There is a growing recognition that the criminal justice system has failed Native Americans and that it is not effective in handling the Native Americans in its care. One strategy is to encourage or require that non-Native American criminal justice personnel at all levels of the system increase their knowledge about Native American cultures and their intercultural communication skills (Ross, 1996).

Second, Native Americans must be more involved in operating the criminal justice system. As mentioned earlier, Native Americans are underrepresented in all aspects of justice service provision, even though many justice organizations have made special efforts to recruit Native Americans. In a 1991 study, the Federal Bureau of Investigation had the worst showing; they would have to hire 34 Native American men and 3 Native American women to attain population representation (0.8% of the general population). The Drug Enforcement Administration would have to hire 3 women; the U.S. Marshals Service 3 men and 1.7 women; the Bureau of Alcohol, Tobacco and Firearms 7 men and 3 women; and the U.S. Secret Service 12 men and 4 women (Reddy, 1995). Although there are few figures available for state or local criminal justice services, New York City reported that in 1992, 28 of its 20,098 officers (or 0.1%) were Native American (Reddy, 1995).

Native Americans can provide criminal justice services through four different routes. The first is that they can be service providers in the dominant system in indigenized positions; that is, they are employed to work within the European-based criminal justice system. This kind of role gives them very little leeway to modify their job descriptions in order to add or substitute culturally sensitive practices, although it paves the way for more sensitive treatment and just decisions.

They could also operate European-based criminal justice services on Native American land, including tribal police forces, courts, jails, probation supervision, and juvenile programs. With a few exceptions, Nations have limited jurisdiction over the type of offenses and the type of offenders these services can handle. Some of these services are under the supervision of the Bureau of Indian Affairs; others report to the Nation's Council. These services must meet state and federal standards for operation, and have incorporated few culturally based processes or values.

The third kind of service provision is Native American–based or European-based justice services operated by Native Americans outside of Native American land. These are relatively rare compared to similar services available to indigenous peoples in other countries, such as Canada and Australia. Indian cultural centers, of which there are dozens around the country (see Furtaw, 1993 for a listing), and local level services such as Native Americans for Community Action, located in Flagstaff, Arizona, are examples of these kind of services, although neither provides strictly justice-related services. Services they may provide include alcohol-abuse education or mental health counseling. Many of these services also suffer from lack of steady funding, making it difficult for them to respond to all of their clients' needs.

The final kind of service provision is that of providing Native American–based services on Native American land. These services are based in socialization processes that the Nation has used since time immemorial. Navajo Peacemaking is probably one of the best known of these initiatives. With the guidance and input of a Peacemaker, disputants talk over the issue and arrive at a plan for resolving it. "Offenses" that have been handled include assault, sexual assault, domestic violence, and wrongful death, as well as more common disputes over grazing rights, boundaries, and other civil matters (see Bluehouse and Zion, 1993; Zion and Zion, 1993; Zion, 1991; Yazzie, 1994; Nielsen, 1998). Many Native American programs are a kind of restorative justice (see Hudson and Galaway, 1996) because they focus on preventing further occurrences through resolving underlying issues, and "healing" the offender, victim, and community. This kind of service provision is not only the most culturally sensitive strategy for helping many Native American offenders and victims, but also may ultimately be the most effective because restorative justice approaches have the potential to help resolve the large issues of marginalization that cause Native American individuals to come into conflict with the criminal justice system in the first place.

In conclusion, the main hope for Native Americans to escape overrepresentation in the criminal justice system is to regain their self-determination so that they can implement more holistic and long-range services that will end marginalization and remove criminogenic conditions. Part of this process will be to establish culturally appropriate, more effective criminal justice services. Whether Native American Nations will be allowed increased self-determination by the government that has so long exploited them is the underlying question (Boldt, 1993). Because of the important natural resources that Native Americans would then control, and especially because of the massive social, economic, and political restructuring that demarginalizing Native Americans would entail, increased self-determination for Native Americans may be perceived by the government to be against the national interests of the country. If this occurs, then Native American overrepresentation in the criminal justice system can be expected to continue indefinitely.

References

Armstrong, T. L., Guilfoyle, M. H., and Melton, A. P. (1996). Native American delinquency. In M. O. Nielsen and R. A. Silverman (Eds.), *Native Americans, crime, and justice*, pp. 75–88. Boulder, CO: Westview.

Bachman, R. (1992). *Death and violence on the reservation: Homicide, family violence, and suicide in American Indian populations.* New York: Auburn.

Bachman, R., Alvarez, A., and Perkins, C. (1996). Discriminatory imposition of the law: Does it affect sentencing outcomes for American Indians? In M. O. Nielsen and R. A. Silverman (Eds.), *Native Americans, crime, and justice*, pp. 197–208. Boulder, CO: Westview.

Bluehouse, P. and Zion, J. W. (1993). Hozhooji Naat'aanii: The Navajo justice and harmony ceremony. *Mediation Quarterly, 10(4),* 327–337.

Boldt, M. (1993). *Surviving as Indians: The challenge of self-government.* Toronto: University of Toronto Press.

Bynum T. and Paternoster, R. (1996). Discrimination revisited. In M. O. Nielsen and R. A. Silverman (Eds.), *Native Americans, crime, and justice*, pp. 228–238. Boulder, CO: Westview.

Deloria, V. Jr. and Lytle, C. M. (1983). *American Indians, American justice.* Austin, TX: University of Texas Press.

Dumont, J. (1993). Justice and aboriginal peoples. In Royal Commission on Aboriginal Peoples (Ed.), *Aboriginal peoples and the justice system*, pp. 42–85. Ottawa: Ministry of Supply and Services.

Ettenborough, K. (1999). Indian inmate's last rites. *Arizona Republic,* February 2, 1999, A1, A12.

French, L. A. (1994). *The winds of injustice: American Indians and the U.S. government.* New York: Garland.

Furtaw, J. C. (Ed.) (1993). *Native Americans information directory.* Detroit, MI: Gale Research.

Harjo, S. S. (1998). Redskins, savages, and other Indian enemies: A historical overview of American media coverage of Native Peoples. In C. R. Mann and M. S. Zatz (Eds.), *Images of color, images of crime*, pp. 30–45. Los Angeles: Roxbury.

Hudson, J. and Galaway, B. (1996). Introduction. In B. Galaway and J. Hudson (Eds.), *Restorative justice: International perspectives*, pp. 1–14. Monsey, NY: Criminal Justice Press.

Hutton, C., Pommersheim, F., and Feimer, S. (1996). I fought the law and the law won. In M. O. Nielsen and R. A. Silverman (Eds.), *Native Americans, crime, and justice*, pp. 209–220. Boulder, CO: Westview.

Grobsmith, E. S. (1994). *Indians in prison: Incarcerated Native Americans in Nebraska.* Lincoln, NE: University of Nebraska Press.

Jennings, F. (1993). *The founders of America: From the earliest migrations to the present.* New York: W. W. Norton.

Lujan, C. (1998). Or, "The only real Indian is the stereotyped Indian." In C. R. Mann and M. S. Zatz (Eds.), *Images of color, images of crime,* pp. 47–57. Los Angeles: Roxbury.

Mail, P. D. and Johnson, S. (1993). Boozing, sniffing, and toking: An overview of the past, present, and future of substance use by American Indians. *American Indian and Alaska Native Mental Health Research Journal, 5(2),* 1–33.

Mihesuah, D. (1996). *American Indians: Stereotypes and realities.* Atlanta, GA: Clarity Press.

Miller, J. R. (1989). *Skyscrapers hide the heavens: A history of Indian-white relations in Canada,* Revised Edition. Toronto: University of Toronto Press.

Morse, B. W. (1985). *Aboriginal peoples and the law.* Ottawa: Carleton University Press.

Nechi Institute and KAS Corporation (1994). *Healing, spirit and recovery: Factors associated with successful integration.* Ottawa: Supply and Services Canada.

Nielsen, M. O. (1998). A comparison of Canadian youth justice committees and Navajo peacemakers: A summary of research results. *Journal of Contemporary Criminal Justice, 14(1),* 6–25.

Nies, J. (1996). *Native American history: A chronology of a culture's vast achievements and their links to world events.* New York: Ballantine.

Pommersheim, F. (1995). *Braid of feathers: American Indian law and contemporary tribal life.* Berkeley, CA: University of California Press.

Reddy, M. A. (Ed.) (1995). *Statistical record of Native North Americans,* 2nd Edition. New York: Gale Research.

Ross, R. (1996). *Returning to the teachings: Exploring aboriginal justice.* Toronto: Penguin.

Silverman, R. A. (1996). Patterns of Native American crime. In M. O. Nielsen and R. A. Silverman (Eds.), *Native Americans, crime, and justice,* pp. 58–74. Boulder, CO: Westview.

Snipp, C. M. (1989). *American Indians: The first of this land.* New York: Russell Sage Foundation.

Snyder, H. N. and Sickmund, M. (1995). *Juvenile offenders and victims.* Washington, DC: Office of Juvenile Justice and Delinquency Prevention.

Stiffarm, L. A. and Lane, P., Jr. (1992). The demography of Native North America: A question of American Indian survival. In M. A. Jaimes (Ed.), *The state of Native America: Genocide, colonization, and resistance,* pp. 23–53. Boston: South End Press.

Trigger, B. G. (1985). *Natives and newcomers.* Kingston: McGill–Queen's University Press.

U.S. Government, Bureau of the Census (1992). *1990 Census of population: General population characteristics, American Indian and Alaska Native areas.* Washington, DC: U.S. Government Printing Office.

U.S. Government, Bureau of Justice Statistics (1999). *American Indians and crime.* Washington, DC: Department of Justice (NCJ-173386).

U.S. Government, Bureau of Justice Statistics (1997a). *Sourcebook of criminal justice statistics, 1996.* Washington, DC: Department of Justice (NCJ-165361).

U.S. Government, Bureau of Justice Statistics (1997b). *Correctional populations in the United States, 1995.* Washington, DC: Department of Justice (NCJ-163916).

U.S. Government, Office for Victims of Crime (1992). Victim programs to serve Native Americans. *OVC Bulletin* (NCJ 133963). Washington, DC: U.S. Department of Justice.

Utter, J. (1993). *American Indians: Answers to today's questions.* Lake Ann, MI: National Woodlands Publishing.

Waldram, J. B. (1996). Aboriginal spirituality in corrections. In M. O. Nielsen and R. A. Silverman (Eds.), *Native Americans, crime, and justice,* pp. 239–253. Boulder, CO: Westview.

Wright, R. (1992). *Stolen continents: The "New World" through Indian eyes.* Boston: Houghton Mifflin.

Yazzie, R. (1994). Life comes from it: Navajo justice concepts. *New Mexico Law Review, 24(2),* 175–190.

Zion, J. W. (1991). The use of Navajo common law in dealing with rape. *Law and Anthropology, 6,* 131–167.

Zion, J. W. and Zion, E. B. (1993). Hozho's Sokee'—Stay together nicely. *Arizona State Law Journal, 25(2),* 407–426.

5 Exclusion, Inclusion, and Violence

Immigrants and Criminal Justice

BARBARA PERRY

The bosom of America is open to receive not only the Opulent and respect-
able Stranger, but the oppressed and persecuted of all nations and religions,
whom we shall welcome to participation of all our rights and privileges.
—George Washington, 1783

A central element of the cultural mythology of the United States is that this is a "nation of immigrants." As this chapter demonstrates, there is some truth to this notion. Periodic waves of immigrants to these shores have transformed this country in numerous ways. However, to characterize the United States in these terms is to ignore two indisputable facts of history that are addressed elsewhere in this book: (1) that this land was inhabited and settled by Native Americans long before its "discovery" (Chapter 4) and (2) that thousands of African "immigrants" arrived here not by choice, but in chains (Chapter 6; Rothenberg, 1997). To understand the United States as a "nation of immigrants" would render invisible the place and contributions of substantial numbers of "nonimmigrants."

Having said that, we are still in a position to recognize the ways in which immigrants from around the world have helped to shape the contours of United States material and cultural reality. It is the rare United States resident who cannot trace his or her ancestry beyond the borders of this country. Each of us thus shares the legacy of immigration. With few exceptions, that legacy is one of struggle, discrimination, and violence. The plight of the immigrant—especially non-European immigrants—has not always been an easy one, in light of the frequent emergence of anti-immigrant sentiment and policy that has characterized United States history.

Immigration Patterns

The history of immigration to what is now the United States began with British colonization in the seventeenth century. Between 1600 and 1775, the colonizing migrants tended to be Puritans, Quakers, entrepreneurs, and unskilled or indentured laborers. In a country where land was plentiful, entrepreneurs also turned to imported slave labor to ensure their profits. Consequently, by the time slavery was legally abolished in 1808, half a million slaves had been imported; many continued to be forcibly and illegally imported throughout the remainder of the century. By the close of the eighteenth century, the United States was peopled by a majority Anglo-Saxon immigrant population. Of the free, nonslave, non-Native population, 60% were English, 14% Scottish (or Scots-Irish), 8.6% German, 3.6% Irish, the remainder constituted largely by Dutch, French, and Swedes. In all, then, nearly 80% of the immigrant population was from the British Isles.

The period between the 1840s and 1870s was a period of expansion in economic and geographic terms. Irish and German immigrants were attracted to the northern United States by the promise of employment in emerging industries such as textile and iron works. This was especially appealing to the Irish—mostly indentured laborers—forced from their homeland by the economic crisis engendered by the potato famine, and by English oppression. As indentured servants, they would receive money for their passage to the United States, and pay it off by working for their sponsor for a specified period of time, after which they could leave to seek their "fortunes."

The westward expansion of the United States had dramatic implications for immigration trends. Irish laborers were joined, often replaced, by cheap Asian laborers from China and Japan. Between 1848 and 1882, more than 200,000 male Chinese workers were imported, largely for employment in the railroads and mines. By the end of this era, however, Chinese immigration was largely halted by the Chinese Exclusion Act of 1882.

With the end of the Mexican–American War, United States demographics once again shifted. The annexation of the Southwest (Arizona, New Mexico, etc.) meant that, without physically moving, many Spanish-speaking Mexicans suddenly became United States immigrants.

The period following the Civil War—the 1880s to the 1920s—was characterized by a dramatic economic and demographic explosion. Employment in agriculture shrank while employment in manufacturing doubled. Racism and discrimination kept many black laborers tied to southern agriculture. The resultant labor shortage meant that northern industrial employers turned to immigrant labor. By 1910, six of ten such workers were foreign born (Feagin and Feagin, 1996). The vast majority of the 21,000,000 immigrants drawn to the United States by these promises of employment were drawn from the impoverished regions of Southern and Eastern Europe. Thus, this era saw the beginning of mass migration of Italians, Poles, Russians, and Eastern European Jews.

The 1930s and 1940s were relatively quiet in terms of immigration. It was not until the 1950s—perhaps owing to the apparent affluence of the United

States—that immigration levels began to climb gradually. Throughout the decades of the 1950s and 1960s, Europeans and Canadians continued to dominate. However, by the 1970s, the trend reversed itself, due in large part to changes in immigration policy. The 1965 Immigration Act eliminated discriminatory country of origin quotas. For the first time in United States history, white European immigrants were the minority (Aguirre and Turner, 1997), representing less than 15% of all newcomers. Instead, Asians and Latin Americans (especially Mexicans) led the queue. Moreover, 1991 represented the century peak for immigration, which reached a high of 1.8 million.

Not surprisingly, postcolonial immigration has often been met with deep suspicion and often mistreatment of the newcomers. Each cohort of "new immigrants" was perceived as the alien and foreign "Other." They have been regarded as outside the boundaries of the imagined community of the United States. Successive groups of immigrants were thought to represent distinct and threatening "races."

Anti-Immigrant Sentiments

Having established themselves as the "nativist" core of the United States, European Protestants were loath to welcome the cultural influence of other immigrants. Although grateful for the cheap labor provided by subsequent immigrants, the English American "founders" nonetheless saw themselves as the only true Americans. Unless and until the "foreigners" subordinated themselves to the ethnic ideology of Protestantism, they would remain outsiders, with the corresponding lack of power. They would be reminded of their inferiority by the actions of organized and unorganized mobs of nativists—anti-immigrant leagues, Ku Klux Klan, even political parties like the Know Nothings (Feagin and Feagin, 1996; Bailey, 1991).

The development of "scientific" racial ideologies in the 1800s legitimated these negative perceptions of immigrants. Anglo-Saxons were constructed as inherently superior to all other races along cultural, intellectual, and political lines. Ironically, these racial exclusions were applied to many groups we would now identify as "white." Irish, Jews, Eastern Europeans, and Mediterraneans were long held to be foreign and defiled "races" (Sacks, 1997). If they could not be assimilated, they must be eliminated. The following is indicative of the sentiment:

> The neighborhood (New York City's Lower East Side), peopled almost entirely by the people who claim to have been driven from Poland and Russia, is the eyesore of New York and perhaps the filthiest place on the western continent. It is impossible for a Christian to live there because he will be driven out, either by blows or the dirt and the stench. (1922—Madison Grant, cited in Sacks, 1997:102)

The ghosts of the 1920s have returned to haunt us in the contemporary era. Now, as then, there is a widespread fear that unbridled immigration will destroy the moral, economic, and (mono)cultural fibre of the United States. We see resurrected a political discourse that seeks also to construct immigrants as dangerous "others" within. In fact, opponents are fond of using the explicitly exclusionary term "alien" rather than "immigrant," presumably to highlight the marginal status of these people. This reflects the historical ambivalence toward immigrants in a nation of immigrants, a notion reinforced by the former governor of Colorado and his coauthor: "Immigration policy was once an asset to this country, helping to make us strong. But its current uncontrolled state will seriously harm this country and its institutions" (Lamm and Imhoff, 1985:49). Currently, the United States is faced with an "immigration crisis." Unlike the cases of the earlier waves of immigration, the current arrivals are not predominantly European, are not even predominantly white. On the contrary, they are overwhelmingly Asians, and Hispanics from South and Central America. On the basis of race alone, these immigrants are not as readily assimilable as their predecessors. This makes people like David Duke (former Louisiana Representative and former KKK leader) nervous:

> The darkening of our nation mimics histories of many other nations. The nations of the Caribbean, Central and South America, are predictive examples of the fate that awaits us. The Third World awaits our children. It is in our streets, in our taxpayer paid–for housing projects, in our jails, and in our mayor's chairs. . . . Our children grow up in an alien society that our forefathers would not recognize. (Duke, online)

Culturally, nonwhite, non-European immigrants are constructed as major contributors to the breakdown of United States' morality, unity, and stability. An integral element of the perceived danger involves the invocation of the theme of "immigrant criminality." Immigrants are presented as the "partners in crime" to the black native-born male. Lamm and Imhoff (1985:49) devote a full chapter to the crime-immigrant nexus. They contend that, "As far as we are from solving our own crime problem, we cannot afford to ignore the lawlessness that comes with the breakdown of our borders. Our immigration policies are exacerbating our national epidemic of crime." Following this warning, the authors introduce three pages of anecdotal evidence to "prove" the contributions of (especially illegal) immigrants to the violent crime rate in this country. In fact, in spite of their assurances to the contrary, Lamm and Imhoff (1985:53) imply that immigrants are inherently criminal. They support this contention, first by generalizing their observation that illegal immigrants are by definition criminal. In addition, however, they marshal evidence from the case of the Mariel boatlift. Relying solely on the arguments of an investigating officer by the name of Detective Alvarez, Lamm and Imhoff (1985) suggest that because so many of these (illegal) immigrants were *probably* criminals, then it is reasonable to assume that, in general, many immigrants are also *probably* criminals.

The association between immigrants and criminality is often supplemented by messages implying that they are also the root of the nation's economic woes.

From this perspective, immigrants—especially Third World immigrants—come to this country for two reasons: to sack the welfare system and to take the jobs of Americans. The former belief underlies Wilson's Proposition 187, which would have excluded illegal immigrants and their children from most state social services, and proposals to exclude even legal immigrants from Social Security payments. Presumably, immigrants are getting rich off the United States' welfare system; it is catapulting them into the middle class, over the heads of long-suffering native-born Americans. It is, however, unclear what computations place welfare recipients in a middle-income bracket.

Immigrants are in a double bind. On the one hand, they are berated for their presumed exploitation and plundering of the social safety net. Yet on the other hand, should they turn instead to legitimate employment—as the vast majority do—they are then reviled for stealing "American" jobs. Meldren Thomas Jr., former governor of New Hampshire, levies both charges in one very direct statement:

> One tax expert estimates that right now the average tax payer pays $259 a year just to support illegal aliens now in the United States. Illegal aliens cost you tax dollars when they get food stamps, welfare benefits, medical and Medicare payments, free bilingual public schooling and social security benefits—illegal immigrants take 3.5 million jobs from Americans. (cited in Simon and Alexander, 1993:259)

Whether framed in economic, cultural, or criminal terms, the underlying message is that war must be declared on the invading force of immigrants. To frame a problem in such terms and call for an armed response plants the seeds of violence in the broader culture. Immigrants are framed as "enemies" of the American way of life. Presumably, they present a threat that can only be contained by extreme means. Consequently,

> Immigrant bashing is a popular activity in assigning blame for the nation's economic problems. When stagnation is evident in the national economy and unemployment exceeds seven percent, a pervasive fear that one's job is on the line often emerges. Anxiety triggers frustration and blame; resentment towards immigrants, documented and undocumented, becomes an ugly side of racism, nativism, and xenophobia. (Ochoa, 1995:227)

A backlash against immigrants is also reflected in public sentiments. In general, the majority (65%) of those polled feel that immigration levels should be decreased (Gallup, 1993a). Unpacking this position, we find rationales that speak to perceived threats associated with immigrants: 55% of respondents felt that immigration "threatened American culture"—in fact, 82% of those who felt immigration should be decreased felt so threatened. Another Gallup poll (1993b) found that 29% of those surveyed feared that immigrants were more likely than other groups to commit crime. Fifty-six percent of respondents indicated their belief that immigration was a drain on the United States' economy (Gallup, 1993a).

Immigrants as Offenders

Illegal Aliens

Contrary to historical and contemporary perceptions of immigrant criminality, immigrants tend not to be overrepresented in crime statistics. The obvious exception to this observation are undocumented immigrants—"illegals," as they have come to be labeled. Undocumented immigrants are, by definition, engaging in criminal behavior. They have either entered the country illegally ("Without Inspection") or have remained here subsequent to legal entry (what the Immigration and Naturalization Service [INS] refers to as "Overstays"). The INS estimates that in 1996, approximately 5,000,000 undocumented immigrants were living in the United States. Nearly half of these were Overstays rather than immigrants Without Inspection. The majority of illegal immigrants (54%) come from Mexico, followed by El Salvador, Guatemala, Canada, and Haiti (Bureau of Justice Statistics, 1996).

The INS is responsible for the apprehension and expulsion of illegal aliens. In an average year, the agency expels 1,000,000 undocumented immigrants, the majority of which tend to be Mexicans. Only a small proportion of those found to be in the country illegally are forcibly deported. Consistently, upwards of 90% take the option of *voluntary return with safeguards.* Although the former is barred from reentering the United States for 5 years, the latter can reenter legally at any time.

Criminal Aliens

Criminal aliens must be distinguished from illegal aliens. The former are noncitizens who have been convicted of such offenses as felonies, drug trafficking, firearms offenses, or offenses endangering national security. These people may be in the United States legally as resident aliens or on visas. However, by virtue of their conviction for law-breaking behavior, they are automatically deportable as well as subject to penalties ranging from probation to long-term incarceration—after which they may still be deported. Moreover, Miller and Moore (1997:318) argue that most noncitizens in federal prisons are not immigrants but are rather international criminals who were in the country temporarily. Consequently, the available data on noncitizens in the criminal justice system must be considered with that caveat in mind.

A recent Bureau of Justice Statistics (BJS, 1996) publication provides a succinct overview of the characteristics of noncitizens in the criminal justice system. Nearly half (48.6%) of all noncitizens convicted of a federal offense in 1994 were from Mexico; 28.8% were from South or Central America; and 2.2% were from

Canada. Those noncitizens who were prosecuted were less likely (44%) than their citizen counterparts (60%) to have a known criminal history.

Noncitizens—some of whom may be immigrants, many of whom are in the country temporarily—are overwhelmingly charged with immigration and drug-related offenses. Together, these categories accounted for 69% of all convictions. Of all federal immigration offenders, the vast majority (66.5%) were convicted for illegal entry or reentry (BJS, 1996). The remainder were convicted of offenses related to smuggling noncitizens or handling fraudulent entry and passport documents.

Noncitizens—immigrants among them—have found themselves caught in the double bind of the war on drugs and anti-immigrant sentiment and policy. The outcome of this has been a dramatic sweep of noncitizen drug offenders. Consequently, 85% of all federal noncitizen inmates and 45% of all noncitizen state inmates were convicted of drug offenses. However, these were not the "hardened traffickers" of popular imagery. On the contrary, the majority of those incarcerated for drug offenses tend to be users and small-scale dealers (Dunn, 1996).

In contrast, few noncitizens appear to be involved in violent offenses, especially at the federal level. Although 35.2% of all noncitizens in state prisons in 1991 were convicted of violent offenses, only 1.9% of those in federal prisons were convicted of the same (BJS, 1996). Again, one must regard these figures with some care, because violent crime rates tend to be more closely associated with nonresident aliens and with international organized crime.

Organized Crime

Increasingly, organized crime in the United States has assumed an international flavor. No longer the preserve of "white ethnics" (e.g., Irish, Italians, and Jews), organized crime now encompasses a cross-section of the "new immigrants" as well. Latin Americans, Africans, Asians, and Eastern Europeans (especially Russians) are all represented in organized crime groups. Marshall (1997) suggests that although many of its members are immigrants, a substantial proportion are also nonresidents in this country with the explicit intent of expanding the domain and markets of organizations that exist in their home countries. Consequently, they are able to exploit "the bonds resulting from a common place of origin and its cultural and social rituals and values . . . to reproduce the same structures of hierarchy, complicity, conspiracy of silence and the same cohesion" with which migrants are familiar (Schmid and Savona, 1996:21). In some sense, then, organized crime in the United States provides a bridge between cultures.

Many of the Asian crime organizations—like the Triads—originally emerged as political or community-oriented organizations. Others, such as the Wah Ching, developed out of more loosely organized street gangs. However, in the contemporary era, these have all come to resemble those explicitly created around criminal activity. The Japanese Yakuza, the Jamaican posses, and the "Russian mafia" increasingly share common characteristics and pursuits. Such syndicates control regionally and often ethnically specific black markets (Tanton and Lutton, 1993). Asian syndicates tend to control much of the drug smuggling, prostitution, and other vice markets on the West Coast and parts of New York and New Jersey. Caribbean cartels, such as those with links to Haiti and Cuba, tend to dominate the southeast United States drug trade in particular. The Russian mafia tends to be less localized, preferring to spread its fraud, extortion, burglary, and other such activities across the nation. Nigerians, operating in small "cells," engage in some heroin smuggling, but more commonly specialize in massive fraud schemes (Tanton and Lutton, 1993).

Immigrants as Victims

In spite of the previously mentioned data, the tendency to assume that immigrants are immoral at best and criminal at worst persists. Consequently, "immigrant bashing" has become a part of the daily reality for those who have reached these shores in search of the promised freedom and opportunity. Unfortunately, there are no concrete data on anti-immigrant violence. Violence against a Korean shopowner, for example, is classified and recorded as anti-Asian violence. However, the connection between the perpetrator's tendency to equate ethnicity with immigrant status is apparent in the verbal assaults that often accompany physical assaults. When East Indians or Haitians are told to "go back where you belong," the assumption is clear: regardless of whether they are first, second, or third generation, those who are "different" are perceived as perpetual foreigners who do not belong here. It is likely, therefore, that a significant proportion of the 355 anti-Asian and 516 anti-Hispanic hate crimes recorded by the FBI in 1995 (FBI, 1996) were motivated by anti-immigrant sentiments. Perhaps even some of the 2,988 antiblack hate crimes were motivated by the perception that the victims were Nigerian, or Haitian, or South African, for example.

The perceived correspondence of race/ethnicity and immigrant status is apparent in the case of the thousands of Hmong refugees who had been resettled in Philadelphia in the late 1970s. By 1985, fewer than 700 remained, a factor many have attributed to the ongoing harassment and intimidation of the refugees. A witness reported to a Human Relations hearing that "It is not uncommon for complete strangers to come up to me and say, 'Are you Chinese?' We are all identified as Chinese. . . . It is not uncommon for a refugee to be accosted with a statement like, 'Chinese go home'" (United States Commission on Civil Rights, nd: 48–49). Similar confusion is evident in the targeting of Hindu temples, which "become the proxy for violence against individual Asians. One such temple in Chandler, Arizona, was spray painted with the message 'No Chinks. Go Home to China.' Gun shots through the door punctuated the message" (United States Commission on Civil Rights, 1992:32). These examples are not atypical of the victimization of those deemed to be "foreign." They reflect the simmering hostility toward those held responsible for economic and social ills alike.

Not surprisingly, there are regional variations in the intensity and frequency of immigrant bashing. It tends to be most prevalent in those areas—the Northeast (especially New York and New Jersey) and the Southwest (especially Arizona, California, and Texas)—with a disproportionate share of newly arrived immigrants. Between 1982 and 1993, nearly 35% of all legal immigrants settled in California; nearly 20% settled in New York and New Jersey (Miller and Moore, 1997:311). In addition, the INS estimated that in 1996, California hosted 2 million of the 2.6 million illegal Mexican immigrants alone (INS, 1997:online).

Consequently, anti-immigrant hate crime is relatively frequent in these areas. In particular, California, Arizona, and Texas see their share of border violence, wherein legal and illegal immigrants are victimized by vigilantes and by Border Patrol agents alike. In the late 1980s, the Arizona Border Patrol was "aided" by a paramilitary group calling itself Civilian Military Assistance (CMA). The KKK continues to burn crosses periodically along the border in an attempt to frighten both legal and illegal immigrants (Nuñez, 1992). At the level of interpersonal violence, in a camp for homeless migrant workers in Alpine, California, a Hispanic man was beaten by six men with baseball bats who later bragged about "kicking Mexican ass" (Southern Poverty Law Center, 1997:223). Nuñez (1992) documents numerous cases of such anti-immigrant bias along the United States–Mexico border, ranging from verbal taunts to rock throwing to shots fired.

There is little the victims can do to defend themselves. Whether legal or illegal, immigrants often fear and mistrust Border Patrol authorities. The threat of secondary victimization is a very real one. Border Patrol and INS agents are not without blame. A report issued by the American Friends Service Committee of Los Angeles documented 55 incidents of brutality (a mere fraction of what is suspected) and misconduct by INS agents, one of which ended in death. Of these, 10 of the complainants were United States citizens, and 27 were legal residents or visitors (Southern Poverty Law Center, 1997).

Undocumented immigrants are at a heightened risk of victimization and revictimization because of their particular fears of reporting abuses by civilians and state agents. They have far more to lose by drawing attention to themselves. A 1979 Task Force finding remains true today: there exists an "extra-legal society whose members are unable to have wrongs redressed through legitimate channels without risking discovery and subsequent deportation" (Interagency Task Force on Immigration Policy, 1979:363–364). Moreover, the people to whom one might report a crime are often the offenders. INS and Border Patrol agents have a job to do: stop illegal border crossings. However, buoyed by a climate of anti-immigrant hostility, officials can be overzealous in their policing of the border. Excessive use of force and unwarranted abuses do occur. An America's Watch report documents several such cases, including that of Francisco Ruiz and his pregnant wife, Evelyn. When Ruiz attempted to protect his wife from an attack by a Border Patrol agent (which included him pressing his foot on her abdomen), he was shot once in the stomach and once in the buttock (Nuñez, 1992:1574–1575).

The border violence experienced by Mexican immigrants in particular is an extension of the broader sense—noted previously—that the United States is in the midst of an "immigration crisis" and that the nation has lost control of the flow of disruptive newcomers. All too often, reports of misconduct are thus met with indifference, if not support. The construction of immigrants as "alien" and as a menace ensures that anti-immigrant violence will persist unless the ideology and action are confronted directly. In short, immigrants require the protections afforded by representation of their interests in and by the criminal justice system.

Immigrants as Service Providers in the Criminal Justice System

Data on immigrants as service providers within the criminal justice system are as meager as those on victimization. Again, immigrant status is collapsed within racial and ethnic categories. Given the paucity of racial and ethnic minorities as employees in the criminal justice system, it is plausible to assume that immigrants are underrepresented. Keep in mind the earlier discussion of the distribution of the "new immigrants"—predominantly Asians, Latin Americans, and Africans. These people of color are not highly visible as criminal justice practitioners (Stokes and Scott, 1996; Flowers, 1990; Shusta, 1995). It is especially troubling that the Border Patrol—with its enforcement emphasis on the United States–Mexico border—has a relatively low proportion of Hispanic officers. The border is the site of some of the most frequent and brutal victimization of legal and illegal residents. Enhanced minority hiring would establish a more empathetic environment. Nuñez (1992) also recommends that the internal review process of the INS and Border Patrol be replaced with an independent civilian review board as a means of establishing accountability.

To some extent, there are legitimate reasons for the slow absorption of immigrants into the criminal justice system. Nonnative born individuals lack the familiarity with United States culture, customs, and legal order that would facilitate immediate entry. Moreover, they are often excluded by reason of language barriers. However, once they have acclimated to the "new world," they would bring numerous advantages to the criminal justice system. Immigrant personnel would act as both cultural and linguistic bridges between immigrants and their native-born counterparts, between the community and the criminal justice system.

Other means of making the criminal justice system accountable and accessible to the immigrant community include the related initiatives of cultural awareness training, language training, and the availability of bilingual officers and/or translators. Long Beach, California, provides a model in that its police department addresses the needs of the community's 17,000 Khmer speakers and several thousand Spanish speakers with two-person patrols consisting of Spanish- and Khmer-speaking officers. In addition, all officers are required to attend a 40-hour cultural awareness training program.

Immigrant social and cultural organizations are also indispensable mechanisms by which to ease the transition for newcomers (e.g., Cambodian Association of America; Japanese American Social Services, Inc.). Such programs represent the interests of immigrants through community organizing, social functions, and the provision of services and service links to social and medical agencies. Communities with particularly large immigrant populations have established settlement centers and organizations. The Haitian Refugee Center, for example, provides counseling and guidance on posttraumatic stress, employment and employment skills, and housing. Perhaps more important in light of the anti-Haitian activities of the INS, the center also protects Haitian immigrants from wrongful expulsion and deportation (Nuñez, 1992).

In response to the harassment and violence often suffered by immigrants, many antiviolence and civil rights groups have emerged. Some, like the Coalition Against Asian Violence and the California Border Violence Delegation Project, serve regionally and ethnically specific interests by monitoring and publicizing violence against them. Others, like the American Friends Service Committee's Immigration Law Enforcement Monitoring Project, have a broader mandate to address violence experienced by all immigrants, regardless of country of origin.

It is unfortunate that the United States still requires the presence of such watchdogs. However, this is a nation grounded in a legacy of racist and anti-immigrant sentiment and practice that is not going to disappear on its own. The civil rights organizations and activists that represent immigrants will continue to play a dominant role in enhancing the perception, place, and power of all newcomers, whatever the color of their face or accent in their speech.

References

Aguirre, A. and Turner, J. (1997). *American ethnicity*. Boston: McGraw-Hill.

Bailey, F. (1991). Law, justice and "Americans:" An historical overview. In M. Lynch and B. Patterson (Eds.), *Race and criminal justice*, pp. 10–21. Albany, NY: Harrow and Heston.

Bureau of Justice Statistics (1996). *Non-citizens in the federal criminal justice system, 1984–94*.

David Duke (nd), untitled, www.duke.org/object.html.

Dunn, T. (1996). *The militarization of the U.S. Mexico border, 1978–1992*. Austin, TX: Center for Mexican American Studies Press.

Feagin, J. and Feagin, C. B. (1996). *Racial and ethnic relations*. Upper Saddle River, NJ: Prentice-Hall.

Federal Bureau of Investigation (1996). *Hate crime statistics, 1995*. Washington, DC: U.S. Department of Justice.

Flowers, R. B. (1990). *Minorities and criminality*. New York: Praeger.

Gallup (1993a). Americans feel threatened by new immigrants. *Gallup Poll Monthly*, (July):2–96.

———. (1993b). Racial overtones evident in Americans' attitudes about crime. *Gallup Poll Monthly*, (Dec.):37–42.

Immigration and Naturalization Service (1997). *Illegal alien resident population*, www.ins.usdoj.gov/stats/illegalalien/index.html.

Interagency Task Force on Immigration Policy (1979). *Staff report*.

Lamm, R. and Imhoff, G. (1985). *The immigration time bomb*. New York: Truman Tally Books.

Marshall, I. H. (1997). Minorities, crime and criminal justice in the United States. In I. H. Marshall (Ed.), *Minorities, migrants and crime*, pp. 1–35. Thousand Oaks, CA: Sage.

Miller, J. and Moore, S. (1997). The index of leading immigration indicators. In N. Capaldi (Ed.), *Immigration: Debating the issues*, pp. 306–322. Amherst, NY: Prometheus.

Nuñez, M. (1992). Violence at our border: Rights and status of immigrant victims of hate crimes and violence along the border between the United States and Mexico. *Hastings Law Journal*, *43*, 1573–1605.

Ochoa, A. (1995). Language policy and social implications for addressing the bicultural experience in the U.S. In A. Dander (Ed.), *Culture and difference: Critical perspectives on the bicultural experience in the United States*, pp. 227–253. Westport, CT: Bergin and Garey.

Rothenberg, P. (1997). Introduction, Pt. II. In P. Rothenberg (Ed.), *Race, class and gender in the United States*, pp. 110–114. New York: St. Martin's.

Sacks, K. B. (1997). How Jews became white. In P. Rothenberg (Ed.), *Race, class and gender in the United States*. New York: St. Martin's.

Schmid, A. P. and Savona, E. U. (1996). Migration and crime: A framework for discussion. In A. P. Schmid (Ed.), *Migration and crime*. Milan, Italy: International Scientific and Professional Advisory Council of the United Nations Crime Prevention and Criminal Justice Program.

Shusta, R. (1995). *Multicultural law enforcement: Strategies for peacekeeping in a diverse society*. Englewood Cliffs, NJ: Prentice Hall.

Simon, R. and Alexander, S. (1993). *The ambivalent welcome*. Westport, CT: Praeger.

Southern Poverty Law Center (1997). Anti-immigrant violence in Virginia. In V. Cyrus (Ed.), *Experiencing race, class and gender in the United States*, pp. 223–228. Mountain View, CA: Mayfield.

Stokes, L. and Scott, J. (1996). Affirmative action and selected minority groups in law enforcement. *Journal of Criminal Justice, 24(1)*, 29–38.

Tanton, J. and Lutton, W. (1993). Immigration and criminality in the USA. *Journal of Social, Political and Economic Studies, 18(2)*, 217–234.

U.S. Commission on Civil Rights (1992). *Civil rights issues facing Asian Americans*.

———. (nd). *Recent actions against citizens and residents of Asian descent*.

Wilson, P. (1994). Securing our nation's borders. Speech presented at Los Angeles Town Hall, April 25, 1994.

6 Historical Injustices, Contemporary Inequalities

African Americans and Criminal Justice

BRIAN J. SMITH

On an early summer evening in 1998, three young men were driving around the town of Jasper, Texas, when one of them spotted James Byrd walking along the road. One of the men knew Byrd from the local parole office, so they gave him a ride. The three men savagely beat Byrd, and then chained him to the back of their pick-up truck. They proceeded to drag him for more than 2 miles, dismembering and killing him (Hohler, 1998). As many may remember, the suspected offenders are white men and James Byrd was a middle-age black man. As would be expected, the public and political leaders were outraged by this brutal crime. Although some called for harmony between blacks and whites, black political groups marched in Jasper and suggested that local blacks arm themselves for self-protection. Today, we consider this lynching to be a heinous crime committed by immoral individuals; yet 200 years ago, James Byrd's body parts could have been legally and publicly displayed to deter against slave rebellion. Even 100 years ago, this lynching would have been legally accepted in Jasper and would have received very little public attention. This incident reminds us of the enduring significance of being black in the United States. Racial differences produce tensions, conflict, inequalities, and violence in the United States. Consequently, racial identity is very important. In the United States, "race matters" (West, 1993).

Historically in the United States, legal, political, public, economic, and social institutions have often treated African Americans as unequal people. Sometimes African Americans' racial identity still causes them to be targets of individual and/or institutional discrimination (i.e., acts and policies that treat them as unequals due to their racial identity). Consider the name for an apparent crime on

Maryland's interstates—"Driving while Black" (Barovick, 1998).[1] Between 1995 and 1997, only 17% of drivers on I95 in Maryland were black, yet they represented 70% of drivers stopped and searched by police. Whites represented 75% of total drivers, but only 23% of those stopped and searched (Barovick, 1998). These disproportionate percentages are the result of police "profiles" of drug couriers; part of the profile seems to be being black. Of course, there has been some progress, some institutional inclusion of African Americans. Slavery is no longer legal, and James Byrd's killers will be harshly punished. African Americans now have access to legal rights and civil liberties, and many live free and decent lives. They can vote and are generally treated more equally by legal institutions; they can be elected to powerful positions in legal and political institutions. Employers and public schools and universities can no longer legally exclude black individuals from their institutions because of their racial identity. However, in spite of these advances, African Americans remain disadvantaged as a group in the 1990s. They are still more likely than whites to suffer from inequalities that are usually no fault of their own; these include the following: childhood and adult poverty, unemployment, inadequate health care, location of residence, educational status, unequal legal treatment, and a lack of economic and educational opportunity. African Americans are also more likely to be in prison, to be homicide victims, and to be victims of personal and property crimes.

This chapter has the following purposes: (1) to show some of the legal injustices and inequalities that blacks suffered from as slaves in the United States; (2) to illustrate some of the legal exclusions of blacks in the post–Civil War era; (3) to note some of the legal progress that has been made; (4) to present the current criminal justice status of African Americans as victims, offenders, and service providers; and (5) to briefly note some suggestions for legal changes and public policies that may help improve African Americans' status in the United States. Much of this chapter emphasizes the power and role of law; this emphasis is especially appropriate regarding the status of blacks. Law's power has been utilized to exclude blacks from meaningful participation in United States social life, and it has also been utilized in attempts to better their social status. African Americans' current disadvantaged and unequal status indicates that they have not yet attained full social, legal, and political inclusion in America.

Legal Historical Context

Goldberg (1995:284) writes that "[r]easonable people generally now agree that it is wrong for both persons and social institutions to discriminate against others . . .

---

[1]This chapter uses "black" and "white" to identify the racial identity of African Americans and European Americans. Scholars (Jones, 1998; Russell, 1998) adopt these terms in their investigations of racial identities. Indeed, the name of the driving offense also shows that for African Americans, being "black" is very significant in the United States. Thus, this chapter utilizes both sets of terms to signify group identity.

on grounds of their race." Historically, blacks have suffered greatly from individual and institutional discrimination. From the initial bonds of slavery to their exclusion from and segregation within various spheres of social life, the United States has often treated African Americans in an extremely unequal and unjust manner. This section provides the historical context that is necessary for understanding the current unequal and disadvantaged status of African Americans.

Slavery

The history of African Americans is a story of inequality, injustice, and exclusion, beginning with slavery. Widespread belief in the natural inequality/inferiority of blacks (i.e., racist ideology) helped underpin discriminatory policies and actions (Bailey, 1991; Flowers, 1988; Russell, 1998). Slavery can be understood as a "system of forced, lifetime labor" (Schwarz, 1988:7). Slaves were not free, but rather were owned by others; they were considered to be economic property, anything but equal human beings. From 1619 to 1865, slaves were subject to states' "slave codes," which declared blacks' inferiority and upheld the exploitation of slaves and their exclusion from American life. The codes banned slaves from enjoying the following rights or freedoms: speech, privacy, association, education, employment, voting, holding political office, or owning property (Turner, Singleton, and Musick, 1984).

Slave codes let plantation owners police and control their slaves, and the owners often punished in cruel and inhumane ways. If a slave was discovered outside of plantation boundaries, he/she could be killed for refusing to answer questions. A dismembered slave's body parts could be publicly displayed, and the codes made it illegal for whites to "actively oppose" the institution of slavery (Russell, 1998). The most common sanction for slaves was whipping, a punishment considered cruel and unusual today (Hindus, 1980; Rabinowitz, 1992). Slaves were also branded for crimes; an example would be the letter "T" for the crime of theft (Russell, 1998). Plantation owners could also punish slaves by denying them fulfilment of basic human needs such as social contact and food (Schwarz, 1988). In sum, the slave codes designated blacks as inferiors, treated them as unequal human beings, and exploited their labor.

Post–Civil War

Three post–Civil War amendments to the Bill of Rights are dramatic legal declarations regarding blacks and citizens' rights. They declare that individuals cannot be enslaved in the United States, and that they have certain legal rights and political freedoms. The 13th Amendment (1866) legally ended the institution of slavery, declaring that people should be free in the United States unless they committed a crime. The 14th Amendment (1868) declared that all citizens have legal rights that cannot be taken away, and also required the law to treat people equally and protect their freedoms. The Supreme Court later interpreted this amendment as prohibiting public or legal policies that discriminate based on racial identity. The

15th Amendment (1870) provided a first step towards granting blacks their right to self-government; significantly, this amendment declared that they had the right to determine who governs them. The amendment declares that the United States cannot "deny or abridge" a citizen's right to vote "on account of race, color, or previous condition of servitude." Despite these official legal declarations, blacks continued to suffer great injustices during the postbellum era. In fact, federal laws would have to restate and enforce the substantive ideas of the three amendments through the mid-1900s. Legal change does not immediately alter social structures (Turner *et al.*, 1984); cultural, social, and economic progress takes time.

Legal Exclusions

In response to the emancipation of African Americans, many states passed "black codes" and "Jim Crow laws" that helped maintain the legal–institutional discrimination of the pre–Civil War era. These laws specifically targeted African Americans, restricting their freedoms and preventing their inclusion into white society. Politically, the codes denied blacks the right to vote or to public assembly (Jones, 1998; Russell, 1998). Economically, the codes did allow freed slaves to enter into contracts and restricted them to menial and inferior employment positions. In apparent contradiction with the 14th Amendment, the Supreme Court ruled that "separate but equal" institutions for blacks and whites were constitutional in *Plessy* v. *Ferguson* (1896). This decision upheld a Louisiana statute that required separate accommodations in public train coaches and helped solidify the legal foundation for the segregationist and exclusionary practices that became commonplace through the first half of the twentieth century in the United States.

Jim Crow statutes created a legally segregated society across the United States, an "American apartheid" (Bailey, 1991); thus, simply "being black" remained a crime during this era (Russell, 1998). Blacks were not allowed to associate with whites in public places such as golf courses, parks, and restaurants. They were not allowed to attend some of the best public schools and universities. Like the earlier slave codes, black codes and Jim Crow statutes allowed blacks to be punished for certain "social actions" such as talking with friends on the street corner or making eye contact with whites (Russell, 1998). Neighborhoods and housing developments enforced covenants that did not allow African American residents in white neighborhoods (Turner *et al.*, 1984). Many blacks were forced to live in dangerous inner-city neighborhoods that had inferior schools (Jones, 1998). In large part through legal institutional discrimination, blacks remained politically and economically excluded during the post–Civil War era; their 15th Amendment right to vote was not upheld by law, but rather by the whim of whites (Jones, 1998). Economic institutions utilized black codes and Jim Crow laws to segregate and exclude blacks through the mid-1900s. Some employers refused to hire blacks, and many powerful unions denied them membership (Jones, 1998). Most employers would not promote blacks above a certain work position, and blacks were more likely to occupy the manual labor work in large companies.

It was extremely rare for a black to occupy a managerial or supervisory position (Jones, 1998).

Discriminatory Criminal Justice System Practices

The black codes and Jim Crow statutes maintained the law's unequal treatment and protection of African Americans; indeed, the very existence of the codes shows that the post–Civil War laws still categorized blacks as different and inferior human beings rather than as equals. The codes continued to allow harsher punishments based on race, and generally did not punish whites for most crimes committed against blacks. The death penalty continued to be practiced in a discriminatory way through the mid-1900s. From the 1800s through the mid-1900s, black offenders who raped white women were often executed. In the vast majority of cases, white rapists were not sentenced to death (Bohm, 1991).

The legal system's discriminatory practices maintained the economic exploitation of blacks. The south made every effort to maintain the economic exploitation of former slaves; thus, in the postbellum south, "crime control meant race control" (Adamson, 1992:11), and race control meant economic power. According to Adamson (1992:6,8), laws were designed to "channel [black] labor into a socially productive use . . . [county] courts were virtual employment bureaus." States developed convict lease systems that exploited blacks' labor power. Correctional systems' policies were grounded in institutional discrimination; blacks were segregated and treated unequally. Whereas whites worked mainly within prison walls, blacks were subjected to harsh working conditions—either under private companies they had been leased to, or on the public chain gang. The separate punishment systems were markedly different. Leased black convicts were subjected to dangerous and brutal living and working conditions on railways and in mines. The law allowed them to be whipped by their captor—the company. Incarceration rates fluctuated with the need for labor power (Adamson, 1992; Myers and Massey, 1991); Myers and Massey's (1991) research illustrates the relationship between increased demands for labor in the cotton fields and increases in the black incarceration rate.

Lynching

The historical phenomenon of lynching during the early part of the twentieth century provides dramatic evidence of institutional *and* individual discrimination against blacks. Lynching can be defined as the "killing of one or more blacks at the hands of an extra-legal mob of three or more individuals" (Beck and Tolnay, 1990:530). Yet in many places, lynchings were "legal" for all practical practices. Police were often present at lynchings, and courts generally did not prosecute whites who lynched blacks (Russell, 1998). The most accurate records indicate that approximately 3,000 African Americans were lynched in the south from the mid-1800s to the early 1900s (Beck and Tolnay, 1990). Lynching was used to symbolically reinforce the inferior economic and social position of blacks; it was often used in times of black threats to white economic dominance and stability (Beck and Tolnay, 1990). Lynching increased dramatically during the economically un-stable post–Civil War decades and peaked in the 1890s, (Beck and Tolnay, 1990; Myers and Massey, 1991; Turner *et al.*, 1984).

It appears that there was a relationship between lynching rates and fluctua-tions in the cotton market. Beck and Tolnay's (1990) research shows that lynching rates were highest when cotton market prices were low. During these time peri-ods, blacks were a direct threat to lower-class whites' economic viability, as these whites needed to sell their labor power in the cotton fields. The prevalence of lynching also varied according to regional factors; for example, Corzine, Creech, and Corzine's (1983) research illustrates that lynching rates were highest in areas with the largest percentage of African Americans. Unable to rely on the law for the maintenance of race relations, whites in such areas often resorted to collective violence. Obviously, there were no concerns about equal treatment or equal pro-tection when blacks were lynched by "extra-legal mobs."

Twentieth-Century Progress

To a certain extent, the United States has made positive strides in its treatment of African Americans. African Americans are generally treated more justly by some social institutions than they have been historically. They have many legal rights, and are often treated equally and protected by the law. There has been some progress made in public and political arenas. Blacks can attend the best public universities, hold political office, have authority in legal institutions, and take part in many public and political activities. Importantly, the law can no longer utilize racial identity as a legitimate reason for limiting these rights and freedoms. In fact, the law has played a crucial role in these changes. The *Brown v. Board of Education* (1954) Supreme Court decision declared the exclusionist separate but equal doctrine unconstitutional due to its violation of the equal protection clause of the 14th Amendment. This case ruled on whether African American children had the right to attend white public schools in Kansas, South Carolina, Virginia, and Delaware. For the court, such separation was a social symbol of an ideology of blacks' inferiority/inequality and limited their life opportunities, and was therefore unacceptable.

The power and progression of the law during this era is also seen in the pas-sage and enforcement of numerous federal civil rights laws during the 1950s and 1960s. The 1957 and 1960 civil rights acts restated that it is the government's re-sponsibility to uphold an individual's right to vote. The landmark 1964 Civil Rights Act restated the unlawfulness of segregated public schools and also out-lawed segregation in public contexts, including restaurants, movie theaters, retail establishments, and sporting events. Title VII of this act sought to promote the economic inclusion of minorities and women. It banned employer policies that discriminate against individuals on the basis of their race, color, religion, sex, or national origin (in areas such as hiring, wages, and promotions). The 1965 Voting Rights Act again declared that race is not a legitimate reason for placing restrictions on an individual's right to political participation.

African Americans, Crime, and the Criminal Justice System

African Americans' legal history in the United States laid the groundwork for their current social status as a racial group—as blacks. Despite the many positive changes since the 1960s, African Americans as a social group continue to be disadvantaged during the 1990s. They are more likely to suffer from numerous economic inequalities. In 1997, 26.5% of blacks were living below the poverty line, compared with 11% of whites (United States Bureau of Census, 1997). In 1992, 46.3% of black children were living in poverty, compared with 16% of white children (Reiman, 1998; Walker et al., 1996). Furthermore, economic disadvantage is linked with other social disadvantages, including inadequate housing and health care, illiteracy, shorter life expectancy, higher infant mortality rates, and less educational and economic opportunity (Russell, 1998; Jones, 1998; Reiman, 1998; Walker et al., 1996). The fact that African Americans are more likely to suffer from economic inequality and all the additional disadvantages that come with it, provides a framework for understanding their increased likelihood of criminal victimization and overrepresentation in the criminal justice system.

Victimization

National victimization survey data illustrate that blacks, as a racial group, are disproportionately disadvantaged by their criminal victimization status. This likelihood is closely linked with their geographic location; in general, the urban poor are more likely to be victims of crime, and African Americans are disproportionately represented among the urban poor. Data from the National Crime Victimization Survey (NCVS) for 1996 illustrate that black households were more likely than whites to suffer from property crime victimization—motor vehicle theft and household burglary and theft (310/1,000 versus 260/1,000; Bureau of Justice Statistics, 1996a). Black households were almost twice as likely as whites to be victims of motor vehicle theft during 1996 (22.2/1,000 versus 21.1/1,000; Bureau of Justice Statistics, 1996a).

Since 1973, victimization data have shown consistently that African Americans are approximately twice as likely as whites to be victims of serious violent crime—homicide, rape, robbery, and aggravated assault. In 1996, the victimization rate for these crimes was 20.5/1,000 for blacks and 11.1/1,000 for whites (Bureau of Justice Statistics, 1998b). The NCVS data from 1992 to 1994 show that blacks were approximately twice as likely to be victims of serious violent crime (Bureau of Justice Statistics, 1997). According to 1996 NCVS data, blacks were more likely to be victims of violence (52.3/1,000) than were any other racial group (Bureau of Justice Statistics, 1998b). Particularly troubling are certain trends since the 1970s. NCVS data indicate that from 1973 to 1992, the likelihood of young black males (aged 12–24) being violently victimized (by robberies and assaults) increased 25%. In 1992, black males aged 16 to 19 were twice as likely as whites in the same age group to be victims of violent crime (Bureau of Justice Statistics, 1994). Data from 1996 indicate that blacks were victimized by robbery at a rate three times higher than that of whites, and were twice as likely to be victims of aggravated assault (Bureau of Justice Statistics, 1996a). Blacks fare no better in statistics on homicide victims. In 1992, blacks represented 12% of the population and 50% of homicide victims (Walker *et al.*, 1996). During the same year, young black males (aged 12–24) were 14 times more likely than the general population to be homicide victims. These males represented 1.3% of the population and 17.2% of single-victim homicides (Bureau of Justice Statistics, 1994). Victimization data for 1996 also illustrate that black males aged 18 to 24 were six times more likely than whites of the same age group to be murdered. Overall, blacks represented 48% of murder victims (Bureau of Justice Statistics, 1996a).

Most crimes committed against blacks are intraracial and are not motivated by racial hate. Still, the large number of black hate-crime victims indicates that they still continue to suffer disproportionately from individual discriminatory actions. There were 8,759 bias-motivated crimes reported to the FBI in 1996, involving 11,039 victims. Approximately 60% of hate-crime victims were attacked because of their race. Blacks were the most common hate-crime victims in the United States, representing 42% (4,600) of all hate-crime victims during 1996 (FBI, 1996b).

Offending

How does contemporary law treat African Americans? Is the criminal justice system still treating blacks unfairly? Again, there has been some improvement; for example, it is illegal for courts and correctional systems to institutionally discriminate against blacks and exploit their labor; blacks are not sentenced to death for crimes that whites are not. Despite these improvements, blacks as a group are still more likely to suffer from disadvantaged criminal justice status. Like criminal victimization status, criminal justice status is significantly linked with one's economic status. Poor individuals are more likely to end up in jail and prison, on probation or parole, and African Americans are disproportionately poor. If one lives in urban poverty, one is more likely to be arrested for street crimes, sit in jail without bail money, be sent to prison, and end up on parole or probation.

Nowhere is this disparity greater than in the overrepresentation of blacks in the criminal justice system. Between 1990 and 1997, the total number of inmates in United States prisons increased from 773,918 to 1,244,554 (Bureau of Justice Statistics, 1998a). Blacks have continued to be disproportionately represented in the criminal justice system during this increase. Blacks make up approximately 13%

of the United States population and represent approximately 50% of the prison population (Chiricos and Crawford, 1995; Bureau of Justice Statistics, 1998a; Tonry, 1995). Data from 1996 indicate that blacks represented 49.4% of state and federal prisoners (Bureau of Justice Statistics, 1996b). Between 1980 and the mid-1990s, the number of blacks in prison tripled (Tonry, 1995). Between 1990 and 1996, the number of black males in prison (with at least a 1-year sentence) increased 55% (to 528,200). The number of black females in prison increased 72% (to 33,900) during the same time period (Bureau of Justice Statistics, 1996b). In 1996, black males were more than eight times as likely to be in prison as their white counterparts (3,098/100,000 versus 370/100,000; Bureau of Justice Statistics, 1998a). Blacks are also overrepresented in United States jails. Black men and women represented 41% of jail inmates in 1996 (Bureau of Justice Statistics, 1996b). Miller (1996) notes that 25% of black males in their 20s are under the control of the criminal justice system on any given day. Year-end data from 1997 show that there were 3.9 million men and women on probation or parole at the end of 1997. The data further indicate that one-third (775,600) of probationers were black and almost one-half (281,000) of parolees were black (Bureau of Justice Statistics, 1998c).

Scholars debate the reasons for African Americans' overrepresentation in the criminal justice system. The disproportionate percentage of blacks under justice system control does not necessarily point to the existence of a discriminatory criminal justice system (Reiman, 1998; Tonry, 1995; Walker et al., 1996). Certain groups may be disproportionately represented in prisons due to their disproportionate involvement in crime. In 1996, blacks represented 30.7% of all persons arrested, 32.4% of persons arrested for property crimes, and 43.2% of all persons arrested for violent crimes (FBI, 1996a). Percentages like these lead some scholars to argue that the main reason for the disproportionate number of incarcerated blacks is that this group is more likely to be involved in crimes that result in imprisonment. Indeed, many researchers believe that the criminal justice system is usually discrimination-free at its various processing stages (Russell, 1998; Tonry, 1995). Some contend that when legal variables are controlled, race is usually not a factor in criminal justice process. Yet, although most researchers agree that the explicit, widespread institutional discriminatory practices of the criminal justice system have lessened, many point to the existence of contextualized institutional discrimination at certain system processing points (e.g., police arrest stage).

Some scholars suggest that although blacks may commit more street crime proportionately, they are targeted by police for certain types of crime such as drug offenses (e.g., "Driving while Black) (Russell, 1998; Reiman, 1998; Walker et al., 1996). Thus, blacks may be institutionally discriminated against by police agencies at the arrest stage. One thing seems certain—increases in African Americans' involvement in street crime do not appear to explain the remarkable increases in their prison numbers. Since the 1970s, black arrest rates have been stable (about 45% of those arrested for rape, robbery, and aggravated assault), but blacks have gone to prison at increasing rates. In 1991, incarceration rates for blacks were seven times higher than white rates (Tonry, 1995).

An extensive amount of research has focused on the relationship between race and sentencing. The findings vary across contexts and are equivocal (Spohn and Cederblom, 1991; Farnworth, Teske, and Thurman, 1991; Miller, 1996; Kramer and Steffensmeir, 1993; Blumstein, 1982; Tonry, 1995; Chircos and Crawford, 1995; Russell, 1998; Walker *et al.*, 1996). For example, it appears that the criminal justice system is often free of discrimination when sentencing individuals for certain violent crimes. Yet a significant amount of research suggests that for some crimes, in some contexts, blacks are discriminated against during the sentencing decision stage for some types of crime. Chiricos and Crawford's (1991) review of 38 studies from the 1970s and 1980s found evidence that race had a direct impact on whether one received a prison sentence for certain felonies, especially in the following contexts: high unemployment rates, in the southern United States, and where blacks make up a greater percentage of the population. Research also indicates that blacks are discriminated against in sentencing decisions for certain lesser felonies (Spohn and Cederblom, 1991).

Certain drug laws and their enforcement indicate systemic discrimination against blacks. Drug war policies have contributed greatly to the increasingly high number of blacks burdened by unequal legal status. Legal changes helped create this increase, rather than any change in black criminal activity. Here, race got mixed in with the "war on drugs" and "get-tough" politicians to wreak devastation on young blacks. Many scholars consider the war on drugs an extremely expensive and wasted effort; without a doubt, it has had dramatic consequences for blacks. According to Miller (1996) the United States has spent $31 billion on the war on drugs. Studies completed on drug usage during the 1970s and 1980s suggest that blacks use drugs "roughly equivalent to their representation in society" (Miller, 1996:80). Despite this, the war on drugs has disproportionately targeted blacks relative to their drug usage or involvement in drug sales (Miller, 1996; Tonry, 1995; Walker *et al.*, 1996).

Federal and state drug statutes have an unfair effect on young African American drug offenders. Federal statutes call for a 5-year mandatory minimum sentence for 5 grams of crack; the same amount of powder cocaine calls for a 1-year minimum mandatory sentence (Miller, 1996:83; Tonry, 1995). In 1991, 90% of the offenders arrested for crack use were minority group members. In contrast, 75% of offenders arrested for powder cocaine were white (Miller, 1996:82). Drug offenses accounted for 30% of the increase in black inmates during 1996 (Bureau of Justice Statistics, 1998a). Tonry (1995:82) writes that drug enforcement tactics and increased sentences for drug offenders "unnecessarily blighted the lives of hundreds of thousands of young disadvantaged black Americans and undermined decades of effort to improve the life chances of members of the urban black underclass."

Service Providers and Support Agencies

African Americans are not only victims and offenders but are also service providers within the criminal justice system. There have been significant increases in the number of African American legal and criminal justice system workers. In 1961, there were 58 black judges; by 1986, there were 841 (Walker et al., 1996). Before the 1970s, many police departments did not hire nonwhites. The total number of black officers has more than doubled since 1972, from about 20,000 to 42,000; in addition, there are now more than a dozen African American police chiefs in major cities (Peak, 1997). Between 1983 and 1992, the 50 largest city departments showed an increase of at least 50% in black officers. In 1993, blacks represented 11.3% of all police officers in local departments in the United States (Bureau of Justice Statistics, 1993). The percentage of blacks employed in corrections has also increased significantly. As of June 30, 1995, blacks represented 20% (49,226) of state and federal correctional employees, a 33% increase from 1990 (Bureau of Justice Statistics, 1995).

Numerous agencies provide support services for black crime victims and offenders. The Office for Victims of Crime, in the United States Department of Justice, provides various types of assistance to crime victims and has special programs to assist minority communities and victims. The National Association for the Advancement of Colored People (NAACP) and the American Civil Liberties Union (ACLU) have numerous programs to assist black citizens and offenders. The National Black United Front (NBUF) has chapters throughout the country that provide educational resources for black inmates.

Policy Considerations

Although there has been progress made regarding African Americans' status in the United States, it is also evident that more is still needed. The law should be utilized as a tool for social progress. To conclude this chapter, I note some legal policies that may help create this progress. First, in regard to the criminal justice system, it is necessary to end the war on drugs and use prisons less. Numerous authors (e.g., Reiman, 1998; Tonry, 1995) suggest that the criminal justice system should, at the very least, not cause more harm than it prevents. Social–legal policies that can help create an equitable opportunity structure that will lead to more educated middle-class blacks and fewer economically disadvantaged blacks, should be explored. Three policies that would be steps towards creating these changes include: (1) the elimination of childhood poverty—the devastating harm of such poverty is well documented (Walker et al., 1996); (2) the creation and maintenance of good juvenile educational and employment programs; and (3) the provision of employment, education, and training to disadvantaged and qualified young adults. These final two suggestions will help give all disadvantaged Americans, including African Americans, an equal opportunity for a decent life free of criminal justice control.

Often, people cannot discuss racial differences and inequalities without having the communication process deteriorate into hostility and ineffectiveness. It is hoped that this chapter presents a contextual framework for both understanding the contemporary criminal justice inequalities that blacks continue to face and exploring practical means of changing these inequalities. This framework suggests that we can use the law to make the United States a better place. The power of the law should be harnessed and utilized to achieve a more just society for all. The United States should be a place of equal opportunity, and the policy suggestions noted here would help move America toward this goal. A childhood of poverty, inferior educational opportunities, being under control of the criminal justice system, and being a victim of crime do not equate with equal opportunity. African Americans began their time here as slaves, and some now have decent opportunities, good employment, and live relatively free lives. Yet, blacks as a racial group continue to be burdened by numerous disadvantages and inequalities in the United States. The power of law should be used to help improve the status of African Americans.

References

Adamson, C. (1992). Punishment after slavery: Southern state penal systems. In P. Finkelman (Ed.), *Race and criminal justice*, pp. 1–15. New York: Garland.

Bailey, F. Y. (1991). Law, justice, and "Americans": An historical overview. In M. J. Lynch and E. B. Patterson (Eds.), *Race and criminal justice*, pp. 10–21. New York: Harrow and Heston.

Barovick, H. (1998). DWB: Driving while black. *Time, 151(23)*, 35.

Beck, E. M. and Tolnay, S. E. (1990). The killing fields of the deep south: The market for cotton and the lynching of blacks, 1882–1930. *American Sociological Review, 55*, 526–539.

Blumstein, A. (1982). On the racial disproportionality of United States' prison populations. *Journal of Criminal Law and Criminology, 73(3)*, 1259–1281.

Bohm, R. (1991). Race and the death penalty in the United States. In M. J. Lynch and E. B. Patterson (Eds.), *Race and criminal justice*, pp. 71–85. New York: Harrow and Heston.

Bridges, G. and Myers, M. (Eds.) (1994). *Inequality, crime and social control*. Boulder, CO: Westview Press.

Bridges, G. and Myers, M. (1994). Problems and prospects in the study of inequality, crime, and social control. In G. Bridges and M. Myers (Eds.), *Inequality, crime and social control*, pp. 3–18. Boulder, CO: Westview.

Brown v. Board of Education (1954). 347 U.S. 483 (1954).

Bureau of Justice Statistics (1998a). *Prisoners in 1997*. Washington, DC: United States Department of Justice.

———. (1998b). *Blacks experience the highest rates of serious violent crime*. Washington, DC: United States Department of Justice.

———. (1998c). *Nation's probation and parole population reached new high last year*. Washington, DC: United States Department of Justice.

———. (1997). *Age patterns of victims of serious violent crime*. Washington, DC: United States Department of Justice.

———. (1996a). *Criminal victimization*. Washington, DC: United States Department of Justice.

———. (1996b). *Profile of jail inmates*. Washington, DC: United States Department of Justice.

———. (1995). *Census of state and federal correctional facilities*. Washington, DC: United States Department of Justice.

———. (1994). *Young black male victims*. Washington, DC: United States Department of Justice.

———. (1993). *Local police departments*. Washington, DC: United States Department of Justice.

Chiricos, T. C. and Crawford, C. (1995). Race and imprisonment: A contextual assessment of the evidence. In D. F. Hawkins (Ed.), *Ethnicity, race, and crime*, pp. 281–309. Albany, NY: SUNY Press.

Corzine, J., Creech, J., and Corzine, L. (1983). Black concentration and lynchings in the South: Testing Blalock's power-threat hypothesis. *Social Forces, 61,* 774–796.

Delong, C. and Jackson, K. (1998). Putting race into context: Race, juvenile justice processing, and urbanization. *Justice Quarterly, 15(3),* 487–504.

Farnworth, M., Teske, R., and Thurman, G. (1991). Ethnic, racial, and minority disparity in felony court processing. In M. J. Lynch and E. B. Patterson (Eds.), *Race and criminal justice,* pp. 54–70. New York: Harrow and Heston.

FBI (1996a). *Crime in the United States.* Washington, DC: United States Department of Justice.

FBI (1996b). *Hate Crime Statistics (1996).* Washington, DC: United States Department of Justice.

Flowers, R. (1988). *Minorities and criminality.* New York: Greenwood Press.

Free, M. D., Jr. (1996). *African Americans and the criminal justice system.* New York: Garland.

Goldberg, D. T. (1995). *Ethical theory and social issues.* Orlando, FL: Harcourt Brace.

Hacker, A. (1992). *Two nations: Black and white, separate, hostile, unequal.* New York: MacMillan.

Hindus, M. S. (1980). *Prison and plantation: Crime, justice, and authority in Massachusetts and South Carolina, 1767–1878.* Chapel Hill, NC: University of North Carolina.

Hohler, B. (1998) Terror in a Texas town. *Boston Globe,* June 14, p. A3.

Jones, J. (1998). *American work: Four centuries of black and white labor.* New York: W. W. Norton.

Kramer, J. and Steffensmeir, D. (1993). Race and imprisonment decisions. *The Sociological Quarterly, 34(2),* 357–376.

Mann, C. R. (1993). *Unequal justice: A question of color.* Bloomington, IN: Indiana University.

Miller, J. G. (1996). *Search and destroy: African-American males in the criminal justice system.* Cambridge, UK: Cambridge University.

Myers, M. A. and Massey, J. L. (1991). Race, labor, and punishment in postbellum Georgia. *Social Problems, 38(2),* 267–286.

Peak, K. (1997). *Policing in America,* 2nd ed. Upper Saddle River, NJ: Prentice Hall.

Plessy v. *Ferguson* (1896). 163 U.S. 537 (1896).

Rabinowitz, H. (1992). The conflict between blacks and the police in the urban south, 1865–1900. In P. Finkelman (Ed) *Race and criminal justice,* pp. 319–332. New York: Garland.

Rabinowitz, H. (1976). From exclusion to segregation: Southern race relations, 1865–1890. *Journal of American History, 63(2),* 325–350.

Rachels, J. (1993). *The elements of moral philosophy,* 2nd ed. New York: McGraw-Hill.

Reiman, J. (1998). *The rich get richer and the poor get prison,* 5th ed. Boston: Allyn and Bacon.

Russell, K. (1998). *The color of crime.* New York: NYU Press.

Schwarz, P. J. (1988). *Twice condemned: Slaves and the criminal laws of Virginia, 1705–1865.* Baton Rouge, LA: Louisiana State University.

Shklar, J. (1991). *American citizenship.* Cambridge, MA: Harvard University.

Spohn, C. (1994). Crime and the social control of blacks: Offender/victim race and the sentencing of violent offenders. In G. S. Bridges and M. A. Myers (Eds.), *Inequality, crime, and social control,* pp. 249–268. Boulder, CO: Westview.

Spohn, C. and Cederblom, J. (1991). Race and disparities in sentencing: A test of the liberation hypothesis. *Justice Quarterly, 8(3),* 305–327.

Tonry, M. (1995). *Malign neglect—Race, crime, and punishment in America.* New York: Oxford University Press.

Turner, J. H., Singleton, R., and Musick, D. (1984). *Oppression: A socio-history of black-white relations in America.* Chicago: Nelson-Hall.

United States Census Bureau Data, 1995–1997. Washington, DC: United States Dept. of Commerce.

United States Civil Rights Acts, 1957. P.L. 85-315, 9/9/57.

United States Civil Rights Acts, 1960. P.L. 86-449, 5/6/60.

United States Civil Rights Acts, 1964. P.L. 88-352, 7/2/64.

United States Constitution, Bill of Rights. First Congress, December 15, 1791.

United States Voting Rights Act, 1965. P.L. 89-110, 8/6/65.

Walker, S., Spohn, C., and DeLone, M. (1996). *The color of justice: Race, ethnicity, and crime in America*. Belmont, CA: Wadsworth.
Welch, M. (1996). *Corrections*. New York: McGraw-Hill.
West, C. (1993). *Race matters*. Boston: Beacon Press.

7

Unwelcome Citizens

Latinos and the Criminal Justice System

ALEXANDER ALVAREZ

The commonly held perception that "every Texas Ranger has some Mexican blood. He has it on his boots" (Murguia, 1975) illustrates well the adversarial and sometimes violent relationship that many Mexican Americans in particular, and Latinos in general, experience with the criminal justice system. Frequently, reported stories of blatant abuse and harassment by law enforcement agents only reinforces the perception that in this society, past and present discriminatory practices are often the norm where Latinos are concerned. This discrimination exists both within the criminal justice system and in the larger population (Aguirre and Turner, 1995). For example, studies in various states have found that judges impose heavier sentences on Latinos and African Americans than they do on whites, even if the offense and prior record are comparable (Holmes and Daudistel, 1984; Petersilia, 1985).

In addition, Latinos are often characterized as foreigners and immigrants (Mata, 1998), a depiction that ignores the fact that many Mexican Americans, for example, never immigrated here, but became U.S. citizens when the border changed. This representation also ignores the reality that Puerto Ricans became U.S. citizens as a direct result of military conquest when the United States defeated Spain in the Spanish–American War. Similarly, a misinformed panic about the "alien invasion" of illegal immigrants from Mexico is a topic of urgent concern for some who perceive a threat to the "American way of life," and frequently apply their xenophobia to all Latinos in the United States (see Perry, Chapter 5, of this book). However, one never hears of the threat of illegal immigration from Canada, which is also a source of large numbers of illegal immigrants (U.S. Immigration and Naturalization Service, 1997).

Subject to dehumanizing popular stereotypes in the entertainment media, Latinos are many times negatively typecast by police officers and other officials of the criminal justice system (Portillos, 1998). Common images of Latinos as greasers, drug dealers, gang members, and other assorted criminals reinforce the notion that Latino populations are dangerous and need to be continuously monitored and controlled.

In short, the Latino experience in the United States has frequently been punctuated by conflict, misunderstanding, racism, and violence. It is, however, a history that in recent years has emerged into our national consciousness. The belated recognition that this country is a multicultural society has exploded onto the political and social scene as issues such as multilingual education, affirmative action, and racism provide fodder for debate and discourse in communities across the nation. This awareness has sparked attention to the impact of race and ethnicity in the criminal justice arena and the role various minority groups play as actors in that domain. One such group is Latinos.

Latino populations have had an impact on the American criminal justice in numerous ways as perpetrators, victims, and practitioners, and that influence is likely to grow in the coming years. Currently, Latino populations comprise approximately 9% of the U.S. populace, or roughly 28 million people (del Pinal and Singer, 1997). In all likelihood, this is an underestimation because official figures do not include illegal aliens and migrant workers (Foggo, 1993). Not surprisingly, these numbers are expected to rise dramatically, due in part to the high levels of legal and illegal immigration coupled with high birth rates. In fact, the Latino population increased by 50% from 1980 to 1990. This trend is projected to continue in the next few decades until Latinos comprise the largest single minority group in the United States (Farley, 1995; Jaret, 1995). It is projected that the Latino population will outnumber African Americans in 2005, and by 2050, the Latino population is expected to reach 100 million (del Pinal and Singer, 1997).

However, even though Latino populations represent a sizable fraction of the American population, relatively little research has focused on Latinos specifically in terms of crime and justice. As Michael Leiber notes, most research on minorities and criminal justice compare only African Americans and whites, or, if other groups are included, classify various races and ethnicities together into an "other" category that does not differentiate between Latinos, Asian Americans, and Native Americans (Leiber, 1994). For all practical purposes, this conflation renders the "other" category meaningless for descriptive or statistical purposes. This is not to say that Latinos have been completely excluded from traditional crime statistics; it is just that their inclusion has been disguised. Specifically, Latinos have typically been categorized as either white or black, depending on self-identification or on skin coloring. Although this misclassification is slowly being remedied, it still makes research on Latinos problematic (Farnworth, Teske, and Thurman, 1991; Lynch, 1990). As far as research on crime and minority groups, Latinos have truly been an "invisible" population for far too long.

There are several other significant issues that must be addressed when studying Latino populations. Even though Latinos are typically referred to as a minority group, they can more accurately be described as being composed of many diverse groups, each with its own unique history, culture, and experience. Mexican Americans comprise the largest single Latino population (64%), followed by Central and South Americans (14%), Puerto Ricans (11%), other Latinos such as Spanish and Dominicans (7%), and Cubans (4%) (del Pinal and Singer, 1997). Although these populations share a common language, they are typically quite distinct in their cultural traditions, heritage, history, and backgrounds. As Himilce Novas writes, "Perhaps no other ethnic group in the United States is as diverse in its culture, physical appearance, and traditions as the Hispanics" (1994:2). Indeed, there is even a great deal of variation within specific Latino populations. Mexican Americans, for example, may be of pure Spanish origin, Indian, or mestizo. Moreover, Pinal and Singer suggest, "a third-generation, college-educated Mexican American may feel little commonality with a recent immigrant from rural Mexico who has little formal education" (del Pinal and Singer, 1997:3).

Accordingly, it is perhaps most appropriate to refer to the specific country of origin designation when discussing Latinos in the United States, because that often provides the most specificity for cultural group and avoids making generalizations that are not accurate for all populations.

Sometimes, however, it is difficult to avoid aggregating Latino groups. Although several terms have been used to describe this aggregate, such as people of Spanish Origin and Hispanic, I use the term *Latino*. As Hayes-Bautista and Chapa argue, "Latino is the best label to describe Hispanics since it preserves national origin of the referents as a significant characteristic, it is culturally and racially neutral, and may be the least objectionable of all possible ethnic labels" (1987:21–22). In addition, it is important to note that when we use the term *African American*, we are referring to non-Latino African Americans. The terms *Anglo* and *white* should be perceived as referring to whites not of Latino origin. For a more complete discussion of these issues, see Marín and Marín (1991), Novas (1994), and Shorris (1992). In addition to the issue of identification, we must also recognize that the present experience of Latino groups is firmly rooted in the events and ideologies of the past.

History

Even though the history of Latinos in the Americas goes back further than practically any other group with the exception of indigenous peoples, their relationship with the Anglo culture has been a difficult and contentious one. The first Spanish colony in the continental United States was established in 1598 at Santa Fe, now in the state of New Mexico (Shorris, 1992), and it was not long before similar Mexican settlements were established in what are now California, Arizona, and Texas. Similarly, Spanish settlements were founded in Florida and in various locations along the southeastern seaboard (Steele, 1994). The Spanish presence in North America, especially in the southwest and southeast, therefore predates the Anglo presence on much of the continent. However, even though their pedigree in North America was long and distinguished, Latinos were often the losers when they came into contact with Anglos. For example, after Mexico lost the Mexican–

American War in 1847 and was coerced into signing the Treaty of Guadalupe Hidalgo a year later, Mexico lost approximately 50% of its sovereign territory as Texas, New Mexico, California, Arizona, Nevada, Utah, and half of Colorado were delivered over to the United States (Novas, 1994). The 80,000 Mexicans in this vast territory became citizens of the United States overnight.

Within a short period of time, these new citizens were made second-class citizens, being deprived of their land, property, wealth, and, in some cases, their lives. The law and agents of criminal justice were often the mechanisms by which this was accomplished (Aguirre and Baker, 1994; Vigil, 1998). As Shorris writes, "Ironically, it was through the use of the new democratic practices of the United States that the once dominant population group was excluded from having any voice in the government. Anglo legislators passed tax laws and land-use laws designed to wrest the huge ranches away from the rich Californians and to take the modest homesites of the poor" (1992:2). Deprived of their economic resource base, Mexican Americans were consigned to the economic underclass of this society, where they have labored for most of this country's history. This would not be the last time that Mexican Americans were exploited and discriminated against. The exploitation of the Braceros work programs, the violence of the Zoot suit riots of 1943, and the more recent demonization and stereotyping of illegal immigrants all indicate as much.

In regards to the issue of immigration, Mercedes Lynn De Uriarte writes, "Mexicans are portrayed as the only illegal-immigrant group. Thus an entire population is criminalized through visual images meant to incite anger and fear" (De Uriarte, 1998:120). Other common images of Mexicans portray them as overweight, sneaky, smelly, lazy, and thieving (Levin, 1975). Many of these racist stereotypes are found in mass-media portrayals and advertisements that serve to propagate and disseminate these negative images on a wide scale. Not surprisingly, agents of the criminal justice system itself accept these constructions and treat Mexican Americans accordingly. Aguirre and Turner (1995:133) state that, "Studies of police tactics in small communities have shown that Mexican Americans are victims of prejudiced attitudes, indiscriminate searches and detentions, and high arrest–conviction rates." Similarly, evidence indicates that Mexican Americans have frequently been the victims of racist-motivated police violence, ritualized ceremonies of degradation, as well as numerous other examples of discriminatory treatment (Garza, 1995; LaFree, 1995; Rodriquez, 1993; Padilla, 1992; U.S. Commission on Civil Rights, 1970).

The history of Puerto Ricans in the United States is also a story replete with examples of economic, social, and legal discrimination. After the United States defeated Spain in the Spanish–American War, Puerto Rico became a U.S. protectorate and, subsequently, in 1917, its people were granted U.S. citizenship, which allowed for unrestricted migration and travel from the island to the mainland. Although American businesses have certainly profited from their association with Puerto Rico, the same cannot be said for its inhabitants, who have traditionally suffered from high rates of poverty and unemployment (Bourgois, 1996; Rodriguez, 1991). Throughout the 20th century, large numbers of Puerto Ricans have migrated to the mainland United States in search of better economic opportunities and have often been recruited to work in the sweatshops of the garment industry (Morales, 1986). In most cases, however, they have merely traded rural poverty on the island for urban poverty in the slums and barrios of New York City and other large eastern cities. Of this deprivation, Bourgois writes:

> Few other ethnic groups, except perhaps Native American Indians, fared more poorly in official statistics than the 896,753 Puerto Ricans who lived in New York City at the time of the 1990 census. They have the highest welfare dependancy and household poverty rates, as well as the lowest labor force participation rates, of any other ethnic group in the city. In fact, in 1989 their poverty rate (38 percent) was double that of New York City's (19 percent). One statistical survey showed their family poverty rate in the late 1980s to be 500 percent higher than New York City's average. (1996:53)

In short, Puerto Ricans are the most economically disadvantaged Latino group in the United States (Myers, Cintron, and Scarborough, 1994). Their experiences with the criminal justice system, similar to those of Mexican Americans, have also been marked by sometimes blatant discrimination. One study, for example, found that Puerto Ricans are more likely to be institutionalized than to receive probation and receive longer sentences than do whites for the same offenses (Sissons, 1979). Given the stereotypes that portray Puerto Ricans as "lazy, submissive, and immoral, with propensities for crime and gang violence" (Aguirre and Turner, 1995:139), the inequities they suffer at the hands of the criminal justice system are hardly surprising.

In marked contrast to both Mexican Americans and Puerto Ricans, the position of much of the Cuban American community in the United States is a relatively privileged and powerful one. There are several specific reasons for this rather peculiar position (peculiar when compared to other Latino groups).

First, Cuban immigrants to this country did not really arrive in any large numbers until the 1950s, as large numbers of middle- and upper-class Cubans sought refuge from Fidel Castro's new society. They, therefore, escaped many of the earliest excesses and images directed against longer-established Latino populations that have colored subsequent relationships with those groups. Many of the dominant negative stereotypes of Mexican Americans, for example, are derived from old animosities embedded in the historic landscape, and Cuban Americans have largely escaped these sorts of traditional negative images. Second, these Cubans were relatively well educated and were largely from the middle and upper tiers of the Cuban economic ladder. The Cuban American community thus arrived with the necessary economic resources needed not only to survive, but also to succeed. This economic clout, when combined with the Cuban American political conservatism and antipathy toward communism, gave this population access to political and social circles not common to most Latino communities (Hess, Markson, and Stein, 1998).

This is not to say, however, that Cuban Americans have not suffered from some of the same racism so endemic to most Latino/Anglo relations. This is especially true for one subgroup of Cubans known as the Marielitos. In 1980, Fidel Castro emptied his prisons of political prisoners and predatory criminals, and the mental hospitals of their patients, and "encouraged" them to emigrate to the United States. Thus was born the Mariel boatlift, named after the Cuban port from which they fled. These latest arrivals were usually "darker skinned, poorer, and often unemployable" (Aguirre and Turner, 1995:143). Whereas only a relatively small number of Marielitos were actually criminals, they were constantly portrayed as dangerous deviants and defectives (Hamm,1995). These new Cuban Americans helped change the way Cuban Americans were perceived and treated. Whereas the older, whiter, and wealthier Cuban Americans are relatively isolated from contact with the criminal justice system, the Marielitos have not enjoyed the same privileged position and consequently have had more conflict with law enforcement agencies and other criminal justice organizations.

To summarize, then, the experience of Latinos in the United States is a varied one that reflects the diversity of Latino populations in this country. One persistent element for the various Latino populations is the role that discrimination has played in their relationship with the criminal justice system. There are, however, other factors that relate to Latino involvement with the criminal justice system.

Latino populations represent at-risk groups for both crime perpetration and victimization because of several specific characteristics these populations share. For example, Latino groups are among the most urbanized collectives in the United States. According to the U.S. Bureau of Census (1992a), approximately 90% of Latinos live in cities. Crime statistics indicate that many types of crime, especially violent crimes, are concentrated in urban areas, especially in central cities, which suggests that Latinos are at high risk for many types of crimes (Baker, O'Neill, and Karpf, 1984; Segall and Wilson, 1993; Wilkinson, 1984; Sampson and Lauritson, 1994). In addition, most criminality revolves around young males, and because the median age for Latino groups is only 25.5 (U.S. Bureau of Census, 1992b), the youngest of any racial or ethnic minority group in the United States, this also suggests that Latino males are particularly at risk for crime perpetration and victimization.

Perpetrators

As perpetrators of crime, Latino populations comprise a relatively little-studied group. What work there is, however, indicates that Latino groups are at a greater risk of perpetration than are non-Latino whites. Generally speaking, although African Americans tend to have the highest perpetration rates for various types of crime and whites the lowest, Latinos often have intermediate rates between the two extremes. For example, the research on homicide in Latino communities in different states and cities generally reveals that the Latino homicide rates are usually above those of whites but below those of African Americans (Block, 1976; Smith, Mercy, and Rosenberg, 1986; Mercy, 1987; Becker *et al.*, 1990; Zahn, 1987; Zahn and Sagi, 1987). Interestingly enough, some research indicates that among Latino populations, it is Puerto Ricans who experience the highest homicide rates (Rodriguez, 1987). This may well be a result of the fact that Puerto Ricans suffer from the highest poverty rates and lowest educational attainment of any Latino group.

Coramae Richey Mann reports that during the mid-1980s, when Latinos comprised roughly 6.5% of the population, they constituted almost 13% of all persons arrested (Mann, 1993). In 1986, this amounted to approximately 1,172,609 Latinos (Flowers, 1990); an arrest rate double their population size. These numbers, it is important to point out, vary widely by region of the country. Not surprisingly, the highest arrest rates come from those regions of the country such as the southwest that have large Latino populations. In 1997, for example, although Latino males comprised 1.4% of all persons arrested in St. Louis, Missouri, 1.8% in Atlanta, Georgia, and 0.5% of all arrestees in Detroit, Michigan, they constituted 46.5% in San Diego, California, 53% in Los Angeles, California, and 76.7% in San Antonio, Texas (U.S. Department of Justice, 1997).

Although Latinos are overrepresented in the official arrest statistics relative to their size in the population, it is noteworthy that this exaggerated representation is only partially due to perpetration. As illustrated earlier, at every stage of the criminal justice process, Latinos may be treated more harshly and punitively than are whites. The discretion available to law enforcement officers and court officials is frequently used against Latinos, and their overrepresentation in arrest statistics reflects this reality.

In terms of the types of crimes for which they are arrested, the evidence indicates that in 1986, the 10 most common offenses for which Latinos were arrested were: DUI, drunkenness, larceny–theft, drug violations, other assaults, disorderly conduct, burglary, liquor law violations, aggravated assault, and weapons violations (Mann, 1993:42). According to Coramae Richey Mann's analysis, these 10 offenses account for more than two thirds of all offenses for which Latinos are arrested. Most of these, it should be noted, are not index offenses. Rather, 5 of the 10 arrest offenses appear to be drug and alcohol related. This certainly does not appear to vindicate the popular stereotypes that portray all Latinos as violent gang members and criminals.

Theoretical attempts to explain Latino patterns of criminality tend to focus on either structural issues of poverty and discrimination or, alternatively, on cultural roles and identity within Latino communities. Many of the structural arguments are guided by the notion that various forms of inequality, including economic and political disparities, influence the perpetration of crime. It is important to note, therefore, that Latino populations are often ranked among the lowest rungs of this society's economy. In 1991, for example, the median family net worth for Latinos was $5,345, only marginally better than that for African Americans ($4,604), and far below that of whites ($44,408) (Walker, Spohn, and DeLone, 1996). A similar pattern is revealed when the median family income is examined.

In 1992, the median family income for Latinos was $23,901, a figure slightly higher than that for African Americans ($21,161), but much lower than that for whites ($38, 909) (Walker, Spohn, and DeLone, 1996).

These aggregates, however, conceal the fact that poverty varies tremendously between Latino groups. For example, although only 16% of Cuban families lived below the poverty level in 1995, 36% of Puerto Rican families and 28% of Mexican American families were also impoverished (del Pinal and Singer, 1997). Similar patterns emerge when educational attainment and unemployment figures are reviewed. We have already discussed the ways in which Latinos have been discriminated against in the criminal justice system, but it is important to note that they are sometimes treated unequally in other contexts as well, such as choice of residency (Massey and Denton, 1987; Santiago and Wilder, 1991). This practice produces increased levels of social, spatial, and economic isolation of Latino communities and, therefore, exacerbates the effects of poverty and other social ills.

Other researchers point to social disorganization within Latino communities (Block, 1985; Valdez and Nourjah, 1987) and difficulties in cultural assimilation and adjustment (Bondavalli and Bondavalli, 1981) as possible explanations for Latino criminality. In short, many Latinos continue to exist at the bottom of this society, economically, politically, and socially, and it is these kinds of conditions that have been linked to criminality in the social science literature (Blau and Blau, 1982; Blau and Golden, 1986; Blau and Schwartz, 1984; Crutchfield, 1989; Harer and Steffensmeier, 1992; Sampson, 1986). It is said that poverty breeds crime, as members of impoverished communities commit crime for either economic advantage (e.g., theft-related crimes), escape (e.g., drug-related crimes), or out of rage, anger, and frustration (e.g., violent crime). Given the economic state of many Latino communities, these arguments go a long way toward explaining many of the crime patterns exhibited by Latino groups.

Many cultural theories of Latino crime revolve around the related concepts of machismo and the subculture of violence thesis. The notion of machismo relates to a specific definition of masculinity in which physical aggression, virility, pride, strength, and courage are all necessary qualities for Latino males (Shorris, 1992; Marín and Marín, 1991; Vigil, 1998). In essence, then, some have suggested that the cultural premiums placed on these male qualities lend themselves to aggression and violence, and involvement in gangs (Erlanger, 1979; Flowers, 1990; Mann, 1993). The subculture of violence thesis, however, suggests that certain regions and/or groups have adopted values that are conducive to the use of violence in order to resolve conflict (Wolfgang and Ferracuti, 1967). Commonly used to explain the violence in African American communities, this argument suggests that Latino cultural values support and encourage the use violence in everyday conflictual situations because it is one way of asserting power in groups that are relatively powerless (Erlanger, 1979).

The difficulty with these cultural arguments is that they do not recognize the very real diversity of culture among Latino populations. It is difficult to understand how one cultural theory is applicable to culturally diverse populations. Nevertheless, it remains a popular way of explaining Latino criminality. It is important to note that many of these cultural explanations of crime have been criticized as victim-blaming strategies and as having racist overtones for suggesting a cultural inferiority among Latino groups. In other words, these arguments implicitly posit dysfunctional or deviance-producing qualities to the cultures of various minority groups, rather than making allowance for the fact that much of the criminality within Latino communities is also seen as deviant by many members of that group. In addition, these cultural arguments ignore the role of the criminal justice system in producing criminal identities. That is, crime is as much a political manifestation as it is a behavioral one. When law enforcement officials target Latino communities for heightened and more punitive attention, they effectively criminalize that population and help to perpetuate the stigmatized identity of the targeted group. In short, these cultural arguments often manifest many of the same discriminatory attitudes so prevalent in this society at large.

Victims

In terms of victimization, the available evidence indicates that Latinos are at extreme risk of victimization for both property and violent offenses. Their rates of victimization often exceed those of non-Latinos. In 1994, for example, the Hispanic rate of victimization for all personal crimes was 63.3 per 100,000, whereas the rate for non-Hispanics was 51.9 (U.S. Department of Justice, 1994). This type of pattern tends to hold when crime types are disaggregated. For the crime of robbery, Latinos are twice as likely to be victimized by this crime as non-Latinos. Specifically, the Latino robbery victimization rate in 1992 was 10.6 per 100,000, compared to a rate of 5.4 per 100,000 for non-Latinos (U.S. Department of Justice, 1992). For the crimes of burglary, household larceny, and motor vehicle theft, Latino households invariably experience higher rates than non-Latino households (U.S. Department of Justice, 1992). In addition, Flowers (1990) reports that Latino men aged 12 to 19 are more often the victims of these crimes than are Latino females of any age.

Recent data also suggest that Latinos continue to be victimized by hate crimes targeted against them specifically because of their ethnicity. Although this is not a new type of victimization for Latinos, its reporting certainly is new. In 1994, there were 337 reported incidents of this type of crime that victimized a total of 471 Latinos (U.S. Department of Justice, 1996c). Whereas this number is relatively small compared to hate crimes against African Americans (2,174 reported incidents in 1994), this number is certainly underreported. Latinos are much less likely to report victimizations to official sources than are non-Latinos (Walker, Spohn, and DeLone, 1996). This marked tendency toward underreporting is largely due to the widespread perception among Latinos that law enforcement is the enemy and unfairly targets and harasses Latinos simply because of their ethnic identity. As the Latino populations continue to grow in the United States and assume ever more visible roles in the shaping of this society, it is likely that hate crimes targeting them will also grow more prevalent.

Practitioners

In recent years, Latinos have made strong strides toward greater occupational representation in the criminal justice system. For example, in 1991, 6.4% of police officers were Latino, an increase from 4.1% in 1988 (Carter and Sapp, 1991; Walker, 1992). In New York City in 1992, 3,688 police officers out of a total of 27,154 were Latino (*USA Today*, 1992). There has been a similar improvement in sheriffs' departments, with 5.8% of all full-time sworn personnel being Latino in 1993 (U.S. Department of Justice, 1996b). This is a tremendous improvement, and as Latino involvement in law enforcement increases, it can be hoped that many of the worst excesses of the past years will decrease.

There have also been similar improvements in other areas of the criminal justice system as an examination of the characteristics of presidential appointees to U.S. District Court judgeships reveals. Under President Nixon, 1.1% were Latinos, and under President Ford, 1.9% were Latinos. President Bush, however, selected Latinos 4% of the time, and President Clinton did so for 6.5% of his nominations (U.S. Department of Justice, 1996a). A similar pattern of increase is also evident in the patterns of presidential appointees to U.S. Courts of Appeals judgeships. The percentage of Latino selectees changed from zero under presidents Johnson, Nixon, and Ford to a high of 10.3% under President Clinton (U.S. Department of Justice, 1996a). Slowly, the representation of Latinos in the criminal justice system appears to be increasing, this time not merely as clients of the system, but as practitioners.

Having criminal justice agents and personnel drawn from the communities they serve, and sensitive to the cultures, ethnic identities, and languages of the various populations and minority groups can only serve to help reduce the conflict, misunderstanding, and outright discrimination that has so often been a part of the Latino history in this country. The Latino population in the United States is here to stay, and the voices of its people are heard increasingly in all arenas of social, economic, and political life. This society must recognize that this is a positive and beneficial reality, not something to be fought against. When the United States embraces this multiculturalism that is so much a fact of modern American life, than perhaps this society can truly begin to live up to its ideals and promises of justice and equality.

References

Aguirre, A., Jr. and Baker, D. (1994). *Perspectives on race and ethnicity in American criminal justice.* Minneapolis, MN: West Publishing.

Aguirre, A., Jr. and Turner, J. H. (1995). *American ethnicity: The dynamics and consequences of discrimination.* New York: McGraw-Hill.

Baker, S. P., O'Neill, B., and Karpf, R. S. (1984). *The injury fact book.* Lexington: D. C. Heath.

Becker, T. M., Samet, J. M., Wiggins, C. L., and Key, C. R. (1990). Violent death in the west: Suicide and homicide in New Mexico, 1958–1987. *Suicide and Life Threatening Behavior, 20,* 324–334.

Blau, J. R. and Blau, P. M. (1982). The cost of inequality: Metropolitan structure and violent crime. *American Sociological Review, 47*, 114–129.

Blau, P. M. and Golden, R. M. (1986). Metropolitan structure and criminal violence. *Sociological Quarterly, 27*, 15–26.

Blau, P. M. and Schwartz, J. E. (1984). *Crosscutting social circles*. San Diego, CA: Academic Press.

Block, R. (1976). Homicide in Chicago: A nine-year study (1965–1973). *The Journal of Criminal Law and Criminology, 66*, 496–510.

Block, R. (1985). Race/ethnicity and patterns of Chicago homicide 1965 to 1981. *Crime and Delinquency, 31*, 104–116.

Bondavalli, B. J. and Bondavalli, B. (1981). Spanish-speaking people and the North American criminal justice system. In R. L. McNeely and C. E. Pope (Eds.), *Race, crime, and criminal justice*. Beverly Hills, CA: Sage Publications.

Bourgois, P. (1996). *Selling crack in el barrio*. New York: Cambridge University Press.

Carter, D. L. and Sapp, A. D. (1991). *Police education and minority recruitment: The impact of a college requirement*. Washington, DC: Police Executive Research Forum.

Crutchfield, R. D. (1989). Labor stratification and violent crime. *Social Forces, 68*, 489–512.

De Uriarte, M. L. (1998). Baiting immigrants: Heartbreak for Latinos. In P. S. Rothenberg (Ed.), *Race, class, and gender in the United States: An integrated study*, 4th ed., pp. 118–121. New York: St. Martin's Press.

Erlanger, H. (1979). Estrangement, machismo, and gang violence. *Social Science Quarterly, 60(2)*, 235–248.

Farley, J. E. (1995). *Majority-minority relations*. Englewood Cliffs, NJ: Prentice Hall.

Farnworth, M., Teske, R. H. C., Jr., and Thurman, G. (1991). Ethnic, racial, and minority disparity in felony court processing. In M. J. Lynch, and E. B. Patterson (Eds.), *Race and criminal justice*, pp. 54–70. New York: Harrow and Heston.

Flowers, R. B. (1990). *Minorities and criminality*. New York: Praeger.

Foggo, J. G. (1993). *Review of data on Hispanics report*. Washington, DC: Defense Equal Opportunity Management Institute.

Garza, H. (1995). Administration of justice: Chicanos in Monterey County. In A. S. Lopez (Ed.), *Latinos in the United States. Vol. 3. Criminal justice and Latino communities*. New York: Garland.

Hamm, M. S. (1995). *The abandoned ones: The imprisonment and uprising of the Mariel boat people*. Boston: Northeastern University Press.

Harer, M. D. and Steffensmeier, D. (1992). The differing effects of economic inequality on black and white rates of violence. *Social Forces, 70*, 1035–1054.

Hayes-Bautista, D. E. and Chapa, J. (1987). Latino terminology: Conceptual bases for standardized terminology. *American Journal of Public Health, 77*, 61–68.

Hess, B. B., Markson, E. W., and Stein, P. J. (1998). Racial and ethnic minorities: An overview. In P. S. Rothenberg (Ed.), *Race, class, and gender in the United States: An integrated study*, 4th ed., pp. 258–270. New York: St. Martin's Press.

Holmes, M. and Daudistel, H. (1984). Ethnicity and justice in the Southwest: The sentencing of Anglo, black, and Mexican American defendants. *Social Science Quarterly, 65*, 265–277.

Jaret, C. (1995). *Contemporary racial and ethnic relations*. Glenview, IL: HarperCollins College Publishers.

LaFree, G. D. (1995). Official reactions to Hispanic defendants in the Southwest. In A. S. Lopez (Ed.), *Latinos in the United States. Vol. 3. Criminal justice and Latino communities*. New York: Garland.

Leiber, M. J. (1994). A comparison of juvenile court outcomes for Native Americans, African Americans, and whites. *Justice Quarterly, 11*, 257–279.

Levin, J. (1975). *The functions of prejudice*. New York: Harper & Row.

Lynch, M. J. (1990). Racial bias and criminal justice: Definitional and methodological issues. In B. Maclean and D. Milovanovic (Eds.), *Racism, empiricism and criminal justice*. Vancouver: Collective Press.

Mann, C. R. (1993). *Unequal justice: A question of color*. Bloomington, IN: Indiana University Press.

Marín, G. and VanOss Marín, B. (1991). *Research with Hispanic populations*. Newbury Park, CA: Sage Publications

Massey, D. S. and Denton, N. A. (1987). Trends in the residential segregation of blacks, Hispanics, and Asians: 1970–1980. *American Sociological Review, 52*, 802–825.

Mata, A. G., Jr. (1998). Immigrant bashing and nativist political movements. In C. R. Mann and M. S. Zatz (Eds.), *Images of color: Images of crime*, pp. 145–155. Los Angeles: Roxbury Publishing.

Mercy, J. A. (1987). Assaultive injury among Hispanics: A public health problem. In J. Kraus, S. Sorenson, and P. Juarez (Eds.), *Research conference on violence and homicide in Hispanic communities*, pp. 1–12. Office of Minority Health, U.S. Department of Health and Human Services: UCLA Publication Services.

Morales, J. (1986). *Puerto Rican poverty and migration: We just had to try elsewhere*. New York: Praeger.

Murguia, E. (1975). *Assimilation, colonialism, and the Mexican American people*. Austin, TX: University of Texas at Austin, Center for Mexican American Studies, Monograph Series No. 1.

Myers, L. B., Cintron, M., and Scarborough, K. E. (1994). Latinos: The conceptualization of race. In J. Hendricks and B. Byers (Eds.), *Multicultural perspectives in criminal justice*, pp. 155–184. Springfield, IL: Charles C. Thomas Publishers.

Novas, H. (1994). *Everything you need to know about Latino history*. New York: Plume Books.

Padilla, F. (1992). *The gang as an American enterprise*. Rutgers, NJ: Rutgers University Press.

Petersilia, J. (1985). Racial disparities in the criminal justice system: A summary. *Crime and Delinquency, 31*, 15–34.

del Pinal, J. and Singer, A. (1997). Generations of diversity: Latinos in the United States. *Population Bulletin, 52(3)*. Washington, DC: Population Reference Bureau, Inc.

Portillos, E. L. (1998). Latinos, gangs, and drugs. In C. R. Mann and M. S. Zatz (Eds.), *Images of color: Images of crime*, pp. 156–165. Los Angeles: Roxbury Publishing.

Rodriguez, O. (1987). Hispanics and homicide in New York City. In J. Kraus, S. Sorenson, and P. Juarez (Eds.), *Research conference on violence and homicide in Hispanic communities*, pp. 67–84. Office of Minority Health, U.S. Department of Health and Human Services: UCLA Publication Services.

Rodriguez, C. E. (1991). *Puerto Ricans: Born in the U.S.A.* Boulder, CO: Westview Press.

Rodriquez, L. J. (1993). *Always running, la Vida Loca: Gang days in L.A.* New York: Touchstone.

Sampson, R. J. (1986). Effects of inequality, heterogeneity, and urbanization on intergroup victimization. *Social Science Quarterly, 67*, 751–766.

Sampson, R. J. and Lauritsen, J. L. (1994). Violent victimization and offending: Individual-, situational-, and community-level risk factors. In A. J. Reiss and J. A. Roth (Eds.), *Understanding and preventing violence*, pp. 1–114. Washington, DC: National Academy Press.

Santiago, A. M. and Wilder, M. G. (1991). Residential segregation and links to minority poverty: The case of Latinos in the United States. *Social Problems, 38*, 492–515.

Segall, W. E. and Wilson, A. V. (1993). Who is at greatest risk in homicides? A comparison of victimization rates by geographic region. In A. V. Wilson (Ed.), *Homicide: The victim/offender connection*, pp. 343–356. Cincinnati, OH: Anderson Publishing Company.

Shorris, E. (1992). *Latinos: A biography of the people*. New York: W. W. Norton and Company.

Sissons, P. (1979). *The Hispanic experience of criminal justice*. New York: Hispanic Research Center at Fordham University.

Smith, J. C., Mercy, J. A., and Rosenberg, M. L. (1986). Suicide and homicide among Hispanics in the southwest. *Public Health Reports, 101*, 265–270.

Steele, I. K. (1994). *Warpaths: Invasions of North America*. New York: Oxford University Press.

U.S. Bureau of Census (1992a). *1990 census of population: General population characteristics, United States*. Report no. 1990CP-1-1. Washington, DC: U.S. Government Printing Office

U.S. Bureau of Census (1992b). *Statistical abstract of the U.S., 1992*. Washington, DC: U.S. Government Printing Office.

U.S. Commission on Civil Rights (1970). *Mexican Americans and the administration of justice in the Southwest*. Washington, DC: U.S. Government Printing Office.

U.S. Department of Justice, Bureau of Justice Statistics (1992). *Criminal victimization in the United States, 1992.* Washington, DC: U.S. Department of Justice.

U.S. Department of Justice, Bureau of Justice Statistics (1994). *Criminal victimization in the United States, 1994,* NCJ-1621126. Washington, DC: U.S. Department of Justice.

U.S. Department of Justice, Bureau of Justice Statistics (1996a). *Criminal victimization in the United States, 1996.* Washington, DC: U.S. Department of Justice.

U.S. Department of Justice, Bureau of Justice Statistics (1996b). *Sheriffs' departments, 1993,* NCJ-148823. Washington, DC: U.S. Department of Justice.

U.S. Department of Justice, Federal Bureau of Investigation (1996c). *Hate crime statistics, 1994.* Washington, DC: U.S. Government Printing Office.

U.S. Department of Justice, Office of Justice Programs, National Institute of Justice (1997). *1997 annual report on adult and juvenile arrestees,* NCJ-171672. Washington, DC: U.S. Government Printing Office.

U.S. Immigration and Naturalization Service (1997). *Statistical yearbook of the Immigration and Naturalization Service, 1996.* Washington, DC: U.S. Government Printing Office.

USA Today, October 7, 1992, p. 8A. Primary Source: USA TODAY research.

Valdez, R. B. and Nourjah, P. (1987). Homicide in Southern California, 1966–1985: An examination based on vital statistics data. In J. Kraus, S. Sorenson, and P. Juarez (Eds.), *Research conference on violence and homicide in Hispanic communities,* pp. 85–100. Office of Minority Health, U.S. Department of Health and Human Services: UCLA Publication Services.

Vigil, J. D. (1998). *From Indians to Chicanos: The dynamics of Mexican-American culture.* Prospect Heights, IL: Waveland Press.

Walker, S. (1992). *The police in America,* 2nd ed. New York: McGraw-Hill.

Walker, S., Spohn, C., and DeLone, M. (1996). *The color of justice: Race, ethnicity, and crime in America.* Belmont, CA: Wadsworth.

Wilkinson, K. P. (1984). A research note on homicide and rurality. *Social Forces, 63,* 445–452.

Wolfgang, M. E. and Ferracuti, F. (1967). *The subculture of violence: Towards an integrated theory in criminology.* London: Tavistock.

Zahn, M. A. (1987). Homicide in nine American cities: The Hispanic case. In J. Kraus, S. Sorenson, and P. Juarez (Eds.), *Research conference on violence and homicide in Hispanic communities,* pp. 13–29. Office of Minority Health, U.S. Department of Health and Human Services: UCLA Publication Services.

Zahn, M. A. and Sagi, P. C. (1987). Stranger homicides in nine American cities. *The Journal of Criminal Law and Criminology, 78,* 377–397.

8

Perpetual Outsiders

Criminal Justice and the Asian American Experience

BARBARA PERRY

A century and a half after their first arrival on the shores of the United States, Americans of Asian descent are still perceived as "foreigners." Whether part of the "old" or "new" immigration, whether fifth or first generation, Asian Americans continue to be constructed as the "Other." As this chapter reveals, this perpetual outsider status has been maintained through legal and extralegal mechanisms such as exclusionary immigration policies, rhetorical images of Asians, and anti-Asian violence.

The 1840s and 1850s marked the beginning of Asian immigration to the United States, starting with the arrival of Chinese in Hawaii and on the mainland West Coast. Initially, laborers found work on the sugar plantations and in the gold mines, and later supplied much of the manual labor for the building of the western leg of the transcontinental railway. By the turn of the twentieth century, the same employment opportunities began to draw increasing numbers of immigrants from other parts of Asia, including Japan, the Philippines, Korea, and India.

However, successive waves of Asian immigration tended to create corresponding waves of anti-Asian sentiment. Labor leaders, temperance activists, and agricultural interests pressed the government to react to the perceived threats that Asians were thought to represent to employment (e.g., wage deflation), morality (e.g., opium use), and hygiene (e.g., prostitution). This agitation was met with increasingly restrictive immigration and naturalization policies that slowed Asian immigration to a trickle throughout the first half of the twentieth century.

The liberalization of immigration policy following World War II brought with it a new wave of Asian immigration. Whereas Asian Americans represented less than one half of 1% of the United States population in 1940, by 1990 they made up nearly 3%, or 7 million. However, Asian Americans are not a homogeneous community. On the contrary, they represent a very diverse population, with regionally and culturally specific language, dialects, traditions, and beliefs. Moreover, each cultural group was drawn (or pushed) to the United States by different motives. Most early immigrants—whether Chinese, Japanese, or Filipino, for example—sought employment as unskilled labor. By the 1960s, this trend began to reverse, as many Chinese and Japanese, in particular, migrated under policies designed to attract skilled laborers and professionals. Those seeking enhanced employment opportunities were later joined by Southeast Asians fleeing the political upheavals in that part of the world. During and after the Korean War (1956–1965), many of those impressed by their view of Americans' affluence, together with political dissidents, fled to the United States. During the 1970s, nearly 200,000 Vietnamese emigrated to the United States—many of whom were admitted with refugee status. More recent immigration of Asians, including that of Asian Indians, has been motivated by educational and professional opportunities. Very often, Asians who come to this country to pursue a university education decide to stay and embark on a career in this country.

The diverse and uneven patterns of migration associated with Asian Americans have resulted in a dramatically heterogeneous Asian "community," representing dozens of Asian identities, ranging from Chinese to Filipino to Laotian to Taiwanese. Those of Chinese and Filipino descent dominate the Asian population, followed by Asian Indians, Koreans, and Vietnamese.

Given the differences between these groups, it is not surprising that their experiences have been quite different in the United States. Asian Americans do not fare equally well in socioeconomic terms. Specifically, Koreans and Vietnamese consistently lag behind Chinese, Japanese, and Asian Indians on most indicators of socioeconomic status. The often-touted belief that Asians are the "successful" minority thus masks the dramatic differences between groups. Although summary statistics do suggest higher education, higher income, and higher occupational status for Asians, what such generalizations fail to reveal are the factors that underlie the trends:

- the concentration of Asians in geographic areas with a high cost of living
- a high proportion of multiple incomes within the household
- low per capita incomes
- with educational levels held constant, Asian Americans earn about the same or less than their white counterparts. (U.S. Commission on Civil Rights, 1992:18)

In other words, discrimination in employment, income, and education continue to affect Americans of Asian descent in ways that are concealed by the cultural emphasis on the "model minority" myth.

Imaging Asian Americans

More so, perhaps, than any other ethnic or racial minority group in the United States, Asian Americans are held up as the model minority—they work hard, they save and invest their earnings, and they succeed in achieving the American dream. By dint of hard labor and "inherent" abilities in maths and sciences, Asians are perceived as the epitome of the "good" immigrant—that is, the model by which all other groups are measured and to which all other groups should aspire.

This seemingly glowing endorsement of Asian Americans is not without its pitfalls. First, as noted, it occludes the dramatic differences between and within the diversity of the Asian population. It denies the reality of those who live in poverty, who do not receive advanced degrees, and who do not attain a middle-class standard of living. Moreover, it renders invisible the related reality of discrimination faced by many segments of the Asian American population: the persistence of the glass ceiling and discriminatory admissions policies in colleges and universities, for example. Consequently, the model minority myth minimizes the tendency—and apparent need—to provide services and resources specific to the problems faced by Asian Americans. As the United States Commission on Civil Rights (1992:20) concluded, "despite the problems Asian Americans encounter, the success stereotype appears to have led policy makers to ignore those truly in need."

This stereotype also has dramatic implications for interethnic relationships, to the extent that it represents a wedge, pitting minority against minority. It discredits other minority groups by reinforcing the ideology of meritocracy: that anyone regardless of race, creed, or color can succeed in the United States. In other words, "people earn (or don't earn) what they deserve" (Nakayama, 1998:184). This plays a valuable ideological role in defending economic and political structures from the claims of discrimination levied by the civil rights movement. As such, it also creates friction between Asian Americans and other disadvantaged minority groups. In particular, African Americans and Hispanic Americans are made to feel inadequate for not having succeeded in the same way as have Asian Americans. This has been most apparent recently in Los Angeles' Chinatown, which shouldered much of the destruction and violence of the L.A. riots in 1992. During the riots, 300 Korean businesses were looted and burned; in all, 40% of the businesses lost were Asian owned (Cho, 1993).

There is also an impressive and disturbing slate of negative stereotypical constructs available by which to reinforce the inferiority of Asian Americans. Dispelled through the media, political rhetoric, and public debate, these images portray Asians in very unsympathetic terms. As noted earlier, Asian Americans are seen as perpetual foreigners, whose loyalty remains with their "homeland," not the United States. There is the persistent question, "Where did you learn to speak English?" Consequently, anti-Asian sentiments fluctuate with the relationship between the United States and the East. When the Japanese auto industry expanded its activity in the United States, for example, regions dependent on United States auto making (e.g., Detroit) witnessed increased hostility. It was in this context, for example, that Vincent Chin was beaten to death with a baseball bat, while his attackers shouted that it was "because of you . . . we're out of work" (United States Commission on Civil Rights, nd:43).

Just as Asian economies are presumed to represent a threat to United States dominance, so too are Asian Americans—as individuals—seen as unfair competitors within United States borders. Like other immigrants, they have come to this country and taken away "our" jobs and "our" businesses. In fact, Asians often create wealth and employment by investing savings in the United States economy and by creating small businesses. Unfortunately, even the latter is often interpreted in negative terms, as Asian business people and Asians in general are depicted as deceitful and devious. In their business dealings, they are not to be trusted; they are said to inflate their prices and minimize their service.

Institutionalized Discrimination Against Asian Americans

The negative images by which Asian American identity is constructed in the United States have consistently legitimated discriminatory treatment, while the model minority myth has rendered it invisible. Evidence of discrimination is apparent on many levels and in many different intersecting institutions.

Immigration and Citizenship

It was not until 1965 that the borders of the United States reopened to welcome immigration of people of Asian descent. Up until that time, successive immigration policy reforms limited and denied immigration and citizenship to those claiming Asian ancestry. Responding largely to public sentiment and political rhetoric that portrayed Asians as unfair labor competition and opium-smoking fiends, the United States Congress passed the Chinese Exclusion Act of 1882. That act accomplished two things: it suspended Chinese immigration for 10 years and it prohibited resident Chinese from attaining U.S. citizenship. The act was regularly renewed. It was finally repealed in 1943.

Japanese immigrants faced similar restrictions after the turn of the twentieth century. Under the 1907 Gentlemen's Agreement between Japan and the United States, admission of skilled and unskilled laborers (and their wives and children) was halted. In 1917, the Immigration Act barred all immigrants from most parts of Asia. The 1924 National Origins Act went even further, to bar admission of Japanese wives, even those whose husbands were U.S. citizens, and to prohibit immigration of aliens ineligible to attain U.S. citizenship. Given the 1922 Supreme Court decision that those of Japanese descent could not become naturalized, the 1924 act effectively halted Japanese immigration.

Japanese Internment

The anti-Japanese sentiments that underlaid the immigration reforms of the 1920s intensified during World War II. Executive Order 9066, signed by President Roosevelt in 1942, initiated the forced evacuation of persons of Japanese descent from the West Coast. Those moved to the "relocation camps" were often given little advance notice. Moreover, they were allowed to take with them only what they could carry. This meant that most were forced to sell their property and other belongings at outrageously low prices. That negative stereotypes underlaid this mistreatment is evident from public statements of the day. For example, California Congressman Rankin declared, "Once a Jap, always a Jap! You can't any more regenerate a Jap than you can reverse the laws of nature. I'm for taking every Japanese and putting him in a concentration camp" (cited in United States Commission on Civil Rights, 1992:10).

Educational Discrimination

In light of the dramatic recent influx of Asian immigrants, primary and secondary schools are confronted with the special problems of first- and second-generation Asian students, many of whom are ill-prepared for the educational experience in this country. Teachers and students unprepared for the diversity introduced by Asian students often create an unfriendly atmosphere that maintains the "difference" and outsider status of immigrant youth.

Problems of a different sort emerge for Asian Americans with aspirations of higher education. In spite of the broad belief in Asian educational success, there is evidence that they are subject to both negative sentiments and treatment at these institutions. Inquiries at a number of postsecondary institutions have uncovered damning evidence of discrimination in recruitment and admissions in particular. For example, the Brown University Corporation Committee on Minority Affairs (1984:4) reported that, "It was clearly stated by all admission staff to whom we spoke that Asian American applicants receive comparatively low non-academic ratings. These unjustified low ratings are due to the cultural biases and stereotypes which prevail in the admission office."

Economic Discrimination

The experience of educational and legal discrimination are reinforced in economic fora, which once again contradicts the success stereotype of Asian Americans. Owing largely to the fears of Asian economic competition and "unscrupulous business practices," many Asian Americans face the glass ceiling. Although highly represented in white-collar occupations, Asian Americans often find that their mobility within these organizations is curtailed. Aguirre and Turner (1998:185) quote an Asian white-collar worker's perceptions of his limited opportunities: "I suspect that the minds of many corporate managers and the senior staff members who have direct control . . . are still in the 1960s. As a consequence, for most of them we Asians are a suspect class, and we usually have to prove that we are better in order to be equal." Research consistently illustrates the validity of these perceptions. There is ample evidence to suggest that management, especially its upper tiers, is off-limits to Asian American professionals (Aguirre and Turner, 1998). Perhaps not surprisingly, income discrimination often follows similar patterns, wherein equally qualified Asian American employees earn less than their non-Asian, especially white, counterparts.

Asian Americans as Offenders

As noted previously, the ironic opposite pole of the model minority stereotype is that of the mysterious, devious, fearsome Asian. Media, politicians, and social commentators too often confuse this stereotype with the reality of Asian criminal activity. If we were to believe the words of Senator Sam Nunn, we might make the mistake of accepting the sensational media images of Asian gangsters: "Chinese organized crime . . . is in many ways as mysterious, if not more so, than its portrayal in movies such as *Year of the Dragon*" (cited in Laidler, 1998:170). According to such portrayals, all Asians are martial arts experts; all are stealthy and silent; all are violent gang members; and all are connected by a network of organized crime. These images consistently mark Asians as "different," as the Other, thereby reinforcing their "foreign" and alien nature. It also makes them something to be feared and, therefore, avoided.

What little is known about Asian criminality refutes these images of Asian violence and stealth. On the contrary, the offenses for which Asian Americans are most likely to be arrested are public order offenses. The contemporary patterns of criminality that emerge are very much in line with the historical evolution of Asian criminality, and with discrimination against Chinese and Japanese immigrants in particular. Earlier restrictions on Asian immigration—especially with respect to women—often meant that Asian immigrant laborers were confined to all-male communities. Antimiscegenation laws around the turn of the twentieth century only exaggerated this tendency. Consequently, Asian workers often turned to prostitutes as a necessary outlet for sex and companionship (Espiritu, 1997:31). By 1870, more than 75% of the nearly 3,000 Chinese women workers in the United States identified themselves as prostitutes. In 1900, most Japanese immigrant women were also prostitutes. With the easing of immigration restrictions later in the twentieth century, there was a transition from the importation of prostitutes to the importation of "picture brides." Both practices were "big business," not for the women themselves but for the men who profited from their labors: procurers, brothel owners, and the officials paid to "look the other way" (Espiritu, 1997:31).

Although initially controlled by individual men (and some women), prostitution ultimately fell under the control of emerging Asian "secret societies" and Chinese *tongs* in particular. These organizations were originally created to meet the needs for community and representation of the isolated Asian male immigrants, in the context of a hostile social climate. However, many evolved into criminal organizations or developed links with Chinese triads. Consequently, the tongs came to dominate prostitution, along with gambling, drugs, and other vice crimes. So, in addition to providing sexual outlets, they also created other opportunities for recreation and escapist behavior.

With respect to the criminal involvement of Asians in public order offenses, Mann (1993:133) observes that "minority people commit the crimes that are created for them." In other words, particular behaviors come to be criminalized as a means of regulating specific communities. For example, turn of the twentieth century opium legislation was clearly an effort to curtail the economic power of Asians. Mann (1993) offers other examples, drawn from Portland, Oregon's, ordinances: prohibiting the use of poles across the shoulders as a means of carrying heavy loads (a Chinese practice); and the "Chinese Theater Ordinance," which prohibited the playing of any instrument other than a guitar in any theater after midnight.

As a result of this discriminatory application of the criminal law, Asians were among the most heavily incarcerated groups on the West Coast during the early part of the twentieth century. However, in the contemporary era, Asian Americans are consistently underrepresented in the crime statistics, unlike other communities of color. In 1993, for example, Asian Americans represented approximately 3% of the population, but only 1% of those arrested. Moreover, they were most likely to be arrested for public order offenses—prostitution or gambling—rather than violent offenses.

The vice crimes for which Asians—especially Japanese, Chinese, and Vietnamese—are most likely to be arrested are lucrative sources of revenue for organized crime groups: Chinese tongs and triads and Japanese yakuza, for example. There is a consensus among scholars and law enforcement agencies that Asian organized crime is growing at a more rapid rate than that of any other cultural group (Flowers, 1990; Mann, 1993; Marshall, 1997; Ho, 1998). Consequently, these groups are assuming a growing share of illegal markets. It is the effort to protect these market shares that is responsible for the recent increases in violent crime associated with Asian Americans.

Sometimes connected to and sometimes independent of Asian organized crime are the growing numbers of Asian youth gangs. Flowers (1990) and Mann (1993) both report that Chinatowns across the United States have recently witnessed dramatic and violent increases in Asian gang membership. Although the triads and yakuza tend to be involved in racketeering, smuggling, and so on, Asian youth gangs are more likely to be involved in localized extortion and robbery, as well as internecine conflicts. The older, more formalized groups tend to include both immigrants and United States born Asians, whereas the youth gangs are dominated by recent immigrants, leading Parillo (1985:251) to conclude:

> The growing problem of youthful militancy and delinquency appears to reflect the marginal status of those in the younger generation who experience frustration and adjustment problems in America. Recent

arrivals from Hong Kong are unfamiliar with the language and culture, they are either unemployed or in the lowliest of jobs, and they live in overcrowded, slum-like quarters with no recreational facilities. Gang behavior serves as an alternative and a way of filling status and identity needs.

Asian Americans as Victims of Crime

Many of the same sentiments that perpetuate anti-Asian discrimination and sensational images of Asian crime also underlie anti-Asian victimization. Moreover, the legacy of discriminatory legislation and activity finds a violent supplement in victimization motivated by anti-Asian bias. The current environment of intolerance—highlighted by California's Proposition 187 and the nationwide impetus for immigration reform—has meant that immigrants are increasingly held up as scapegoats, thereby encouraging and legitimating violent acts perpetrated against these "invading foreigners." Might there not be a link between the following scenarios?

> New York City Councilwoman Julia Harrison referred to the growing Asian American population in Queens as "an invasion, not an assimilation." Moreover, she laid the blame for such widespread problems as crime and high real estate prices at the feet of Asian Americans. For her, the changing face of her community was "very upsetting, very discombobulating." (National Asian Pacific American Legal Consortium, 1996:14)

> New York City has one of the highest and fastest growing rates of anti-Asian violence in the country. One example of such violence includes the attack by three white youths on a Chinese American man. The assault was prefaced by their exclamation that "I don't want you Chinks thinking you own the world." (National Asian Pacific American Legal Consortium, 1996:14)

Anti-Asian violence accounts for a relatively small proportion of all racially motivated hate crime. However, it does represent a growing proportion. Many sources suggest that it constitutes the most dramatically and rapidly growing type of racial violence (United States Commission on Civil Rights, 1992; nd; NAPALC, 1996; FBI, 1997). The most comprehensive source of data on violence against Asian Americans is the National Asian Pacific American Legal Consortium (NAPALC) yearly audit. The range of their data sources is broad and varied: telephone and intake sessions, newspaper reports, community-based organizations, churches, human rights commissions, bar associations, and government agencies. Their annual audits are veritable treasure troves of information. They provide summary counts, synopses of cases, information on legal action taken by

NAPALC, analyses of regional and national trends, and extensive policy recommendations.

Owing to the variation in reporting methods and agencies, the NAPALC data are not to be taken as accurate in terms of absolute numbers. However, the trends and analyses offered in the audits are nonetheless informative and indicative of underlying patterns. The most recent audit seems to confirm what anecdotal evidence and intuitive observations have suggested: riding a wave of anti-immigrant sentiments, anti-Asian violence is consistently on the rise in the 1990s. As is often the case with hate crime, anti-Asian incidents disproportionately involve assaults and intimidation: that is, violations of the person. For example, in 1995, assaults accounted for 28% of all incidents reported to NAPALC.

It is interesting to note that a substantial number of suspected offenders involved in violence against Asian Americans are African American or Hispanic. In 1995, these two groups accounted for nearly 45% of offenders (NAPALC, 1996). The interethnic hostilities noted earlier in this chapter also manifest themselves in interethnic violence, wherever other minority groups feel further alienated and marginalized by "newcomers" who appear to have surpassed them in their pursuit of the American Dream. For example, in Washington, DC, between 1984 and 1995, 9 Korean-owned businesses within a three-block area in a predominantly black neighborhood were firebombed. Although police failed to investigate these as racially motivated, Koreans in the neighborhood had little doubt as to their motivation, given the intensity of black hostility toward Korean shopowners.

The NAPALC (1996) audit of anti-Asian incidents provides ample evidence of the relationship between anti-Asian themes and violence. Consider just a few illustrative examples; first, Asians as foreigners: "An East Indian woman was approached by her white neighbors and told 'You Hindu bitches, why did you have to move into here?' The victim also found a flag, used in religious ceremonies, broken in her yard" (NAPALC, 1996:32). Second, Asians as economic competitors: "A Chinese American man was assaulted in a supermarket parking lot. A white male stabbed him four times, resulting in multiple injuries, including a punctured lung. The assailant justified his actions when he confessed that he sought to kill an Asian person because 'they got all the good jobs'" (NAPALC, 1996:8).

These examples are not atypical. Asians—regardless of the longevity of their ties to the United States—are frequent victims of violence, ranging from offensive bumper stickers, to verbal harassment, to assault, to murder. Moreover, it is only recently that the problems faced by Asian Americans have been acknowledged and finally addressed by advocacy groups and state agencies alike.

Asian Americans as Service Providers

Increasingly, the particular needs of Asian communities, victims, and offenders are being recognized in the context of criminal and social justice concerns. This task is complicated by the distrust of criminal justice agents on the part of many

Asians. One of the contributing factors here is the traditional reliance on private resolution of conflicts, which excludes police involvement. In addition, there is often a great fear of authority figures, especially among recent immigrants from autocratic or war-torn countries. We must also recognize the very real fear on the part of victims of retaliation in the event that they point accusing fingers at their offenders.

Some efforts have been made by law enforcement agencies to overcome the barriers between Asian communities and police departments. Cultural awareness training has been implemented as a means of improving police officers' understanding and treatment of Asian Americans. Interpreters have been hired where numbers warrant. Community policing initiatives have been implemented as a means of integrating police and public. One of the greatest disappointments in police–Asian relations has been in the area of representation in police departments. Stokes and Scott's (1996) review of hiring practices found that in spite of affirmative action initiatives, Asian Americans are dramatically underrepresented among police officers, even in communities in which Asians make up a substantial proportion of the population. Most cities with a sizable Asian population had negligible representation on police forces. Even San Francisco and Oakland, California, with 29% and 15% Asian populations, respectively, had a very low proportion of Asian officers.

Some police departments across the country are making admirable efforts to enhance the accessibility and civility of their personnel. San Diego and Oakland, California, for example, have established Asian Advisory Committees that act as liaisons between the police department and the Asian communities. The committees bring concerns to the police departments and mobilize community support for the police force. San Diego and Los Angeles have introduced Civilian Community Service Officers who work out of storefront offices in the Asian communities. Their role is to act as buffers between the two communities by taking reports, attending community events, offering crime prevention and counseling programs, and other similar community oriented services. Although such efforts represent valuable innovations, they demand long-term commitment to ensure that they do not become merely token initiatives meant to quell public complaint.

As supplements—or more often alternatives—to criminal justice agencies, Asian communities across the nation have begun to establish their own advocacy and action groups, intended to represent and protect Asian interests. This is a dramatic step, given the historical failure of Asian Americans to protest or speak out against their plight. Perhaps buoyed by the gains of other civil rights movements and by the findings of recent civil rights commissions' reports, Asian Americans have begun to mobilize their growing numerical strength into political and social power. In addition to Pan–Asian umbrella organizations like the NAPALC and employment, resettlement, and workers' organizations, Asians have established several legal centers geared toward assisting and advocating for the community. American Citizens for Justice was originally founded in 1983 in protest of the lenient sentences given to Vincent Chin's murderers. It continues to fight for the civil rights of all Americans, and especially Asian Americans, by engaging in legal consultations, the monitoring of anti-Asian violence, and the provision of educational services. The Asian American Legal Defense and Education Fund is similarly committed to promoting the civil rights of Asian Americans. It has established an Anti-Asian Violence Project, which litigates and provides counseling for victims of hate crime and police brutality. The Asian Immigrant Women Advocates (AIWA) recognizes and addresses the particular problems of immigrant women who are often exploited and subjugated by both their originating culture and that of the United States. AIWA seeks to empower these women by providing job training and counseling as well as education on their rights in their new home.

One could go on endlessly. There are literally hundreds of local, regional, and national organizations committed to enhancing the place and power of Asian Americans in the United States. Given the historical and systemic nature of violence and discrimination against this community, they are correct in recognizing that meaningful and lasting change requires activity on the part of the many Asian communities—singly and collectively.

References

Aguirre, A. and Turner, J. (1998). *American ethnicity*, 2nd ed. Boston: McGraw-Hill.

Brown University Corporation Committee on Minority Affairs (1984). *Report to the Corporation Committee on Minority Affairs from its Subcommittee on Asian Americans*.

Cho, S. (1993). Korean Americans vs. African Americans: Conflict and construction. In R. Gooding-Williams (Ed.), *Reading Rodney King, reading urban uprisings*, pp. 196–211. New York: Routledge.

Espiritu, Y. L. (1997). *Asian American women and men*. Thousand Oaks, CA: Sage.

Federal Bureau of Investigation (1997). *Hate crime statistics, 1996*. Washington, DC: U.S. Department of Justice.

Flowers, R. B. (1990). *Minorities and criminality*. New York: Praeger.

Ho, T. (1998). Vice crimes and Asian Americans. In C. R. Mann and M. S. Zatz (Eds.), *Images of color, images of crime*, pp. 195–204. Los Angeles: Roxbury.

Kim, B. H. (1998). Asian Americans and the black-white paradigms. In C. R. Mann and M. S. Zatz (Eds.), *Images of color, images of crime*, pp. 188–194. Los Angeles: Roxbury.

Laidler, K. J. (1998). Senator sir, meet Susie Wong and the inscrutable Fu Manchu. In C. R. Mann and M. S. Zatz (Eds.), *Images of color, images of crime*, pp. 169–179. Los Angeles: Roxbury.

Mann, C. R. (1993). *Unequal justice*. Bloomington, IN: Indiana University Press.

Marshall, I. H. (1997). Minorities, crime and criminal justice in the United States. In I. H. Marshall (Ed.), *Minorities, migrants and crime*, pp. 1–35. Thousand Oaks, CA: Sage.

McClain, P. and Stuart, J. (1995). *Can we all get along? Racial and ethnic minorities in American politics*. Boulder, CO: Westview.

Nakayama, T. (1998). Framing Asian Americans. In C. R. Mann and M. S. Zatz (Eds.), *Images of color, images of crime*, pp. 179–187. Los Angeles: Roxbury.

National Asian and Pacific Americans Legal Consortium (1996). *Audit of violence against Asian Pacific Americans*.

Parillo, V. (1985). *Strangers to these shores: Race and ethnic relations in the U.S.* New York: John Wiley.

Stokes, L. and Scott, J. (1996). Affirmative action and selected minority groups in law enforcement, *Journal of Criminal Justice, 24(1)*, 29–38.

U.S. Commission on Civil Rights (1992). *Civil rights issues facing Asian Americans.* Washington, DC: U.S. Government Printing Office.

———, (nd). *Recent actions against citizens and residents of Asian descent.* Washington, DC: U.S. Government Printing Office.

9 Class, Difference, and the Social Construction of Crime and Criminality

RAYMOND J. MICHALOWSKI

The crime that I've always been fighting is violent crime—the rapists, the murderers, the child molesters, the bank robbers. Those are the people who are a danger to society. The issue we are dealing with here has to do with nuances of financial reporting, no theft of money or anything like that. So, it's different.

With these words, J. Fyfe Symington, millionaire, land developer, and former governor of Arizona, rejected the idea that his 1997 conviction on seven counts of felony fraud constituted *real* crime (Natchtigal, 1998). By claiming that his crimes were not a "danger to society," Symington dramatized the way social class influences how we define crime and deal with criminals in the United States. Typically, when people of high social status commit white collar crimes—even felony offenses like Symington's that defraud hundreds of working people of millions of dollars—they do not see themselves as *real* criminals, nor are they treated as real criminals by others. Furthermore, many of the harmful acts that can be committed only by those of high social status are never even defined as crimes. Millions of Americans, for instance, have contracted chronic or fatal diseases because people of high social status, such as corporate managers or government officials, either knowingly exposed them to hazardous substances, deliberately hid the truth about the risks these substances posed, or both (for details, see Braithwaite, 1984; Hawkins, 1997; Kauzlarich and Kramer, 1998; Mintz, 1985; Rebovich, 1992; Wright, 1996). Even so, very few people have ever been charged with criminal offenses for the illness and death resulting from this type of wrongdoing (Hills, 1987). Instead, we reserve the label of "real crime" for behaviors typically associated with people of lower social status, even when their offenses are relatively minor or lack immediate victims, such as drug use or prostitution (Chambliss and Seidman, 1982; Michalowski, 1985).

This chapter explores how social class as a critical arena of difference in the United States helps ensure that most of the people who are victims of crime and the majority of those who are arrested, go to court, and find their way to America's currently overcrowded prisons and jails are poor (Bureau of Justice Statistics, 1993, 1998). Specifically, this chapter focuses on three aspects of the relationship between social class differences and crime: (1) how social class shapes the definition of crime, (2) how social class influences patterns of victimization and wrongful behavior, and (3) how fundamental changes in our society are presently altering the way the criminal justice system deals with lower-income populations. Before examining these topics, it is useful to explore the meaning of the term social class.

What Is Social Class?

When people talk about social class, they frequently use terms like "upper class," "middle class," "lower class," "working class," and "underclass." These words typically characterize social groups according to their access to economic, social, and/or life-style resources. Economic resources consist of the wealth and/or income controlled by different social groups. Social resources constitute the degree to which groups can exert political influence and/or cultural authority. Political influence is the ability of groups to shape the actions of governmental institutions either as members of the government or by influencing political processes from positions of power outside of government. Cultural authority is the ability to shape popular consciousness through access to mass media, education, or other platforms of public communication. Finally, "life-style" resources refers to the degree to which group-based patterns of behavior and belief are valued or devalued within a society. These include such things as modes of speech, style of dress, expressed attitudes and values, and preferred and/or available pleasures. As both William Wilson (1987) and Philippe Bourgois (1995) show in their respective studies of ghetto youth, the less individuals can look, talk, dress, and act in the approved middle-class manner, the less likely they are to be hired, even when they have the necessary skills for a job.

There have been many attempts to create precise definitions of various social classes and determine just where one class ends and another begins (see, for example, Bartley and Briggs, 1979; Szymanski, 1983; Wright, 1985). Rather than treat social classes as distinct groups bounded by precise lines, however, I suggest that the central elements of social class—economic resources, social resources, and life-style resources—constitute intersecting characteristics that combine to place individuals somewhere on a social class continuum that ranges from the least- to the most-advantaged Americans.

The uppermost reaches of social class formation in the United States are inhabited by individuals who own large shares of the nation's wealth, exert direct influence over the making and implementation of laws and governmental policy, can use both their wealth and the political power to shape the content of mass media, and who live the kinds of life-styles that many people envy and would like to emulate. Nearer the bottom are individuals who earn very little, have no wealth, enjoy little direct influence over government or media, and whose style of speech, dress, and conduct are seen as maladjusted, eccentric, or "dangerous" by those from more advantaged sectors of the society. In the middle of this continuum is a broad range of individuals who enjoy differing configurations of economic, social, and life-style resources.

For our purposes, what is significant about this differential distribution of resources is how it influences the justice process. Specifically, it enables resource-advantaged groups to create and implement definitions of crime that ensure that everyone will be victims of upper-class wrongdoing, whereas less-advantaged groups will bear the weight of street crime both as victims and as criminals targeted by the justice system.

Why Do We Have Social Classes?

The United States, like most of the world, is based on a political–economic system organized around free-market competition, that is, *capitalism.* One of the essential features of competitive market systems is that some people win a larger share of the society's resources than others. There are many factors that can influence why some people obtain more than others. Some are healthier than others. Some start life with more cultural advantages than others. Some have more hope. Some work harder than others. And so on. Whatever the *individual* reasons for success or failure, however, when societies are organized around economic competition, the division of society into haves, have-somes, and have-nots is an inevitable, *structural* outcome (Poulantzas, 1975). Thus, although individual differences are the *means* for creating inequality, they are not the *reason* for it. That reason lies in a social system organized around the principle that people who are more fortunate in terms of health, background, skill, or energy should be able to acquire more than those who are less fortunate.

This division of society into social classes is both an uneven and a cumulative process. The more resources individuals and groups can bring to the game, the more they can win. The more they have won in the past, the more they are likely to win in the future. For instance, if Microsoft stock rose by 10%, the person with $1,000 of Microsoft stock would earn $100, whereas the person with $10,000 invested would net $1,000. The first person's wealth would have grown from $1,000 to $1,100, and the second person's from $10,000 to $11,000. In other words, a 10% gain for each person increased the wealth gap between them by $900. In the same manner, unless there are powerful redistribution mechanisms, economic growth typically means that the gap between the rich, the middle class, and the poor becomes wider, not narrower. For instance, between 1979 and 1993, during a period of exceptional economic growth, 60% of American workers saw their annual incomes *decline*. Moreover, the richest one-fifth of the population were the only group to enjoy substantial gains, with an 18% increase in their income. At the same time, the average incomes of the poorest one-fifth of the population declined by 15% (Bluestone, 1995).

A similar process occurs with respect to *social capital;* that is, the nonmonetary resources people bring to the game. Children who grow up in advantaged homes where they are introduced to important developmental experiences such as reading, writing, analytic reasoning, arts, and travel at an early age typically do better in school, gain higher levels of education, obtain better jobs as adults, and earn more money in their lifetime than do children who grow up in less-advantaged surroundings (Macleod, 1995; Lusane, 1991). It is true that some individuals start out with few resources yet succeed beyond all expectations, whereas some who had every advantage fail. For most of the people, most of the time, however, social class origins significantly shape the character of their adult lives.

This process of uneven competition ensures that income and wealth concentrate within relatively small segments of the population, thus solidifying economic differences between groups and ensuring the continuation of social class differences. In 1995, for instance, the richest 10% of the American population owned 68% of everything of value in the nation, and one third of this was owned by only *one-half of one percent* of the population. This left less than a third of the nation's wealth (32%) for the remaining 90% of the population (see Figure 9.1). In other words, if the United States were a village with 1,000 people with a total wealth of $1 million, the richest five individuals would each have $54,000, the next 95 people would have $3,368 apiece, and the remaining 900 people would each have $456.

Although an uneven distribution of wealth and cultural advantages is inevitable in competitive market societies, just how uneven this distribution will be is shaped by political forces. Government policies can either intensify or lessen class inequalities. Progressive taxation of income and capital gains can be used to finance policies and programs that help improve the chances of people who are less advantaged while reducing the income and wealth gap between social classes. Or governments can implement more regressive taxes, such as sales taxes, which tend to make the poor poorer and the rich richer. Governments also develop and implement policies to address the criminogenic consequences of income and wealth inequality. In doing so, they can pursue preventative or punitive strategies. Preventative strategies such as Head Start, housing subsidies, income support policies for poor families, and drug rehabilitation programs are designed to reduce the negative effects of inequality and lessen the number of the least advantaged who may be attracted to crime. Punitive strategies attack the crime problem through "get tough" tactics such as determinate sentencing, wars on crime and drugs, and removal of rehabilitation programs from prisons. Either way, state and federal governments play important roles in determining the meaning and consequences of social class inequality for the problems of crime and crime control.

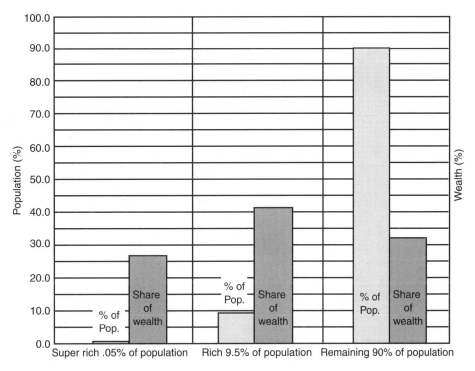

FIGURE 9.1   Distribution of Wealth in the United States, 1995.

Source: Unpublished Federal Reserve Technical Paper, July 1, 1995.

Social Class and the Definition of Crime

Social class divisions involve the unequal distribution of political power and cultural authority as well the distribution of wealth. On a one-for-one basis, people whose money comes primarily from investments or high-status occupations tend to have more ability to influence the formal institutions of the United States—including the justice system—than do ordinary wage workers, the poor, the unemployed, the young, or the undereducated. If you doubt this, examine the composition of the U.S. Senate, Congress, or any state legislature. You will find that the vast majority of elected officials are either wealthy, have high-status professional careers, are business owners, or manifest some combination of these characteristics (Parenti, 1977). What you will not find are very many factory workers, sales clerks, low-level managers, truck drivers, housewives, students, unemployed, homeless, or any of the other folk who comprise the vast majority of the American social landscape. Consequently, the laws and policies that shape how we define crime are more likely to reflect the values, life experiences, and interests of the upper echelons of society.

I am not suggesting that laws and policies reflect *only* the interests of upper echelons of society. There are many areas of agreement between social classes over the definition of crime. Both the rich and the poor agree that murder, rape, theft, and burglary should be treated as crimes. It is where there are disagreements that social class exerts its influence over the definition of crime. For instance, the majority of Americans view deliberate acts of white-collar crimes that lead to death or injury as serious as street crimes that lead to death or injury (Rossi, 1974). Lawmakers, however, come primarily from the strata of society that has the *exclusive ability* to commit white-collar crimes. As a result, the prosecution and punishment of white-collar, corporate, and political crimes have always been more lenient than the treatment of street crimes.

In addition to frequently prevailing in cases of specific disagreements with less-advantaged classes, the resource-rich have always played an important role in shaping broadly held visions of right and wrong. In *The Search for Criminal Man*, Ysabel Renee (1979) details how the cultural understanding of who is "dangerous" historically has focused on individuals whose behavior challenged established economic and cultural hierarchies. During the Middle Ages, when royalty and the Catholic Church constituted the ruling classes, "republicans" (those who believed in political equality) and "heretics" (those who refused to accept Papal interpretations of scripture) were viewed as the most dangerous of criminals. During the early stages of mercantile capitalism, those who refused to be evicted from hereditary feudal lands, refused to work for wages, or who violated the new rights of private property were defined as dangerous and deserving of harsh punishments (Chambliss, 1964; Hall, 1935). With the rise of industrialization, the growing population of poorly paid and unemployed urbanized, industrial workers were labeled the "dangerous classes," and it came to be taken for granted that their pleasures were "vices" that should be criminalized and repressed (Brace, 1880; Helmer, 1975).

In nineteenth century America, the new class of industrial workers threatened the established political, economic, and cultural hierarchies. Their efforts to organize into syndicates and unions challenged the authority of the business class to determine wages and living conditions (Boyer and Morais, 1955). Historical records indicate that the rise of urban police in the United States was influenced by the desire to control worker organization and unrest as much as by a desire to control typical "street" crimes (Harring, 1983). Rising populations of poor and/or unemployed workers also threatened the cultural authority of the proponents of America's "democratic" version of capitalism (Livingston, 1986; Sklar, 1988). The frequently squalid living conditions of nineteenth century industrial workers called into question the claims of business, governmental, and moral leaders that the emergent order was a just and fair one. By defining the pleasures *available* to the working class such as getting drunk, gambling, and "illicit sex" as both immoral and illegal, the elite and middle classes shifted the blame for the social problems resulting from urbanization and industrialization onto the personal failings of the people who benefited least and suffered most under the emerging factory system. The combination of police control of "street" crime and public welfare campaigns against vice contributed to this process in two ways. First, the idea of vice came to be associated with the pleasures of the poor, not those of the elite. Second, vice became an easy way to blame the poor for their own poverty. In other words, if it wasn't for their drinking, or gambling, or sexual promiscuity, and so forth, those who were poor could have been middle class. At the same time that the poor were being blamed for their poverty, the "captains of industry" who sent children into factories at an early age, consigned injured workers to permanent unemployment with no compensation, and who paid wages that drove many to drink, desperation, and violence were heralded as the brave leaders of a new society, while the harms *they* caused were placed both legally and culturally beyond the reach of criminal law.

Since the middle of the nineteenth century, the American justice system has promoted definitions of behavior and morality that paint the poorer parts of society as overrepresented by dangerous people and deviant behavior, whereas the middle and upper classes are presumed to be primarily industrious and moral. As Edwin Sutherland (1949) noted in his landmark volume, *White Collar Crime,* when people of "high social status" do wrong in the course of pursuing profit, the legal system "administratively segregates" their wrongdoing from *crime.* Harmful behaviors committed in the pursuit of profit are typically defined as "regulatory violations," which carry neither the stigma nor the punishments associated with *real* crime (for details, see Edelhertz and Geis, 1974; Michalowski, 1998; Reiman, 1996). This occurs even though the damage to health, wealth, and life caused by these offenses *vastly exceeds* damages caused by routine criminals from poorer social classes. As the populist folk singer of the 1930s, Woody Guthrie, wrote: "Some men rob you with a six gun, some with a fountain pen." The criminal justice system, however, is designed almost exclusively to control those who "rob you with a six gun."

The long-term cultural effects of this process are substantial. Regardless of social class, many people think of the vices and street crimes of lower-income groups as the essence of *real* crime, and as the appropriate, primary focus for law enforcement. The reason for this, however, is not because these activities are the most harmful ones occurring in the United States. It is because this is what our society, by example and by rhetoric, has taught us to believe about crime since we were children. We rarely hear of white-collar offenders being imprisoned for their crimes, but the media regularly treats us with stories of lower-income street criminals being processed through the halls of justice (Barak, 1994; Ericson, Baranek, and Chan, 1991). Consequently, it is easier to believe that burglars, robbers, drug dealers, and auto thieves pose a far greater threat to our well-being than do corporate criminals. When political leaders repeatedly denounce gangs as a fundamental threat to social order, but rarely, if ever, use their cultural authority to condemn corporate officials who deliberately poison and impoverish large segments of the world's population in pursuit of "economic growth," we are likely to believe that it is more important to control young men showing gang colors than those who believe profit justifies human suffering (Michalowski, 1998). The more the criminal justice system focuses on people from poorer and culturally disdained backgrounds, the more it appears as if the poor are the crime problem.

The criminal justice system's focus on the crimes of the poor obscures the far greater harm done by white-collar and corporate criminals. Consider the following. A U.S. Department of Justice study estimated that the total cost of serious crime in the United Sates in 1992 amounted to $17.6 billion. Although this represents a substantial loss, it is only a fraction of the costs that white-collar criminals impose on the United States. According to the U.S. General Accounting Office, fraud and abuse account for 10% of the total money spent on health care in the United States, with most of this fraud being committed not by health care users, but by insurance companies, health care professionals, and health care organizations. In 1995, the cost from this one area of fraud alone was estimated to be *$100 billion,* nearly seven times greater than the cost of all street crime (Davis, 1995; Thompson, 1992). According to the Association of Certified Fraud Examiners, the annual cost of all frauds within business in United States is approximately *$400 billion, 22 times higher* than the total cost of serious street crime (Geis, 1998).

The typical argument posed against comparisons like those presented here are that although white-collar and corporate crimes cost people money, even a lot of money, they do not involve the personal injury and suffering caused by street crime. Claims of this sort, however, do not take into account the deaths and injuries that result each year from corporate lawbreaking in the workplace, in the marketplace, and in the environment, and the real human suffering caused by things such as unaffordable health insurance, fraudulent investment schemes, and raided pension funds.

Each year between 9,000 and 10,000 people die due to work-related accidents, and according to the most conservative estimates, between 50,000 and 70,000 die from diseases contracted due to toxins in the workplace (Occupational Safety and Health Administration, 1997). Using the lowest estimates, this means that at least 59,000 people die each year due to workplace hazards. Certainly, not all of these deaths result from violations of law. Some are due to worker carelessness or exposure to unknown hazards. However, according data from the U.S. Government Accounting Office (1996), 69% of workplaces under government contract that were inspected by the Occupational Safety and Health Administration (OSHA) were guilty of at least one willful violation of workplace safety laws serious enough to pose "a risk of death or serious physical harm to workers" (emphasis added). Insofar as government contractors are more closely supervised by OSHA than other workplaces, 69% of the deaths due to work-related injury or illness (41,125 deaths) is a reasonable estimate of the number of people who die annually due to corporate lawbreaking in the workplace. If we compare these 41,125 criminal workplace deaths with the 24,330 homicides in 1990, the peak year for homicides during the 1990s, we find that the odds of dying due to work are almost double those of being murdered, if we generalize these figures to the entire population. However, because the workforce is less than one-half of the population, these figures actually mean that for workers the chance of being killed by a job-related accident or illness are roughly four times greater than the likelihood of being murdered. For the friends and relatives of those killed, these deaths are very real, very painful losses made all the more so because, like homicide in the street or the home, they result from the criminal activity of others.

If we turn our attention to workplace injuries we find a similar picture. According to the FBI, in 1995 the rate of violent crime in the United States was 635 per every 100,000 people (Sourcebook, 1998). By comparison, OSHA estimated there were roughly 6,800 nonfatal workplace injuries requiring medical care per 100,000 workers (OSHA, 1997). In other words, the odds of being the victim of an injury-causing workplace incident is nearly eleven times greater than the risk of being the victim of a violent crime. These comparisons only touch on the ways white-collar and corporate crime harm us in our everyday life. The financial costs and physical harms resulting from illegal environmental pollution, the deliberate marketing of unsafe products, and the vast array of scams that take not only people's money but destroy their financial security and emotional well-being exceed the physical and financial costs of street crime by a wide margin every year (Reiman, 1996). Yet it is street crime and street criminals that the law targets most energetically. This is the long legacy of social class bias in the American system of criminal justice.

Class, Criminality, and Victimization

There is considerable disagreement within criminology and criminal justice regarding whether individuals from lower classes are more likely to commit crime than are those from the middle and upper classes. If we ask who is more likely to cause *harm* to the society, as discussed previously, it would appear that the upper- and middle-class sectors pose the greatest danger to our health, life, and economic well-being. If we stick to the question of who commits the crimes that the justice system pays the most attention to, the picture becomes less clear.

Annual FBI reports of the characteristics of people who are arrested in the United States provide information regarding gender, age, race, and ethnicity, but little regarding social class characteristics such as income, occupation, or residence. Consequently, the best information we have regarding the social class characteristics of street criminals is based on surveys of prison inmates. According to these surveys, there is little question that the vast majority of those serving time for criminal offenses come from the poorest segments of the society. They show that criminal offenders are less well educated, far less likely to be employed, and earn far lower incomes than the general population. For instance, although 78% of the general population had graduated from high school, only 33% of the prisoners surveyed had done so. At a time when 7% of the total labor force was unemployed, 45% of those in prison had been without jobs at the time of their arrest. Finally, although the average yearly wage for full-time employed workers was $27,000, and even the *poorest* 10% of full-time workers earned an average of $13,000 a year, 53% of those in prison had incomes of $10,000 or less before being arrested (Bureau of Justice Statistics, 1993). Although these statistics may be somewhat skewed by the fact that better-off offenders charged with street crimes are more likely to avoid imprisonment, there is little reason to believe the degree of error is substantial. All one need do is spend a few days in any urban police station to know that very few middle- or upper-class citizens are being brought to the bar of justice for common street crimes. Clearly, the criminal justice net hauls in the poorest of the poor. What this tells us about the link between social class and criminal behavior, however, remains controversial.

Attempts to explain the relationship between social class and criminality has produced three types of explanations: individual defect theories, social interaction theories, and structural outcomes theories. Currently, the dominant individualistic explanation for higher rates of street crime among the poor focuses on family failings and personal morality. *Body Count*, a highly influential conservative assessments of crime trends in the 1990s, argues that crime is the result of "moral poverty." The authors contend that high crime rates occur when families fail to impose clear moral understandings of right and wrong on the next generation (Bennett, DiJullio, and Walters, 1996). By focusing on "street criminals," the authors make it clear that they are primarily concerned with the "moral poverty" of the poorer classes, not the moral poverty of corporate and political wrongdoers. This approach is a modern-day equivalent of the nineteenth-century writers who blamed the working class for their poverty, rather than asking why industrial workers earned so little. Even if the proportion of families able to pass on moral messages to the next generation has declined in recent decades, why is this? Might it have anything to do with the substantial decline in family wages among the poorest 40% of the population? Or the emergence of a new cybertech society that offers few opportunities for the children of today's inner-city poor? Explanations that focus on the belief systems of criminals tend to be circular insofar as they claim (1) that individuals commit crime because they lack good values, and (2) we know they lack good values because they commit crime. By placing the locus of responsibility for crime at the individual level, these explanations minimize the importance of societal changes that alter the context within which individuals learn their values and select their behaviors. In the end, individualistic explanations for crime are much like focusing on a ping-pong match when there are elephants wrestling underneath the table.

Social interactionist approaches argue that if were not for the maladroit intervention of the justice system, the poor would appear just as law-abiding as the affluent. They contend that "criminals" (that is, those who show up in official statistics) are disproportionately poor because (1) the justice system focuses on controlling poor communities, and (2) this practice increases the likelihood of future criminality by "labeling" residents of these areas, particularly young men, as "criminals" at an early age (Matza, 1969; Currie, 1993; Irwin and Austin, 1994). A typical example put forth is that the proportion of drug users among college students is no less than in poor communities, yet college students have a far lower risk of serving time as drug offenders than do residents of poor communities because they are not the targets of the "war on drugs"—which is really a war on poor people (Chambliss, 1995; Currie, 1998). Although there is some merit to this approach, the question that remains is, *why* does the criminal justice system do this? Is it merely a reflection of the discriminatory attitudes of those who work in the justice system? Or are they, as good workers, simply pursuing the goals set out for them by a broader political and economic system?

Structural outcomes perspectives generally argue that poor communities will manifest higher rates of criminal behavior, just as they manifest increased levels of other problems such as hypertension, alcoholism, and diabetes, not because of individual failings, but because of the physical and emotional pressures of poverty. Higher rates of property crime are typically explained in terms of the structurally induced gap that people experience between their material wants and the resources they have to fulfill them. This notion of *structural strain*, first formalized by Robert Merton in the 1930s, contends that although desires for the "good things" in life cut across all social classes, the poor have fewer resources to obtain them. Some individuals resolve this pressure by resorting to illegal means to fulfill their culturally learned desires (Merton, 1938). When it comes to nonutilitarian crimes such as interpersonal violence or drug use, structural outcomes models shift the focus toward how the daily frustrations of living poor can increase tendencies toward aggression or to self-medication with illegal drugs to ease the sadness and difficulties of daily life (Bernard, 1990). A common criticism of strain models of criminality is that they do not explain why the majority of individuals subjected to these pressured do not become criminal (Gottfredson and Hirschi, 1990).

The problem with most efforts to explain the link between social class and criminality is the tendency to focus on a single level of analysis. It is more useful, however, to think about the relationship between social class and crime as an interaction between different levels of social life. The broadest level is the organization of society according to the competitive market relations of capitalism. This leads to the division of society into social classes with differing levels of economic, social, and life-style resources. This, in turn, has behavioral, political, and justice system consequences. At the behavioral level, resource-rich and resource-poor classes develop differing ways of life. Each group utilizes the resources available to them to resolve the problems or take advantage of the opportunities their social positions offer them. This includes differences in the typical ways members of these groups do harm and find pleasures. At the political level, however, resource-rich classes are able to establish laws that define the harms and pleasures of resource-poor population as criminal while leaving the harms and pleasures of their own groups largely beyond the scope of the criminal law. This, in turn, leads to a justice system focused on poorer populations. The *face* of crime comes to be seen as that of poor people using crude means such as theft or force to obtain some desired good, or reacting in frustration or sadness to the difficulties of their lives through drug use or violence in their personal relationships. This sets up a feedback loop whereby the public comes to believe that the street crimes and vice crimes of the poor are the primary threat to social order, and thus they demand more control over these crimes. This leads to more poor criminals, which leads to more demands for crime control, and so on.

Although there is some debate about the relationship between criminality and social class, the data regarding social class and criminal victimization are well

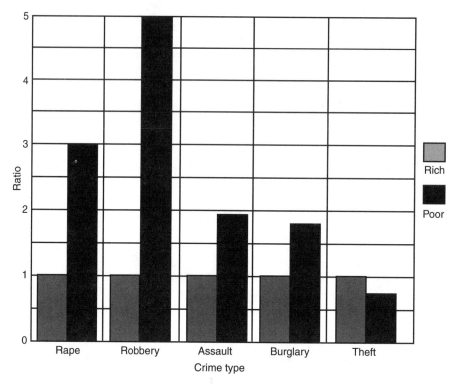

FIGURE 9.2   Number of Poor Crime Victims for Every Rich Victim of Crime.

Source: National Criminal Victimization Survey, 1998. B.J.S. Washington, DC.

established. Since 1973, the Bureau of Justice Statistics has conducted the National Crime Victimization Survey (NCVS), which uses a representative sample of households nationwide to estimate the rate of criminal victimization in the United States each year. The data provided by NCVS indicate that although the link between social class and victimization varies according to crime, overall, the less well off tend to bear a greater burden as crime victims, particularly with respect to crimes of violence (see Figure 9.2). For instance, in 1996, households earning less than $7,500 were three times more likely to contain someone who had been raped that year and five times more likely to contain someone who was the victim of a robbery than were households with incomes above $75,000. In most cases, middle-income households fell between the richest and the poorest categories. For instance, households earning between $15,000 and $50,000 were 80% more likely to contain victims of rape or robbery than rich households and 80% less likely than poor households to have had one or more of their members raped or robbed. The difference between the rich and poor households as victims of property crime is less dramatic, although for the more serious crime of burglary, poor households face greater risks than rich ones. According to the NCVS, for every 18 burglaries of poor homes there are 10 burglaries of rich ones. Only the least serious crime reported—theft without personal contact—recorded greater victimiza-

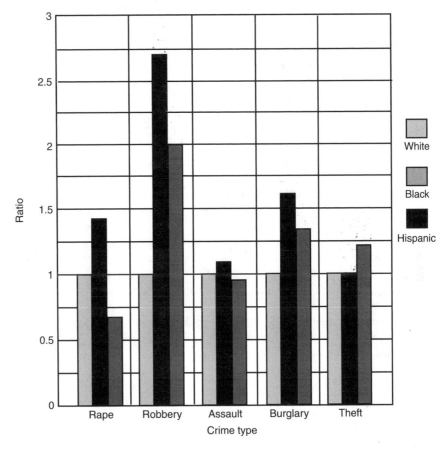

FIGURE 9.3   Number of Black and Hispanic Victims for Every White Victim of Crime.

Source: National Crime Victimization Survey, 1998. B.J.S. Washington, DC.

tion of rich households than poor ones. Rich households had a 20% greater chance than poor households of being victims of a theft that did not involve either illegal entry or personal contact (Bureau of Justice Statistics, 1998). Although the popular image of street crime is often that of the poor preying on the rich, the reality of crime is most people tend to commit crime within a relatively short distance of where they live. Thus, if the poor are more likely to commit street crimes, it means that the poor are more likely to be the victims of these crimes.

A similar pattern holds for the black/white victimization ratio as for the rich/poor ratio (see Figure 9.3). Members of black households were 40% more likely to report rape, 270% more likely to report robbery, 10% more likely to report assault, and 60% more likely to report burglary. For the crimes of rape and assault, Hispanic households had lower rates of victimization than did white or black ones, although the Hispanic rate of victimization for robbery and burglary fell between that of white and black households. Once again, only the crime of

theft without contact or forced entry demonstrated comparable rates of victimization among the three categories. Overall, the NCVS data indicate that the chances
of being a crime victim increase as one moves down the social ladder, and become
particularly high for African American households.

Conclusion: Social Class, Social Welfare, and the Future of Criminal Justice

The contemporary justice system and those who work in it face a dilemma. The
United States *does have* high levels of street crime in comparison with the rest of
the developed world, and this crime *is* disproportionately concentrated in lower-
income communities (Braithwaite, 1981). Reducing the pain, loss, fear, and sadness caused by these crimes is a worthy goal for anyone who undertakes a career
in criminal justice. Some important underlying features of contemporary society,
however, make it a goal with a dark side.

It is not popular these days to talk about the "root causes of crime." Not talking about them, however, does not make them go away, even if business and political leaders choose to act like little children who cover their eyes and then say:
"You can't see me!" Regardless of whether we want to see it, our world is changing in ways that are increasing the production of both poor people and crime and
that are intensifying the social class bias of the criminal justice system. Rapid increases in hypertechnology and global competition mean that growing numbers
of people are being closed off from work that pays a living wage (Rifkin, 1995). A
depressingly familiar feature of many inner-city communities is a near total absence of decent jobs. Significant numbers of people have been rendered part of a
"surplus population" who are simply not needed by the work world. Equally disturbing is the fact that we have come to accept high levels of unemployment
among inner-city youth as normal, just as we have come to accept the homeless as
a normal feature of urban life. Yet there was a time in recent U.S. history when
neither of these things were commonplace. As William Wilson (1996) details in
When Work Disappears, when young people do not see adults working and being
rewarded for legitimate work, they are more likely to pursue illegitimate routes to
income or to compensate for their lack of hope by pursuing the street comforts of
alcohol, drugs, casual sex, and gang membership. This search for alternative (and
often illegal) means to material goods and belonging is intensified in the contemporary world where the ability to purchase life-style commodities has become a
key element in the construction of personal identity (see Ewen, 1988; Fiske, 1996;
Unger, 1990).

Economic indicators point to a continued growth in the surplus population—what some people call the "underclass"—over the coming years (Carlson
and Michalowski, 1997). Historically, the United States has responded to the
problem of controlling surplus populations with one of two strategies—criminal
justice in the form of police and prisons, and social welfare in the form of jobs
programs and cash or in-kind public assistance (Piven and Cloward, 1977). The

current political climate favors a strategy based largely on using the criminal justice system, particularly prisons, to deal with the problems posed by a growing underclass. According to the Bureau of Justice Statistics, currently 28% of African American men and 16% of Hispanic men—men who have been disproportionately affected by the disappearance of good-paying industrial jobs—will spend some time in a state or federal prison over the course of their life. White men, by comparison, face a lifetime risk of imprisonment of only 4.4% (Bureau of Justice Statistics, 1997). This disparity reflects both the racial biases built into the justice system (see Free, 1996; Hawkins, 1997; Mann, 1993; Mann and Zatz, 1998; Miller, 1996) *and* the powerful ways in which race and class intersect, with the result that the least advantaged bear the brunt of both crime and crime control. Not being white increases the likelihood of being poor in the United States. Being poor, in turn, increases the likelihood of engaging in the activities and living in the neighborhoods toward which the criminal justice system devotes the majority of its attention. By deviantizing and criminalizing large numbers of youth from low-income (and typically minority) communities, often for relatively minor offenses, the justice system ensures a growing number of poor offenders, just as the poverty of their neighborhoods ensures a growing number of poor victims. This poses several dilemmas for justice system workers. The first dilemma is whether working in the justice system is an honorable career devoted to protecting people from the ravages of crime, or a career merely devoted to keeping the lid on the consequences of social class inequality so that those who are better off can enjoy their larger shares of the pie in relative peace and with the confidence that *they* are not part of the problem. Of course, things are never that simple or clear cut. Crimes occur. They harm people physically and emotionally. They disrupt community life in a multitude of ways. In a society whose social structure produces high rates of crime, someone must help those who would be its victims. Even if these efforts do not substantially stem the flow of crime—and there is little evidence that 30 years of a war on crime and 20 years of a war on drugs has brought many real victories—they are worth making. Every crime prevented, every victim helped, every offender rehabilitated, every addict detoxed is another human being whose suffering has been lessened. At the same time, it is important that both citizens and those who work in the justice system are not blinded by the goodness of these acts into thinking that they represent a solution to, or even major gains against, the crime problem.

The justice system helps many people, but it alone cannot produce *justice* in the society. Real justice is *social justice*. A large criminal justice system cannot compensate for a lack of social justice. This brings us to the second dilemma facing justice system workers and others today. Should we continue to support "get tough" policies that will certainly create more jobs for justice system workers, but do so at the expense of real justice? Or should we dedicate ourselves to creating a more just society, one that can live with a smaller justice system because it is less divided by class inequalities? We can continue to treat the poor parts of our society as battle zones. This will certainly keep justice system employment high. However, if we are truly dedicated to reducing the human tragedy of crime, we need to cease the violent rhetoric of our various "wars" against crime and begin to look for ways of reducing social inequality and creating genuine opportunities for dignified, materially adequate, and socially accepted lives for all. In the final analysis, if we want peace, we must work for social justice. The alternative is perpetual war.

References

Bartley, R. L. and Bruce-Briggs, B. (Eds.) (1979). *The new class?* New Brunswick, NJ: Transaction Books.

Bennett, W. J., DiJullio, J. J., and Walters, J. P. (1996). *Body count.* New York: Simon & Schuster.

Barak, G. (Ed.) (1994). *Media, process, and the social construction of crime: Studies in newsmaking criminology.* New York: Garland.

Bernard, T. J. (1990). Angry aggression. *Criminology, 28(1),* 73–96.

Bluestone, B. (1995). *The polarization of American society: Victims, suspects, and mysteries to unravel.* New York: Twentieth Century Fund Press.

Bourgois, P. (1995). *In search of respect: Selling crack in el barrio.* New York: Cambridge University Press.

Boyer, R. and Morais, H. M. (1955). *Labor's untold story.* New York: Cameron Associates.

Brace, C. L. (1880). *The dangerous classes of New York, and twenty years' work among them.* New York: Wynkoop & Hallenbeck.

Braithwaite, J. (1984). *Corporate crime in the pharmaceutical industry.* Boston: Routledge & Kegan Paul.

Braithwaite, J. (1981). The myth of social class and criminality reconsidered. *American Sociological Review, 46(1),* 36–57.

Bureau of Justice Statistics (1998). *Sourcebook of Criminal Justice Statistics, 1997.* Washington, DC: U.S. Government Printing Office.

Bureau of Justice Statistics, U.S. Department of Justice (1997). *Lifetime likelihood of going to state or federal prison NCJ-160092.* Washington, DC: U.S. Government Printing Office.

Bureau of Justice Statistics, U.S. Department of Justice (1993). *Survey of Inmates of State Prisons. NCJ 136949.* Washington, DC: U.S. Government Printing Office.

Bureau of Justice Statistics, U.S. Department of Justice (1998). *National Crime Victimization Survey.* Washington DC: U.S. Government Printing Office.

Carlson, S. and Michalowski, R. (1997). Crime, unemployment, and social structures of accumulation: An inquiry into historical contingency. *Justice Quarterly, 14(2),* 209–241.

Chambliss, W. (1964). A sociological analysis of the laws of vagrancy. *Social Problems, 12,* 67–77.

Chambliss, W. (1995). Another lost war: The costs and consequences of drug prohibition. *Social Justice Summer, 22(2),* 101–124.

Chambliss, W. and Seidman, R. (1982). *Law, order and power.* Reading, MA: Addison-Wesley.

Currie, E. (1993). *Reckoning: Drugs, the cities, and the American future.* New York: Hill and Wang.

Currie, E. (1998). *Crime and punishment in America.* New York: Holt.

Davis, L. J. (1995). Medscam. *Mother Jones* at http://bsd.mojones.com/mother_jones/MA95/davis.html

Edelhertz, H. and Geis, G. (1974). *Public compensation to victims of crime.* New York: Praeger.

Ericson, R. V., Baranek, P. M., and Chan, J. (1991). *Representing order: Crime, law, and justice in the news media.* Toronto: University of Toronto Press.

Ewen, S. (1988). *All consuming images: The politics of style in contemporary culture.* New York: Basic Books.

Fiske, J. (1996). *Media matters: Everyday culture and political change.* Minneapolis, MN: University of Minnesota Press.

Free, M. D. (1996). *African Americans and the criminal justice system.* New York: Garland.

Geis, G. (1998). *Association of Certified Fraud Examiners: Report to the nation.* Austin, TX: Association of Certified Fraud Examiners.

Gottfredson, M. R. and Hirschi, T. (1990). *A general theory of crime.* Stanford, CA: Stanford University Press.

Hall, J. (1935). *Theft, law and society.* Boston: Little Brown.

Harring, S. (1983). *Policing a class society: The experience of American cities, 1865–1915.* New Brunswick, NJ: Rutgers University Press.

Hawkins, D. F. (Ed.) (1995). *Ethnicity, race and crime.* Albany, NY: SUNY Press.

Hawkins, M. F. (1997). *Unshielded: The human cost of the Dalkon Shield.* Toronto: University of Toronto Press.

Helmer, J. (1975). *Drugs and minority oppression.* New York: Seabury Press.

Hills, S. L. (Ed.) (1987). *Corporate violence: Injury and death for profit.* Totowa, NJ: Rowman & Littlefield.

Irwin, J. and Austin, J. (1994). *It's about time: America's imprisonment binge.* Belmont, CA: Wadsworth.

Kauzlarich, D. and Kramer, R. (1998). *Crimes of the nuclear state.* Boston: Northeastern University Press.

Livingston, J. (1986). *Origins of the Federal Reserve System: Money, class, and corporate capitalism, 1890–1913.* Ithaca, NY: Cornell University Press.

Lusane, C. (1991). *Pipe dream blues: Racism and the war on drugs.* Boston: South End Press.

Macleod, J. (1995). *Ain't no makin' it: Aspirations and attainment in a low-income neighborhood.* Boulder, CO: Westview Press.

Mann, C. R. (1993). *Unequal justice: A question of color.* Bloomington, IN: Indiana University Press.

Mann, C. R. and Zatz, M. (Eds.) (1998). *Images of color: Images of crime.* Los Angeles: Roxbury.

Matza, D. (1969). *Becoming deviant.* Englewood Cliffs, NJ: Prentice-Hall.

Merton, R. (1938). Social structure and anomie. *American Sociological Review, 3,* 672–682.

Michalowski, R. (1985). *Order, law, and crime.* New York: Random House.

———. (1998). International environmental issues. In M. Clifford (Ed.), *Environmental crime,* pp. 315–340. Gaithersburg, MD: Aspen Publishers.

Miller, J. (1996). *Search and destroy: African-American males in the criminal justice system.* New York: Cambridge University Press.

Mintz, M. (1985). *At any cost: Corporate greed, women, and the Dalkon Shield.* New York: Pantheon Books.

Nachtigal, J. (1998). My non-violent offenses "different," Symington says: Draws distinctions between his doings and robbers, rapists. *The Arizona Republic,* February 4:A1.

Occupational Safety and Health Administration (1997). *Strategic plan.* Washington, DC: U.S. Government Printing Office.

Parenti, M. (1977). *Democracy for the few.* New York: St. Martin's Press.

Piven, F. F. and Cloward, R. (1977). *Poor peoples' movements .* New York: Pantheon Books.

Poulantzas, N. (1975). *Classes in contemporary capitalism* (translated from the French by D. Fernbach). London: NLB.

Rebovich, D. (1992). *Dangerous ground: The world of hazardous waste crime.* New Brunswick, NJ: Transaction Publishers.

Reiman, J. (1996). *The rich get richer and the poor get prison: Economic bias in American criminal justice.* Boston: Allyn and Bacon.

Renee, Y. (1979). *The search for criminal man.* Boston: Sage.

Rifkin, J. (1995). *The end of work: The decline of the global labor force and the dawn of the post-market era.* New York: G. P. Putnam Sons.

Rossi, P. (1974). The seriousness of crimes: Normative structures and individual differences. *American Sociological Review, 39(1),* 224–237.

Sklar, M. (1988). *The corporate reconstruction of American capitalism, 1890–1916: The market, the law, and politics.* New York: Cambridge University Press.

Sutherland, E. (1949). *White collar crime.* New York: Dryden Press.

Szymanski, A. (1983). *Class structure.* New York: Praeger.

Thompson, L. H. (1992). Heath insurance: Vulnerable payers lose billions to fraud and abuse. Report to Chairman, Subcommittee on Human Resources and Intergovernmental Operations, U.S. House of Representatives. Washington, DC: United States General Accounting Office.

Tunnel, K. (Ed.) (1993). *Political crime in America.* New York: Garland.

Unger, P. (1990). *Identity, consciousness, and value.* New York: Oxford University Press.

Wilson, W. J. (1987). *The truly disadvantaged: The inner city, the underclass, and public policy.* Chicago: University of Chicago Press.

Wilson, W. J. (1996). *When work disappears.* New York: Knopf.

Wright, E. O. (1985). *Classes.* London: Verso.

———. 1996. *Class counts: Comparative studies in class analysis.* New York: Cambridge University Press.

Wright, L. (1996). *Corporate abuse: How "lean and mean" robs people and profits.* New York: Macmillan.

10 Women and Criminal Justice

Wielding the Tool of Difference

KARLA B. HACKSTAFF[1]

On February 3, 1998, Karla Faye Tucker was executed by the state of Texas for pick-axing two people to death when she was in a drug-induced frenzy. Most notable about her execution was the public debate it provoked about the death penalty. Some claimed that Tucker did not deserve death because she had become a good wife, a devout Christian, and a role model to the women in her prison. In contrast to a brutal murderer, she was described as "attractive, sweet-natured" and having a "big smile, dark eyes and flowing dark curls" (Graczyk, 1998; Gwynne-Austin, 1998). Because most death row inmates are neither women nor white, were "sweet-natured" and "big smile" asides or do they indicate how gender and racial identities enter into constructions of "innocence" and "criminality"?

No one explicitly argued that Ms. Tucker should be spared death *because she was a woman*—an argument used earlier in U.S. history, before women obtained political rights (Jones 1996). At that time, it was commonly accepted that women were more different from than similar to men. Today, "equality," which stresses women's and men's similarity, compels the death penalty. If Tucker were spared death, commentators reasoned, it would represent special treatment as a white woman and a default to "difference."

Tucker's case reveals the typical "dilemma of difference" (Minow, 1984; Jaggar, 1994; Messerschmidt, 1997; West and Zimmerman, 1987; Young, 1990). Women's "difference" or "sameness" are like tools, used by both the empowered and disempowered to advance their respective interests as the situation demands. Women's experience of the criminal justice system (regardless of race, class, sexu-

[1]Special thanks to Phoebe Morgan for her insightful, careful, and thorough criticism and to Barbara Perry for her extensive and helpful editing suggestions. I would also like to thank Dr. Morgan, Dr. Perry, Marianne Nielsen, Neil Websdale, and Hollie Vargas for sharing the resources of time, labor, and books that were necessary for writing this chapter.

ality, or age) has been different; they have been defined as different and subject to laws not of their own making. For that reason, women confront a "dilemma of difference." To emphasize similarity to men has often meant succumbing to a male standard; in the Tucker case, if men have faced the death penalty, so too should women. To emphasize women's difference from men, is to obscure how women vary by race, class, sexuality, and in other ways. If Tucker had been lesbian or a recently converted Black Muslim daughter of Islam, would she have received the same measure of sympathy? History reveals that the process of criminalization is not neutral about these attributes, but a process infused with the power dynamics of differentiating social groups.

This chapter focuses on women as victims, offenders, and workers and suggests that the concept of "difference" has been a tool used by those in power to marginalize women as well as a tool used by women to resist and to regain power. The tool of difference has been a double-edged sword for women. Whether difference has been emphasized or deemphasized, women have found it difficult to break free of male standards as victims, makers, and/or breakers of the law.

Women and the Criminal Justice System: A Historical Overview

In the past, women's difference from men has most often been constructed as a biological difference. Women's biology has been used to construct women as "natural" rather than "cultural," irrational rather than rational, childlike rather than adult-like, sexually passive rather than sexually aggressive, care givers rather than warriors, and, as shown in this chapter, morally superior based on childbearing capacities. Also, constructions of women have been invariably based on a portrait of "ladies" or the white, middle-class woman's experience. Biological theories of sexual and racial deficiency have been used as tools of difference to legitimize the oppression of men of color and all women. White men have used this tool to exclude women from the making and enforcing of law, and to deny women jobs, criminalize women, and justify their victimization.

From Nonpersons to Persons in Their Own Right

During the colonial era, women were legally defined as less than full persons and thereby excluded from both legal protection and prosecution. Until the turn of the twentieth century, women were not allowed to vote, sue, serve on juries, control their own wages, or enter into contracts; they did not have legal rights to their children, their ability to own property was limited, and they were dependent on the legal identities of their fathers if unmarried, or husbands if married, rather than their own (Pollock, 1995:8). White women of the middle classes were afforded some protection and opportunity that African American women (and men) under slavery and Native American women (and men) under conquest were not (Dill, 1988:416). Although women of color faced additional obstacles to personhood, white women's legal status as nonpersons was primarily circumscribed by the legal constructions of heterosexual marriage.

The English common law doctrine of *coverture* prevailed in the United States until the 1970s; this was the legal assertion that the husband and wife became a single legal entity upon marriage and that entity was the husband (Jones, 1996:73–74). Wives were legally bound to be submissive to and obey husbands. The rights of husbands to "correct" wives by physical force, understood as "domestic chastisement," were varied by the end of the nineteenth century, but reflected the idea that women were the property of their husbands (Gordon, 1988:256, 364; Kurz, 1989:496).

Fathers or husbands served as women's legal representatives because women were not viewed as persons who could "intend" in general, or in matters of crime (Sokoloff and Price, 1995a:24). White women were accorded a chivalrous although condescending exemption from prosecution or severe sentences. Yet such chivalrous protections were never extended to slaves, ex-slaves, poor or working-class women (Sokoloff and Price, 1995a:24). White women's status was both a privilege and a curse with the rise of the ideology of "separate spheres."

The growth of industrialization from the eighteenth to nineteenth centuries brought with it a middle-class family ideal—the ideology of separate spheres— that polarized men's and women's activities. As men increasingly "went out" to do paid labor for wages, women were associated with the unpaid labor in the home—feeding, clothing, caring for family members, and thereby sustaining the labor force. Mothers became constructed as different due to their superior moral capacities, and these capacities were rooted in biology. As motherhood was glorified, women made claims about their special womanly qualities. Women used the tool of difference, that is, their claims to superior morality, to advance the abolitionist, suffrage, and temperance movements and ultimately to expand their own legal personhood. Rights to child custody and property ownership were secured in the nineteenth century and the vote early in the twentieth century. More recently, women have become legal persons in their own right. In 1971, women were granted recognition by the Supreme Court as "persons" in the case of *Reed* v. *Reed* (Sokoloff and Price, 1995a:23). A second Women's Movement in the 1970s and new legislative action have advanced women's rights, yet women have not escaped the dilemma of difference. Our society's approach to contending with crimes against women reveals that women continue to experience less power to construct behaviors as crimes and determine who is a criminal.

Crimes Against Women

Women's and men's victimization have one thing in common: they are mostly victimized by men. What makes crimes against women different from those against men? Women are most often victimized through crimes against their persons, in their homes, and in their personal lives. As Dobash and Dobash (1992:269) report, "Whether it be sexual assault, rape or physical assault, females are at a greater risk from fathers, husbands, boyfriends and acquaintances than from strangers, and there is almost no risk from other women." These behaviors have resisted definition as crimes partly because it has not been in men's immediate interests to do so. The legacy of separate spheres, wherein men are conceived as having prerogatives as household heads and the home is conceived of as private and inviolable, has made it difficult for many to recognize that the home is not simply a "haven," but also a site of crime. Women have rallied every political and legal resource to redefine such harmful behaviors as crimes. Indeed, words like "battered woman," "wife abuse," and "marital rape" were not even known concepts as recently as the 1970s, and incest was perceived to be pathological and rare (Aulette, 1994).

Both girls and boys are subject to neglect and abuse by mothers who remain primary caretakers of children, although men's role in child and elderly abuse is surprisingly high given their secondary role (Gordon, 1988). However, a disproportionate number of incest victims are girls. In fact, 96% of people who had experienced incest indicated that it involved an older man and a girl (Finkelhor, cited in Aulette, 1994:400). Sexually abused girls are in a double bind: They are victimized by the very people who are their protectors. Incest is a key link to eventual offending by females, and parallels women's victimization by intimates in adulthood.

Research shows that both wives and husbands commit violent acts—they kick, hit, and throw objects at their partners (Straus, Gelles, and Steinmetz, 1980). Yet, research also shows that men initiate the violence, whereas women act in self-defense and are overwhelmingly among the injured (Kurz, 1989). Dobash and Dobash (1992:269) report, "from police and court records, national crime surveys and historical documentation all confirm the asymmetrical pattern of male violence directed at female partners." "In a given year, anywhere from 10 to 25 percent of women are beaten by a male intimate, and a quarter to a half of all women will experience violence at the hands of a male intimate in their lifetime" (Kurz, 1995:52).

Russell has shown that more women are raped than are beaten by their husbands (1990:90). Rape is the brutal use of difference to dominate and control others. Until 1977, when Oregon became the first state to repeal marital exemptions in its rape statute, rape was legally impossible in marriage. This marital exclusion reflected the historical perception of women as nonpersons, as property to whom husbands had a right, and rape as an offense against the woman's husband or father, rather than the woman herself. Frieze (1983) found that one-third of her sample of women had experienced rape in addition to physical violence (cited in Dobash and Dobash, 1992:270). For a woman raped by her partner, who must fear for her safety even while asleep in her bed, her home is not a haven.

Perhaps the most frequently asked question when it comes to wife abuse is: Why don't women leave? This question overlooks the fact that most women do leave, and it reveals a social resistance to constructing "the husband" as an "offender." Given who is harming, we should ask: Why aren't men compelled to leave? Wondering why women do not leave reveals a stubborn unwillingness to see how women's different economic, legal, and social status makes departing difficult. Women who leave must make "choices" within a limited structure of options. Leaving not only increases her risk of attack (Browne, 1995:230), but she must secure alternative income, housing, social supports, and schools for her children. These difficulties can be particularly acute for poor and rural women (Websdale, 1998).

Women of color face additional obstacles to protection. Having witnessed brutality and racism by police, trust in police is rare, and battered women of color are more likely to turn to health care systems (Richie and Kanuha, 1993). Language barriers, sustaining the honor of their communities, and awareness of the disproportionate criminalization of men of color are all additional obstacles for women of color who seek to escape domestic violence (Rasche, 1988; Richie and Kanuha, 1993). These obstacles to "leaving" suggest that it is extraordinary when women escape abuse and forge new lives for themselves.

Of course, women are not just victimized in the context of marriage. Most research indicates that about one-quarter of women will experience a rape in their lifetime (Scully, 1995:199); thus, it is not simply an act committed by a "pathological" fringe group (Johnson, cited in Scully, 1995). The idea that rapists are different from other men overlooks the numbers of men who would like to rape. Research that asked college men if they would rape if they could be assured they would not be caught revealed that anywhere from 28 to 37% reported they would rape, and another 30% would use force (Briere and Malamuth, 1983; Tieger, 1981, cited in Scully, 1995:207).

A stubborn belief is that men are different from women because they are sexually aggressive by nature; indeed, sociobiologists try to substantiate this belief (Hubbard, 1995). Yet, attributing rapist behaviors to biology absolves rapists of responsibility and prevents a social analysis of men's sense of powerlessness. This essentialist notion of manhood is complemented by the construction of women as sexually passive and aroused by the use of force. Such a construction of women suggests that no means yes, that women ultimately desire rape, and that women act to provoke rape; this, in turn, holds women accountable and "blames the victim" (Karmen, 1995; Scully, 1995). It is no wonder that the majority of rapes go unreported; women know they will have to account for their behavior and deportment to significant others, the police, and in the courts (Konradi, 1996). A sex worker or prostitute rarely reports rape, knowing that others presume she not only "asked for it," but "got paid for it."

Although the prevailing image of stranger rape influences women's daily lives, research repeatedly shows that most rape in the United States occurs in the context of personal relationships (Herman, 1979; Scully, 1995). The U.S. Department of Justice reported in 1994 that approximately 55% of all rapes are acquaintance rapes—that is, sexual intercourse coerced by someone the victim knows (Renzetti and Curran, 1995:341). It has been estimated that among all rapes, less than 40% end in arrest, and among these, only 3% result in conviction (Renzetti and Curran, 1995:342). Sentencing is generally lenient, but this depends on the race of the perpetrator as well as the victim. When perpetrators are black men and victims are white women, black men can expect the harshest treatment of all (LaFree, 1980, cited in Renzetti and Curran, 1995:343). White men raping black women receive the most leniency—exposing the power of difference.

Another myth is that rape is a sexual rather than a fundamentally violent act. Clearly, sexuality cannot be extricated from rape. Yet, the use of rape in wars to subdue conquered populations across cultures, the use of rape to control black slaves' behavior and procreation in U.S. history, and the use of rape by men against men in prisons reveal that the goal is dominance. Such histories reveal rape for what it is: an act of concerted violence for purposes of social control and not a result of losing sexual control.

Constructing Criminality: The Woman as "Criminal"

Although constructions of "difference" have impeded criminalizing behaviors that harm women, in recent years the construction of women as criminals has gained momentum and resulted in an explosion of imprisoned women (Chesney-Lind, 1995:106). Although women still only constitute 6.4% of the total prison population, their rates of imprisonment have grown immensely: in 1970, there were 5,635 women in prison, but by 1997, there were 78,067 women in prison (Bureau of Justice Statistics, 1998:4). Chesney-Lind and Pollock (1995) deemed this trend "equality with a vengeance," meaning that in aiming to treat women the "same" as men, we have lost sight of constructed differences. Both "sameness" and "difference" have been tools for constructing women's criminality. Still, what are all these women doing?

Women who kill, such as Karla Faye Tucker, may seem to represent increased "criminality" among women, but violent crimes like murder are not representative of the *growth* in women's incarceration. Indeed, women's share of homicides declined from 17% in 1960 to 10% by 1990 (Steffensmeier, 1995:94). Like men, most women who are arrested and imprisoned have primarily committed property- and drug-related crimes. Women constituted a larger percentage of newly committed inmates for drug offenses every year in the 1980s and "a higher percentage of female prison inmates than of male inmates were under the influence of drugs or alcohol at the time of their current offense" (Steffensmeier, 1995:102).

The portrait of imprisoned women that emerged from the American Correctional Association's (ACA) national survey in 1991 found that "overwhelmingly they were young, economically marginalized women of color (57%) and mothers of children (75%), although only a third were married at the time of the survey" (Chesney-Lind, 1995:110). The overrepresentation of women of color in prison is most striking. "Women of color were 61.4% of all incarcerated females in state institutions and 64.5% of women in federal prisons" in 1991 (Mann, 1995:129). Latinas and African American women are overrepresented in jails, state prisons, and in federal prisons where their numbers are three times their proportion in the general female population (Mann, 1995:130).

How is criminality constructed through social, legal, and institutional processes? At every step of the criminal justice system, behaviors and groups go through differentiating processes. Self-report surveys, for example, show that white girls are fully as "delinquent" as nonwhite girls, but are not similarly represented in detention rates (Chesney-Lind and Shelden, 1998:27). Among adults, more whites report drug use than do African Americans, but whites are less likely to be arrested (Mann, 1995:120). More African American women are arrested for prostitution than whites—perhaps reflecting street workers' visibility and vulnerability to arrest (Mann, 1995:119). Some studies show that whereas the proportion of white women moving through the criminal justice process appears to decrease at each step—from their proportion in the population, to their proportion booked, to their proportion returned to jail, to their proportion receiving sentences—the proportion of African American women increases (Mann, 1995). The "seriousness" of the offense does not explain this disparity (Mann, 1995:125). Thus, racism and poverty are structured into the process of criminalization from arrest to sentencing (Wonders, 1996). The tool of difference simultaneously creates an intersection of difference by race, class, and gender that subordinates the poor and racial–ethnic minorities.

Despite economic gains for some women since the 1970s, the impoverishment of women continues to grow. Women still predominate in jobs distinguished by low pay, low job security, and few benefits or promotional opportunities; women still make only about 70% of what men earn (Reskin and Padavi, 1994:104). Also, women increasingly live in female-headed households, supporting children without access to a male wage. Economic marginalization helps explain some of the growth in women's property crimes. Also, new systems of social control—surveillance systems, computer record keeping, more police officers—help to explain this growth (Steffensmeier and Streifel, 1992:92). Perhaps most striking, the crackdown on drug offenses has worked to construct the new female criminal: a drug-dependent, poor mother of color is most representative of the enormous growth in imprisoned women.

In 1986, the Narcotics Penalties and Enforcement Acts targeted street dealers at the expense of wholesalers at the international level; sentencing guidelines mandated 5 years of imprisonment whether a person had sold 5 grams of crack or 500 grams of cocaine (Mahan, 1996:31). Female crack users have paid a higher price for their addictions than have crack-addicted fathers because they are often primary caretakers of children. Pregnant African American women are targeted for drug tests by medical providers even before they encounter the police; pregnant white women show the same rate of drug use, yet escape testing due to their race, middle-class status, and their drug of choice being marijuana (Humphries *et al.*, 1995:174). In 1989, Jennifer Johnson was the first woman convicted of drug trafficking charges through the umbilical cord to her newborn daughter. Although the Florida Supreme Court recognized that an umbilical cord was not the intent of laws on the delivery of controlled substances and did not uphold her conviction, there is an "eerie reflection of the past" when crimes unique to women were prosecuted (Pollock, 1995:18).

At least half of incarcerated women share a history of disadvantage as girls (Chesney-Lind, 1995:110). About one-half of all girls who encounter the juvenile justice system are arrested for larceny–theft or status offenses such as running away (Chesney-Lind and Shelden, 1998:10). Status offenses are "crimes" applied only to juveniles, including curfew regulations, running away, truancy, and incorrigibility, and girls have been and continue to be subject to these offenses disproportionately. For example, in 1991, "girls made up 61 percent of young people appearing in juvenile courts charged with running away from home, and they are about half (41 percent) of all youths charged with a status offense; by contrast, girls made up only 19 percent of those in juvenile court for criminal offenses" (Chesney-Lind and Shelden, 1998:3). Although girls and boys run away from home in equal numbers, girls appear to be held more accountable for that behavior than do boys—by parents, police, and society in general.

Historically, status offenses have served to control girls' sexuality. Yet it is not the girls' sexuality that needs controlling. Two-thirds to three-quarters of girls that end up in juvenile detention facilities or runaway shelters have been sexually abused (Chesney-Lind and Shelden, 1998:3). The girl who tries to escape this victimization by running away from home becomes arrested for "status offenses" and thereby criminalized (Chesney-Lind and Shelden, 1998; Arnold, 1995). These girls are caught between victimization in families or by the criminal justice system. This double bind has led some girls to construct new "families" in gangs.

Girls in gangs are increasingly constructed as violent and "masculine" offenders looking for a fight armed with guns, knives, and razor blades. The *New York Times* reports that girls are "more violent, they get angry quicker, they are trying to prove they are just as tough as the boys" (cited in Maher and Curtis, 1995). Violence perpetrated by females relies on a male standard of crime; violent females become, by definition, less than feminine and, therefore, "masculine." According to Messerschmidt (1997), we need to recognize that girls in gangs are attempting to forge alternative femininities and not simply mimicking masculine standards. To assume like many theorists that certain behaviors, like violence, represent masculinity fails to recognize the variations among females and to perceive the overlap between female and male experiences (Connell, 1987; Messerschmidt, 1997). Girls and boys alike share the need to construct a sense of family or belonging, confront racist education and a dearth of legitimate economic opportunities, and have an interest in resisting the society that marginalizes them. Girls in gangs resist society's devaluation of their class and racial identities as do "home boys," yet the girl "gangsta" must regularly contend with sexualization by home boys as well as by white, middle-class, mostly male, legal authorities. Ironically, many heterosexual girls use the tool of difference, their sexuality, as a means to power and economic survival, even though they have been sexually abused in their families. If more criminal justice workers were women, might they be more sensitive to the double bind facing young girls or women?

Women Working at the Borders of Crime and Justice

Since the late 1970s, women have become visible as workers in the criminal justice system. For the first time in our history, women are represented on the United States Supreme Court, thereby participating in shaping law. The appointments of Sandra Day O'Connor in 1981 and of Ruth Bader Ginsburg in 1993 to the U.S. Supreme Court have been crucial symbolic developments. Women have traveled an enormous legal distance since the nineteenth century, when women could not enter into contracts or vote, let alone become judges (Pollock, 1995). By the end of the twentieth century, women had secured these rights and young girls had models through which they could imagine their presence on the Supreme Court.

The Supreme Court represents a pinnacle of power in the criminal justice system, but the number of women workers has grown throughout the system. Women's entry into legal work, corrections, and policing is notable because these professions have all been dominated by men and are considered "masculine" professions. In spite of the growth, female underrepresentation continues. Pollock reports that "women still comprise only a fraction in any subsystem of criminal justice: approximately 10 percent of sworn police officers, 18 percent of lawyers and judges, and 11 percent of federal correctional officers" (1995:26).

Like most professional occupations that came to be constituted by men since the nineteenth century, a male-based structure underlies law, policing, and corrections in the criminal justice system. Culturally, these occupations are widely recognized as "masculine." Lawyers are constructed as aggressive, tough, and rational—a privileged form of masculinity in our society. Correctional and police officers are constructed as physically strong and able to engage in violence; as blue-collar occupations, they represent alternative masculinities—less privileged than lawyers, but still more valued than femininity. Women who are constructed as aggressive, tough, rational, strong, or violent are seen and treated as "different." Thus, women face a double bind; they must negotiate the dilemma of difference whether they mirror or repudiate the traits associated with the masculine traits of the job or with feminine traits.

MacKinnon (1987) argues that women should use the tool of difference to create laws and policies based on women's experiences of injuries or harm. For example, sexual harassment law was the first law made by and for women that criminalizes behaviors that women experience as harmful. However, other legal scholars have argued that the conservative nature of the law—such as the accumulated history of case law—will impede change in the legal apparatus regardless of the number of women who are in, use, or challenge the criminal justice system (Smart, 1989). Yet, if women cannot rely on the tool of difference, can they rely on "sameness," which is likely to be based on a male standard? To examine the dilemma of difference for workers, we begin by looking at the legal profession.

Women in Law

Increases in women law students suggest women's equal participation is on the horizon. For example, the number of female law students has reached parity with the number of male law students since the mid-1980s or so (Pollock and Ramirez, 1995:82). Despite their numbers and solid academic records, the career trajectories of female lawyers suggest that women will not change the legal profession in the immediate future. Currently, women constitute only 21% of practicing attorneys, and only 8% hold the rank of partner in the top 250 law firms (Pollock and Ramirez, 1995:85). Women's choices are made within a structure of opportunity that channels their specialties, professional relationships, and perceptions of their competence, and influences their strategies for contending with "gendered organizational logic" (Acker, 1990). Female attorneys cluster in different occupational locations and describe different experiences in the practice of law than do men (Anleau, 1995; Pollock, 1995). In private practice, corporate firms, and in government, women "choose" arenas of legal practice that minimize obstacles based on a male standard—as they seek flexible hours to attend to their competing domestic responsibilities and lower rates of sexual harassment (Martin and Jurik, 1996:120). Yet, these same positions also result in lower pay and prestige, fewer promotions, as well as less power in the profession overall (Pollock, 1995:26).

Can we expect the presence of women attorneys in the courtroom to make a "difference"? Research comparing women's and men's interpretation of the law has yielded inconsistent results so far (Pollock and Ramirez, 1995:92). Practicing female attorneys still report biased treatment by a mostly male judiciary (Martin and Jurik, 1996:220). For example, judges do not necessarily treat behaviors the same when performed by men and women. A combative style in the courtroom may be interpreted as appropriately aggressive if a man, but too shrill or aggressive if a woman; a soft-spoken, noncombative style may be interpreted as a negotiating skill if a man, but as an incapacity for aggression if a woman (Martin and Jurik, 1996:124). Thus, gender influences how women and men go about performing their job and the responses their acts elicit. Interpretations of the same behavior are changed when we look through the lens of gender.

The adversarial system has been described as at odds with women's greater negotiating and cooperative style. The adversarial system emphasizes winners and losers by using a language of rights; in contrast, "accommodation or meeting needs is foreign to the adversarial nature of law" (Pollock and Ramirez, 1995:82). Panel participants at the American Judiciary Society in 1990 suggested that women tend toward a more participatory and men towards a more hierarchical management style, and that women are more willing to acknowledge fears and emotions that lead to a different courtroom atmosphere (Pollock and Ramirez,

1995:92). Time and research will be required to assess whether such anecdotes describe women's difference.

Women in Policing and Corrections

Law enforcement and correction officers stand in contrast to the white-collar legal professions. They are treated together here because traditionally, they have been blue-collar occupations, and have only recently gained a semiprofessional status through increased training and educational criteria—in part to advance more humane practices (Martin and Jurik, 1996:160). In contrast to attorneys where workers are "about one-quarter female but only about one percent black female" (Sokoloff and Price, 1995b:327), in policing and corrections racial–ethnic women experience greater representation. Whereas minority women are approximately 18.4% of the U.S. adult female population, they represent about 40% of all women police officers (Sokoloff and Price, 1995b:326). Still, women of color are "virtually absent" in supervisory positions (National Center for Women and Policing, 1998:5). Minority women's pursuit of jobs in policing and corrections is related to the financial and educational hurdles associated with legal careers as well as the higher wages and job security of these occupations compared to traditional female jobs, like clerical work or waitressing.

Until the 1960s, women working in policing were treated in terms of "difference"—receiving special assignments, titles, and lower pay than male officers (Pollock, 1995:27). Women took a variety of actions to be treated the "same": they sued for equal pay, challenged a male standard of physical height and weight requirements, and sued for the right to take promotional exams (Pollock, 1995). Also, in 1973, the Crime Control Act "made it illegal to discriminate against women if the agency or organization received Law Enforcement Assistance Administration funds" (Pollock, 1995:27).

Sexual harassment and discrimination in police work is less blatant and systematic today due to these legal advances, yet female police officers continue to face hostility, resistance, and sexual harassment from male colleagues and supervisors (National Center for Women and Policing, 1998:2). In contrast to the female lawyer, who might face sexist remarks in the courtroom that undermine her authority, the female police officer can face threats to her life as well as her authority if other officers fail to back her up at the scene of a violent crime. Research has found that white women are more likely to be protected than black women by fellow male officers who are predominantly white (Martin, 1995:391). A woman of color cannot always tell if hostility by coworkers or the public is related to her sex, her race, or both at once because these structures of disadvantage intersect. Women of color face discrimination in white-dominated occupations and, with white women, encounter hostility in male-dominated occupations in which they are unwanted and/or perceived as a threat.

One perceived threat for men is that women introduce an alternative organizational culture through a different approach to conflict. Some women draw on their negotiating skills as a tool of "difference" to defuse inmate conflict. More-over, some female corrections workers have been shown to prefer "treatment" over "custodial" approaches to offenders. Similarly in police work, the efforts to hire and treat women the "same" as male officers were also accompanied by an increased emphasis on interpersonal skills in police work to improve community relations (Jurik, 1985). These new emphases seem to revalue "different" traits con-ventionally associated with women, yet they have also met with resistance. Poli-cies, training, and evaluations still do not emphasize the interpersonal skills that might benefit women (National Center for Women and Policing, 1998).

Even as more women enter policing and corrections, they appear to confront a "glass ceiling" when it comes to promotions. Policies, practices, and assump-tions that sustain gendered organizations continue to privilege the upward mo-bility of men—particularly white men. Assignments affect women's promotional and career opportunities. Gratch reports in policing: "Women are assigned more often to nonpatrol areas; few are in mid-level management positions; and almost none are in command positions" (1995:69). Evaluations also affect promotions. Although women and men have equal performance evaluations in policing, a male standard for promotion endures (Martin, 1995). Evaluations are based on a male standard to the degree that they emphasize aspects of the work that men value: currently, the dangerous aspects of policing are emphasized in evaluations and promotions. Thus, for example, Chicago's police department stresses the number of arrests rather than public service and crime prevention when assessing quantity of work (Martin and Jurik, 1996:86). It is telling that only 2.6% of police duty time is spent in crimes against persons and 14.82% in crimes against prop-erty; in contrast, 50.19% of police work time is spent in administrative duties (Gratch, 1995:67). In short, promotions are often based on performance in less than a quarter of the overall job.

Similar patterns emerge in corrections. Britton (1997) analyzed the effect of policies on women and men corrections officers in women's and men's prisons. Britton found that prison training and evaluations were predicated on the worker being male, that the skills perceived as unique to men were more valued, and that male workers were disproportionately benefited by policies and practices—al-though not all men had equal access to higher rewards (1997:813). Officer training assumed a "male officer" in a "men's prison." Interpersonal strategies, prepara-tion for sexual harassment from inmates, and the different conditions in women's prisons (such as smaller and different designs and the warden's latitude in women's prisons) were all ignored. Training appeared to be gender neutral, yet it was gendered in its content and consequences: "the rewards of gender-neutral training essentially accrue to male officers who will for the most part be em-ployed in men's prisons. They are better prepared; able to see their work environ-ment as normative; and are perceived by coworkers, supervisors, and the administration as possessing the basic requisites to be successful officers" (1997:807)

Britton also found that many assignments presumed a need for men. Men's stereotypical "strength" was perceived to be crucial not only in men's prisons, but also in women's prisons. Ironically, the physical strength of female prisoners was emphasized, even as female correctional officer's physical strength was discounted. This reveals how men can use the tool of difference in contradictory ways to disadvantage women workers. Furthermore, although the rhetoric in training films emphasized the prison as a site of "unimaginable violence," when asked to describe the job of correctional officer, workers depicted the job as more of a mental job than a physical one (Britton, 1997:803–804).

This section focuses on the more privileged and male-dominated occupations in the criminal justice system. Women's numbers in all these occupations have grown, yet they remain in the minority, and the verdict is still out whether women will change these occupations or these occupations will change women.

Conclusions: Women for Justice

Aristotle perceived that "justice consists not only in treating like cases alike but also in treating different cases differently (Jaggar, 1994:19). For women, both approaches have yielded justice in various contexts and eras. Arguments for justice that focus on either women's difference or sameness are doomed. To stress "difference" succumbs to reinforcing stereotypes, whether by race or sex, whereas to stress sameness invariably relies on established standards, such as a hegemonic masculinity or prevailing racial projects.

In the case of female victims, it has been crucial to recognize how women's victimization is different from men's: they are more often harmed in the context of personal relationships. To not only criminalize but also enforce laws against men who rape, beat, harass, stalk, or commit incest with female victims, is to not only recognize women's different experience, but also to insist that harm is harm, whether committed by a husband or a stranger. The Women's Movement has used the tool of difference in public education, policy formation, and in the initial development of rape crisis centers and shelters for abused women and their children. The increase of victim/witness, rape crisis, and battered women shelters since the 1970s has brought recognition and remedy to crimes against women. By emphasizing women's different needs, they have empowered women. Such programs speak to women's rejection of passive victimization and ability to actively secure resources to turn victims into survivors—in spite of the power differentials in society at large.

Still, there are limits to temporary shelters and counseling supports. Women require training, education, jobs, health care, homes, and support for child care responsibilities to become survivors. Furthermore, judges, police, and prosecutors also need education to take crimes against women seriously. The Violence Against Women Act (VAWA) of 1994 made federal funds for state and local governments contingent on a "stronger commitment to arresting and prosecuting offenders"; it made it a federal crime to cross states lines to intimidate a partner or in violation of a protection order; it incorporated a civil rights remedy so that women can sue and receive compensatory damages if the crime is motivated by gender; and it made funding and protections available to rural and immigrant women (Hirshman, 1994:46; Pollock, 1995:24; Websdale, 1998). Although the VAWA was an important step, in 1998 new legislation, known as VAWA II, was introduced to expand the services still required by domestic violence victims. If passed, this law would reauthorize programs that have been successful under the first Violence Against Women Act, such as the National Domestic Violence Hotline, and would launch new initiatives such as funds for more battered women shelters and new workplace initiatives (Ireland, 1998).

In addition to services created by and for women, services for men who commit acts of violence are equally important. Some efforts to prevent violence by men have arisen across the country from Emerge in Cambridge, Massachusetts, to the Oakland Men's Project (OMP) in California. The OMP, formed in 1979, aims to "eradicate male violence, racism, and homophobia" (Allen and Kivel, 1994:50). Such projects do not simply aim to cure individual men of violence, but rather to educate men "how power, inequality, and the ability to do violence to others are structured into social relationships in this country" (Allen and Kivel, 1994:52). Cross-cultural research suggests that "rape-prone" societies, like the United States, are characterized by women's devaluation and a lower social and economic status relative to the men of their group (Scully, 1995:204–205). Thus, our remedies for crimes against women should not simply focus on blaming the offender rather than the victim; as Karmen (1995) argues, we need to focus on the social structures that construct such individuals.

The case of Karla Faye Tucker forces us to recognize that women are as capable of violent behaviors as men, even if they are underrepresented in our prisons. To some degree, gender stereotypes may prevent us from "seeing" women's violence; yet women may act in less violent ways, not because they are "naturally" less violent, but because they have been subject to different means of social control through femininities constructed in families, schools, and the media. Females are neither taught nor expected to be in control of others in the way males are in this society. Still, the geometric increase in female offenders suggests we may not only be witnessing "equality with a vengeance" (Chesney-Lind and Pollock, 1995), but also new means for social control of women.

Incarcerated women have increasingly been treated the same as incarcerated men. This approach has yielded educational and vocational programs that had been offered previously to male but not to female inmates (Merlo, 1995b:253). It is clear that women and men similarly need education and training if they are to create alternative ways of making a living after imprisonment. Yet, as Chesney-Lind and Pollock (1995) point out, the circumstances of female offenders are also different. First, women's health care includes gynecological needs. Second, most incarcerated women have been the primary caretakers of children. If mothers are expected to build a life after imprisonment, they need facilities and policies that enable them to sustain relations with children, particularly if they are nonviolent offenders. Third, unlike male offenders, women tend to be less violent and less of a threat to the community.

The overwhelming connection between drugs and crime for women inmates demands a new approach. Beyond decriminalizing drug abuse, custody without treatment does not make sense knowing, as we do, that drug users relapse into drug use and criminal means for economic survival. Drug treatment that addresses the economic, psychological, and social reasons for women's drug use would be a much more efficient use of tax dollars than the building of additional prisons. Yet drug treatment programs are scarce for women and even scarcer for pregnant women (Humphries *et al.*, 1995). Furthermore, criminal justice workers must eliminate the discriminatory treatment accorded women drug users on the basis of their race. Diversity across all occupations in the criminal justice system would help.

Gendered organizational logic continues to shape the culture and the structure of occupations that are either prototypically male or female (Acker, 1990). There are several ways to change the conservative bias of gendered occupations. One way is to increase women's presence in male-dominated occupations—a solution that reflects the aim of affirmative action policies that assume that women are just like men if only they are given the opportunity. Another approach is to change the remuneration in female-dominated occupations through "comparable worth" policies; these would revalue female jobs and move beyond a male standard of valuation and embrace women's difference. Still another approach would be to extend career ladders; clerical and service workers could move through "bridge" positions into administrative positions if the criminal justice system were to promote it (Kanter, 1977; Reskin and Padavic, 1994:98).

The law remains an important tool for social change. For example, although acknowledging the limits of sexual harassment law—only a small percentage of those who file charges of sexual harassment have their day in court and even fewer win—Phoebe Stambaugh argues that women are empowered through their efforts to harness a law made by and for women (Stambaugh, 1997). Also, a recent assessment of women's status in policing found that women's gains in policing have been at an "alarmingly slow rate" and that the gains have occurred when departments have been under "court ordered consent decrees to hire more women or minorities as the result of lawsuits initiated by women's organizations or by women who experienced discrimination" (National Center for Women and Policing, 1998:6).

Whether women avail themselves of the tool of difference or sameness depends on the circumstances in which they find themselves. Sometimes it will be more just to recognize gender differences and other times more just to insist on sameness. Above all, future criminal justice workers, educated in feminist criminology, should encourage new theoretical questions about and research on constructions of gender. Such efforts could help to eventually reconstruct, if not eradicate, the dilemma of difference.

References

Acker, J. (1990). Hierarchies, jobs, bodies: A theory of gendered organizations. *Gender and Society, 4(2)*, 139–158.

Allen, R. and Kivel, P. (1994). Men changing men. *Ms. Magazine,* September/October, 50–53.

Anleau, S. L. R. (1995). Women in law: Theory, research, and practice. In B. R. Price and N. J. Sokoloff (Eds.), *The criminal justice system and women: Offenders, victims, and workers*, 2nd ed., pp. 358–371. New York: McGraw-Hill.

Arnold, R. (1995). Processes of victimization and criminalization of black women. In B. R. Price and N. J. Sokoloff (Eds.), *The criminal justice system and women: Offenders, victims, and workers*, 2nd ed., pp. 136–146. New York: McGraw-Hill.

Aulette, J. R. (1994). *Changing families*. Belmont, CA: Wadsworth Publishing Company.

Bray, R. (1994). Remember the children. *Ms. Magazine*, September/October: 38–41.

Britton, D. M. (1997). Gendered organizational logic: Policy and practice in men's and women's prisons. *Gender and Society, 11(6)*, 796–818.

Browne, A. (1995). Fear and the perception of alternatives: Asking "why battered women don't leave" is the wrong question. In B. R. Price and N. J. Sokoloff (Eds.), *The criminal justice system and women: Offenders, victims, and workers*, 2nd ed., pp. 228–245. New York: McGraw-Hill.

Bureau of Justice Statistics (1998). *Prison and jail inmates at midyear 1997*. Washington, DC: U.S. Department of Justice, January 1988, NCJ-167247.

Chesney-Lind, M. (1995). Rethinking women's imprisonment: A critical examination of trends in female incarceration. In B. R. Price and N. J. Sokoloff (Eds.), *The criminal justice system and women: Offenders, victims, and workers*, 2nd ed., pp. 106–117. New York: McGraw-Hill.

Chesney-Lind, M. and Pollock, J. M. (1995). Women's prisons: Equality with a vengeance. In A. V. Merlo and J. M. Pollock (Eds.), *Women, law, and social control*, pp. 155–176. Boston: Allyn and Bacon.

Chesney-Lind, M. and Shelden, R. B. (1998). *Girls, delinquency, and juvenile justice*, 2nd ed. Belmont, CA: West/Wadsworth.

Connell, R. W. (1987). *Gender and power*. Stanford, CA: Stanford University Press.

Dill, B. T. (1988). Our mothers' grief: Racial ethnic women and the maintenance of families. *Journal of Family History, 13(4)*, 415–431.

Dobash, R. E. and Dobash, R. P. (1992). *Women, violence and social change*. New York: Routledge.

Gordon, L. (1988). *Heroes of their own lives: The politics and history of family violence, Boston 1880–1960*. New York: Viking Press.

Graczyk, M. (1998). Hope fading for woman on death row. *Arizona Daily Sun*, February 3, p. 14.

Gratch, L. (1995). Sexual harassment among police officers: Crisis and change in the normative structure. In A. V. Merlo and J. M. Pollock (Eds.), *Women, law, and social control*, pp. 55–78. Boston: Allyn and Bacon.

Gwynne-Austin, S. C. (1998). Why so many want to save her. *Time*, January 19, p. 56.

Herman, D. (1979). The rape culture. In J. Freeman (Ed.), *Women: A feminist perspective*, 2nd ed., pp. 41–63. Palo Alto, CA: Mayfield Publishing Company.

Hirshman, L. (1994). Making safety a civil right. In *Ms. Magazine*, September/October: 44–47.

Hubbard, R. (1995). Sexism and sociobiology: For our own good and the good of the species. In *Profitable promises: Essays on women, science and health*, pp. 103–121. Monroe, ME: Common Courage Press.

Humphries, D., Dawson, J., Cronin, V., Keating, P., Wisniewski, C., and Eichfeld, J. (1995). Mothers and children, drugs and crack: Reactions to maternal drug dependency. In B. R. Price and N. J. Sokoloff (Eds.), *The criminal justice system and women: Offenders, victims, and workers*, 2nd ed., pp. 167–179. New York: McGraw-Hill.

Ireland, J. (1998). Data and demand show need for VAWA II. A statement by the President of the National Organization for Women, 3-19-98. http://www.now.org/issues/violence/vawa/need.html

Jaggar, A. M. (1994). Sexual difference and sexual equality. In A. Jaggar (Ed.), *Living with contradictions: Controversies in feminist social ethics*, pp. 18–27. Boulder, CO: Westview Press.

Jones, A. (1996). *Women who kill*. Boston: Beacon Press.

Jurik, N. C. (1985). An officer and a lady: Organizational barriers to women working as correctional officers in men's prisons. *Social Problems, 32(4)*, 375–387.

Kanter, R. M. (1977). *Men and women of the corporation*. New York: Basic Books.

Karmen, A. (1995). Women victims of crime. In B. R. Price and N. J. Sokoloff (Eds.), *The criminal justice system and women: Offenders, victims, and workers*, 2nd ed., pp. 181–196. New York: McGraw-Hill.

Konradi, A. (1996). Preparing to testify: Rape survivors negotiating the criminal justice process. *Gender and Society, 10 (4)*, 404–432.

Kurz, D. (1989). Social science perspectives on wife abuse. *Gender and Society, 3(4)*, 489–505.

Kurz, D. (1995). *For richer, for poorer: Mothers confront divorce*. New York: Routledge.

MacKinnon, C. (1987). Sexual harassment: Its first decade in court. In B. R. Price and N. J. Sokoloff (Eds.), *The criminal justice system and women: Offenders, victims, and workers*, 2nd ed., pp. 297–311. New York: McGraw-Hill.

Mahan, S. (1996). *Crack cocaine, crime, and women: Legal, social, and treatment issues* (Drugs, Health, and Social Policy Series, Vol. 4). Thousand Oaks, CA: Sage.

Maher, L. and Curtis, R. (1995). In search of the female urban "gangsta": Change, culture, and crack cocaine. In B. R. Price and N. J. Sokoloff (Eds.), *The criminal justice system and women: Offenders, victims, and workers*, 2nd ed., pp. 147–166. New York: McGraw-Hill.

Mann, C. R. (1995). Women of color and the criminal justice system. In B. R. Price and N. J. Sokoloff (Eds.), *The criminal justice system and women: Offenders, victims, and workers*, 2nd ed., pp. 118–135. New York: McGraw-Hill.

Martin, S. (1995). The interactive effects of race and sex on women police officers. In B. R. Price and N. J. Sokoloff (Eds.), *The criminal justice system and women: Offenders, victims, and workers*, 2nd ed., pp. 383–396. New York: McGraw-Hill.

Martin, S. E. and Jurik, N. C. (1996). *Doing justice, doing gender: Women in law and criminal justice occupations*. Thousand Oaks, CA: Sage Publications.

Merlo, A. V. (1995a). Female criminality in the 1990s. In A. V. Merlo and J. M. Pollock (Eds.), *Women, law, and social control*, pp. 119–134. Boston: Allyn and Bacon.

Merlo, A. V. (1995b). Female criminality in the 1990s. In A. V. Merlo and J. M. Pollock (Eds.), *Women, law, and social control*, pp. 241–264. Boston: Allyn and Bacon.

Messerschmidt, J. (1997). *Crime as structured action: Gender, race, class, and crime in the making.* Thousand Oaks, CA: Sage.

Minow, M. (1984). Learning to live with the dilemma of difference: Bilingual and special education. *Law and Contemporary Problems, 48(2)*, 157–211.

National Center for Women and Policing, a Division of the Feminist Majority Foundation (1998). Equality denied: The status of women in policing, 1997.

Pollock, J. M. (1995). Gender, justice, and social control: A historical perspective. In A. V. Merlo and J. M. Pollock (Eds.), *Women, law, and social control*, pp. 3–35. Boston: Allyn and Bacon.

Pollock, J. and Ramirez, B. (1995). Women in the legal profession. In A. V. Merlo and J. M. Pollock (Eds.), *Women, law, and social control*, pp. 79–96. Boston: Allyn and Bacon.

Rasche, C. (1988). Minority women and domestic violence: The unique dilemmas of battered women of color. In B. R. Price and N. J. Sokoloff (Eds.), *The criminal justice system and women: Offenders, victims, and workers*, 2nd ed., pp. 246–261. New York: McGraw-Hill.

Renzetti, C. and Curran, D. (1995). *Women, men and society*, 3rd ed. Boston: Allyn and Bacon.

Reskin, B. and Padavic, I. (1994). *Women and men at work*. Thousand Oaks, CA: Pine Forge Press.

Richie, B. E. and Kanuha, V. (1993). Battered women of color in public health care systems: Racism, sexism, and violence. In M. B. Zinn, P. Hondagneu-Sotelo, and M. A. Messner (Eds.), *Through the prism of difference: Readings in sex and gender*, pp. 121–129. Boston: Allyn and Bacon.

Russell, D. (1990). *Rape in marriage*. Bloomington, IN: Indiana University Press.

Scully, D. (1995). Rape is the problem. In B. R. Price and N. J. Sokoloff (Eds.), *The criminal justice system and women: Offenders, victims, and workers*, 2nd ed., pp. 197–215. New York: McGraw-Hill.

Smart, C. (1989). *Feminism and the power of law*. London: Routledge.

Sokoloff, N. J. and Price, B. R. (1995a). The criminal law and women. In B. R. Price and N. J. Sokoloff (Eds.), *The criminal justice system and women: Offenders, victims, and workers*, 2nd ed., pp, 11–29. New York: McGraw-Hill.

Sokoloff, N. J. and Price, B. R. (1995b). Women workers in the criminal justice system. In B. R. Price and N. J. Sokoloff (Eds.), *The criminal justice system and women: Offenders, victims, and workers*, 2nd ed., pp. 321–331. New York: McGraw-Hill.

Stambaugh, P. M. (1997). The power of law and the sexual harassment complaints of women. *National Women's Studies Association Journal, 9(2)*, 23–42.

Steffensmeier, D. (1995). Trends in female crime: It's still a man's world. In B. R. Price and N. J. Sokoloff (Eds.), *The criminal justice system and women: Offenders, victims, and workers*, 2nd ed., pp. 90–104. New York: McGraw-Hill.

Steffensmeier, D. and Streifel, C. (1992). Time-series analysis of the female percentage of arrests for property crimes, 1960–1985: A test of alternative explanations. *Justice Quarterly, 9* (March), 77–103.

Straton, J. C. (1994). The myth of the "battered husband syndrome." In M. B. Zinn, P. Hondagneu-Sotelo, and M. A. Messner (Eds.), *Through the prism of difference: Readings in sex and gender,* pp. 118–120. Boston: Allyn and Bacon.

Straus, M., Gelles, R., and Steinmetz, S. (1980). The marriage license as a hitting license. In A. Skolnick and J. Skolnick (Eds.), *Family in transition*, 8th ed., pp. 202–215. New York: HarperCollins.

Websdale, N. (1998). *Rural woman battering and the justice system*. Thousand Oaks, CA: Sage.

West, C. and Zimmerman, D. H. (1987). Doing gender. *Gender and Society, 1(2)*, 125–151.

Wonders, N. (1996). Determinate sentencing: A feminist and postmodern story. *Justice Quarterly, 13(4)*, 611–648.

Young, I. (1990). *Justice and the politics of difference*. Princeton, NJ: Princeton University Press.

11 Constructing Sexual Identities

Gay Men and Lesbians in the Criminal Justice System

BARBARA PERRY

For centuries, gay men and lesbians in the United States have been stigmatized as sinners and perverts, diseased in mind and body. As a result, they have historically been silenced at best, brutally beaten to death at worst. It is only since the late 1960s that gay men and lesbians in the United States have begun to break out of these constraining images and empower themselves socially and politically. This has often been accomplished in spite of, rather than because of, the criminal justice system. Law enforcement agents, judges, and most other actors within the justice system have long been resistant to accept homosexuality as legitimate. Consequently, the criminal justice system has offered little in the way of protection or redress. As this chapter illustrates, the criminal justice system represents, at best, an ambiguous site for gay and lesbian struggles.

Investigating Homosexuality

The stigmatization of homosexuality is not historically or cross-culturally universal. Biery (1990:10) suggests that what we now refer to as homosexuality really "began in the nineteenth century when the word was used for the first time." However, "a label does not give birth to something. Same-sex affection and eroticism have existed since the beginning of recorded history—and probably long before that."

The social and moral assessment of same-sex relationships varies dramatically by time, place, and culture. Such relationships have flourished in cultures as diverse as Ancient Greece, Medieval England, and contemporary Polynesia. Native Americans have long held flexible and fluid views of sexuality. In fact, many Native American traditions refer to the "Two Spirited" as those who are valued because of their inherent combination of both the male and female spirits (Tafoya,

1997:8). Some Asian cultures share this tolerant outlook on sexual diversity. Historically, same-sex relationships have permeated the upper echelons of Japanese society, including the wealthy urban classes, Buddhist clergy, and the military. However, while this tradition was readily accepted for centuries, it seems to have become latent since the turn of the twentieth century, a phenomenon Miller (1995) attributes to the Westernization of Japan—a process that included a transition in sexual morality.

Nonetheless, there remains a significant distinction between Asian and Western reactions to homosexuality. Miller (1995) and Greene (1997) both assert that Asian resistance is grounded, not in homophobia or heterosexism, but in pressure to marry. Asian American men and women are held accountable to family rather than gender expectations. Homosexuality is thus a punishable threat to the family line and name. This may be especially important for Asians living in the United States, where the Western culture generally poses a threat to the continuation of the traditional Asian family line and values.

Family also provides a context for anti-gay sentiment among Latinos and Latinas, yet in a different and generally more intense manner (Greene, 1997). In Latino American communities, the family has primacy. Associated with this are narrowly defined gender roles. Masculinity is rigidly enacted through the patriarchal family roles of provider and protector, whereas femininity is associated with passivity and virtue. Homosexual men, however, are regarded as effete, and both incapable and unwilling to assume these roles. Lesbians are perceived to threaten male dominance and control. Consequently, both gay men and lesbians are labeled as traitors to the family as well as to the culture itself.

However, this homophobia is not without its contradictions. Often, homosexual behavior is less threatening than the explicit assumption of a homosexual identity (Greene, 1997). Drawing on anthropological evidence, Almaguer (1995) asserts that the Chicano understanding of homosexuality revolves around sexual acts rather than sexual preferences per se. For men, a distinction is drawn between *activo* and *pasivo,* with stigmatization and ridicule reserved for the *pasivo.* The latter is deemed to be enacting a passive, subservient, feminine identity, very much out of line with the favored *activo,* who is by definition active, aggressive, and very "male."

Homophobia among African Americans, according to Greene (1997) is multiply determined by sexism, Christian religiosity (especially Southern Baptist), and external and internalized racism. By virtue of their long experiences within a white Christian society, African Americans have also internalized the norms and values associated with white patriarchal notions of sexuality; yet by virtue of their class and race subordination, poor black male youths, in particular, do not have access to the resources by which they might "appropriately" enact acceptable gender-specific behavior.

Regardless of the varied conceptions of homosexuality across cultures, the dominant United States view has been shaped by the social and moral agenda of the Euro-Christian majority. Drawing on the English common law, the Colonial state determined that "what was sinful in the eyes of the church was illegal in the eyes of the state" (Biery, 1990:10). Consequently, "sodomy" and "buggery" came to be seen as immoral acts, and "crimes against nature."

Although there are still proponents of the "homosexuality as sin" perspective, this religiously grounded view has been supplemented, if not supplanted, by the more "scientific" view of same-sex relations as "illness." This interpretation, "which also sees homosexuality as wrong and deviant, maintains that sexual acts are symptoms of a sickness. In contrast to the sin conception, the sickness view sees the desire to engage in homosexual activity inhering in the individual's identity" (Editors of the *Harvard Law Review,* 1990:4). It was this designation of "deviant" that facilitated the persistence of the criminalization and pathologizing of same-sex relations. Consequently, gay men and women were harassed, persecuted, and disempowered for their difference: they continued to be marked as the sexual Other.

Although it was science that labeled homosexuality as an illness, it was also science that began to break down the notion that homosexual behavior was abnormal. In 1948, Dr. Alfred Kinsey published the groundbreaking book *Sexual Behavior in the Human Male.* It was Kinsey's work that revealed that same-sex relationships and behaviors were far more common than had previously been imagined. His work suggested that more than one-third of all adult males had engaged in homosexual activity at least once, and that 10% to 12% of the general population saw themselves as homosexual.

Kinsey's research was one among many factors that enabled an emerging gay and lesbian movement to systematically challenge the dominant negative perceptions of same-sex relations. The cause was furthered by the broader momentum of the civil rights and women's rights movements of the 1960s. Gay activists came to share in the demand for a revolutionary vision of United States democracy. Although the gay rights movement has been very effective in establishing civil and legal rights, gay men and lesbians continue to struggle against the persistence of stigmatizing stereotypes, legal persecution, and violent victimization.

Gay Mythology

Contemporary imagery and stereotypes surrounding gay men and women often resurrect the historical construction of homosexuality as sin and illness. Former Oklahoma City Representative Graves openly stated his repulsion of gays. He claimed that he, like the "majority" of people, knows that, "Gays are the reason for the AIDS plague." He added, "It is not the city's place to subsidize immorality. The next thing you know, why, we'll have paedophiles in day care" (NGLTF, 1994:31–34).

Graves' statement contains references to the three most egregious sins for which gays are held accountable: the spread of AIDS, ungodliness, and pedophilia. Similar sentiments abound in this culture. It is still possible, for example, to find evidence of publicly expressed views that mirror the generations-old words of Justice Blackstone, who set precedents for British and United States' interpretations of sodomy. In the early 1800s, and still in the late 1900s, there are public figures who would describe sodomy as "the infamous crime against nature," "a crime not fit to be named" (Blackstone, 1811:215). A 1973 Arkansas district court decision reiterated Blackstone's sentiments in much more graphic terms: "It will be unnecessary for us to set out the sordid testimony about the (alleged homosexual) act, which appeared so revolting to one of the two deputies sheriff . . . that he vomited thrice during the evening" (cited in Goldyn, 1981:34). This was reinforced in 1993 when an Ohio Supreme Court judge—in a case of a gay man's parole violation—railed against the "evils" and "immorality" of homosexuality (NGLTF, 1994:34). It is reinforced regularly by Dallas District Court Judge Jack Hampton, whose views on homosexuality are no secret: "I don't care for queers cruising the streets picking up teen-age boys . . . I've got a teen-age boy. . . . Those two guys wouldn't have been killed if they hadn't been cruising the streets picking up teen-age boys" (cited in Bissinger, 1995:82). Hampton is best known for his quip that, "I put prostitutes and queers at the same level . . . and I'd be hard put to give somebody life for killing a prostitute" (cited in Berrill and Herek, 1992:294). Given such pervasive negative sentiments, especially on the part of government officials, it is perhaps not surprising the gay men and lesbians still suffer considerable legal discrimination within the criminal justice system.

Gay Men and Lesbians as Offenders

To an alarming extent, gay men and lesbians remain outside the law. Restrictions on their sexuality, relationships, and civil rights means that gay men and women typically do not enjoy the same freedoms as their heterosexual counterparts. This interventionist stance is in contrast to the practices of many other Western democratic nations. Canada's former Prime Minister Pierre Trudeau once claimed that the state "has no place in the bedrooms of the nation." In addition, compare the national backlash to Hawaii's legalization of same-sex marriages to the normalization of such relationships in the Netherlands.

Herek (1992:91) summarizes the marginal legal status of gay men and lesbians as follows:

> Except in four states . . . and several dozen municipalities, discrimination on the basis of sexual orientation is not prohibited in employment, housing, or services. Gay relationships generally have no legal status, and lesbian and gay male parents often lose legal custody of their children when their homosexuality becomes known. Nearly one half of the states outlaw private consenting homosexual acts and their right to do so was upheld by the U.S. Supreme Court in 1996.

The Supreme Court decision to which Herek refers was *Bowers* v. *Hardwick* and is held to be the most significant contemporary statement of the status and rights of gays (Editors of the *Harvard Law Review*, 1990; Mohr, 1988; Leiser, 1997). In that case, the court upheld the constitutionality of Georgia's sodomy statute. In his majority opinion, Chief Justice Warren Burger concluded that, "To uphold that the act of homosexual sodomy is somehow protected as a fundamental right would be to cast aside millennia of moral teaching." With these words, he denied the legal right to private, consensual, same-sex sodomy. Moreover, he reaffirmed the moral prescriptions against homosexuality as defined by Christian canons.

Georgia is not alone in its proscriptions against sodomy. As Herek noted, such statutes are widespread. Until 1961, all states outlawed homosexual sodomy, and most classed it as a felony. Twenty states continue to criminalize same-sex sexual relations, referring to them variously as "sodomy," "unnatural intercourse," "deviate sexual conduct," "sexual misconduct," "unnatural and lascivious acts," and "crimes against nature."

Although prosecutions under these various statutes are rare, their presence nonetheless has a dramatic impact on gay men and lesbians. Symbolically, this legislation and the terminology used both marginalizes and stigmatizes a whole community. They send the message that same-sex activity is "unnatural," "deviant," and not to be tolerated. At the practical level, these laws are "frequently invoked to justify other types of discrimination against lesbians and gay men on the grounds that they are presumed to violate these statutes" (Editors of the *Harvard Law Review*, 1990:11). So, for example, the "criminality" of gay men or lesbians has been used to refuse parental rights, or the right to adopt, or the right to marry. The legally ambiguous status of gay men and women can even be invoked as a means of denying them freedom from discrimination in employment and job benefits (e.g., domestic partner benefits).

As noted earlier, sodomy statutes are rarely enforced. In 1990, for example, 150 lesbians and gay men were arrested under such legislation; fewer still were eventually charged or convicted (Singer and Deschamps, 1994). Much more likely to be enforced are sexual solicitation laws (Mohr, 1988; Editors of the *Harvard Law Review*, 1990). The Editors of the *Harvard Law Review* (1990) imply that solicitation laws are more zealously employed against gay men, in particular, than against heterosexual men or women, and often constitute entrapment. Police officers may "haunt" gay bars, or "cruise" gay parks, specifically seeking suspects who by word or deed appear to be soliciting illegal, but nonetheless noncommercial, consensual same-sex sexual activity.

The regulation of "public sex" has become particularly pronounced in the current era, thanks largely to the emergence of AIDS as a public health issue. Although AIDS is not only a "gay disease," gay men are certainly an at-risk group, and are publicly perceived to be the predominant carriers. Consequently, New York City, for example, has become the site of a crusade against commercial sex establishments (e.g., bath houses) and public sex of all kinds—with the result that such locations and behaviors are becoming heavily policed under both criminal and public health laws. Consequently, "regulatory laws collapse public sex with unsafe sex, promiscuity with the spread of HIV, and legality with public health" (Dangerous Bedfellows, 1996:17).

Ultimately, the persistent criminalization of homosexual behavior leaves gay men and lesbians vulnerable to public and private persecution. This is especially evident in the contemporary data on violence against gay men and lesbians.

Anti-Gay Victimization

What are ya', a fag? Come on sissy, fight me. Don't touch me, ya' homo!

Such are the epithets teenagers thoughtlessly hurl against friends and foes alike in their less-enlightened adolescent years. Yet for many, the underlying message that homosexuality is an inherently undesirable identity remains, and may in fact reemerge in much more violent ways. It is important to note at the outset that violence against homosexuals is not a new problem (Bensinger, 1992). Historically, it has been a legally sanctioned policy, as in medieval Europe or the colonial United States, where sodomy was punishable by various forms of mutilation or even death. Homosexuals were imprisoned and exterminated alongside German Jews in Nazi death camps. Some American "liberators," noting the pink triangles worn by gay men in the camps, returned the "deviants" to their prisons in sympathy with the Nazis' intentions (Herek and Berrill, 1992:1).

Gay men and lesbians continue to suffer as victims of violence, harassment, and hatred. It is difficult, however, to determine the extent of change in hate and bias crimes directed against gays and lesbians. In spite of the federal Hate Crime Statistics Act of 1990, there still exist no systematic nationwide data on which to base such judgments. Data from the National Gay and Lesbian Task Force (NGLTF), New York City Gay and Lesbian Anti-violence Project, and police department bias units across the country have all documented dramatic increases since the mid-1980s (Berrill, 1993; Jenness, 1995). However, it is not at all clear whether this reflects a "real" increase in such violence or a greater willingness to report victimization.

Nonetheless, together, data from the Uniform Crime Report, from NGLTF reports, and from other regional and national victimization surveys paint a disturbing picture of widespread violence against gay men and women. Victimization surveys, for example, consistently find upwards of 60%—often as high as 80 or 90%—of subjects experiencing verbal abuse; physical abuse is as high as 30%. Moreover, rates of victimization and the proportion of victimizations involving assaultive offenses, are dramatically higher than for the general population (Berrill, 1992, 1993).

Attacks against homosexuals tend to be among the most brutal acts of hatred. They often involve severe beatings, torture, mutilation, castration, and even sexual assault. They are also very likely to result in death (Comstock, 1991; Levin and McDevitt, 1993). This feature of violence against gays may account for its emergence as a recognizable social problem, worthy of public attention. Jenness's (1995) examination of gay and lesbian antiviolence projects seems to support this contention, in that many of them were initiated in response to particularly dramatic cases.

What accounts for the persistence of violence against gays? Perhaps a consideration of the common traits shared by its perpetrators provides some insight. Consistently, the data show that they are "predominantly ordinary young men" (Comstock, 1991:2; Hamm, 1994). In particular, they are young white men or adolescents, often from working-class or middle-class backgrounds (Berk, Boyd, and Hamner, 1992; Berrill, 1992; Hamm, 1994). Anti-gay violence, then, may serve to define, regulate, and express sexuality, and masculine sexuality in particular. Acts of violence perpetrated against gays serve to reaffirm gendered hierarchies by asserting the superiority and strength of the perpetrators while sanctioning those seen to violate the standard gender and sexual boundaries.

Violence against lesbians appears to be less pervasive than violence against gay men. To be sure, they are often victims of homophobic violence, but at a much lower rate than gay males (Berrill, 1992; Comstock, 1991; National Gay and Lesbian Task Force, 1992, 1993, 1994). Berrill (1992:28) identifies several pragmatic reasons why lesbians may appear to be at lower risk of victimization: the fact that men, in general, are at a greater risk of violence; the higher visibility of gay men as opposed to gay women; the earlier recognition and "outing" of gay men; gay women's greater tendency to alter behavior and, therefore, vulnerability to assault; and the difficulty in distinguishing antiwoman violence from antilesbian violence.

von Schulthess's (1992) study of antilesbian violence in San Francisco reveals close links between antiwoman and antilesbian violence. In fact, she argues that antilesbian violence is an extension of misogynistic sentiment in general. Thus, the two are difficult to untangle. Nonetheless, once identified as gay, lesbians are subject to similar social censure. Pharr (1988:181) reminds us that, "To be a lesbian is to be *perceived* as someone who has stepped out of line, who has moved out of sexual/economic dependence on a male, who is woman identified."

Nationwide, religious and political movements have intensified the victimization of gay men and lesbians. Scriptural interpretations have engendered hostility and violence against gay men and lesbians. Leviticus is held to be the authoritative Biblical decree outlawing homosexuality. It is there that we find the often-cited passages thought to prohibit homosexuality as sin: "You shall not lie with a male as with a woman; it is an abomination" (Leviticus 18:22). "If a man lies with a male as with a woman, both of them have committed an abomination; they shall be put to death, their blood is upon them" (Leviticus 20:13).

Comstock (1991) and Biery (1990) contest the literal reading of these passages as prohibiting same-sex relations in general. Instead, they cite favorably scholars who argue that "because these verses are immediately proximate to prohibitions against the cultic practices of other nations, they condemn only . . . male temple prostitution and idolatry" (Comstock, 1991:121). Whether accurate or not, the more literal translation has nonetheless been used to justify state policy (as in *Hardwick* v. *Georgia*) and anti-gay violence.

The contemporary mainstreaming of homosexuality through civil rights protections "shook the foundations of orthodox religious belief. . . . The increasing acceptance of homosexuality . . . became a sign of godlessness and impending calamity" (Herman, 1997:4). The consequent anti-gay backlash in recent years has been so intense as to be characterized as a "crusade" (Comstock, 1991:26). Scripturally grounded homophobic rhetoric is correlated with a heightened incidence of anti-gay violence, and anti-gay violence is consistently accompanied by Biblical references. Offenders are frequently reported to refer to victims as "sinners," as "unnatural," as "violators of God's law," or as "going against the Bible" (Comstock, 1991; NGLTF, 1994, 1995).

Concurrently, recent anti-gay ballot initiatives have played on all of the fears and stereotypes mentioned earlier—of sexual predators, of disease carriers, of destroyers of families—in their calls for the denial of civil protections for gays. Oregon, Maine, Arizona, and Florida are among those states that have been the sites of bitter political campaigns oriented around the prevention or repeal of what Far Right representatives have inaccurately termed "special rights" for gay men and lesbians. The anti-gay rhetoric at the heart of these explicitly political campaigns has fanned the flames of homophobia:

> Far Right operatives created an atmosphere of loathing and contempt for lesbian, gay and bisexual people by poisoning communities with rhetoric and misinformation that vilify and demonize lesbians, gay men and bisexuals as sexual predators and undeserving of basic human rights and protections against discrimination. (They) portrayed gay people as degenerate, un-American, privileged, sexually perverse and subhuman. (NGLTF, 1994:16–17)

The first of such campaigns was perhaps the most vicious in its assaults on gays. The 1992 Oregon measure explicitly defined homosexuality as "abnormal, wrong, unnatural, and perverse" (Moritz, 1995:57). The title of the ballot measure, "Minority Status and Child Protection Act," openly equates homosexuality with pedophilia. During Colorado's campaign in the same year, Pastor Pete Peters—on the basis of his Scriptural interpretation—called for the death penalty for gays. Concerned Maine Families, the primary sponsor of the Maine anti-gay initiative, explicitly vilified homosexuals as pedophiles and as the transmitters of AIDS.

There is ample evidence that some citizens took these threats seriously. The NGLTF (1994) documented a frightening increase in violence against gays corresponding to Colorado's November 1992 initiative. Similarly, Maine's Attorney General logged elevated numbers of attacks on homosexuals in that state, leading up to the November 1995 vote (Maine Attorney General office, personal communication; February, 1996).

In part, then, the elevated rates of violence against gays in recent years may be a reaction to their increasing visibility and activism. Similarly, the recent emergence and spread of AIDS—originally called GRIDS (Gay Related Immune Deficiency Syndrome)—has drawn negative attention toward the community. The association of AIDS and HIV with gay men provides yet another justification—not cause—for already existing homophobia. Just as gay activism elicits a violent response, so too does the presence of AIDS. Berrill (1992:38) cites the Presidential Commission on the Human Immunodeficiency Virus Epidemic in support of this contention: "Increasing violence against those perceived to carry HIV, so called 'hate crimes,' are a serious problem. The commission has heard reports in which gay men in particular have been victims of violent acts that are indicative of a society that is not yet reacting rationally to the epidemic." National Gay and Lesbian Task Force (NGLTF, 1994, 1995) annual reports also support the link between anti-gay violence and HIV. Their data reveal that violence against people with AIDS or HIV is increasingly widespread. Individual victims are often assaulted and taunted with such labels as "AIDS faggot" or "plague-carrying faggot." AIDS service providers are also often victimized, as in the case of a Burlington, Vermont organization whose building was burned down.

As is the case with other minority victims of crime, gay victims are reluctant to report their experiences to police. In particular, they are reluctant to come forward because of their fear of secondary victimization, which occurs when "others respond negatively to a crime survivor because of his or her sexual orientation" (Berrill and Herek, 1992:289). If the victims are not yet "out" as gay, they may fear disclosure to friends, family, coworkers, or employers. Given the paucity of anti-discrimination laws protecting gay men and lesbians, this disclosure could very well lead to loss of job, housing, or child custody. It could result in violence as well. Moreover, gay victims may legitimately fear violence at the hands of police. Distrust of law enforcement agents is another factor that gays often share with other minority groups, given the history of police intolerance for gay men and lesbians (Leinen, 1993). Gay men and lesbians are mindful of police harassment, extortion, and beatings of gay victims.

Gay victims of crime may also fear the courtroom experience. Judicial statements noted above—about the "unnaturalness" of homosexuality—remind victims that they may not receive a sympathetic hearing. Moreover, recent years have seen increasing use of the homosexual panic defense, whereby perpetrators of violence posit their fear of a homosexual advance as a mitigating circumstance in the assault. It is, oddly, presented as a form of self-defense. Symbolically, such a defense reaffirms the broader cultural stereotype of gay men and women as sexual predators (Berrill and Herek, 1992). You may recall the recent homicide of a young gay male who had appeared on a nationally televised talk show to proclaim his "crush" on the straight male. The latter claimed to have murdered out of shame and embarrassment at having been identified as the object of a gay man's affection.

Neither primary nor secondary victimization of gay men and women will be eliminated in the absence of concentrated efforts to counter the homophobia and heterosexism that motivate such violence. We turn now to a consideration of criminal justice interventions that may play a role in enhancing the status and role of gay men and lesbians, and that serve the needs of this community.

Service Provision

It may appear paradoxical to expect change to occur on the "frontlines"—that is, within police organizations. In general, police departments remain militaristic organizations whose officers are expected to symbolize the essence of aggression and "manliness." Gay men, in particular, are erroneously assumed to be the antithesis of this—weak and effeminate. Resistance grounded in this perceived contradiction is exaggerated by the corollary fact that "police also tend to see themselves as upholders of society's social and moral order and to view homosexuals as a serious threat to that order" (Leinen, 1993:xi). Consequently, gay men and women who do decide to join the force face a serious dilemma: remain closeted, and thus lead a double life; or come out, and risk harassment or restricted promotions (Leinen, 1993; Burkhe, 1996).

In spite of all this, increasing numbers of gay men and women are opting for careers in law enforcement. In fact, some cities with especially large and visible gay communities—New York City and San Francisco, for example—have begun to actively recruit gay and lesbian officers (Leinen, 1993; Arnott, 1994; Burkhe, 1996). As the numbers of openly gay officers increase, support organizations are also emerging in the law enforcement community. Among these are such gay police fraternal organizations as the Society of Law Officers (SOLO) in San Diego, and the nationwide Gay Officers Action League (GOAL).

It is not just personnel within the criminal justice system who benefit from service organizations. Victims and alleged offenders also warrant special attention. As an outgrowth of the emergence of a viable gay rights movement, recent years have seen the parallel development of gay rights organizations (Jenness and Broad, 1997). As Wertheimer (1992:229) proclaims, "the lesbian and gay community has taken upon itself the tasks of identifying and defining the problem of violence against its members, providing appropriate services to individuals in need, and working to heal the injuries that violence can create in the larger community." Such bodies serve two primary roles relevant to the current context: lobbying for the elimination of discriminatory law and practice (e.g., ACLU Lesbian and Gay Rights Project, Lambda Legal Defense and Education Fund); and monitoring and responding to anti-gay violence (e.g., New York City Gay and Lesbian Anti-violence Project). Consequently, they are important actors working in the interests of both criminalized and victimized gays.

Virtually every community with an identifiable gay presence—even college campuses—hosts a gay and lesbian coalition of some kind. Jenness (1995) catalogs a number of these organizations and the role they have played in constructing violence against gays and lesbians as a social problem. However, the most active and visible of such organizations at the national level is the National Gay and Lesbian Task Force. Since 1973, NGLTF has been actively gathering data on the extent, nature, and dynamics of hate crime. Moreover, the organization acts as a clearinghouse for information on anti-gay violence. As the NGLTF Mission Statement asserts, this body addresses the full range of anti-gay initiatives outlined in this chapter:

Since its inception, NGLTF has been at the forefront of every major initiative for lesbian, gay, bisexual and transgender rights . . . NGLTF is the front line activist organization in the national gay and lesbian movement. As such, it serves as the national resource center for grassroots lesbian, gay, bisexual and transgender organizations that are facing a variety of battles at the state and local level—such as combating anti-gay violence, battling Radical Right anti-gay legislative and ballot measures, advocating an end to job discrimination, working to repeal sodomy laws, demanding an effective governmental response to HIV and reform of the health care system and much more. (NGLTF, www.ngltf.org)

As history attests, the grassroots and national activities of gay rights organizations will be crucial to the continuing recognition of gay men and lesbians as a vital part of the broader community. In light of widespread misunderstandings and misperceptions of what it is to be gay, this cultural group must overcome similar barriers to those faced by racial and ethnic minorities throughout the history of the United States. That will require ongoing and persistent mobilization for changes in attitude and policy alike.

References

Adam, B. (1995). *The rise of a gay and lesbian movement*. New York: Twayne Publishers.

————. (1992). The construction of a sociological "homosexual" in Canadian textbooks. In W. Dynes and S. Donaldson (Eds.), *Sociology of homosexuality*, pp. 19–32. New York: Garland Publishers.

Almaguer, T. (1995). Chicano men: A cartography of homosexual identity and behavior. In M. Kimmel and M. Messner (Eds.), *Men's lives*, 418–431. Boston: Allyn and Bacon.

Arnott, J. (1994). Gays and lesbians in criminal justice. In J. Hendricks and B. Byers (Eds.), *Multicultural perspectives in criminal justice and criminology*, pp. 211–232. Springfield, IL: Charles C. Thomas.

Bensinger, G. (1992). Hate crime: A new/old problem. *International Journal of Comparative and Applied Criminal Justice, 16*, 115–123.

Berk, R., Boyd E., and Hamner, K. (1992). Thinking more clearly about hate-motivated crimes. In G. Herek and K. Berrill (Eds.), *Hate crimes: Confronting violence against lesbians and gay men*, pp. 123–143. Newbury Park, CA: Sage.

Berrill, K. (1992). Anti-gay violence and victimization in the United States: An overview. In G. Herek and K. Berrill (Eds.), *Hate crimes: Confronting violence against lesbians and gay men*, pp. 19–45. Newbury Park, CA: Sage.

Berrill, K. (1993). Anti-gay violence: Causes, consequences and responses. In R. Kelly (Ed.), *Bias crime: American law enforcement and legal responses*, pp. 151–164. Chicago: Office of International Criminal Justice.

Berrill, K. and Herek, G. (1992). Primary and secondary victimization in anti-gay hate crimes: Official responses and public policy. In G. Herek and K. Berrill (Eds.), *Hate crimes: Confronting violence against lesbians and gay men*, pp. 289–305. Newbury Park, CA: Sage.

Biery, R. (1990). *Understanding homosexuality*. Austin, TX: Edward-William Publishing.

Bissinger, H. G. (1995). The killing trial. *Vanity Fair,* (Feb.):84–88; 142–145.

Blackstone, W. (1811). *Commentaries on the laws of England*, Vol. 4. London: William Reed.

Burkhe, R. (1996). *A matter of justice: Lesbians and gay men in law enforcement*. New York: Routledge.

Comstock, G. (1991). *Violence against lesbians and gay men*. New York: Columbia University Press.

Concerned Maine Families (1994). STOP special gay rights status (Newsletter).

Connell, R. (1987). *Gender and power*. Stanford, CA: Stanford University Press.

Dangerous Bedfellows (1996). Introduction. In Dangerous Bedfellows, *Policing public sex*. Boston: South End Press.

Editors of the *Harvard Law Review* (1990). *Sexual orientation and the law*. Cambridge, MA: Harvard University Press.

Feagin, J. and Feagin, C. B. (1996). *Racial and ethnic relations*. Upper Saddle River, NJ: Prentice-Hall.

Goldyn, L. (1981). Gratuitous language in appellate cases involving gay people: "Queer-baiting" from the bench. *Political Behavior, 3(1)*, 31–48.

Greene, B. (1997). Ethnic minority lesbians and gay men: Mental health and treatment issues. In B. Greene (Ed.), *Ethnic and cultural diversity among lesbians and gay men*, pp. 216–239. Thousand Oaks, CA: Sage.

Hamm, M. (1994. *American skinheads*. Westport, CT: Praeger.

Harry, J. (1992). Conceptualizing anti-gay violence. In G. Herek and K. Berrill (Eds.), *Hate crimes: Confronting violence against lesbians and gay men*, pp. 113–122. Newbury Park, CA: Sage.

Herdt, G. (1997). *Same sex, different cultures*. Boulder, CO: Westview.

Herek, G. (1992). The social context of hate crimes: Notes on cultural heterosexism. In G. Herek and K. Berrill (Eds.), *Hate crimes: Confronting violence against lesbians and gay men*, pp. 89–104. Newbury Park, CA: Sage.

Herek, G. and Berrill, K. (1992). Introduction. In G. Herek and K. Berrill (Eds.), *Hate crimes: Confronting violence against lesbians and gay men*, pp. 1–10. Newbury Park, CA: Sage.

Herman, D. (1977). *The anti-gay agenda*. Chicago: The University of Chicago Press.

Hopkins, P. (1992). Gender treachery: Homophobia, masculinity, and threatened identities. In L. May and R. Strikwerda (Eds.), *Rethinking masculinity: Philosophical explorations in light of feminism*, pp. 111–131. Landham, MD: Rowman and Littlefield.

Jenness, V. and Broad, K. (1997). *Hate crime: New social movements and the politics of violence*. New York: Aldine de Gruyter.

———. (1995). Social movement growth, domain expansion, and framing processes: The gay/lesbian movement and violence against gays and lesbians as a social problem. *Social Problems 42(1)*, 145–170.

Leinen, S. (1993). *Gay cops*. New Brunswick, NJ: Rutgers University Press.

Leiser, B. (1997). Homosexuality and the "unnaturalness argument." In L. Gruen (Ed.), *Masculinities and crime*. Lanham, MD: Rowman and Littlefield.

Levin, J. and McDevitt, J. *Hate crimes*. New York: Plenum Press.

Miller, N. (1995). *Out of the past: Gay and lesbian history from 1969 to the present*. New York: Vintage Press.

Mohr, R. (1988). *Gays/justice*. New York: Columbia University Press.

Moraga, C. (1996). Queer Aztlán: The reformation of Chicano tribe. In D. Morton (Ed.), *The material queer*, pp. 297–304. Boulder, CO: Westview.

Moritz, M. J. (1995). The gay agenda: Marketing hate speech to mainstream media. In R. K. Whillock and D. Slayden (Eds.), *Hate speech*, pp. 55–79. Thousand Oaks, CA: Sage.

National Gay and Lesbian Task Force (1995). *Anti-gay/lesbian violence, Victimization and defamation in 1994*. Washington, DC: NGLTF Policy Institute.

———. (1994). *Anti-gay/lesbian violence, victimization and defamation in 1993*. Washington, DC: NGLTF Policy Institute.

———. (1993). *Anti-gay/lesbian violence, victimization and defamation in 1992*. Washington, DC: NGLTF Policy Institute.

———. (1992). *Anti-gay/lesbian violence, victimization and defamation in 1991*. Washington, DC: NGLTF Policy Institute.

NGLTF. (nd). www.ngltf.org.

Pharr, S. (1988). *Homophobia: A weapon of sexism*. Inverness, CA: Chardon Press.

Philadelphia Lesbian and Gay Task Force (1992). *Discrimination and violence against lesbian women and gay men in Philadelphia and the Commonwealth of Pennsylvania*. Philadelphia, PA: PLGTF.

Sheffield, C. (1995). Hate violence. In P. Rothenberg (Ed.), *Race, class and gender in the United States*, pp. 432–441. New York: St. Martin's Press.

Singer, B. and Deschamps, D. (1994). *Gay and lesbian stats*. New York: The New Press.

Tafoya, T. (1997). Native gay and lesbian issues: Two spirited. In B. Greene (Ed.), *Ethnic and cultural diversity among lesbians and gay men*, pp. 1–10. Thousand Oaks, CA: Sage.

von Schulthess, B. (1992). Violence in the streets: Anti-lesbian assault and harassment in San Francisco. In G. Herek and K. Berrill (Eds.), *Hate crimes: Confronting violence against lesbians and gay men*, pp. 65–75. Newbury Park, CA: Sage.

Weissman, E. (1992). Kids who attack gay. In G. Herek and K. Berrill (Eds.), *Hate crimes: Confronting violence against lesbians and gay men*, pp. 170–178. Newbury Park, CA: Sage.

Wertheimer, D. (1992). Treatment and service intervention for lesbian and gay male crime victims. In G. Herek and K. Berrill (Eds.), *Hate crimes: Confronting violence against lesbians and gay men*, pp. 227–240. Newbury Park, CA: Sage.

12 Old Enough to Know Better?

Aging and Criminal Justice

CAROLE MANDINO

Because of the portrayal of elderly persons as frail and easily deceived, they have become prime targets of crime. Many elderly persons may live alone and may suffer from loneliness, making them targets for phone fraud. The era that today's elderly grew up in is much different than the current era. New con games and access to personal information through the Internet offer criminals more ways to scam the elderly.

Beyond scams, the elderly also suffer abuse from others. Many frail or vulnerable elderly persons are physically or emotionally unable to protect themselves from abuse by others. Many are abused by people they know, while others are abused by personnel who are supposed to be providing them care. The physical abuse some elderly persons experience can be more severe depending on their medical condition. Furthermore, neglect constitutes serious abuse if the elderly person is unable to care for themselves. Psychological and financial abuse or exploitation may also have very devastating results for elderly victims.

The population of criminals also has its share of elderly. Just as everyone ages in their profession, so do some criminals. Many times it is all they know how to do for a living. Often, older people may be at the center of a crime organization, having worked their way up from doing crime to ordering crime. Then there are aging inmates, people sentenced to crimes for long periods of time, living out their days in prison.

In this chapter, discussion centers on the following: elder abuse, crime committed against the elderly, elderly criminals, and aging prisoners.

Who Are the Elderly?

An unprecedented shift in the demographics of the United States is occurring. As a result of medical advancement, the lowering of the infant mortality rate, decreasing birth rates, and the baby boomers advancing in age, a larger portion of the population is classified as older adults (age 60+). According to the Administration on Aging, what they refer to as the "older population" (those age 65+) totaled 33.5 million people in 1995. That figure represents 12.8% of the United States population. One in approximately eight people living in the United States is age 65 or older. It is predicted by the U.S. Census Bureau that by the year 2040 one of every five people (Barrow, 1996), or 21.7% of the population (Thorson, 1995), will be age 65 or older.

Average age in the United States in 1990 was 32.7 years old. By the year 2050, it is predicted that the average age of the population will be 50 years old. As can be seen by the preceding figures, the population of the United States is growing older, and crimes committed against and by elderly will also increase.

Crimes Committed Against the Elderly

Elder Abuse

What exactly constitutes elder abuse? Elder abuse was only recently defined by the Older Americans Act (OAA) in 1987, although these definitions are not widely utilized by all states. However, we review them here for use in this chapter.

Physical abuse includes the intentional use of physical force or the infliction of pain or injury, including beating, pushing, choking, burning, restraining, sexual abuse or assault, slapping, hitting, forced feeding, and physical neglect. Physical abuse may cause bruises, broken bones, bed sores, internal bleeding, complications to existing conditions, and pain.

Psychological or *mental abuse* is conduct that causes mental anguish. Abuses can include verbal assaults, threats, intimidation, humiliation, and isolation. Results from psychological or mental abuse may include confusion or disorientation, embarrassment, shame, loss of self-respect, and/or loss of dignity. Psychological abuse is about control.

The failure of the caregiver to provide the basics of life constitutes *neglect*. The denial of food, shelter, or necessary health or dental care may be included under neglect. Neglect may be intentional, such as withholding food; or unintentional, such as simply not being able to provide food or shelter. Neglect is the most common form of abuse (Barrow, 1996).

Self-abuse or *neglect*, although not a crime, is the elderly person's failure to give proper care, either intentionally or unintentionally, to themselves. Results could be lack of proper clothing or shelter, weight loss, or improper health or dental care. When investigating neglect, authorities may need to be cautious in determining whether the person committed self-neglect or whether neglect was committed against the individual.

Illegally or improperly using or mismanaging funds, property or other resources of another resulting in the personal gain to a financial advisor, caretaker, family member, or a con artist comprises *financial exploitation* or *abuse*. Financial exploitation can result in the loss of independence for a senior if they have lost their home or their financial freedom.

Personal freedom includes the right to personal space and freedom of movement. Restraining someone to their bed or to only a closet or room may violate their personal freedom. Elderly persons, like all others, should be able to feel safe in the home in which they live.

Physical and/or mental abuse affects more than 1 million elderly persons each year. However, it is thought that approximately only one in six cases of elder abuse are reported. Those who are being abused may not be able to report the abuse, or may be embarrassed to report the abuse. The most likely abusers are family members or caretakers. Within the family structure, the most likely to commit abuse are sons (21%) and daughters (17%), followed by spouses, other family members (e.g., grandchildren), and caretakers (LaRue, 1992).

Stress is one factor contributing to a family member committing abuse against an older family member. Stress may be due to the loss of income or may be due to taking care of an incapacitated elder. Resistance levels may be down when there is financial strain, which may increase the odds of abuse (Wolf, 1996). Stress can also contribute to emotions being out of control and expressed through violence or intimidation or withdrawal of love, support, or communication. A family history of violence, or revenge against earlier violence perpetrated by the elder person to the caretaker in the past may also contribute to physical or mental abuse. (The cycle of violence theory has not been confirmed in elder abuse cases; see Wolf, 1996.) Other factors that may contribute to physical and/or mental abuse may include strained family ties, addiction to alcohol or drugs, and/or psychiatric illnesses. Those abused may be reluctant to report the abuse due to shame, loss of dignity, fear of being placed in a nursing home, or fear of retaliation from the abuser. Victims may even feel they warrant some of the blame for the abuse.

Mandatory reporting does not always solve the problem of elder abuse. Help may be administered through professional counseling for the family or through receiving respite care for the main caretakers. Awareness of their rights helps the abused identify when things are wrong (LaRue, 1992). Police must be sensitive to elder abuse, and need to be aware that arresting the abuser may mean placing the victim in a nursing home (Plotkin, 1996). In many cases, Adult Protective Services (APS) workers may be best at assessing what course of action to follow and may be best equipped to respond to the victim's needs.

Abuse also happens within nursing institutions, private group homes, and other long-term care facilities. Abuse is not always easy to detect, and usually occurs when family members or other staff are not present. Abuse in institutions may include such things as unsanitary conditions, dental or medical neglect, overmedication or oversedation, the use of psychotropic drugs to quiet patients, physical mistreatment or abuse, utilization of physical restraints, the lack of proper nutrition or stimulation, and sexual abuse.

Workers in such institutions many times are overworked and underpaid. Although most states require background checks on workers in such facilities, some states still do not require these checks. Job demands may be demeaning, such as emptying bed pans, turning and bathing patients, or feeding patients. Many times the abuse may not be intentional—for example, improper feeding techniques—but happens nonetheless. If patients are not properly cared for or are neglected, bed sores—also called pressure sores—may develop and become problematic. If not treated properly or within a reasonable time frame they can require surgery, cause irreversible damage, or become life-threatening.

Patients cannot always eat as quickly as a caregiver would like or may not be able to feed themselves. If caregivers do not spend the proper time feeding the patient and neglect the patient's nutritional needs, drastic weight loss may occur, which may be life-threatening. Severe dehydration can also be problematic and a form of neglect or abuse if the patient is not supplied with water or the means to obtain it. Often times, because patients may be incontinent, workers do not want to give them water, as they may have to change them more if fully hydrated (Harter and Nichols, 1997).

Many times, it is very hard to press charges against care facilities. It is difficult to prove intent, and sometimes the witnesses (the patients) have already died or are unable to be reliable witnesses as they may be too afraid or confused. Death certificates only identify the major cause of death, and rarely list dehydration or bed sores as causes (Harter and Nichols, 1997).

Workers and care homes are not the only ones to blame. Many times, families abandon their incapacitated elders after putting them in institutions. Time constraints and the inability to communicate with the elderly are poor excuses used by family members who abandon their elderly members.

In a series published in 1997, the *Arizona Republic* reported that many of those employed by "board and care facilities" may be ex-convicts who may be guided by their parole agents toward elder care roles. In some states, board and care facilities do not conduct background checks, the jobs do not require much skill, and the caregiver may not be required to have a licence (Harter and Nichols, 1997). The most vulnerable, those who are unable to care for themselves, may be put under the care of those who have been convicted of past crimes.

Neglect is still the largest form of abuse from private homes to care homes, with 58.5% of all cases falling in this category. Physical abuse accounts for 15.7% of reported cases, followed by financial exploitation (12.3%); psychological, emotional, or mental abuse (7.3%); and other forms of abuse (6.2%) (Harter and Nichols, 1997).

Attention to means for the prevention of elder abuse is on the rise. There are many agencies and organizations that can help the abused and the abuser. Prevention programs are more prevalent, with background checks being mandatory in more states. Training for staff and caretakers is also given more frequently. However, the number of elderly persons is expected to rise tremendously in the future, with those in the 85 and older age category showing the largest percentage of growth. With the increase in the number of women in the workforce and with many families with two wage earners, this may lead to many more elderly persons being institutionalized or receiving care from someone coming into their home, which could lead to more elder abuse (LaRue, 1992).

Other Crimes Committed Against the Elderly

Many elderly persons have a great fear of crime, so much so that one would believe that crime affects the elderly more so than the young. However, the elderly are less likely to be victims of crime than are those who are younger. Violent crimes such as rape, robbery, and assault affect those who are younger more frequently than those who are older. Although 33 million elderly persons make up the population of the United States, only about 2% of them fall victims to crime (Bureau of Justice Statistics, 1994). There are notable exceptions to this trend. Purse snatching occurs more frequently to older victims. Older adults have more that $1 trillion in assets, and many scam artists are aware that the elderly as a group have money (West, 1998).

As with all age groups, the elderly cannot be thought of as homogeneous. Some fear crime more than others. The elderly with the highest fear of crime are females, followed by those who are low income, African Americans, city dwellers, those who are physically challenged, and those who are socially isolated (McCoy, 1996).

Victimization of elderly persons is more frequent near where the older victim resides. Older adults tend to stay close to home when shopping and tend to stay home in the evenings. They also tend to avoid dangerous places. However, because the elderly are more vulnerable and they may bear more bodily injury, they tend to take more precautions against crime (McCoy, 1996). They may be more likely to purchase security systems and to install bars on their windows and doors.

The elderly are often portrayed as victims of crime and as being a highly vulnerable population. Society usually assigns the role of victim to "women, children, and the elderly" (Bichler-Robertson, 1997). Younger offenders may see the elderly as defenseless and unable to protect themselves, thus targeting the elderly as victims. The media are also likely to report attacks on the elderly. Some elderly persons live in high crime neighborhoods such as "city" or "project" housing and are vulnerable to young offenders. Robbing an elderly person is often referred to as a "crib job" because it is said to be like taking candy from a baby (Barrow, 1996). When confronted by crime, the elderly are more likely to give a burglar what is wanted as they may be fearful for their lives. However, some elderly crime victims do fight back successfully. Not all elderly persons are vulnerable, and with the changing demographics and the aging of the "baby boomers," more elderly are stronger and take measures to protect themselves against crime.

As with all victims, crime can destroy self-esteem and emotional well-being. With the elderly, crime can also take away independence if family members believe they may be vulnerable or if they have been robbed and the family is afraid it will happen again.

Although the elderly comprise only 13% of the total population, they comprise 30% of victims of fraud (Barrow, 1996). There are many different types of fraud schemes committed against the elderly, ranging from companies who send prize notices in the mail to those who call after seeing obituaries in the newspaper.

Those in grief may be very vulnerable to scam artists who prey on survivors, many times presenting "false" bills of items the dead had ordered "special" for the survivor prior to death, or they may sell unnecessary or unneeded items to survivors. There have been news reports about states suing magazine companies making false prize claims. Some elderly persons have flown across the country to claim prizes only to find they have not won. These companies make money preying on the elderly and other victims. Elderly persons living alone may be more vulnerable to telephone solicitors and may be in need of hearing a "friendly" voice or may be too polite to interrupt, allowing the solicitor to give their pitch.

The elderly may be conned into thinking they are doing a good deed by helping others. Some well-known schemes include the "bank auditor," "the pigeon drop," and the "concerned citizen" or "repair person."

There are many other fraud schemes committed against the elderly. Among them may be the following: social, land, home equity, mail order, telephone, credit card, and neighborhood frauds. These frauds against elderly persons may go unreported, as the victim does not want to lose self-esteem, dignity, or their independence. Those who do report crimes of this nature may suffer from embarrassment, and many times do not want family members to know. The crime becomes more than just theft of money—it is a crime involving theft of self-value and worth.

Elderly Criminals

Impossible as it may seem, the "nice" old man or woman down the street could be a criminal. Criminologists used to laugh at the thought of elderly criminals. In fact, it was gerontologists, or those who study aging, who brought out the issue of elderly offenders (Chanels and Burnett, 1989). Just as with every other age group, one cannot tell a criminal by their looks or daily behavior. Arrest records are dominated by those aged 16 to 24. Most offenders tend to quit committing crimes in their early to mid-thirties (Newman *et al.*, 1984). Younger adults are 10 times more likely than elderly persons to commit crimes (Barrow, 1996). Those older than age 65 commit only 1.5% of violent crimes, such as murder or manslaughter, and less than 1% of rapes. They also commit less than 1% of crimes involving major thefts such as vehicular thefts or bank robberies (Barrow, 1996). Nonetheless, elderly criminals may be the heads of organized crime and can commit high pay-off crimes. In the movie *The Sting*, the character played by Paul Newman was a prototype of several real-life older criminals, one of whom was Joseph Weil, last arrested when he was 72 years old.

Elderly persons do make up a small percentage of those arrested for driving while intoxicated (DWI), shoplifters, homicide offenders, sex offenders, and those arrested for elder abuse. Let's take a quick look at each of these areas (although elder abuse has been previously covered earlier in this chapter).

Elderly and DWI

The majority of arrests of older adults is for DWI. Males with long-term substance abuse problems and histories of alcohol-related crimes are the most likely to be offenders in this category. Age-related theories, such as disengagement theory, suggest that because of social isolation, widowhood, illness, and the effects of limited incomes, many older adults may turn to substance abuse for their problems. However, most substance-abuse offenders are those with long-term abuse problems that did not start in old age. Older adults make up only about 5% of DWI arrests (Newman *et al.*, 1984). Many elderly persons consider themselves to be social drinkers, not serious substance abusers. More research is needed in this area.

Elderly and Shoplifting

Larceny dominates the field of those age 60 and older who commit crimes. Shoplifting fits under the general category of larceny. Although shoplifting may be thought of by some as a crime committed by more females than males, "with increasing age there is no difference between the proportion of men and the proportion of women among the elderly shoplifting population" (Newman *et al.*, 1984). Interestingly, shoplifting is a crime that seems to increase with age. Shoplifting among the elderly is not always in proportion to income. More of those who are middle-income earners tend to be shoplifters than are those who are lower-income earners. Items shoplifted are not for sustenance of life, but are more likely to be extra items, such as clothing and cosmetics.

It is also often thought that the elderly have memory loss and forget to pay for the item shoplifted. However, in 48% of incidences, more than one item was taken, negating forgetfulness. When asked, 75% of the elderly respondents knew they were guilty of shoplifting.

Elderly and Homicide

The elderly commit fewer and different types of homicides than do younger offenders. Sex and race are factors that must be taken into account when looking at elderly offenders. Elderly Anglo females account for approximately one tenth of 1% of all elderly committed homicides, compared to 19.25% for elderly African American males (Newman *et al.*, 1984). One must remember that elderly persons commit less than 1% of all homicides in the country. Often, these homicides are a form of euthanasia, committed when a spouse is suffering from prolonged illness or incapacitation.

Elderly and Sex Offenses

"Dirty old man" is an ageist phrase often associated with the elderly. It is believed that sex offenses involving children are a common crime with older adults, usually by first-time offenders (Newman *et al.*, 1984). Grandparent figures tend to be trusted by young children, who may be unable to defend themselves.

Elderly sex offenders usually engage in more passive sexual activity and rarely use force against their victims. Offenses are commonly committed in the home of the victims, as the offenders may be friends of the victim's parents. Occasionally, offenses also occur within day-care facilities, which can be either in a large commercial setting or within a private home. Only about 1% of elderly sex offenders serve any prison time for their crime.

More often than not, elderly persons convicted for the first time are usually sexual offenders. Jonathon Turley, professor of law at George Washington University Law School and the founder of the Project for Older Prisoners (POPS), states that, "child molestation is unique in that while other types of crime fall away as people age, child molestation remains a certain constant" (Bowers, 1996).

The Incarcerated Elderly

The population of today's prisons is changing. With tougher sentencing mandates, more time is being spent behind bars. Longer sentences beget an aging prison population. Many prisoners are middle aged, and some are in their 60s and 70s. Approximately 3% of the prison population is aged 55 and older, whereas those aged 35 to 54 make up approximately 27% of the prison population (Mergenhagen, 1996). The number of prisoners who are aged 55 or older rose from 9,000 in 1986 to more than 30,000 in 1996. Older prisoners are more costly to care for, estimated to cost more than $2 billion per year. Each inmate aged 55 and older costs approximately $69,000 to imprison (Coalition for Federal Sentencing, 1998). In the future, states may need to set up geriatric care units in prison. In 1995, the state of Colorado considered opening a nursing home for inmates only; however, the plan did not go through.

The option of sending elderly prisoners into conventional nursing homes does not always work. There are only a limited number of beds, and not all nursing homes are willing to take prison inmates.

POPS is a group whose primary focus is special needs of elderly prisoners. The POPS program has successfully petitioned parole for elderly prisoners who have gone on to lead successful lives in their communities. No act of recidivism has been committed by a POPS parolee (POPS Website, 1998).

Although more research is needed regarding the causes of recidivism, the likelihood of committing new offenses is reduced as a person ages. However, not everyone fits this mold and those who are convicted of crimes committed when they are older are less likely to be reformed. Each case needs to be viewed individually.

Colorado's Territorial Prison developed a hospice program for terminally ill inmates. More than 12 inmates went through the hospice program, although not all were elderly. Since the infirmary at Territorial cannot maintain life-support systems, inmates needing such are sent to nearby private hospitals. In 1996, the Utah Legislature required the Utah Department of Corrections to develop a plan for incarcerated frail elderly and terminally ill prisoners to provide for medical care and mental health, grief, and family support, keeping in mind the economic practicality of imprisoning the elderly (Baird, 1996). With the elderly, as a whole, not at risk for recidivism, is it wise to spend extra dollars to keep them incarcerated? As Jonathon Turley points out, "the simple fact is that our prison population is graying and prisons make perfectly horrible nursing homes" (Bowers, 1996).

As the population continues to age, it will affect all aspects of criminal justice. There will be more abuse and neglect of the elderly, more elderly persons who are scammed, more elderly persons involved in crime, and more elderly prisoners. Those working in the field of criminal justice may want to prepare themselves for this change by taking course work or seminars in aging.

References

Baird, B. (1996). Old folks in prison: A not so wonderful life for the growing population of incarcerated elderly [online publication]. *Private Eye Weekly.* http://www.sweekly.com/news/story/story_961226_1.html.

Barrow, G. M. (1996). *Aging, the individual and society*, 6th ed. Minneapolis/St. Paul: West Publishing Company.

Bichler-Robertson, G. (1997). Review of the book *Violence in Canada: Sociopolitical perspectives. Social Pathology, 3, 3,* 245.

Bowers, K. (1996). Stealing time [online publication]. *Denver Westword.com.* http://www.westword.com/1996/080196/newsfeat.html.

Bureau of Justice Statistics (1994). *Elderly crime victims: National crime victimization survey* [online]. http://www.ojp.usdoj.gov/pub/bjs/ascii/ecv.txt.

Chanels, S. and Burnett, C. (1989). *Older offenders: Current trends.* New York: The Haworth Press.

Coalition for Federal Sentencing (1998). *Elderly prisoner initiative* [online]. http://www.sentencing.org/elder.html.

de Kok, D. A., Worden, M. A., and Wright, B. A., *et al.* (1998). *Meeting the challenges and opportunities of Arizona's growing senior population*, 72nd Arizona Town Hall. Phoenix, AZ: Arizona Town Hall.

Elder Abuse and Victimization Statistics (1998). *Elder abuse and crime against the elderly* [online]. http://www.nvc.org/stats/elderly.htm#rea.

Harter, V. and Nichols, J. (1997). Homes without hope, preying on the elderly. Special Report. *The Arizona Republic,* reprint EC5-24, June 8–12.

LaRue, G. A. (1992). *Gero-ethics: A new vision of growing old in America.* Buffalo, NY: Prometheus Books.

McCoy, H. V. (1996). Lifestyles of the old and not so fearful: Life situation and older person's fear of crime. *Journal of Criminal Justice, 24,*3:191–205.

Mergenhagen, P. (1996). *The prison population bomb* [online publication]. www.demographics.com/publications/AD/96_AD/9602_AD/AD880.HTM.

National Victim Center (1998). *Infolink: Elder abuse* [online]. http://www.nvc.org/infolink/ info18.htm.

Newman, E. S., Newman, D. J., Gewirtz, M. L., *et al.* (1984). *Elderly criminals.* Cambridge, MA: Oelgeschlager, Gunn & Hain, Publishers, Inc.

Plotkin, M. R. (1996). Improving the police response to domestic elder abuse victims. *Aging Magazine, 367:28.*

POPS Website (1998). *Project for older prisoners (POPS)* [online]. http://www.law.umich.edu/ students/orgs/pops.htm.

Thorson, J. A. (1995). *Aging in a changing society.* Belmont, CA: Wadsworth Publishing Co.

West, M. (1998). Investigators join forces to expose elder killings. *The Arizona Republic,* March 16, pp. A8, B3.

Wolf, R. S. (1996). Elder abuse and family violence: Testimony presented before the U.S. Senate Special Committee on Aging. *Journal of Elder Abuse & Neglect, 8(1),* 81.

13 Dancing Apart

Youth, Criminal Justice, and Juvenile Justice

JEFF FERRELL

Since late in the nineteenth century, young people and the criminal justice system have danced together in an odd and often contentious interplay of crime, criminalization, and control. At times young people have taken the lead in this dance, inventing new forms of collective activity and collective visibility that have drawn the attention and condemnation of legal authorities. More often the criminal justice system itself has taken the first step, by inventing new categories of illegality and new forms of social and legal control aimed specifically at the young. In either case, however, the dance has long been one of mutual engagement, with each party to a large degree constructing the reality of the other. Without the remarkable and growing collective presence of young people in modern social and cultural life, the criminal justice system would not have taken its present shape, and most certainly would not have spun off a major subsidiary: the juvenile justice system. Yet at the same time, it is this very juvenile justice system and its legal concepts of youthful behavior and misbehavior that have largely defined the meaning of youth in modern society and constructed youth as a category of difference. The dance of young people and the legal system designed to regulate and control them has profoundly shaped both participants and the larger society in which both reside. And, for good or bad, the dance continues today, with each inventing new steps for the other.

Historical and Cultural Constructions of Youth and Delinquency

Profound social, cultural, and economic changes emerging in the late nineteenth and early twentieth centuries reshaped the reality of everyday life in the United States. The development of an industrialized economy and an industrial workforce and the related movement of the population from small town and country-side to great urban centers laid the foundation for the modern mass society that would emerge. At the same time, these broad changes reconstructed the immediate experience of daily work, the meaning and practice of family life—and the social understanding and social status of the young. As the social and economic roles of children changed within new patterns of adult work, within new family relations, and within new neighborhood ecologies—as, for example, parents were increasingly forced into long hours of factory labor outside the home and away from their children—so did understandings of children's identity change as well. Now, in response to these changes, there emerged ideologies advocating a concern with child welfare, and promoting the "child-centered family" and the "ideal child"—a child morally pure and purposefully protected from the increasing evils of the adult world. In a sense, then, these ideologies together led during this period to the *invention of childhood*. That is, they helped develop the modern notions that children are distinctly different from adults; that they occupy a separate, subordinate reality outside the world of adult society; and that they therefore demand both protection from adult influences and yet, because of their inferiority and vulnerability, control by adult authorities.

As Platt (1998) and others (Lerman, 1995) show, these ideologies provided the impetus for the progressive "child-saving movement" that took shape during this time, and they in turn provided the rationale for a juvenile justice system that now emerged in many ways distinct from the existing adult justice system. This new juvenile justice system embodied and enforced the belief that children deserved different treatment than did adults—that they deserved greater protection and also greater control. The architects of this new system put this protective control model into practice as they began to identify childhood attitudes and behaviors that they defined as indicating "delinquency." In their zeal to "save" children from bad influences and bad behavior, they even sought to identify and control "predelinquents"—children who, by general attitude or circumstance, appeared somehow to have the potential for delinquency. Significantly, then, the new juvenile authorities categorized as "delinquent" or "predelinquent" not only specific violent or criminal acts by children, but also a wide variety of acts and attitudes seen somehow as violating adult notions of morality or showing disrespect for adult authority. Thus, a host of everyday youthful activities involving problems with parents or teachers, being out late at night (especially with the "wrong" people), hanging out at dance halls or pool halls, or otherwise failing to conform to the model of the "ideal child" came under the surveillance and control of the juvenile justice system. As Platt (1998:12) notes, this new system "brought within the ambit of government control a set of youthful activities that had been previously ignored or dealt with on an informal basis." In this way, the new juvenile justice system not only participated in the period's broader invention of childhood—by creating new legal categories for perceiving, understanding, and controlling youthful activities, it also participated in the *invention of juvenile delinquency*.

The construction and control of "delinquent" children in turn emerged as part of larger social developments during the period. The United States' transition to an industrial, mass society was hardly a smooth one. Torn by deep class and ethnic divisions, the United States of the early twentieth century witnessed new forms of social conflict and social control, and the juvenile justice system became an important setting for these battles. With its emphasis on the protective control and social salvation of children, the juvenile justice system incorporated innovative forms of "soft control." This new "soft" control went beyond simple physical punishment; it was designed around a larger goal of reshaping or "reforming" the wayward values and identities of delinquent children. Thus, under a medical or therapeutic model that incorporated fewer legal safeguards than did adult legal models, delinquent children received indeterminate sentences to "reformatories"—sentences without a set time limit, to be served until such time as the children submitted to being re-formed in the image of institutional values and identities. Not by accident, these new values and identities that the reformatories taught revolved around industry, discipline, punctuality, and obedience—the very values that the public schools, the YMCAs, and other just-emerging institutions of "scientific management" were teaching (Ferrell 1990), and the very values necessary to convert "undisciplined" children (and adults) into an efficient industrial workforce.

Moreover, the new forms of control that the juvenile justice system incorporated were aimed most directly at children whose identities were not only undisciplined, but were also culturally marginalized. From the first, the child-saving movement and the juvenile justice system targeted the children of "the dangerous classes"—the children of the poor and of recent ethnic immigrants to the United States. Seen as innately criminal, or at least as innately disposed to crime and delinquency, these children bore the brunt of the juvenile justice system's surveillance and control, and it was their characteristic behaviors that were most likely to be labeled "delinquent" or "predelinquent." As Chesney-Lind (1989), Chesney-Lind and Shelden (1998), and Schlossman and Wallach (1998:43) show, the juvenile justice system likewise targeted young women, and especially "ethnic girls—immigrants or daughters of immigrants [who] were seen as inherently more predisposed to immoral conduct than Yankee girls." Prosecuted in the majority of cases for "immorality" and "immoral" behavior such as coming home late or using obscene language, such girls were sent in great numbers to reformatories, to be taught not only obedience and discipline, but also the gendered ideology of proper domesticity.

In beginning, in the late nineteenth century, to construct categories of childhood and juvenile delinquency, then, the juvenile justice system aided in constructing and enforcing other categories of identity and difference as well. From the start, the juvenile justice system forged an understanding of youthful delinquency out of social conflict and inequality, and intertwined this understanding with societal anxieties about social class, gender, and ethnicity. As shown later in this chapter, however, the juvenile justice system took these steps not only as it began its dance with young people; it followed these steps throughout the century to come.

Youth, Identity, and Difference

As the early operations of the juvenile justice system begin to show, the concept of "youth" in modern society denotes much more than simple chronological age; it defines a socially constructed category of collective identity and difference. Similarly, the category of acts and attitudes labeled as "juvenile delinquent" exists today not because such acts and attitudes are inherently or universally criminal, but because the juvenile justice system has constructed this category out of its own ideological imperatives and internal operations. Interestingly, in examining other areas of social life, sociologists and criminologists generally embrace this sort of social constructionist understanding of identity and difference. They tend to reject "essentialist" views regarding gender, ethnicity, or social class—that is, views that see women and men, ethnic groups, or rich and poor as each defined by inherent and immutable internal characteristics. Instead, such scholars mostly agree that gender, ethnicity, and social class are categories of difference, identity, and collective experience that emerge out of social interaction, and out of the ongoing exercise of power and resistance between groups. When it comes to young people, however, this important lesson is sometimes forgotten. Scholars, students, the public—we all tend to forget that the category of youth has not only been constructed through the same sorts of social processes as other categories of difference, but also in conjunction with them. We tend to forget that the category of youth has been forged out of inequality, out of the power of adult authorities over the young, and that it therefore exists in many ways as a category of subordination, of "protection and control." We thus tend to forget an essential link between young people and the criminal justice system: the powerful role of the justice system in sorting youthful activities into domains of legality and illegality, and thereby shaping the boundaries and the meaning of youth.

The dance between young people and the criminal justice system, however, has never been quite this simple. Historically, young people resisted their legal and social construction as a subordinate group, in response inventing alternative, shared solutions to their collective crises of identity. In the context of historical circumstances that emerged during and following World War II in the United States, this collective counterstep by young people took on remarkable new dimensions. As a postwar "baby boom" produced millions of children, and as educational and economic changes extended and enriched young people's shared experience of adolescence, youth subcultures began to emerge among them with a collective power not seen before. "Zoot-suiters" and Hell's Angels, beats and hippies, rock 'n' rollers and rappers, skateboarders and snowboarders, street gangs and graffiti crews—all have emerged among young people since the 1940s as potent, if sometimes flawed, manifestations of collective identity and empowerment.

In response, however, the criminal justice and juvenile justice systems have countered with their own collective strategy: the criminalization and control of both individual young people engaged in subcultural activities and the larger subcultures to which they belong. During the 1940s, for example, black and Latino/a zoot-suiters were demonized in the media and were regularly rounded up and arrested by the police (Turner and Surace, 1956; Cosgrove, 1984; Moore, 1985). In the 1950s, rock 'n' roll was branded as seditious "race music," and performers and distributors were arrested on obscenity charges. In the 1960s, aggressive legal campaigns were launched against groups ranging from the Hell's Angels (Thompson, 1967) to hippies and anti-Vietnam War protesters. From the 1970s to the 1990s, producers and performers of punk, rap, and heavy metal music have faced countless charges of obscenity, "lewd and dissolute conduct," and contributing to the delinquency of minors (Ferrell, 1998). During this same period, skateboarders, lowriders, homeless "gutter punks," and others have seen increasing legal regulation of their activities, and graffiti crews and street gangs have faced highly orchestrated legal and media campaigns against them, and ever harsher legal penalties in response to their activities (Ferrell, 1995b, 1996, 1997b). Together, these and other cases show the remarkable power of young people to create their own collective and subcultural identities—but at the same time, the vast power of the criminal and juvenile justice systems, working in conjunction with the mass media, to criminalize these subcultures and create "moral panic" about them (Cohen, 1972; see Hollywood, 1997; Schissel, 1997).

In all of these cases, we also see the importance of subcultural symbolism and style as a point of tension between young people and the criminal and juvenile justice systems (Ferrell, 1995a; Hebdige, 1979; Willis, 1977). In the years since World War II, subcultural styles of music, clothing, hair, and comportment have taken on tremendous meaning for young people as markers of subcultural turf, exhibitions of subcultural membership, and, in many cases, defiant displays of nonconformity against prescribed roles and identities. For young people, these forms of music or clothing therefore offer participation in a portable, stylistic community, and moreover generate a sense of subcultural and individual identity to some degree outside the bounds of young people's usual subordination. In response, however, the criminal and juvenile justice systems have made subcultural style an issue—and, ironically, for many of the same reasons. Juvenile justice officials increasingly investigate and catalog subcultural styles as a means of surveillance and street identification, and moreover attempt to suppress these styles because of the disrespect they allegedly show legal authorities and the violence and lost opportunities they allegedly foster (Ferrell, 1995a; Miller, 1995). As Miller (1995) shows, for example, gang probation officers enforce court orders prohibiting gang-style clothing, confiscate gang paraphernalia, and even display their confiscated collections on their office walls. In the odd dance between young people and the justice system, then, subcultural styles both defy and invite control, as their meaning moves back and forth between the two groups. Moreover, because these styles of clothing and music and modes of stylized behavior are most often displayed by young people in shared public settings, young people and legal authorities increasingly fight a parallel battle over "cultural space" (Ferrell 1997b)—that is, over the symbolic meanings and symbolic control of street corners and city streets, suburban shopping malls, and recreational zones.

In addition, in these and other cases we see that the juvenile justice system has continued a pattern established at its origins: the enforcement of prescribed identity and the punishment of marginality and difference. As these cases show, young people who participate in street-level ethnic cultures and traditions, who affiliate with alternative musical or political subcultures, who are unfortunate enough to be visibly destitute or homeless—remain the most likely to find themselves under the surveillance of the juvenile justice system and to find their everyday activities criminalized. Similarly, young women remain the most likely to have their categories of delinquency defined within a sexualized framework, to have everyday survival strategies (such as running away from abusive family situations) criminalized (Chesney-Lind, 1989, 1999; Chesney-Lind and Shelden, 1998), and thus to be twice victimized—first at home or on the streets, and next by a juvenile justice system that continues to enforce gendered roles and expectations (Rosenbaum, 1989). Thus, we see that the juvenile justice system—allegedly designed not only to control young people, but also to protect them from child abuse and neglect, child prostitution and pornography, homicide, and other increasingly prevalent forms of victimization—has in many ways offered to young victims more in the way of control than of comfort. Thus, we see that since the late nineteenth century, the juvenile justice system has continued to target those "dangerous classes" defined by poverty, ethnicity, and gender, and along the way has helped to create a new sort of "dangerous class": young people themselves.

Youth, Politics, and Criminal Justice Policy Today

Since the late nineteenth century, the criminal justice system, in helping to construct youth as a category of difference and to construct young people's identities and activities as emerging domains of danger and threat, has played a central role in an even more disturbing social construction: youth as *enemy*. From the early redefinition of everyday youthful activities as "delinquent" to the endless string of legal and media campaigns and "moral panics" focused on youth subcultures since the 1940s, young people have undergone a remarkable transformation of cultural meaning. Increasingly, young people—and especially young people already marginalized by inequalities of social class, ethnicity, or gender—have come to be seen not as society's sons and daughters, not as its dream for a better future, but as its worst nightmare. Put bluntly, they have today come to be seen as the enemy—the enemy of adult certainty and commitment, of everyday decency and respect, and of safe neighborhoods and sobriety.

This presentation and perception of youth as enemy established the foundation for a recent sharp shift in juvenile justice policy toward a more punitive model of control. By the logic of this model, young people who defy conventional moral and legal codes, who by their identities and behaviors threaten the very basis of "civilized" society, must be met by the most aggressive of social and legal responses; they must be punished if they are to be controlled. In public rhetoric and in juvenile justice practice, then, existing models promoting delinquency prevention, diversion of delinquents into alternative programs, or rehabilitation of delinquent youth have increasingly been supplanted by those promoting punishment as both legalized retribution and legal control.

These twin ideologies of youth as enemy and youth as deserving of ever-increasing control and punishment have in turn flourished in the context of broader contemporary social and political developments. Changes in family and work that have emerged in a climate of conservative political policy and increasing corporate control of the economy have reinforced the perception of young people as an enemy potentially out of control. As single-parent and two-career families have proliferated, so have the numbers of women and children in poverty and the fears that young people lacking parental supervision or family support will turn to their own subcultures for comfort. As a downsized, part-time economy has emerged, employers' own lack of responsibility has, ironically, been attributed to the young workers it victimizes, who are themselves increasingly portrayed as lacking in morality, motivation, or commitment. In addition, the ascendence of conservative and reactionary politics over the past two decades has promoted in response to these sorts of changes a host of punitive adult justice initiatives—mandatory sentencing, the harsh policing of welfare programs and recipients, a racist "war on drugs," and the resultant explosion of the U.S. prison population—all of which make enemies out of marginal or powerless groups, popularize punishment-based "solutions" to social problems, and thus legitimate similar responses to the young. As was the case when it emerged in the late nineteenth century, the juvenile justice system today both reflects and contributes to the social, economic, and political climate within which it operates.

The present juvenile justice model of aggressive legal control and harsh punishment has spun-off an astounding array of heavy-handed responses to youthful activity. Despite expert recommendations in earlier decades to abolish youth curfews due to their discriminatory and even unconstitutional nature, curfews now regulate the movements and activities of young people in almost all large and small U.S. cities (Ruefle and Reynolds, 1995). Similarly, "gutter punks" and others among the growing number of homeless kids confront not only poverty and hunger, but also a host of new and newly enforced laws prohibiting public sleeping, public lodging, public vending, panhandling, loitering, vagrancy, and trespass. Young people engaged in other sorts of street activities—from skateboarders and "skate punks" to street musicians—likewise face complex new regulations and stepped-up enforcement of statutes regarding trespass, destruction of public and private property, and public nuisance. Lowriders and other members of youthful "cruising" subcultures run up against street barricades, new legal bans on cruising, and indirect legal harassment through aggressive enforcement of curfew, trespass, and even "car stereo volume" laws. Young hip hop graffiti "writers" now encounter police surveillance teams armed with night-vision goggles and infrared cameras, helicopter patrols, sophisticated sting operations, and a plethora of harsh new civil and criminal penalties (Ferrell, 1996, 1997b). Most remarkably, young people determined by legal officials to meet the criteria of "gang member" are placed on "gang lists" or entered into "gang-tracking databases," which are then circulated among law enforcement officials, landlords, and others. These criteria of "gang membership" are so vague and all-inclusive (and so often based on a misreading of subcultural style) that vast numbers of young people—especially ethnic young people—find themselves on these lists regardless of whether they have committed a crime. Formal identification as a gang member in turn makes these young people vulnerable to gang roundups, deportation (Rodriguez, 1994), and a new wave of "civil gang injunctions," which police and prosecutors utilize to prohibit all manner of alleged "gang activities"—in one typical case, "standing, sitting, walking, driving, gathering, or appearing anywhere in public view with any suspected gang member" (Siegal, 1997:28).

Significantly, these and other contemporary strategies are designed not only to punish and control young people, but also to publicly humiliate them and their subcultures; in other words, these strategies are utilized as mean-spirited "degradation ceremonies" (Garfinkel, 1956; see Cohen, 1972; Cosgrove, 1984) intended to deflate the social status of the young. Thus, in addition to curfews and civil gang injunctions, politicians and justice system managers today call for public paddling and caning of delinquents, and even symbolic mutilation (for example, cutting off the fingers of graffiti writers, or spray painting their genitals) (Ferrell, 1995b, 1996). Moreover, these and other coercive approaches proliferate in an ongoing atmosphere of inadequate legal representation and uncertain legal rights for young people. In a recent American Bar Association study (Puritz *et al.*, 1995), for example, young people were found to be particularly vulnerable to aggressive legal procedures, given that they were regularly represented in juvenile court by inexperienced defense lawyers carrying loads as high as 500 cases or by no lawyer at all.

The effects of these aggressive strategies and of this imbalance of legal and political power are predictable. Juvenile lock-ups fill and overflow with convicted delinquents, and in this engorged state breed hard-edged inmate subcultures that internalize and reflect the desperation of the institutional situation (Feld, 1981). Politicized by the legalized abuses and legal inequities they encounter, graffiti writers, gutter punks, gang members, and other young people increasingly turn their on-the-street subcultures into countercultures and engage in acts of symbolic resistance against legal and political authority (Cohen, 1955; Ferrell, 1995b, 1996). In this way, as before, the juvenile justice system creates those whom it seeks to control; in constructing young people as the enemy, and punishing them for it, the system pushes them towards the very sorts of behaviors and identities it expects. This context—this dance—in turn provides important perspective on reported increases in the number of young people arrested for crimes of all sorts, and especially for violent crimes (U.S. Department of Justice, 1996). Perhaps punitive models have to some degree emerged in response to higher rates of violence or aggression among young people. More likely, however, harshly punitive approaches to the young have been as much cause as effect, generating their own self-fulfilling patterns of resentment, aggression, and violence among those they target. Moreover, as Chesney-Lind (1999) and others show, punitive models produce harsher enforcement and legal categorization practices that themselves increase the number of young people arrested for "violent" offenses, even while young people's behaviors have not changed. Thus does the contemporary dance between young people and the justice system get faster and more frantic.

A final punitive approach to the young, among the most popular today, adds an ironic twist to this ongoing dance of identity. Across the United States, more and more young people now face mandatory transfer from the juvenile justice system to the adult court and prison system for a wider and wider range of offenses, and at younger and younger ages. Based once again on a set of punitive assumptions—that young people committing "adult-level" crimes deserve not youth-centered rehabilitation, but adult-level punishment—this approach blurs the legal and social boundaries between young person and adult, and thus calls into question the very categories of "childhood" and "juvenile delinquency" that the juvenile justice system itself historically helped to construct. In so doing, it leaves young people hanging in a legal netherworld, caught between the subordinate status of youth and the criminal culpability of adulthood, and continuing in either case to serve as enemy and other.

Toward Decriminalization and Rehabilitation

Clearly, the dance begun in the late nineteenth century between young people and the justice system has produced damaged identities and spiraling social harm. Defined first as delinquents, demonized later at the level of subculture and style, and finally punished as dangerous enemies of adult society, young people and their collective experiences have time and again been confined within categories of criminality. As part of this same process, the juvenile justice system has emerged as an expansive machinery of social control, situating in the daily lives of young people what Foucault (cited in Cohen, 1979:339) once described as "hundreds of tiny theatres of punishment." As the dance has continued, then, it has become not a positive partnership, but a mutual paroxysm of resentment and fear. It is time for new steps, and a new dance.

This new dance can begin with the broad decriminalization of youth. Everyday problems with teachers or parents, day-to-day survival strategies, casual circumstances of collectively hanging around in public—these and other youthful behaviors must be freed from narrow and all-too-suggestive categories of "predelinquency," "delinquency," or "immorality." Similarly, the complex subcultural styles and activities of young people must somehow escape a justice system response that both reduces them to simplistic categories of obscenity or public nuisance, and at the same time falsely amplifies their meaning as part of a panicky "dramatization of evil" (Tannenbaum, 1938). Given the century-long justice system and media construction of youthful identity as criminal, however, this decriminalization requires more than the repeal of specific statutes; it also requires a *cultural decriminalization* (see Ferrell, 1998), a broad reconceptualization and reinterpretation of young people and their activities. Thus, as young people encounter or engender problems in everyday living, these can appropriately elicit cooperative adult aid and the support of a responsible community, rather than a reaction mixing criminalization with adult-imposed "protection and control." As other young people encounter or engender more extreme forms of violence or harm, these too can be addressed in ways that promote social reintegration and the responsible reduction of social harm, rather than simplistic models of punitive retribution. In this way, decriminalization of the young cannot only alter and enrich the meaning of their everyday situations; it can perhaps begin to slow or stop the long-term spiral of resentment and counter-aggression that criminalization sets in motion.

However, this is not enough. After a century of constructing youth as a marginal and threatening category of identity, we owe young people more than decriminalization. We owe them rehabilitation—not the enforced rehabilitation of young people in the reformatory, but instead the rehabilitation of *adults* and of adult understandings of young people and adult relationships with them. Rather than marginalizing young people as somehow inferior because they are not yet adults, for example, we might marvel at the creativity and courage they bring to an increasingly uncertain future, and learn from the exuberant vitality of those less confined by adult convention. Rather than fearing (and thus criminalizing) the otherworldliness of youth subcultures, we might honor and inquire into the politics of these collective endeavors, celebrating rather than denigrating moments of shared self-invention and resistance to inequitable authority (Ferrell 1995b, 1996). Rather than constructing young people as perpetrators of crime and enemies of social safety, we might more productively collaborate with young people in constructing safe social environments and working toward social justice by building on emerging programs that involve young people in community organizing, public health research, policy development, and city planning (Ashley, Samaniego, and Cheun, 1997; Meucci and Redmon, 1997; Salvadori, 1997; Schwab, 1997) and that utilize young people as public peacekeepers ("Youth Patrols," 1998). To the extent that this rehabilitation of adults occurs—to the extent that adults are able to achieve a sense of *verstehen* (Ferrell, 1997a), of empathic understanding, with the collective problems and collective solutions of young people—the dignity of young people, and the essential relationship between young people and adults, will also be rehabilitated.

In the same way, then, that categories of "youth" and "delinquency" have been socially constructed, they can now be reconstructed. Moreover, given the historical emergence of these categories along fault lines of gender, ethnicity, and social class, the reconstruction of youth can contribute significantly to new understandings of other marginalized groups as well, and to a broader empathy for all "dangerous classes" and all those relegated to them. In 1962, Kelley (vii, 145) noted "the continuous assaults in our courts, our jails, through our mass media by adults on our own young," and added that he had been forced by this "to the conclusion that adults do not really like their own young; that youth and age are in conflict; and adults always strike the first blow." In response, he proposed that we "try something different: Acceptance of all of our young as worthy, valuable, uniquely blessed with some gifts. . . . Involving youth in what is to be undertaken. . . . Cooperation and democracy in place of authoritarianism." As valid now as they were then, his words suggest a new dance, one in which adults in and out of the criminal justice and juvenile justice systems show young people the same respect they demand from them.

Let's dance.

References

Ashley, J., Samaniego, D., and Cheun, L. (1997). How Oakland turns its back on teens: A youth perspective. *Social Justice, 24(3)*, 170–176.

Chesney-Lind, M. (1989). Girls' crime and woman's place: Toward a feminist model of female delinquency. *Crime and Delinquency, 35(1)*, 5–29.

———. (1999). Media misogyny: Demonizing "violent" girls and women. In J. Ferrell and N. Websdale (Eds.), *Making trouble: Cultural constructions of crime, deviance, and control*, pp. 115–140. Hawthorne, NY: Aldine de Gruyter.

Chesney-Lind, M. and Shelden, R. (1998). *Girls, delinquency, and juvenile justice*, 2nd ed. Belmont, CA: West/Wadsworth.

Cohen, A. K. (1955). *Delinquent boys: The culture of the gang*. New York: Free Press.

Cohen, S. (1972). *Folk devils and moral panics*. London: Macgibbon and Kee.

———. (1979). The punitive city: Notes on the dispersal of social control. *Contemporary Crises, 3*, 339–363.

Cosgrove, S. (1984). The zoot-suit and style warfare. *Radical America, 18(6)*, 39–51.

Feld, B. (1981). A comparative analysis of organizational structure and inmate subcultures in institutions for juvenile offenders. *Crime and Delinquency, 27(3)*, 336–363.

Ferrell, J. (1990). East Texas/western Louisiana sawmill towns and the control of everyday life. *Locus, 3(1)*, 1–19.

———. (1995a). Style matters: Criminal identity and social control. In J. Ferrell and C. R. Sanders (Eds.), *Cultural criminology*, pp. 169–189. Boston: Northeastern University Press.

———. (1995b). Urban graffiti: Crime, control, and resistance. *Youth and Society, 27(1)*, 73–92.

———. (1996). *Crimes of style: Urban graffiti and the politics of criminality*. Boston: Northeastern University Press.

———. (1997a). Criminological *verstehen*: Inside the immediacy of crime. *Justice Quarterly, 14(1)*, 3–23.

———. (1997b). Youth, crime, and cultural space. *Social Justice, 24(4)*, 21–38.

———. (1998). Criminalizing popular culture. In F. Bailey and D. Hale (Eds.), *Popular culture, crime, and justice*, pp. 71–83. Belmont, CA: West/Wadsworth.

Garfinkel, H. (1956). Conditions of successful degradation ceremonies. *American Journal of Sociology, 61*, 420–424.

Hebdige, D. (1979). *Subculture: The meaning of style*. London: Methuen.

Hollywood, B. (1997). Dancing in the dark: Ecstasy, the dance culture, and moral panic in post ceasefire Northern Ireland. *Critical Criminology, 8(1)*, 62–77.

Kelley, E. C. (1962). *In defense of youth*. Englewood Cliffs, NJ: Prentice-Hall.

Lerman, P. (1995). Delinquency and social policy: An historical perspective. Reprinted in P. M. Sharp and B. W. Hancock (Eds.), *Juvenile delinquency: Historical, theoretical, and societal reactions to youth*, pp. 3–12. Englewood Cliffs, NJ: Prentice-Hall.

Meucci, S. and Redmon, J. (1997). Safe spaces: California children enter a policy debate. *Social Justice, 24(3),* 139–151.

Miller, J. (1995). Struggles over the symbolic: Gang style and the meanings of social control. In J. Ferrell and C. R. Sanders (Eds.), *Cultural criminology,* pp. 213–234. Boston: Northeastern University Press.

Moore, J. (1985). Isolation and stigmatization in the development of an underclass: The case of Chicano gangs in East Los Angeles. *Social Problems, 33,* 1–12.

Platt, A. (1998). The child-saving movement and the origins of the juvenile justice system. Reprinted in P. Sharp and B. Hancock (Eds.), *Juvenile delinquency: Historical, theoretical, and societal reactions to youth,* 2nd ed., pp. 3–18. Upper Saddle River, NJ: Prentice Hall.

Puritz, P., Burrell, S., Schwartz, R., Soler, M., and Warboys, L. (1995). *A call for justice: An assessment of access to counsel and quality of representation in delinquency proceedings.* Washington, DC: American Bar Association.

Rodriguez, L. (1994). Los Angeles' gang culture arrives in El Salvador, courtesy of the INS. *Los Angeles Times,* May 8, M2.

Rosenbaum, J. L. (1989). Family dysfunction and female delinquency. *Crime and Delinquency 35(1),* 31–44.

Ruefle, W. and Reynolds, K. (1995). Curfews and delinquency in major American cities. *Crime and Delinquency, 41(3),* 347–363.

Salvadori, I. (1997). A dragon in the neighborhood: City planning with children in Milan, Italy. *Social Justice, 24(3),* 192–202.

Schissel, B. (1997). Youth crime, moral panics, and the news: The conspiracy against the marginalized in Canada. *Social Justice, 24(2),* 165–184.

Schlossman, S. and Wallach, S. (1998). The crime of precocious sexuality: Female juvenile delinquency in the progressive era. Reprinted in P. Sharp and B. Hancock (Eds.), *Juvenile delinquency: Historical, theoretical, and societal reactions to youth,* 2nd ed., pp. 41–63. Upper Saddle River, NJ: Prentice Hall.

Schwab, M. (1997). Sharing power: Participatory public health research with California teens. *Social Justice, 24(3),* 11–32.

Siegal, N. (1997). Ganging up on civil liberties. *The Progressive, 61(10),* 28–31.

Tannenbaum, F. (1938). *Crime and community.* Boston: Ginn.

Thompson, H. S. (1967). *Hell's Angels.* New York: Ballantine.

Turner, R. H. and Surace, S. (1956). Zoot-suiters and Mexicans: Symbols in crowd behavior. *American Journal of Sociology, 62,* 14–20.

U.S. Department of Justice (1996). *FBI uniform crime reports—1995.* Washington, DC: U.S. Department of Justice.

Willis, P. (1977). *Learning to labor.* New York: Columbia University Press.

Youth patrols on buses a success, SF mayor says (1998). *The Arizona Republic,* February 15, B5.

14 The Invisible Minority

Individuals with Disability

CYNTHIA BAROODY HART

This book attempts to address diversity in the criminal justice system by attending to the differences and similarities among individuals of various groups defined by the social science disciplines as "minority groups." What gets defined as majority and minority is a social construct. Historically, a focus on differences and similarities has sought to deal with the question of what is "normal" in terms of individual characteristics, capabilities, values, behaviors, and interactions with others. In talking of minority/majority relations, minority gets defined in terms of power differentials, not the size of the groups in question.

The process of definition entails the development of a we/they dichotomy: "we" are the same; "they" are different. "We" understand others who are similar to us, not those who are different from us. Similarity is familiar, normal, and comfortable; difference is not. Many of the groups discussed in this text are groups of individuals with common characteristics that are seen as different. In addition, although there is diversity across groups, there is also much diversity within these groups. We are all both different and similar to others. In order to do justice in the operation of the criminal justice system it is necessary to find commonality with those who are defined as different who work in and are processed by the justice system. An understanding of the diversity within the justice system facilitates the operation of the system. To see these differences among us as commonality begins with an understanding of the historical experiences of these groups.

Disability

This chapter addresses individuals with disability who work in and are clients of the criminal justice system. For the purpose of this chapter, people who are visually impaired, hearing or speech impaired, developmentally/learning disabled, and those who face physical and mental challenges are defined as individuals with disability. Individuals with disability participate in all aspects of the criminal justice system: they are judges, lawyers, law enforcement officers, offenders, victims, dispatchers, and counselors, among other things.

The subject matter of this chapter is incredibly broad; it encompasses a very diverse group of individuals reflecting many types of impairments as well as the many roles included in the operation of the criminal justice system. The merging of these two broad areas into one is, no doubt, incomplete. However, it is crucial for students of criminal justice to be sensitive to the issue of individuals with disability as equal participants within criminal justice.

With respect to people with disability, society focuses on a defining status, or "master status," that serves to define the individual by their disability. A master status (Goffman, 1959) is a pivotal position in society, one that is permanent and defining in interaction. For example, one's gender is most notably a master status that is a pivotal identity and dictates social interaction. It is the first thing someone recognizes about an individual. A person interacts with, attributes different characteristics to, and makes different assumptions about an individual based on that status. Disability is most definitely a master status. Ones' inability to hear, walk, learn, or see is extended to every other ability. The folly of this perception is easily dispelled by mentioning the accomplishments of a few extraordinary individuals with disability who are more than able. Ironically, Beethoven was hearing impaired and Einstein was learning disabled. There are many more examples: Stevie Wonder, Ray Charles, Steven Hawkins, and President Franklin Delano Roosevelt, to name a few. It should not be necessary to point to individuals that have made such extraordinary contributions in order to recognize the abilities of individuals with disability.

People attribute many characteristics to individuals with disability. If you are unable to walk, people may talk loudly as if you were unable to hear, or slowly as if you were unable to understand. Historically, individuals with disability have been seen as nonentities, having no role in "mainstream" society. There is a paternalism in interacting with individuals with disability, in that they come to be defined as unable to think for themselves or be involved in self-determination (Scotch, 1989). In essence, they are perceived to be unworthy of equal treatment. Even our language defines individuals with disability as not valid (invalid). The lack of a meaningful role necessitates that disabled individuals accommodate to society, rather than that society should accommodate to the individual.

Paternalism is also reflected in social interactions. The person without disability (if there is such a thing) always knows best, and the individual with disability is, of course, deemed not capable of making their own decisions. People "help," assuming they know what will help without asking. This paternalism, along with "prejudicial attitudes and exclusionary practices are far greater barriers to social participation for many disabled people than are [their] physical or mental impairments" (Scotch, 1989:380).

On the basis of these perceptions and attitudes, individuals with disability have been discriminated against. People with disability have been "invisible"—hidden out of sight "for their own good" or so as not to offend others (Thomas,

1990). Unlike most groups presented here, individuals with disability have not been recognized as "minority" in terms of power differential, even though they most clearly meet that definition (Scotch, 1989; Shakespeare, 1993; Theirs, 1994; Young, 1998). The community of individuals with disability is a diverse community, sharing, as do all of us, similarities and differences. Individuals with disability have all of the social, cultural, and religious identities that accompany other statuses associated with the individual (Backman, 1974). To be disabled and black, disabled and Asian, disabled and Latino/a, and so on, carries different "baggage" for the individual.

Discriminatory laws, termed the "ugly laws," have excluded individuals with disability from participation in society. These laws encoded a variety of prohibitions against specific activities: restrictions on immigration to the United States on the basis of disability, presentation of self in public, regulations against marriage, and even forced sterilization.

To reiterate, the community of individuals with disability is a diverse community that shares, as do all of us, similarities and differences. According to Scotch (1989) and Young (1998), the diversity and the isolation within the disabled community have prevented a sense of collective identity, slowing the development of the disability movement as a social movement. The disability movement will ultimately lead to equal treatment and self-determination. Young (1998) traces the disability movement through five stages, from stigmatization to political/legal action, seeing it as analogous to other social movements such as civil rights, women's, Native American, and gay rights movements. Self-determination is the most crucial issue: the ability of individuals to have control over their own lives. To traverse this stage successfully requires the willingness of others to "lose" the paternalistic approach so common in peoples' dealings with individuals with disability and to fully and equally include these individuals within the community. In addition, it is necessary for individuals with disability to collectively identify their own and others' common status problems. This call to collective social action is embodied in the disability rights movement, which has existed since the late 1970s.

The disability rights movement has engaged in political and legal action using tactics similar to the civil rights and women's movements. This political and legal activism is gradually helping to change the lives of people with disability. The necessary changes for full and equal participation are twofold: to change the physical and structural barriers in the environment and change negative social attitudes regarding individuals with disability. The historical antecedents of the disability rights movement are: (1) the Civil Rights Act of 1964; (2) the Rehabilitation Act of 1973; and, most notably, (3) the Americans with Disability Act (ADA) of 1990. Although it is not possible to legislate attitude, the ADA legislates equal access for all to counter the functional discrimination against individuals with disability that has existed historically.

As a society, we have just begun to deal with the issue of access for people with disability. The ADA influenced various social institutions, businesses, public social services, such as public works and transportation, to provide to people with disability access that most of us take for granted. However, certain social institutions are resistant, if not antagonistic, to this change. The literature is replete with articles debating whether the law is an annoyance or an accommodation, characterizing ADA as a "nightmare," a "quagmire," a "burden," and a "threat." In its short existence, there has already been a backlash to the law. Ironically, parts of the criminal justice system have been very reluctant to accommodate clients and workers with disability.

The ADA is designed to make the environment more accessible for individuals with disability. We all adjust our environments to facilitate the requirements of life and work. In a building that accommodates a number of individuals, we provide more than one door to accommodate easy entry into the building; we do not require individuals to climb ropes to gain access to the second floor of buildings. The disability rights movement has "espoused the philosophy that it is the limitations of the inaccessible environment, not the handicap itself, that makes a disability limiting" (Theirs, 1994:21).

Disability and Criminal Justice

There are 54 million permanently disabled and 10 million temporarily disabled individuals in the United Stated today. Even though there is little demographic data available on this group, it is clear that these individuals are more likely to be poor and undereducated, consequently having fewer opportunities than others in society. These individuals may work within or use the services of the police, the courts, and correctional agencies. Security and safety issues that may be in conflict with access issues could well be the primary concerns in these environments. There are recognizable physical barriers to individuals with disability in many criminal justice agencies. Signs that people cannot see, warnings that cannot be heard, stairs that people cannot climb, and facilities and equipment that are unusable are barriers to full and equal participation.

Access to police departments may involve barriers for many disabled offenders, victims, and employees. The phone call for a hearing-impaired person, signage for a visually impaired person, procedures such as fingerprinting and picture taking set-ups for a person who is mobility impaired are problematic. The barriers for employees of the criminal justice system in general are discussed later in the chapter.

Individuals with Disability as Victims in the Criminal Justice System

Individuals with disability are often assumed to be "victims" in many contexts. There is an element of truth to this idea in that some individuals with disability are particularly vulnerable to victimization because of their actual or perceived inability of "fight or flight" (Office for the Victims of Crime, 1998). With respect to conventional crime, individuals with disability are "easy targets." According to the National Organization of Victim Assistance (NOVA), individuals with disability are more likely to be victims of crime than are individuals without disability. Individuals with developmental disabilities are at particularly high risk for physical and sexual abuse. For example, nearly three-quarters of women with developmental disabilities are sexually assaulted in their lifetime—a rate 50% higher than that for women without disability (Office for the Victims of Crime, 1998). Moreover, victimization—and revictimization—is often at the hands of family members, caregivers, and organizations that are designed to serve the disabled community. A recent Office for Victims of Crime (OVC) report (1998) suggests that nearly half (48.1%) of the perpetrators of sexual assault against people with disability gained access to their victims through disability agencies.

There is an underreporting of crime by individuals with disability. The reticence of individuals with disability to report their victimization is understandable in light of the fear of retaliation as well as the dependence of many individuals on their victimizers. The accessibility to many criminal justice agencies is often limited, making it difficult for victims to use the criminal justice services available to individuals without disability. In addition to questions of equal access based on physical barriers, individuals face negative attitudinal barriers as well.

The following anecdote illustrates the complex interplay between victimization, revictimization, and reporting:

> An elderly woman who was unable to walk was cared for at home by family members. Her grandson, a drug user, frequently stole money from her, especially after the third of each month, when her Social Security Disability Income check arrived. The woman would tuck her money under her to hide it from her grandson. Once, in a state of anger when he could not find her money, he flipped her over and she fell out of the bed onto the floor. She sustained several bruises but was not seen by a doctor. She did not report the abuse or the theft to the police out of fear that her family would no longer want to care for her. (OVC, 1998:4)

Such events are often the trigger for increased suffering on the part of the victim. The physical harm was evident in the bruising. What may not be so evident is the emotional damage done. Victimization, and revictimization in particular, may enhance one's sense of vulnerability, fear, and distrust while reaffirming one's experience of stigmatization, isolation and lowered self-esteem.

Individuals with Disability as Offenders in the Criminal Justice System

Although it is common to assume that people with disability are likely victims, it is less common to assume that they are likely offenders. The paternalistic perceptions noted earlier often mean that society believes people with disability to be "incapable" of engaging in criminal behavior. Although persons with severe mental and physical disabilities are unlikely to be represented in arrest data, those whose disability is less severe do engage in rule-breaking behavior. Activists in the disability rights movement, for example, have seen their share of arrests for civil disobedience, just as did women and people of color. However, people with disability also engage in the more mundane conventional crimes, such as shoplifting and larceny, as well as more serious violent offenses, such as homicide and assault (Miller and Hess, 1998; Kardasz, 1995). The latter offenses are often associated with people experiencing mental disorders that leave them violent and aggressive if untreated.

Individuals with disability as offenders in the criminal justice system are often seen as least eligible for any type of accommodation. Like any other individuals who break the rules, offenders with disability are viewed as undeserving of any accommodation. Consequently, access to court and courtroom procedures remains problematic. For the physically impaired, access to the court itself may be difficult. The symbolic architecture of many courthouses include many steps rising to a plateau. Transportation to court and passing through metal detection devices may be difficult for offenders, witnesses, and observers with a variety of different disabilities. Communication in the courtroom for speech- and hearing-impaired individuals may require sign language interpreters or various available high-tech equipment.

Incarceration in juvenile facilities, jails, and prisons at both state and federal levels requires appropriate living accommodations for any number of individuals with a variety of impairments. In actuality, individuals with disability face dangerous obstacles when seeking access to basic needs. Many horrific cases of blocked access and lack of accommodation have occurred. For example, one man who had been arrested and placed in a local county jail was separated from his prosthesis for months. He was required to hop around without his leg—a threatening and potentially dangerous situation. A wheelchair-bound inmate required to use bathroom facilities not wide enough to accommodate his wheelchair and without adequate grab bars is another dangerous situation. A female hearing-impaired inmate who was denied an interpreter at a grievance hearing was a violation of 14th Amendment guarantees. In addition, given the limited living accommodations for inmates in these environments, there is a question as to whether there is sufficient (equal) access to treatment and programming for rehabilitation.

The supreme court in *Pennsylvania Department of Corrections* v. *Yeskey* (June 15, 1998) found that ADA protections cover state prison inmates. The first legislative step in attempting to erode protection of the ADA comes from senators Jessie Helms and Strom Thurmond. S. 2266, called the "State and Local Prison Relief Act," seeks to exclude all jails, prisons, and juvenile facilities housing physically and mentally disabled adults and children as well as employees of such facilities from compliance with ADA. Helms and Thurmond refer to disabled offenders and employees as seeking "special treatment" rather than an equal playing field.

What better way to erode the protections of the ADA than to attack it using those seen as "least eligible" for accommodation? Who could argue with that logic, even though employees are included under their inappropriately named legislation?

Another extremely serious issue regarding offenders with disability deals with punishment of individuals with developmental and mental impairment. The question of exception to intent must be addressed. We need to particularly question the use of capital punishment, the most extreme punishment, in regard to developmentally and mentally disabled individuals, lest the justice system further victimize these individuals on the basis of their disability.

Individuals with Disability as Employees in the Criminal Justice System

Any of us can become disabled, either temporarily or permanently, at any point in time. It does not fundamentally change who we are, our knowledge, or our training. If an individual is qualified for a position, they cannot—ethically or legally—be denied that position on the basis of a disability. The same types of accommodations made for visitors and the general public must be made for employees. Disabled employees of criminal justice agencies face the physical and social barriers faced by victims and offenders. Accommodations such as ramps and wide doorways for mobility-impaired people as well as telecommunications devices for speech- and hearing-impaired individuals are examples of accommodations. In addition to these accommodations, special equipment such as high-technology telephones (TDD), speech-synthesized computers, and modified training manuals and work schedules, for example, may be required. It may be necessary to change the way certain procedures are done to accommodate an employee with a disability. Any services provided for employees without disabilities must also be provided for employees with disability. In an adaptation to the workplace, innovation is the key.

It is easier to change environments than attitudes. Perceptions of disability and individuals with disability make a difference—negative attitudes of coworkers and clients can be problematic. Seeing the individual as less capable and pitiable interferes with an individual doing their job. "Society hasn't yet made the jump where it's OK for a person [with disability] to be your boss or your brother-in-law"(Theirs, 1994:23).

References

Americans with Disabilities Act of 1990. Public Law 101-336, 101st Cong., 2nd sess. (26 July 1990).
Backman, E. (1994). Is the movement racist? *Mainstream*, (May), 24–31.
Goffman, E. (1959). *The presentation of self in everyday life.* Garden City, NY: Anchor/Doubleday.
Helms, J. and Thurmond, S. 2266 State and local prison relief act, proposed July 17, 1998.

Kardasz, F. (1995). Apprehending mental patients. *Law and Order,* (November), 91–92.

Miller, L. and Hess, K. (1998). *The police in the community: Strategies for the 21st century.* Belmont, CA: West/Wadsworth.

Office for Victims of Crime (1998). *Working with victims of crime with disabilities.* (September). Washington, DC: U.S. Department of Justice.

Pennsylvania Department of Corrections v. *Yeskey* (141 L.Ed. 2d 215, 118 S. Cp. 1952) 1998.

Scotch, R. K. (1989). Politics and policy in the history of the disability rights movement. *The Milbank Quarterly, 67,* (Suppl. 2, Pt. 2), 380–400.

Shakespeare, T. (1993). Disabled people's self-organisation: A new social movement? *Disability, Handicap and Society, 8, (3),* 249–263.

Shapiro, J. P. (1993). *No pity: People with disabilities forging a new civil rights movement.* New York: Times Books.

Theirs, N. (1994). Beyond pity: Americans' perceptions of citizens with disabilities. *OT Week,* (April 94), 20–24.

Thomas, S. (1990). The disability rights movement to stop protecting y'all from me. *The Guild Practitioner, 25,* 33–41.

Tucker, B. P. (1993). Discrimination on the basis of disability: The need for a third wave movement. *Cornell Journal of Law and Public Policy, 3,* 253–264.

Watson, S. D. (1993). An alliance at risk. *The American Prospect, 12* (Winter), 60–67.

Young, J. (1998). *The genealogy of a social movement: Disability rights in comparative perspective.* Paper presented at the meeting of the Western Social Science Association, Denver, CO.

15

In Whose God We Trust?

Religious Difference, Persecution, and Criminal Justice

BARBARA PERRY

From the time European settlers landed on the shores of what is now the United States, there has been a close connection between the "immigrant experience" and religion. For many ethnic groups arriving in this new land, religion has provided the basis for continued (albeit often short-lived) solidarity and sense of community. It has often served as the glue that would reinforce group identity. At the same time, religion has been a frequent source of divisiveness between groups, where religious beliefs and practices have defined worshipers of other faiths as "different."

The "normative standard" against which religious communities have been measured has historically been British Protestantism, which includes denominations such as Anglicans, Presbyterians, Baptists, and Quakers. After the American Revolution, successive waves of non-Protestant immigrants broke this religious monopoly. Eastern European Jews, Irish, German and Mexican Catholics, and diverse religions of the East have contributed to the contemporary religious pluralism of the United States. Consequently, the picture of religious affiliation in the United States is a dizzying mosaic consisting of dozens of major religions, each with its own sects and divisions. Christianity remains dominant, accounting for about 90% of all who profess an affiliation, followed by Muslim, Jewish, and Eastern Orthodox faiths. Within Christianity, Catholics constitute the majority (approximately 60%), followed by Baptists, Methodists, and Pentecostals (National Council of Churches, 1998).

Nonetheless, Protestantism was so deeply embedded prior to the American Revolution that its dominance and influence on cultural values remained intact. The impact of early religious beliefs on all aspects of civil society—including the criminal justice system—was pervasive and long lasting. Friedman (1993:32) maintains that, "It would be hard to over-emphasize the influence of religion in shaping the criminal codes, in framing the modes of enforcement, and, generally, in creating a distinctive legal culture. The criminal justice system was in many ways another arm of religious orthodoxy." Consequently, under colonial rule, there was little if any distinction between sin and crime. The laws of God were also the laws of humankind; offenses against humans were offenses against God. The Laws and Liberties of Massachusetts, for example, specified capital offenses, and included scriptural references justifying the inclusion of both the crime and its attendant punishment. The criminal codes and court dockets throughout the colonies were replete with proscriptions and punishments for what we now think of as "morals" offenses: blasphemy, violating the Sabbath, misbehaving in church, consorting with the Devil, or fornicating. In 1758, Abel Wood of Plymouth was tried for "irreverently behaving himself by chalking the back of one Hezekiah Purrington in church, playing and recreating himself in the *time of public worship*" (emphasis added, Massachusetts Records of 1758, cited in Friedman, 1993:33).

By the end of the eighteenth century, religious orthodoxy had largely lost its hold on the criminal justice system. Increasing diversity and secularization were accompanied by the rationalization and bureaucratization of the legal system, as personified in the constitutional separation of Church and State. Nonetheless, remnants of the country's religious past remained intact within the criminal justice system for some time: the exclusion of religious minorities from citizenship, the courts' religious oath, and criminalization of religious practices, for example. As shown throughout this chapter, religious difference has also often provided the foundation and rationale for persecution, victimization, and criminal acts of violence.

Victims of Religious Persecution

It is ironic that a country resettled by people seeking freedom from religious persecution has had such an extensive history of religious bigotry and violence. It is equally ironic that although the First Amendment guarantees religious freedom, some religious minorities have been met with considerable legal and extralegal intolerance. From Puritan persecutions of "heathens" and "heretics" to contemporary acts of anti-Muslim violence, religious difference has inspired periodic waves of hostility, often culminating in violent victimization of the "other." For example, Mormons, although never overwhelming in terms of absolute numbers, have nonetheless inspired remarkable animosity, resulting in victimization so dramatic and extensive that they fled New York, Ohio, Missouri, and Illinois in turn (Parrillo, 1997; Newton and Newton, 1991). The legacy of religious bigotry is both lengthy and broad. This chapter seeks to provide but a few illustrative cases.

Native Americans

The first to suffer the impact of European religious bigotry in the United States were Native Americans. In the absence of such European religious trappings as churches, shrines, or chalices, Columbus and his followers assumed Native Americans to be without religion, and thus in need of "salvation." Stannard (1992) characterizes Columbus as a typical European religious fanatic who saw it as his divine duty to eliminate "difference" through the conversion, conquest, or execution of non-Christians. He was "a man with sufficient intolerance and contempt for all who did not look like or believe as he did, that he thought nothing of enslaving or killing such people simply because they were not like him" (Stannard, 1992:200). Subsequent evangelists to the Americas took up Columbus' mission to "civilize" the natives by Christianizing them. It was those who steadfastly resisted conversion—individually and collectively—who would suffer the violence of Christian intolerance.

It was the imagery of natives as "savages" and "wild men" that allowed their persecution. Drawing on the emerging notions of social Darwinism, Europeans in the Americas constructed Native Americans as "less than human." Some went so far as to characterize them as consorts of the Devil. Rather than acknowledge the validity and richness of Native American religions, Europeans characterized them as heathens to be saved or eradicated. All too often, the latter was the case. In the Spanish Southwest, for example, Pueblo practitioners risked beatings and even death if they dared to practice traditional rituals (Mihesuah, 1996).

Although violence against Native Americans persists today, it is less apt to be motivated by religious difference than by broader ethnic differences. Similarly, anti-Catholic violence has largely receded into the history books. Nonetheless, it is important that we remember this part of our not-too-distant past in order to minimize the likelihood of repetition.

Catholics

That Catholics were once considered a deceitful, untrustworthy people is almost a forgotten fact. So great was the Protestant intolerance of Catholics that the colonies passed legislation that dramatically restricted the political rights of Catholic immigrants. In 1700, New York banned Catholic clergy and threatened them with imprisonment; subsequent reentry was deemed a capital offense. The primary source of the historical resistance to Catholicism was the hierarchical structure of the Church. It was feared that the Pope, as head of the Church, conspired to be head of the United States government as well. Practitioners, nuns, and priests were thus seen as emissaries of the papacy. In addition, Latin mass was looked on with suspicion, as was the vow of celibacy. The latter, in particular, gave rise to lurid tales of "unnatural" sexual practices within the confines of churches, convents, and parochial schools (Parrillo, 1997). Exacerbating the hostility during the nineteenth century was the ethnicity of so many Catholics: Irish and Eastern and Southern Europeans. As noted in Chapter 5, each of these groups were hated in their own right; their religious affiliation seemed to seal their fate as vulnerable minorities.

Anti-Catholic sentiment frequently erupted into anti-Catholic violence, often instigated by anti-Catholic organizations like the Know-Nothing Party, the

American Protective Society, and the Ku Klux Klan. In May 1844, Philadelphia was the site of untold assaults on Irish Catholics, and the burning of 50 of their homes, two of their churches, a school, and several Irish Catholic businesses (Kleg, 1997). In November 1917, the parish house of a St. Paul church was burned; in October 1924, an Oakland, Michigan, seminary was the site of cross burnings and exploding bombs (Newton and Newton, 1991). Infrequent but troubling episodes of anti-Catholic violence continue to occur at the end of the twentieth century. Corry, Pennsylvania, for example, was the site of a campaign of anti-Catholic vandalism in 1985, when churches, cemeteries, and homes of Catholics were victimized.

For the most part, contemporary Catholics in the United States need not fear persecution on the basis of their religion. The election of John F. Kennedy—the first Catholic president of the United States—is often considered the turning point for the acceptance of Catholics, who have since been fully integrated into broader United States culture and politics. In contrast, whereas Jewish Americans have enjoyed a similar political and economic success, they continue to be victims of crimes ranging from harassment to murder.

Jews

Of all religious minorities, Jews may hold the dubious distinction of having the longest history of persecution. Moreover, they are probably the most vulnerable to contemporary victimization, individually and collectively. Jews have been attacked and even massacred for holding their beliefs since the days of the Roman occupation of Israel. In the modern era, anti-Semitism reached its tragic zenith with the Holocaust in Nazi Germany. In fact, it was Nazi persecution that motivated the great migration of European Jews to the United States in the early part of the twentieth century.

American Jews occupy an ambiguous and often difficult position in the United States. On the one hand, they are among the "white ethnics" to which Gould refers in Chapter 3. On the other hand, they are also perceived as a "people apart." By virtue of skin color, they are relatively privileged; by virtue of their religion, they are subordinate. There is one particularly tenacious element of "white anti-Semitism" that seems indissoluble: "that is the general American belief that the Christian faith is superior to all others, that Jews stubbornly refuse to accept the truthfulness of Christianity, and that until they do, . . . as a group they can never be given the respect that Christians receive" (Dinnerstein, 1994:xii). From this perspective, Jews are "unworthy" because of the fallibility of their beliefs. They are not the "chosen ones" after all. Moreover, anti-Semites have long suspected Jews to engage in horrific practices and rituals, befitting the "vulgar" beliefs of Judaism: child sacrifices and drinking the blood of Christians, for example. Consequently, the perceived economic success of Jews as a group is deemed to be undeserved. Instead, they are thought to have achieved their success through deceit and conspiracy.

Anti-Semitic violence has been relatively persistent throughout the history of Jews in the United States. Since 1979, the Anti-Defamation League (ADL) of B'nai B'rith has been generating annual audits of anti-Semitic victimization, not only in the United States but worldwide. The ADL includes among its data "incidents" that may not fit the traditional definition of crime. It tracks murders, assaults, and arsons to be sure, but this is supplemented with attention paid to other offenses such as harassment, anti-Semitic slurs, and distributing neo-Nazi literature.

An overview of several audits reveals an especially disturbing trend: since 1991, anti-Semitic violence has been increasingly more likely to involve personal rather than property crimes. Historically, this has been a group victimized by crimes against property, such as synagogue or cemetery desecrations. However, the tide has begun to turn. In addition, the decline in the number of anti-Semitic incidents beginning in 1995 has corresponded to an increase in the intensity of the violence associated with the incidents. In 1995, for example, an arson in New York City resulted in several deaths. In November of that year, the FBI fortunately foiled an attempt by the TriState Militia to bomb several ADL offices.

Another disturbing trend is the growth in campus incidents of anti-Semitism. Institutions of higher learning, in particular, have seen an alarming increase in the amount of anti-Semitic violence, vandalism, and leafleting. It is disheartening to imagine this generation of students as the next generation of leaders. They will set the tone for the rhetoric and policies of tolerance or intolerance.

Muslims

A relatively recent arrival to the United States is the Muslim faith. This predominantly black denomination is grounded in staunch moral conservatism, which has often served as a boundary between American Muslims and Americans of other faiths. For Muslims,

> religious beliefs and the social mores of public conduct and private experience are all inseparable. Submission to the will of Allah means a prescribed code of conduct in every facet of life. . . . Conservative in their values and attitudes, Muslims also reject the preoccupation of Americans with materialism and their self-indulgent pleasures at the expense of obligations to family and community. (Parrillo, 1997:462)

Significantly, Americans have come to associate the fundamentalism of Islam with fundamentalist violence, believing that followers of Islam will do anything that is deemed the "will of Allah." Consequently, Muslims are suspected of being foreign and domestic terrorists. Exacerbating this is the tendency to collapse all Muslims with Arabs and to paint all with the same tainted brush. Stereotypes of the "crazed" and "religiously fanatical" Arab/Muslim abound. A blatant media example was a *New York Post* editorial cartoon featuring a Statue of Liberty, flanked by three men in turbans with a bomb and a burning United States flag. The caption read, "Give us your tired, your poor, your huddled masses, your terrorists, your murderers, your slime, your evil cowards, your religious fanatics." In this light, it is not surprising that politicians and public alike so willingly and incorrectly cast the early blame for the Oklahoma City bombing on Muslim terrorists.

As identifiable symbols of Islam, mosques are frequent targets of anti-Muslim crime. The American–Arab Anti-Discrimination Committee (ADC, 1996) reports that in 1995, at least seven mosques were burned downed or seriously vandalized. The UCR (FBI, 1996) reported six cases of destruction/damage/vandalism to Islamic property for the same year. A typical example occurred in Atlanta, Georgia, where a mosque was desecrated with satanic symbols. One surprising finding to emerge from the UCR for 1995 is that nearly as many Muslims—33—reported religiously motivated violence as did Catholics—38. Given that there are only about 25 million Muslims in the United States, it is apparent that they are disproportionately victimized.

Religious minorities, then, have been identifiable victims of personal and property crimes. The preceding was a cursory glance at but a few such cases. We might also explore the experiences of the Amish, the Rastafarians, and other marginal groups for evidence of religious persecution. Time and space preclude more extensive examination. Instead, we turn now to look at the other side of the equation. Minority and majority religious beliefs have motivated criminal (sometimes legal) offending, not only against other religious groups, but also against others who might be practicing "intolerable" behavior.

Offenses Motivated by Religious Belief

Religion has always played some role in defining difference in the United States. In the language of deviance theorists, religion is a mechanism of boundary maintenance by which behaviors are defined as acceptable or unacceptable, moral or immoral, appropriate or inappropriate. Those who transcend those boundaries are constructed as the "Other"—often dangerous, always notably different. Religious communities are especially apt at this, because they generally subscribe to a rigid doctrine that explicitly defines these boundaries: the Ten Commandments is one such typology of proscriptions.

Where proselytizing and other forms of "persuasion" have not convinced the "deviants" to change their ways, violence justified by scripture has frequently taken its place. Offenders have often seen it as their religious duty to police the boundaries of acceptable moral conduct in the United States. Again, the examples are legion. I have chosen but a small sample to illustrate the theme here.

Puritan Campaigns Against Sin

The Puritan preoccupation with piety and sin set the stage for rigid intolerance of religious difference, but also of nonconforming behavior in general. Haught

(1990) goes so far as to characterize the Puritan colony as a "religious police state" driven by an obsessive aversion to "doctrinal deviation." In other words, "there was a high degree of consensus over proper behavior. The central norm was obedience to authority: first to God, then to clergy, and finally to the male head of the household" (Walker, 1998:15–16). It is this context that we can make sense of the crimes perpetrated by Puritans against Quakers, and later, against witches.

The colonial Quakers' democratic vision threatened the Puritan vision of an ordered world. Boorstin (1992) identifies three particular traits that set the Quakers in dangerous opposition to Puritanism. First, their belief in equality clearly contradicted the Puritan hierarchy that privileged God, clergy, and men, and especially white men. Second, their informality of dress, language, and comportment was directly opposite the Puritan traditions of formality in all spheres. Third, the Quaker tradition of tolerance flew in the face of Puritan demands for conformity.

This hostility engendered by these differences would take on a viciously punitive face. The first two Quakers to arrive in Massachusetts in 1656—two women from the Barbados—were forcibly expelled almost before they disembarked from their ship. Before their expulsion, they were "jailed, stripped and searched for signs of witchcraft, their books publicly burned" (Newton and Newton, 1991:13). Quaker "heretics" would henceforth be subject to brutal punishments, including floggings, mutilations, imprisonment, and hanging. In 1657, two Quaker men were arrested and immediately received 30 lashes with a knotted whip; subsequently starved in a bare prison cell for 3 days; imprisoned for 9 winter weeks, during which they received weekly lashings; and then finally banished by ship to the Barbados. By 1661, at least four Quakers had been executed for their beliefs.

Similar treatment awaited suspected witches. In fact, the threats represented by Quakers and witches seemed indistinguishable to Puritans. Both were heretics—consider the fate of the first two Quakers who had been checked for "signs of witchcraft." Witches—women in particular—presented similar challenges to the authority of God, clergy, and men:

> the war against witches was also a war against women: or at least against disorderly, troublesome deviant women. . . . Those who rebelled against order "were the very embodiment of evil." The "subordination of women" was part of the natural order; the witch symbolized or embodied a kind of double rebellion—of women against men, and women against Godly society. (Friedman, 1993:46–47)

Women-as-witches provided convenient scapegoats at a time when the rigid religious homogeneity and conformity were coming to an end. It was believed that such women entered compacts with the Devil, and that their rewards were supernatural powers and earthly riches. It is no coincidence, therefore, that so many of those accused were women of property. Their wealth was taken as a sign of the subversion of both God's and man's patriarchal authority. For this, they would suffer. Ultimately, between May and September of 1692, 21 people (mostly women) and several domestic animals would die in the midst of the witchcraft hysteria. Most were hanged; many suffered mutilation and confessional torture before their death.

Abortion Clinic Violence

Although the seventeenth-century witch hunts were short-lived and narrowly confined to Massachusetts, a contemporary parallel has been raging since the early 1970s. The modern equivalent is abortion clinic violence, which also arises out of the combined influence of religious beliefs and resistance to women's changing roles. Some religiously guided anti-abortionists see it as their "mission" to restore God's will across the nation.

The violent fringe of the anti-abortion movement has relied heavily on interpretations of scripture that justify abortion clinic harassment and violence. Groups like the Lambs of Christ, Missionaries to the Preborn, Army of God, and Operation Rescue include among their membership convicted or alleged perpetrators of arson, bombing, and homicide. What these groups and individuals share is the belief that abortion is murder and murder is sin. It is but a small step for these same zealots to make the claim that preventing abortion "by whatever means necessary" is, in fact, their Christian duty.

The first attempt to plead "justifiable violence" in court emerged in the case against two couples charged with the bombings of two Pensacola, Florida, abortion clinics. The offenders insisted that they were justified in their use of violence to stop the "sin" and "moral evil" represented by abortion. Activists have gone so far as to claim that the rash of homicides in the mid-1990s are also justifiable homicide. In defending Michael Griffin in the killing of Dr. Gunn in 1993, a Catholic priest wrote in the anti-abortionist newsletter *Life Advocate:* "You see how stupid it is for the U.S. bishops to call an act in self defense in favor of unborn infants, murder? . . . The bishops should have condemned the abortions that the doctor performed and praised the heroic act . . . by the pro-life man."

Anti-abortion violence seemed to reach its peak in 1993 and 1994, the same years in which Michael Griffin, Paul Hill, and John Salvi allegedly assassinated five clinic personnel. During the same years, the Feminist Majority Foundation's national survey of clinics found that more than 50% of all clinics experienced severe criminal violence, including invasions, bombs and bomb threats, arson and arson threats, and chemical attacks. Since then the violence has declined, due in large part to the efforts of pro-choice activists, the implementation of the Freedom of Access to Clinic Entrance (1994), and enhanced law enforcement. However, by 1996, nearly a third of all clinics continued to be victimized. Death threats and stalkings have declined most dramatically, although bombings and chemical attacks appear to have become more common (Feminist Majority Foundation, 1997). Although not all abortion clinic violence is perpetrated by members of religiously grounded organizations, it is likely that glorification in the name of religion sets the tone and climate for such crimes to occur. The increase in criminal attacks on clinics and their personnel between the mid-1980s and mid-1990s coincided with the increased visibility and vitriol of right-wing religious anti-abortionists (Diamond, 1996; CDR, 1995; Novick, 1995).

Christian Identity Churches and RAHOWA

Perpetrators of religiously motivated anti-abortion violence are often connected to groups that advocate violence "in the name of God." Frequently, such groups are associated with Christian Identity theology, which identifies the enemies of God in very broad terms. Moreover, it is the Christian Identity movement that leads the calls for RAHOWA, or the Racial Holy War.

The anti-Semitism and racism that characterize so many hate groups—and not just the Identity Churches—can be traced to the theocratic principle of Christian Identity. On the basis of a creative reading of biblical scripture, those advocating this perspective claim the white race to be the direct descendants of Ancient Israel, and therefore God's chosen people:

> WE BELIEVE that Adam, man of Genesis, is the placing of the White Race upon this earth. Not all races descend from Adam. Adam is the father of the White Race only. (Aryan Nations, online)

In contrast to the glorification of the white race, Jews are seen to be the source of all evil, spawned as they are by the Devil himself:

> WE BELIEVE that there are literal children of Satan in this world today . . . WE BELIEVE that the Canaanite Jew is the natural enemy of our Aryan (White) Race. The Jew is like a destroying virus that attacks our racial body to destroy our Aryan culture and the purity of our race. (Aryan Nations, online)

As a corollary of this, the anti-Semites often portray African Americans as the pawns of the Jewish conspiracy. Black-on-white crime, for example, is also seen as a phenomenon orchestrated by Jews as a means of cowing whites. After Jews, then, blacks are perceived to be the greatest threat to the purity and safety of the white race:

> Today you can escape the terror of black ghettos and Brown Barrios. Your children and your children's children will have no refuge. The DEATH OF THE WHITE RACE is neither imaginary nor far off in the distant future. (Aryan Nations, online)

Nowhere is the racist sentiment more evident than in the second "Bible" of the Identity movement, *The Turner Diaries*, a blueprint for racial violence. It is a fictional account of the long hoped-for revolution against the "corruption of our people by the Jewish-liberal-democratic-equalitarian plague which afflicts us" (MacDonald, 1996:42). *The Turner Diaries* has been used as a guide for a series of racially motivated crimes, including robberies, arsons, and assassinations, and for the Oklahoma City bombing.

The belief systems of Christian Identity lead many hate groups to the conclusion that, through organized action, the white race must reverse the trends represented by the myriad forms of white racial "suicide" and "genocide." All traces of the nonwhite presence must be erased from the United States through RAHOWA—RAcial HOly WAr. Only by winning the battle against evil—whether defined as Jew, black, or "mud races"—can supremacists restore the divine order as given by God. Consequently, representatives of the various hate groups are explicit in their call to arms. Consider the following illustrative exhortation:

> WE BELIEVE that the White Race, its Biological and Cultural Heritage, is now under attack by our mortal racial enemies: Jews, niggers and the mud races. WE BELIEVE that RAHOWA (RAcial HOly WAr) . . . is the only road to the resurrection and redemption of the White Race. (World Church of the Creator, online)

It is this call to RAHOWA that puts minorities most at risk, because it attempts to justify violence by appealing to God's will. When it is believed that the "subhuman" and "soulless" races are closer to Satan than to God, it becomes acceptable to attack them in the name of ridding the world of evil. Supremacists claim a moral right to engage in crime and violence as a means of restoring God's law and the white race to its rightful place in the United States' racial hierarchy.

Service Providers

In contrast to those organizations that exploit religious belief to justify oppressive violence against others are religiously grounded organizations that use their beliefs to further the interests of justice. One rallying point continues to be the struggle for religious freedom within the criminal justice system. The Religious Freedom Restoration Act (RFRA) of 1993 represents an uncertain victory in this arena. The Act seeks to significantly increase inmates' freedom to exercise their religious beliefs and rituals. Yet this will not be an easy task:

> Engulfed in problems—prison gangs, overcrowding, violence and riots—and exacerbated by limited finances, outdated facilities, and a soaring inmate population, prisons must accommodate the demands of a panoply of faiths. Outside the prisons, religious adherents can select their own diets, places of worship, and religious leaders, but in prisons, these aspects of religious life must be supplied and regulated by the penal institution. (Solove, 1996:462–463)

Prison administrators have traditionally offered an array of untested assumptions to support their failure to recognize religious freedom: disruption of prison routine; elevated religious animosity between groups; loss of control and discipline over inmates; excessive costs; and lack of resources, space, and personnel.

Nontraditional—that is, non–Judeo-Christian—religions have been most significantly affected. Muslim and Buddhist offenders have been refused the right to wear ritual symbols of faith, or denied the use of prison chapels. Rastafarians, Native Americans, and Orthodox Jews have been forced to shed their traditional-length locks or beards. For the most part, the RFRA has failed to live up to its potential, largely because courts continue to be uninformed and insensitive about prisoners' religious rights and freedoms (Solove, 1996).

One area of particular concern in the context of freedom of religion has been the freedom of Native Americans to practice traditional ways of spirituality. In spite of the 1978 American Indian Religious Freedom Act and the 1993 RFRA, Native American inmates still face obstacles in their attempts to worship according to tradition. Four particular issues stand in their way. First, Native American prisoners are often incarcerated away from their homes, making it difficult to maintain contact not only with family and friends, but with spiritual leaders as well. Second, many prison officials continue to deny religious ceremonies such as sweat lodges. Third, Native Americans are generally denied access to sacred objects such as herbs, pipes, feathers, and long hair. Fourth, officials fail to recognize the natural and cyclical rather than linear nature of the schedule of Native American religious ceremonies.

There is, nonetheless, hope for progress. There is a growing recognition that freedom of religious practice may in fact serve the rehabilitative goals of corrections. In the debates preceding the RFRA, senators as disparate as Bob Dole and Edward Kennedy acknowledged the value of religion in prisons. Dole insisted that, "If religion can help just a handful of prison inmates get back on track, then the inconvenience of accommodating their religious beliefs is a very small price to pay." Kennedy shared the sentiment: "We would encourage prisoners to be religious. There is every reason to believe that doing so will increase the likelihood that a prisoner will be rehabilitated" (cited in Solove, 1996:472).

Religious activists and, to a lesser degree, prison officials have recognized the utility of religious programming in the prison context. Consequently, a variety of prison ministries have emerged nationwide. An Internet search for Prison Ministries identified 20 predominantly Christian and nondenominational ministries, many of which are committed to helping inmates to "find Christ" and subsequently to helping them to reintegrate into their communities. Even the omnipresent 12-step programs, such as Alcoholics Anonymous, have found their way into prison rehabilitation programs. These, too, are grounded in spiritual notions of faith in a higher power (Skotnicki, 1996:41).

On the other side of the prison fence are those religious organizations committed to preventing crime and breaking the links that contribute to crime and violence. Churches often see it as part of their mission to combat the violence, prejudice, and abuses that characterize their congregants and the communities in which they live. Although informed by religious precepts, such organizations are not limited to proselytizing. Many provide food to those who might otherwise steal it, training for those without job skills, rehabilitation programs for those addicted to drugs, or shelters for those victimized by domestic and family violence. Following is just a small sampling of such groups:

- Muslims Against Family Violence offers an educational campaign intended to increase awareness of, and eliminate the problem of, family violence (www.mpac.org/mafv).
- Islamic Relief of Los Angeles seeks to feed, clothe, and find employment for underprivileged Islamics, as well as providing an alternative to gangs and life in prison (amahelp.com/lamission.htm).
- The Social Concern Ministry of the Catholic Church operationalizes church teaching "as it relates to issues of human rights, justice and the empowerment of the poor and disenfranchised in our society" (www. cathcharitiesffldcty.com/SocialCo.html).
- Churches Taking a Corner is an interfaith organization "fighting substance abuse, violence, racism and prejudice in every community where we work" (www.ctacusa.org.html).

As the presence of such organizations suggests, religion has the potential not only to inspire violence, but also to inspire its opposite: peace, tolerance, and justice. As criminal justice practitioners, we might learn from the peacemaking efforts of the religions of the world.

References

American–Arab Anti-Discrimination Committee (1996). *1995 Report on anti-Arab racism*. Washington, DC: ADC.

Anti-Defamation League (1995). *Annual audit of anti-semitic incidents*. New York: ADL.

Aryan Nations: www.stormfront.org/an.html

Biery, R. (1990). *Understanding homosexuality*. Austin, TX: Edward–William Publishing.

Boorstin, D. (1992). *The Americans: The colonial experience*. New York: Vintage Books.

Butler, J. (1990). *Awash in a sea of faith: Christianizing the American people*. Cambridge, MA: Harvard University Press.

Center for Democratic Renewal (1995). *Women's watch: Violence in the anti-abortion movement*. Atlanta, GA: CDR.

Comstock, G. (1991). *Violence against lesbians and gay men*. New York: Columbia University Press.

Dolan, J. (1988). The immigrants and their gods: A new perspective in American religious history. *Church History, 57*, 61–72.

Diamond, S. (1996). *Facing the wrath: Confronting the right in dangerous times*. Monroe, ME: Common Courage Press.

Dinnerstein, L. (1994). *Anti-semitism in America*. New York: Oxford University Press.

Erickson, K. (1966). *Wayward puritans*. New York: John Wiley & Sons.

Federal Bureau of Investigation (1996). *Hate crime statistics, 1995*. Washington, DC: U.S. Department of Justice.

Feminist Majority Foundation (1997). *National Clinic Violence Survey.* Arlington, VA: Feminist Majority Foundation.

Friedman, L. (1993). *Crime and punishment in American history.* New York: Basic Books.

Haught, J. (1995). *Holy hatred.* Buffalo, NY: Prometheus.

———. (1990). *Holy horrors.* Buffalo, NY: Prometheus.

Kleg, M. (1997). Anti-Catholicism. In Prejudice Institute, *Perspectives: The newsletter on prejudice, ethnoviolence and social policy, 2,* 4–6.

———. (1993). *Hate prejudice and racism.* Albany, NY: SUNY Press.

MacDonald, A. (1996). *The Turner diaries.* New York: Barricade Books.

MacLean, N. (1994). *Behind the mask of chivalry: The making of the second Ku Klux Klan.* New York: Oxford University Press.

Moore, L. (1986). *Religious outsiders and the making of America.* New York: Oxford University Press.

Morris, R. (1997). What though our rights have been assailed? Mormons, politics, same sex marriage, and cultural abuse in the Sandwich Islands. *Women's Rights Law Reporter, 18(2),* 129–203.

Mihesuah, D. (1996). *American Indians: Stereotypes and realities.* Atlanta, GA: Clarity Press.

National Council of Churches (1998). *1997 Yearbook of American and Canadian churches.* New York: Roundtable Press.

National Gay and Lesbian Task Force. (1996). *Anti-gay/lesbian violence, victimization and defamation in 1995.* Washington, DC: NGLTF Policy Institute.

———. (1995). *Anti-gay/lesbian violence, victimization and defamation in 1994.* Washington, DC: NGLTF Policy Institute.

———. (1994). *Anti-gay/lesbian violence, victimization and defamation in 1993.* Washington, DC: NGLTF Policy Institute.

Newton, M. and Newton, J. A. (1991). *Racial and religious violence in America: A chronology.* New York: Garland.

Novick, M. (1995). *White lies, white power.* Monroe, ME: Common Courage Press.

Parrillo, V. (1997). *Strangers to these shores: Race and ethnic relations in the United States.* Boston: Allyn and Bacon.

Ridgeway, J. (1995). *Blood in the face.* New York: Thunder's Mouth Press.

Skotnicki, A. (1996). Religion and rehabilitation. *Criminal Justice Ethics,* Summer/Fall, 34–42.

Solove, D. (1996). Faith profaned: The Religious Freedom Restoration Act and religion in the prisons. *Yale Law Journal, 106,* 459–491.

Stannard, D. (1992). *American holocaust.* New York: Oxford University Press.

Subbagh, S. (1990). *Sex, lies and stereotypes: The image of Arabs in American popular fiction.* Washington, DC: ADC.

Walker, S. (1998). *Popular justice: A history of American criminal justice.* New York: Oxford University Press.

West, C. (1994). *Race matters.* New York: Vintage Books.

World Church of the Creator. www.rahowa.com

PART THREE

Reframing Difference

16

Widening the Workforce

Diversity in Criminal Justice Employment

MARILYN D. McSHANE

The videotape televised throughout the country showed an African American motorist struggling with a group of Anglo officers. In another tape, a group of Mexican youths attempting to enter the United States illegally are unnecessarily beaten by American Border Patrol officers. In a busy New York Drug Enforcement Agency office, a $1 million sting operation falls apart when none of the agents can interpret Cantonese.

Different cultures, different languages, and different appearances all create barriers to the successful operation of the criminal justice system. When citizens interact with the criminal justice system, there is often tension, fear, and conflict. Victims, witnesses, offenders, parents, and criminal justice personnel must all coordinate together effectively to resolve issues of crime and justice. The quality and success of each interaction is dependent on each person's perception of the system's legitimacy. When members of minority groups see themselves represented in public service, when their needs and feelings are understood, they may feel more at ease and their sense of belonging may be confirmed.

Over the years, commissions studying civil unrest, riots, and prison disturbances have all attributed imbalances in racial representation to problems in the criminal justice system. Also, the lack of integration in law enforcement can be viewed as contributing, albeit indirectly, to problems of corruption. Experts studying police subcultures, malfeasance, and corrupt practices have pointed to the hiring of friends, relatives, and political patrons as a contributing factor. Legislation (Law Enforcement Assistance Administration) derived from some of these commission reports have dedicated efforts toward increasing diversity within criminal justice agencies.

One could argue that true diversity in work and in educational opportunities has a direct impact on the number of competitively qualified minority candidates entering criminal justice employment. In the past, arrest records, conviction records, educational requirements, experience requirements, licensure requirements, height and weight requirements, credit checks, English-language requirements, and drug and alcohol use have all been used in prequalification screening for applicants (Sedmak and Vidas, 1994).

The number of minority group members who are admitted to colleges and professional schools determines who later has an impact on the criminal justice system at the supervisory and management levels of law enforcement organizations as well as in the courts. Finding that barriers still exist in private companies and law firms, minority professionals often turn to the civil service for employment opportunities.

Government Intervention in Labor

In the private sector, the Commerce Clause in the Constitution gives the government the power to regulate business practices where goods or services involve interstate transactions. Because this incorporates so many daily facets of American business, it is fair to say that the government's authority extends to most workplaces and the people who inhabit them.

Over the years, legislation, local actions, court decisions, administrative rulings, and a series of executive orders have continued to shape the practices of private business as well as public sector employment, including the criminal justice system. One of the major areas for regulation has been protection against discrimination in employment. For example, in 1935 under the Wagner Act, employers were obligated to "undo" past intimidation or harassment of union organizers and union members and take positive steps toward relieving conflict regarding labor unions. Also, perhaps the most notable piece of legislation, the 1964 Civil Rights Act provided for remedial action in cases in which intentional bias is established.

The Civil Rights Act and the Equal Employment Opportunity Commission

Title VII of the Civil Rights Act, probably the most cited language, forbids employment or membership discrimination by employers, employment agencies, or unions on the basis of race, color, religion, sex, or national origin. Subsequent amendments to the Civil Rights Act such as the Age Discrimination Act of 1975, the Pregnancy Discrimination Act of 1978, and the Americans with Disabilities Act of 1990 have broadened its impact and set up procedures for filing and settling disputes.

The Civil Rights Act also authorized the implementation of the Equal Employment Opportunity Commission (EEOC), which developed legal procedures for filing complaints. The EEOC averaged more than 90,000 claims per year in the early 1990s (Sedmak and Vidas, 1994), and in 1994 the total number of employment discrimination complaints filed with all federal, state, and local governments was more than 150,000 (Oppenheimer, 1996). The basis for complaints include discrimination by age, race, religion, disabilities, sexual preference, gender, or country of origin. The work issues most likely to generate claims are those of hiring, scheduling, termination, wages, type of work assignments, geographic areas of assignment, transfers, and promotions.

Affirmative Action

The term *affirmative action* comes from Executive Order 10925, issued by President Kennedy, regarding equal opportunity employment where "The contractor will take affirmative action to ensure that applicants are employed and that employees are treated during employment without regard to their race, creed, color or national origin." Although the wording implied that employers must do more than passive nondiscrimination, it was never articulated what affirmative action really meant. The 1972 amendments to the Civil Rights Act extended prohibitions against discrimination and made public employers responsible for using "affirmative action" to insure equal access to job opportunities (Martin, 1991).

Not long after, the Department of Labor's Office of Federal Contract Compliance began to enforce federal regulations that prohibited discrimination on the basis of sex, marital status, or childbearing status on projects for which federal contractors, subcontractors, or anyone received federal funding. These actions put an end to job advertisements that were separated into male and female categories and required all contracts to contain specific affirmative action plans. Cases that were litigated on discrimination issues could result in a number of positive outcomes for the plaintiffs including preliminary injunctions, back pay, front pay, compensatory and punitive damages, attorney's fees, and equitable remedies such as reinstatement or promotion (Sedmak and Vidas, 1994).

Perhaps because it was never defined and because it encompasses such a wide range of activities and policies, the concept of affirmative action is often misunderstood. As Johns (1998a:H3) explains:

> People often talk about affirmative actions as if it is one monolithic federal program that forces employers to hire less than qualified minorities and women. It is however, more like a smorgasbord of measures that may be used by federal, state or local governments. Some have been court ordered, but most are created voluntarily to increase diversity in the workplace or in educational institutions.

Over the years, affirmative action has meant everything from quotas and targets to incentives and career counseling.

Efforts to clarify the meaning of affirmative action or at least address the many attempts to circumvent equal opportunity employment often came from the courts (Weiss, 1997). The justices in *Griggs* v. *Duke Power Company* (1971) ruled against the use of *de facto* discriminators such as test scores, educational requirements, and so on that had a disparate impact on members of constitutionally protected groups. The court placed the burden on organizations to show that such requirements really were *bona fide* occupational qualifications (BFOQ). Such a qualification must be valid, job-related, and reasonably necessary to the normal operation of that agency. The decision even went so far as to say that despite the absence of any intent to discriminate, policies that had such an adverse impact would be viewed as suspect. Over the years, however, erosions of this vigilant protection of Title VII have shifted the burden onto employees to demonstrate that any employment disparities are directly caused by discriminatory company policies. Today, affirmative action policies must pass strict scrutiny to ensure that they are really necessary and valid. In addition, plans cannot be implemented to simply achieve balance and equity in the workplace, but must address a specific discriminatory practice (see *City of Richmond* v. *J. A. Croson*).

The Backlash Against Affirmative Action

Some critics argue that the original target of civil rights legislation, discrimination, which involved intent or purpose in action, was redefined over time to mean any statistically disproportionate effects (U.S. Department of Justice, 1987). In other words, the law went from seeking to protect against deliberate unlawful practices to challenging any employment arrangement that resulted in a less than proportionate racial distribution. Continued controversy over the meaning of affirmative action as well as conservative political movements for "less government" have led to many attempts to diminish programs and policies that have provided services and protections to less powerful groups (i.e., welfare mothers, alien residents, the disabled, and members of minority groups). Although one may argue that some concerns are fiscal, others are philosophical and have implications for the very fabric of our country's race relations. At the heart of the affirmative action debate are misleading buzzwords such as "preferences," "quotas," and "reverse discrimination."

According to Williams (1996), dominant economic movements since the late 1960s led to the backlash of criticism over affirmative action. First, rising unemployment rates (averaging 4.8% in 1960 and 7.3% in the 1980s) began the undercut of popular support. In addition, changes in industry meant the development of a higher skilled, technologically based workforce that those who were losing industrial jobs were not prepared to compete in. Finally, the economic policies of the Reagan–Bush era (1980–1992) meant lower taxes for the rich, cuts in domestic spending, and less protection for unionized workers who found their wages and job protections diminishing (Williams, 1996:248).

In California, years of economic hardship have set the tone for a competitive work environment that targets scapegoats for public ire and legislative reprisals.

Proposition 187 severely restricted public services for illegal immigrants, and a few years later, Proposition 209, ironically titled the California Civil Rights Initiative, outlawed race and gender preferences in state hiring contracts and public education. A poll conducted in the Phoenix area found that 70% of voters approved of a similar measure for Arizona (Johns, 1998b). A 1997 survey of incoming freshman college students found that 50% believed that affirmative action should be abolished in the college admission process (UCLA, 1998).

Although cases of discrimination in the workplace are heard daily, most are settled on an individual case basis. However, appeals courts and Supreme Court decisions often pave the way for major changes in the way public and private employers operate through their interpretations of civil rights law and responsibilities under existing affirmative action policies. In addition, the higher courts also hear cases that challenge new legislation regarding workplace practices and rule on their constitutionality. These cases have implications for the way the criminal justice system handles personnel issues.

The Status of Women and Minorities in Criminal Justice

Gender and Policing

As late as the 1970s, many women police officers had to wear heeled shoes, were only allowed to work with juvenile offenders, and often were not allowed to ride in patrol cars after dark. Women were denied access to what were considered "dangerous" assignments by minimum height, weight, and strength requirements.

As women surmounted barriers and began to join the police force in greater numbers and in a wider range of assignments during the 1970s, a series of newspaper and magazine surveys as well as government reports found that public acceptance of females in a traditionally male, dangerous, and physically demanding occupation was mixed. Although many believed in equal opportunities and the performance strengths of both sexes, there was still skepticism about violent situations and those requiring more physical strength (Bloch and Anderson, 1974; Leger, 1997). In addition, research on male officers continued to demonstrate persistent negative stereotypes of women on the job, fears of their safety when partnered with women, and concerns about job security and career progression threatened by competing female officers (Lord, 1986; Remmington, 1981). This is ironic given that at the same time, other articles highlighted the benefits of women on patrol, in that they were more effective in communication, were better able to deescalate crisis situations, had similar rates of arrests leading to conviction as male officers, and had fewer formal complaints (McDowell, 1992; Bloch and Anderson, 1974).

Today, women still represent less than 12% of sworn police officers and less than 5% are women of color (National Center for Women and Policing, 1998).

Women are also twice as likely to be found in city- and county-level police positions than in state law enforcement. According to the National Center for Women and Policing, the underrepresentation of women in policing may result in higher incidences of police brutality and expensive lawsuit resolutions, less-effective responses to domestic violence, negative community–police relations, and costly sexual discrimination and sexual harassment litigation. As Doerner and Patterson (1996) note, it is mostly external forces such as the courts and lawsuits that have been responsible for the hiring of even that small percentage of women. Barriers to women in policing still exist, including physical fitness tests that emphasize traditional measures of male strength, recruitment policies that favor venues disproportionately populated by men (such as the military), and styles of policing that reward aggression and force (National Center for Women and Policing, 1998). It is not surprising that today, women represent only 8% of the supervisory ranks in policing (rank of sergeant or higher) (National Center for Women and Policing, 1998).

Gender and Corrections

Because nearly 95% of the inmate population is male, most correctional jobs are in male institutions. Ironically, the early controversy concerning gender and correctional work involved men working with female inmates. In the 1800s, reform groups protested the use of men to supervise female prisoners and advocated the use of matrons who would also serve as appropriate role models. The first separate institution for women was designated in 1873, and the staff who lived on the premises were required to be "single, virtuous, and able to handle their charges in a ladylike manner" (Pollock, 1986).

Since the late 1970s, lawsuits have sought to clarify the balance between the privacy needs of the inmate (freedom from observations by officers of the opposite sex) and the rights of employees to have access to all tasks necessary for promotion and pay increases within the system. The first case to directly address this issue was *Dothard* v. *Rawlinson* in 1977. In this case, Rawlinson was denied a correctional job because she did not meet the minimum height and weight requirements of the Department of Corrections. She challenged this rule on the grounds that it excluded a disproportionate number of women and that it was not essential to the job performed. Also challenged was the departmental rule preventing women officers from being in "continual close proximity" to maximum security male inmates (Hawkins and Alpert, 1989). Although the court did strike down the use of minimum height and weight requirements in general, it also held that in this specific Alabama prison, conditions were so violent and dangerous that it was basically unsafe for women, and the court would not sanction their being allowed into that particular setting. To some analysts, this case backfired on the state, because its defense drew additional attention to prison conditions that had been found unconstitutional in an earlier decision. Alabama's prison system was under orders to be reformed for the sake of the men as well as the women who would eventually work there.

Since the 1970s, women have gradually expanded their work roles in institutions for male inmates. Although women were first employed as clerical assistants and searchers of female visitors, they are now involved in most aspects of corrections work. According to the U.S. Department of Justice (1991), 23% of correctional positions in jails are held by women. Still, of the 207,000 direct custody officers employed in state correctional institutions today, only 21% are female, and less than 2% are in supervisory positions. Even fewer women are in supervisory positions within the Federal Bureau of Prisons (ACA, 1998). Currently, women hold 18% of the warden and superintendent positions in adult corrections and almost that same percentage in juvenile facilities. Ironically, although the Federal Bureau of Prisons is headed by a woman, women hold only 8 of the 94 warden positions (ACA, 1998).

A study by Zupan (1986) found that there was no significant different between men and women officers in their perception of inmate needs, their ability to identify inmate needs accurately, and the levels of job tension each experienced in the work environment. Zupan's explanation for these findings is that the recruitment process may have weeded out those women who were significantly different from men, selecting only those women who were already "most like" men in their attitudes and perceptions. It is also hypothesized that although women and men may have initial differences in attitudes about their job (perhaps because of socialization differences), over time, the women are more likely to reflect traditional correctional officer (male) attitudes. In a study by Simon and Simon (1988), the authors sought to establish the legitimacy of female officers' control by comparing the disposition of disciplinary cases they wrote with those written by their male counterparts. Both male and female officers wrote disciplinary reports at similar rates, and their charges were processed and substantiated (by findings of guilt) at similar rates. Because there was no apparent differences in the authority of the two sexes, as administered by the disciplinary committees, the authors concluded that the female correctional officer is considered as legitimate as her male colleague.

The issue of women working as correctional officers in male prisons seems to have changed from arguments of safety to those of inmate privacy. In *Gunther v. Iowa* (1979), the court found that the privacy rights of inmates should not supersede the female officers' right to promotion opportunities. This implies that the administration should develop ways to allow women to work in all phases of custody without compromising an inmate's dignity. Finding the medium security Iowa facility far less dangerous than the "peculiarly inhospitable" conditions in Alabama, the court believed the department could accommodate basic inmate privacy concerns without violating Title VII of the Civil Rights Act. Decisions over the next few years have somewhat limited the inmate's right to privacy claims, with courts ruling that female officers can do pat-down frisks, even for Muslims (whose religion prohibits women from touching men who are not their husbands) if no male officers are available. In fact, in *Bagly v. Watson* (1983), the court ruled that a woman's right to equal opportunity employment supersedes an inmate's right to privacy (Zimmer, 1986). In a right to privacy case filed by female inmates, the court concluded that when attempts are made to protect privacy by other means, inmates have no right to same-sex guards (*Forts* v. *Ward*). However, since then, the court has recognized that in the case of female inmates with histories as victims of physical assault and sexual abuse, searches and pat-downs by male correctional officers may constitute cruel and unusual punishment and that institutions must find alternative security procedures for these special cases (Weinstein, 1993).

The field of community corrections has done considerably better than both law enforcement and institutional corrections in the recruitment and hiring of a workforce that is balanced in gender. In many probation and parole agencies, the ratio between male and female employees approaches 50–50. However, the predominantly male client population creates problems for both the female officer and her supervisors. The growing emphasis on surveillance and enforcement in probation and parole has highlighted problems ranging from differences in physical strength between female officers and male clients to issues of privacy in the enforcement of certain conditions of release.

Probation and parole officers working the increasingly high-risk felony caseloads may frequently make arrests for violations. Inadequate training of officers in self-defense techniques and the assessment of danger may leave the female officer at greater risk of injury in an arrest. Consequently, many male–female teams have been created for enforcement visits. Also, the transportation of juvenile offenders often requires that same-sex officers be assigned. In rural communities where there are long drives to detention facilities, staffing and scheduling problems often arise when already small numbers of employees are reassigned according to gender and task.

The issue of a client's right to privacy has been raised in discussions of proper procedures for urine testing to detect the use of illicit drugs. Because a positive finding is a common cause for revocation, offenders may be creative in their efforts to deceive officers, often devising an apparatus or technique to produce a "clean" urine sample when they have been using drugs. Official preference for direct observation in the collection of samples poses obvious problems for the female officer. Male officers often complain that predominantly male caseloads and privacy issues have unjustly burdened them with bathroom detail and urine sample surveillance.

Race/Ethnicity and Policing

The Law Enforcement Assistance Act of 1965 led to more proactive recruiting of African Americans, and between 1960 and 1970 the number rose 138%. Although the actual number of African American police has steadily increased (Kuykendall and Burns, 1986), progress is usually measured by percentage of the total police positions held and the degree to which the percentage of minority officers reflects their representation in the general population or workforce. Using this criteria, according to Hacker (1992), in the 15 cities with the largest African American populations in the United States, none had representation on the police force in proportion to the number of African Americans in their area. In addition, across the board, the employment of minority women progresses at a much slower rate than that of African American men (Free, 1996:140).

Some researchers have linked the slow progress of integration in law enforcement with the number of minority applicants having prior criminal records, the fact that many potential minority recruits do not like the police or the profession, and that poor educational backgrounds have meant lower test scores on examinations (Kratkoski and Walker, 1984).

Although many police departments across the country appear to have made significant improvements in obtaining racial balances, there are still many areas of concern. Whereas the number of black officers has increased significantly in the 10 years between 1983 and 1992 in some of the major cities, gains for Hispanic officers have been more modest (Sourcebook, 1995). In addition, minority officers most often hold positions in the lower ranks of the organization and are underrepresented among the rank of sergeant and higher (Pope, 1991; Polk, 1995).

As expected, then, many lawsuits against law enforcement agencies have dealt with promotion rather than hiring. In 1988, the Federal Bureau of Investigation (FBI) lost a discrimination lawsuit filed by Latino agents. Four years later, the FBI settled out of court with African American agents. Rather than admitting to discrimination, the FBI offered 83 African American agents retroactive relief in the form of promotions, back pay, assignments, training, and newly created positions. Many others received payments to offset shortfalls in awards and bonuses. The FBI also accepted plans formulated by outside consultants that would overhaul promotion, evaluation, and reassignment practices.

Race/Ethnicity and Corrections

Dramatic differences in the racial composition of prisoner and officer groups has long been cited as a contributing factor to riots, disturbances, and grievances. At the time of the 1971 Attica riot, approximately three-quarters of the inmates were minority males, yet there were only two minority staff members out of 500 employees. Although the lessons of that and other major riots convinced administrators that a more integrated staff was the key to reducing tensions, some argue that it began the slow and painful process of building a cohesive multicultural workforce (Carroll, 1996). In states such as California and New York, corrections officer unions opposed affirmative action plans and engaged in litigation to block their implementation. As a result, many minority officers formed professional groups to fight discrimination and lobby for inclusion (Jacobs, 1983). However, other research indicates that as in policing, officers often display "working personalities" that find them more alike than different in attitudes toward offenders, the system, and the job (Jurik, 1985). Theorists argue that this is not surprising. The nature of the job tends to attract as well as retain those with similar world views, and those that do assimilate into that shared value structure seem to adapt to the job, whereas those that do not, drop out.

By 1998, African Americans and Hispanics made up 49% of all of those employed in any position in juvenile corrections, 32% of all state correctional officers in adult facilities, and about 25% of the wardens in adult state prisons. The most significant improvements in minority representation can be found in the Federal Bureau of Prisons, where minority group members are now approximately 33% of the workforce (ACA, 1998).

Race/Ethnicity and Gender and the Courts

Unlike law enforcement and corrections, the ability to secure jobs in federal and state courts is often tied to political parties and networks of influence. The positions of one's relatives, the prestige of one's law school, and the contributions made to local and state political committees are all variables in the formula for success in the courts. As minority members find more representation in these various spheres of influence, they will find it easier to gain access to the milestones: good schools, good law schools, good jobs, important connections, opportunities for political involvement, and elections and appointments to the bench.

Today, women represent about 30% of all attorneys and judges (Statistical Abstract of the United States, 1996). Of that number, roughly 2% are of Asian decent, 3% of Hispanic origin, and 6% are identified as African American (1990 Equal Opportunity File). Overall, African Americans, Asian Americans, Hispanics, and Native Americans make up only 12% of the country's law students, less than 8% of the lawyers, 8% of law professors, and 2% of partners in large U.S. law firms (Russell, 1997). In addition, according to the National Black Prosecutor's Association, only 3% of the country's prosecutors and 4% of defense attorneys are African American (Russell, 1997).

Clearly, the careers of federal judges can be traced through their presidential appointments, and we learn much about each administration by the types of justices installed. For example, during the Reagan administration, 92% of the justices appointed to the U.S. Courts of Appeals were male and 93% were white. Under the Bush administration, 80% were male and 89% were white. In the first 3 years of the Clinton administration, 70% were male and 72% were white. With the exception of one Asian male, all of the Nixon and Ford administration's appointees were white males. Although the appointments of Federal District Court Justices yielded a slightly higher percentage of minorities, the Republican years were, by far, much tougher on minority candidates (Sourcebook, 1996).

Summary

Ironically, for the criminal justice system, a single employee lawsuit, because of its scope and impact, often is far more expensive and time consuming than all lawsuits filed by suspects and prisoners combined. However, far more attention and resources seem to be devoted to warding off the latter rather than the former. Historically, criminal justice agencies have not been proactive or consistent in minority hiring efforts. Whereas today many more underrepresented groups enter into the ranks of the workforce through more inclusive hiring policies, the steps toward equality in promotion and assignment opportunities are still slow and inconsistent.

As the criminal justice system becomes more complex, formalized, and professional, employment will be tied in even stronger ways to education, training, and testing. In order to be competitive, candidates from all backgrounds will have to have access to quality education programs that prepare them for the jobs of the future. Agencies should periodically review all of their personnel policies to ensure that procedures are not only legally viable, but also in the spirit of promoting true diversity.

References

American Correctional Association (1998). Directory of juvenile and adult correctional departments, institutions, and paroling authorities. Lanham, MD: ACA.

Bagley v. Watson. 579 F.Supp. 1099 (Federal District Court, Oregon) 11 July 1983.

Balkin, J. (1988). Why policemen don't like policewomen? *Journal of Police Science and Administration, 16(1),* 29–37.

Bloch, P. B. and Anderson, D. (1974). *Policewomen on patrol: Final report.* Washington, DC: The Police Foundation.

Carroll, L. (1996). Racial conflict. In M. McShane and F. P. Williams (Eds.), *Encyclopedia of American prisons,* pp. 377–381. New York: Garland.

City of Richmond v. J. A. Croson. 488 US 321 (1977).

Doerner, W. and Patterson, E. (1996). The influence of race and gender upon rookie evaluations of their field training officers. In D. Kenney and G. Cordner (Eds.), *Managing police personnel,* pp. 79–91. Cincinnati, OH: Anderson.

Dothard v. Rawlinson. 433 U.S. 321 (1977).

Free, M. (1996). *African Americans and the criminal justice system.* New York: Garland.

Forts v. Ward. 621 F. 2d 1210 (1980).

Griggs v. Duke Power Co. 401 U.S. 424 (1971).

Gunther v. Iowa. 462 F. Supp 952 (1979).

Hacker, A. (1992). *Two nations: Black and white, separate, hostile, unequal.* New York: Scribner's.

Hawkins, R. and Alpert, G. (1989). *American prison systems.* Englewood Cliffs, NJ: Prentice Hall.

Jacobs, J. (1983). *New perspectives on prisons and imprisonment.* Ithaca, NY: Cornell University Press.

Johns, C. (1998a). Supreme Court poised to kill affirmative action. *The Arizona Republic,* 11 January, H3.

———. (1998b). Beyond affirmative action: Debate ignores depth of racial divide. *The Arizona Republic,* 11 January, H1–2.

Jurik, N. (1985). Individual and organizational determinants of correctional officer attitudes toward inmates. *Criminology, 23,* 523–539.

Kratcoski, P. and Walker, D. (1984). Recruiting minority officers. In P. Kratcoski and D. Walker (Eds.), *Criminal justice in America,* pp. 197–201. New York: Random House.

Kuykendall, J. and Burns, D. (1986). The black police officer: An historical perspective. *Journal of Contemporary Criminal Justice, 1,* 4–12.

Leger, K. (1997). Public perceptions of female police officers on patrol. *American Journal of Criminal Justice, 21(2),* 231–249.

Lord, L. K. (1986). A comparison of male and female peace officers' stereotypic perceptions of women and women peace officers. *Journal of Police Science and Administration, 14,* 83–96.

Martin, S. E. (1991). The effectiveness of affirmative action: The case of women in policing. *Justice Quarterly, 8(4),* 489–504.

———. (1993). Female officers on the move? A status report on women in policing. In R. G. Dunham and G. P. Alpert (Eds.), *Critical issues in policing,* pp. 327–347. Prospect Heights, IL: Waveland Press.

McDowell, J. (1992). Are women better cops? *Time, 139(7),* 70–72.

National Center for Women and Policing (1998). *Equality denied: The status of women in policing.* Washington, DC: Feminist Majority Foundation.

Oppenheimer, D. B. (1996). Understanding affirmative action. *Hastings Constitutional Law Quarterly, 23,* 926–973.

Polk, O. E. (1995). The effects of ethnicity on career paths of advanced/specialized law enforcement officers. *American Journal of Police, 18(1),* 1–21.

Pollock, J. (1986). *Sex and supervision.* Westport, CT: Greenwood.

Pope, T. (1991). Department lags in hiring practices despite 10-year old court agreement. *The San Bernardino Sun,* 26 May, 12A.

Remmington, P. (1981). *Policing: The occupation and the introduction of female officers.* Washington, DC: University Press of America.

Russell, M. M. (1997). Beyond "sellouts" and "race cards": Black attorneys and the straightjacket of legal practice. *Michigan Law Review, 95(4),* 766–794.

Sedmak, N. and Vidas, C. (1994). *Primer on equal employment opportunity,* 6th ed. Washington, DC: BNA Books.

Simon, R. and Simon, J. (1988). Female C.O.s—Legitimate authority. *Corrections Today, 50(5),* August, 132.

Stokes, L. and Scott, J. (1996). Affirmative action and selected minority groups in law enforcement. *Journal of Criminal Justice, 24(1),* 29–38.

UCLA's Higher Education Research Institute (1998). *The American freshman.* Cited in E. Woo, Poll finds disparate views of state of education. *Los Angeles Times,* 14 January, B2.

United States Bureau of the Census (1990). Equal Opportunity File. Washington, DC.

U.S. Department of Justice (1987). *Report to the attorney general. Redefining discrimination: Disparate impact and the institutionalization of affirmative action.* Washington, DC: U.S. Government Printing Office

U.S. Department of Justice, Bureau of Justice Statistics (1995). *Sourcebook of criminal justice statistics.* Washington, DC: Department of Justice.

U.S. Department of Justice, Bureau of Justice Statistics (1991). *Census of local jails.* Washington, DC: U.S. Government Printing Office.

U.S. Department of Justice, Bureau of Justice Statistics (1996). *Sourcebook of criminal justice statistics.* Washingotn, DC: Department of Justice.

U.S. Government Printing Office (1996). *Statistical Abstract of the United States.* Washington, DC.

Weinstein, H. (1993). Court limits searches of jailed women. *Los Angeles Times,* 26 February, A3, A28.

Weiss, R. J. (1997). *We want jobs: A history of affirmative action.* New York: Garland.

Williams, L. F. (1996). Tracing the politics of affirmative action. In G. E. Curry (Ed.), *The affirmative action debate,* pp. 241–257. Redding, MA: Addison-Wesley.

Zimmer, L. (1986). *Women guarding men.* Chicago: University of Chicago Press.

Zupan, L. (1986). Gender-related differences in correctional officers' perceptions and attitudes. *Journal of Criminal Justice, 14(4),* 349–361.

17 Educating for Change

Cultural Awareness Training for Criminal Justice

LARRY A. GOULD

In the summer of 1997, Abner Louima, a Haitian immigrant, was arrested outside a Brooklyn nightclub after a fight had broken out. When Louima protested his arrest, the arresting officers stopped twice on the way to the station house and beat him with their fists. Once at the station house, Louima was taken to a men's room, where his pants were removed and he was assaulted with the handle of a toilet plunger. First, the plunger was shoved into his rectum and then into his mouth, breaking his teeth. All the while, the police officers were shouting racial slurs at him. Later, Louima was taken to a hospital with a puncture in his small intestine and injuries to his bladder. While the New York Police Department quickly investigated the case, identified the offending officers, and took swift punitive action, the fact remains that one of the causes of this incident was the cultural insensitivity of the officers. When the officers were faced with an assault on their own cultural sensibilities—anger because some of the clubgoers had fought with the police—they responded with violence to this apparent attack on the status quo.

Finding a solution to discriminatory, harassing, insensitive, and/or uncivil behavior through training or education is a complex task involving complex and emotion-laden issues that will continue to cost justice agencies in terms of time and resources. Not addressing the issue will cost justice agencies in terms of litigation, loss of status in the community, loss of employee productivity, and loss of diversity, leading to continued insensitivity on the part of the organization. Through the use of a multipronged approach that addresses the needs of the diverse group of service providers, victims, and offenders, the likelihood of success is increased.

This chapter focuses on three related areas concerning the applicability of cultural diversity education in criminal justice. First, there is a brief review that provides a historical context that relates the problems of the past to those of today. Second, there is a review of some of the points of resistance to cultural diversity training. Finally, there is a review of some of the techniques used to overcome that resistance. When discussing diversity training, it is important to consider much more than just race and gender. In fact, to focus on only race and gender simply serves to alienate those whom you most need to reach, thus dooming the training to inevitable failure. In this chapter, as is the case with the remainder of the book, the term *diversity* is used in its broadest sense so as to include age, socioeconomic status, culture, gender, race, sexual orientation, religion, and ethnicity. The overall approach taken is to recognize how similar we are while not forgetting that we should also be respectful of our group and individual differences. This means that, to effect any change, we must use a multipronged approach to address those issues that continue to keep us separate and thus mistrustful and disrespectful of each other.

This chapter starts with five overlapping assumptions that have been drawn from previous research. The first is that a diverse justice system is a more effective justice system. The second assumption is that an increased understanding of diversity issues can begin with education or training that, in part, asks people to question how and why they have come to hold certain opinions. The third assumption is that the method of achieving a justice system that is sensitive to diversity is equally as important as the message being conveyed. The fourth assumption is that, in teaching cultural diversity, one may at times speak in general terms; however, particular attention must be paid to teaching not only about the differences *between* groups, but also about the differences *within* groups. The fifth assumption is that attitudes concerning cultural sensitivity/diversity can be changed if the methods and techniques of delivering the message are appropriate. This assumption focuses on those factors and/or characteristics of the audience to whom the message is directed. The impact of these five assumptions on the teaching of cultural diversity are more fully discussed after a brief historical review of the attempts to sensitize justice systems' personnel to the different cultures in which they work.

Historical Context

It is certainly a historical truism that various groups of service providers, victims, and offenders have all suffered disparate treatment as a result of a lack of sensitivity to differences by members of the dominant group(s) in the justice system. Whether those differences result from gender, race, ethnicity, religion, region of the country, or any of the other things that make us different as groups, research suggests that the negative impact of groupings could be reduced, if not eliminated, through the use of proper training or education for justice system service providers at the appropriate time. It is also true that the methods by which we have brought attention to diversity issues and the methods by which we have set about providing solutions to these issues have changed over time.

Historically, the various components of the justice system are replete with failed attempts to increase the sensitivity level of the service providers toward minority groups,[1] through either education or training. It should be noted at this point that the term *justice system* refers not only to police, corrections, and the courts, but also to other members of the system, including lawyers, social workers, and victims.

Until recently, the police, courts, and corrections have been largely unsympathetic to the differing needs not only of the various "client" communities they serve, but also of many of the employees within the system. In fact, the three parts of the justice system have often been openly hostile to those individuals or groups who have either sought membership in or needed the services of the justice system (Martin and Jurik, 1996; Skolnick and Fyfe, 1993). Walker, 1992, for example, suggests that it was commonly believed by many police officers during the late 1800s and early 1900s that the immigrant population was largely composed of "the mentally and morally unfit of Europe" (1929:27), and points out that, "Special training in race relations was virtually unthinkable in an era when most police departments offered no formal training of any sort" (Walker, 1992:166).

Although diversity considerations in the training of justice system personnel have varied in importance since the mid-1800s, the message to justice personnel has also changed over time. For instance, it was not that long ago that police departments had police–community relations units. These units usually consisted of two or three officers in a medium-size department. One of the stated goals of these units was to achieve a more harmonious relationship with minority communities through contact with the community leaders. It should be emphasized that there was little effort on the part of the members of these units to contact members of minority communities other than the supposed leaders. Another of the stated goals of such a unit was to help other officers to transcend the differences between the individuals they were sworn to protect by reducing the separation between the police and the community (Miller and Braswell, 1983). This remains one of the goals of community-based policing today; however, the methods of achieving that goal are much different than in the past. A third stated goal was to apprize the community leaders of the reason for certain police actions in the community. In other words, to inform the community leaders of the police side of any story in a sometimes thinly veiled attempt to deflect criticism of the department. It was very rarely the role of the police–community relations unit to attempt to understand the inner workings of the community. In short, informa-

---

[1] For the purposes of this chapter, the author is content with the definition of *minority group* provided by Louis Wirth (1945:347): "A group of people who, because of their physical or cultural characteristics, are singled out from others in the society in which they live for differential and unequal treatment and who therefore regard themselves as objects of collective discrimination." The author recognizes that there may be some problems with this definition; however, those arguments are better left for other discussions.

tion control was paramount. It is not being suggested here that the police–community relations units have been completely abandoned; they have not. Their role has, however, changed over time, to the point that they are now more involved in planning and research concerning issues of police responsiveness to community needs.

The justice system continues to suffer from a tendency to look for quick and simple solutions to problems that are deeply rooted in our social structures and communities (Hennessy, 1994). By this, we mean that the justice system has a tendency to be reactive and responsive to problems using short-term solutions rather than attempting to be proactive and providing longer-term problem solving. Thus, attempts on the part of justice agencies to make the necessary changes that would lead to a true understanding of diversity were, of course, doomed to failure.

There were five major errors made by the agencies. The first was their failure to truly understand diversity. Protection of the *status quo,* or of a particular and narrowly defined standard of living, was often at the forefront of enforcement efforts. A part of this problem was that the police were more interested in "bringing" members of the minority community "up" to the standards of the white community, as opposed to understanding that being different does not necessarily equate with being "wrong." As this writer heard so many officers say time and again in the 1970s and 1980s, "Why can't you people learn to act more like white people?" or, equally offensive, "Let's find a way to keep the 'natives' happy."

The second error was the inability to distinguish between one minority community and another; that, is to recognize that there may be different communities of African Americans, Hispanics, or other minority groups. This often resulted in one or two so-called community leaders being identified as the spokespeople for a large number of people who were really of different communities. This often led to a "one approach fits all problems" method of problem solving.

The third error concerned the method used in training the new service providers. The course of study was often structured in such a way as to afford various minority representatives an opportunity to address rookie trainees or in-service officers. This meeting usually took place in a training seminar in which there was either a one-way monologue delivered by the minority representative or a confrontational dialog between the minority representative and the trainees. The goal was to induce a change in trainee attitudes by having them learn more about the minority representatives' points of view (Hennessy, 1994). This approach usually resulted in a strident and emotional challenge to participants that often led to a deepening of their anger and resentment (Work, 1989). Even when possible avenues for discussion developed, discussion did not occur because the various participants had by then become too emotionally entrenched in their own views.

The fourth error was and continues to be that administrators in general, and justice system administrators in particular, have made the mistake of primarily using minorities and women to teach cultural diversity. It is important that the best people are used regardless of their race or gender (Hennessy, 1994). It is also important to prevent the perception of "a vested interest" on the part of these groups.

The fifth error often made by administrators has been to rely simply on the development of rules and punishment for violation of the rules. Hemphill and Haines (1997) suggest that diversity training has failed to eliminate discrimination and harassment because it has focused on *awareness, understanding, and appreciation* of differences. Hemphill and Haines (1997) do acknowledge that it is useful to recognize and acknowledge unique differences, but they contend that it is far more essential to address effective and appropriate workplace behaviors, often through enforcement of rules by use of punitive measures. Given the general psychological profile of justice agency workers, particularly that of the police officers, Hemphill and Haines' (1997) suggestions hold some interest. Although some disagree (Barlow and Barlow, 1993, 1994; Gould, 1996a) with Hemphill and Haines' single-track approach, there are some useful tactics to be learned from their research in terms of errors that have been often been credited to the failure of cultural diversity courses. Hemphill and Haines suggest that the failure of the current form of cultural diversity training results from:

- Participants finding many training programs to be divisive, disturbing, and counterproductive;
- Diversity trainers were often inexperienced and ineffective;
- Minority groups' expectations were raised, and then disappointed;
- White males were often stereotyped and blamed;
- There was reverse discrimination and reverse stereotyping;
- Sensitive and personal issues were brought out in hostile public settings;
- Participants experience unnecessary anxiety and emotional upheaval;
- Increased distrust was engendered;
- Many participants were resistant to attending further diversity training programs; and,
- Little or no transfer of learning took place from teaching about differences to changing discriminatory and harassing behaviors. (1997:5–6)

The Effect of Psychosocial Development on Minority Relations

Police, courts, and corrections are generally conservative in nature and they tend to have a *status quo* orientation, both of which are reflected in the culture of the organization and, to a certain extent, the culture of the dominant members of society. It is important to any attempt at changing the attitudes and behaviors of justice system personnel to understand the organization and individual cultures with which a trainer or educator will be dealing. Failure to take the psychosocial variables into consideration in developing an approach to teaching cultural diversity will certainly decrease the likelihood of success and may even decrease the likelihood of success for later attempts.

There are three major theoretical approaches to the question of the possible existence of an identifiable organizational culture that have an impact on the individual development and individual personality that a person brings to the job. For the purposes of this discussion, the development of the police personality is used as an example of psychosocial development. This discussion could also be applied to correctional officers, probation/parole officers, judges, prosecutors, and even defense attorneys.

The first approach to understanding the police personality views police departments as organic social systems created by and composed of human beings: They are microcosms of the society at large and provide a sociocultural milieu in which people interact with and influence one another as they pursue common goals and objectives (More, 1992). The individual police officer is the fundamental subsystem around which the police organization is built. Individuals consist of interdependent physiological and psychosocial systems that work in concert with environmental factors to produce distinctive behavior. The dynamic interdependence between the human police officer and the environmental factors (the public and the department) helps to account for the complexity of the behavior of the officer (Roberg and Kuykendall, 1990).

According to this approach, officers bring an already existing set of attitudes to their work, but those attitudes have not necessarily been set in actual behavior. It is the interaction between the officers and their environment that generates the actual behavior of the officers.

The second approach explains cynical, bigoted, indifferent, racist, authoritarian, and/or brutal behavior on the part of police officers by positing that policing attracts individuals who already possess these qualities (Balch, 1992; Smith, Visher, and Davidson, 1984). The adherents to this view suggest that the "power of the badge" attracts those individuals who seek power, have a poor self-image, or have hidden agendas.

The third approach explains aberrant police behavior by a combination of the previous two theories. Those advocating this position suggest that some individuals who seek to become police officers already possess those qualities that make them cynical, bigoted, indifferent, authoritarian, and/or brutal in nature, whereas other police officers adopt one or more of these qualities as a result of the policing environment (Roberg and Kuykendall, 1990; More and Unsinger, 1987). This body of research further suggests that those individuals possessing these qualities prior to beginning a career in policing generally become even more negative as a result of the policing experience (More, 1992; Roberg and Kuykendall, 1990). It should be noted, however, that these officers are also more likely to drop out of policing in the first 5 years of the job experience (Evan, Coman, and Stanley, 1992; Terry, 1981; Wright et al., 1980).

Consistent with any of these explanations for poor police attitudes, particularly toward minority groups, is research that suggests that the problem that exists between the public and the police is the result of a growing view, on the part of the police, that the public *is* the problem (Walker, 1992; U.S. Government, 1990). Researchers have also reported that police officers are typically suspicious, aloof, cynical, and authoritarian in their dealings with the public, particularly minorities (Evans, Coman, and Stanley, 1992; Kroes, 1985; Violanti and Marshall, 1983). As far back as 1967, Niederhoffer suggested that police officers were more cynical than the public in general. This cynicism, according to Niederhoffer, explains in part the indifference, alienation, bigotry, and brutality with which the police sometimes treat the public. It should be noted at this point that a "healthy" dose of cynicism is necessary for the survival of the officer, both mentally and physically. It is when the level of cynicism reaches such a point that it has almost complete control over how the officer views the world that the cynicism becomes a problem. Niederhoffer was criticized for not considering other explanations and for not properly controlling for the length of service of the officers in his research. Research suggests, however, that cynicism remains one of the critical variables in determining police behavior (Balch, 1992). The more cynical officers are, the less likely they are to be willing to change their perception of the world. If anything, they are going to be heavily invested in maintaining the *status quo* with which they have become comfortable.

Continuing to use police officers as an example, research into Myers–Briggs Cognitive Styles, based in Jungian Personality Type Theory and data from other cognitive studies, suggests that the majority (65%) of police officers prefer to take in information and process it through their five senses rather than through intuition. This means that they are "bound in reality"; they are not likely to be convinced by anything but reasoning based on tangible facts. This is one reason that appeals to the heart, a method often used in older forms of teaching police–community relations, may appear to be too "touchy–feely" (Hennessy, 1994).

To fully understanding how the solutions can work to improve the levels of sensitivity to cultural diversity, it is necessary to understand the emotions surrounding this issue. Gould (1996a,b; 1997) found that more experienced white male officers and, to some extent, African American male officers felt that cultural diversity training was an attempt to emasculate policing or to turn police officers into social workers. The intensity of these feelings was expressed in a series of intensive interviews. As one African American male officer said, "Sure, I will try this stuff for a while. If it works, fine; if not, screw it." A white male officer was a bit more vehement in his view, "This is bunch of crap. Will it be useful? Hell, no. While I am doing this social work shit on somebody, they are trying to figure out how to fuck me or the system. What you people need to do is spend more time making the asshole learn the rules. I already know them." Another experienced officer (white male) commented:

OFFICER: "Yeah, I am informed. I am informed that nobody cares about us. It is also clear to me that some of the other people here liked to hear this stuff."

INTERVIEWER: "Which other people?"

OFFICER: "The blacks and the women."

INTERVIEWER: "What stuff do they like to hear?"

OFFICER: "That policing should be something other than what it is. Man, we are supposed to throw people's asses in jail, not treat them like a social work case."

INTERVIEWER: "Who doesn't care about you?"

OFFICER: "The people, the female cops and the blacks."

It appeared that many of the white male and some of the African American male officers felt that their position and behavior as officers was being challenged and/or changed not only by having to take this class, but by some of the actions of the African American and female officers also attending this class. As part of a successful solution to getting people to understand the need for cultural diversity training, it is important to remember that some individuals will be asked to redefine who they are in the context of their jobs. As previously noted, some individuals come to a career with a preconceived notion of what the job is about. These notions or images are defined in part by the individual's personality. Other individuals develop much of their "working personality" on the job; that is, their personality is impacted by their experiences on the job. When the correctness of some of the negative behaviors that are a part of the individual's working personality are called into question, the individual has to either continue to suffer criticism or change the behavior, thus redefining who they are.

It should be noted that Gould (1996a) found that cadets, less-experienced officers, and female police officers (both African American and white) were much more receptive to cultural diversity training and they also recognized that the training could have some very positive outcomes for them as police officers. For example, one white female officer stated:

OFFICER: "Of course the course will be useful to me as an officer. I learned two things. First, I learned that just because a person is different does not mean that they are wrong. Second, I learned that I don't have to act like the meanest person on the block to get many of the people that I deal with to do what I want them to do. I just have to figure out how to understand them and get them to understand me."

INTERVIEWER: "What else did you learn that might be useful?"

OFFICER: "I guess that I learned that I don't have to be one of the guys to be a good cop. I can be me."

An African American female officer, who apparently had been the brunt of some abuse on the job, commented:

OFFICER: "Those motherfuckers just don't get it, this is for them."

INTERVIEWER: "Which motherfuckers are you referring to?"

OFFICER: "Those dumb white boys."

INTERVIEWER: "What is it that they don't get?"

OFFICER: "That this training is for them. It will help them if they would let it work. They are the reason that we are here, the way they treat people."

INTERVIEWER: "How else would it help?"

OFFICER: If those guys got enough of this training they would quit treating people bad. Maybe they would even be nicer to me."

Given the wide range of responses of the officers quoted, it should be apparent that an understanding of the personality of the justice system service provider is vitally important to the success of any program of study intended to change the attitudes of the service provider toward minority groups (Gould, 1996a). Gould (1996a), based on a study of the effect of a training course on cultural sensitivity, suggests that the teaching of cultural diversity also means the "unteaching" of some already existing culturally insensitive attitudes and behaviors. A change in behavior will not generally result from sitting through one cultural diversity course. Gould's work suggests it would be easier to teach tricks to a "new pup" (new police officers) than to an "old dog" (experienced police officers) unless the trainer and educators learn to respect the needs of the "old dog." The respect comes from an understanding of the life experiences of the established criminal justice service provider. Gould (1996a) suggested that, as a matter of policy: (1) the training of experienced officers should include the training of administrators in the same classroom setting; (2) experienced officers' training should include more time for venting of frustrations centering on the cultural diversity training; (3) cultural diversity training should begin early in an officer's career; (4) the training should be reinforced throughout the officer's career; and (5) the training should be aimed toward explanation and discovery concerning cultural differences, rather than appearing simply to place blame for police–community conflict on the individual officer.

The Beginning of a Solution

Barlow and Barlow (1993, 1994) and Gould (1996a) found patterns of behavior similar to those discussed in the previous section, in response to cultural diversity training among police officers; however, they viewed the criticisms as a springboard for refining rather than discarding the training. In particular, Barlow and Barlow (1993, 1994) and Gould (1996a) suggest that channeled venting, which results from the criticisms listed by Hemphill and Haines (1997), actually leads to healthy discussion in which behavior can be changed.

Despite the limited view presented by Hemphill and Haines (1997), they do provide useful additions to the "tool belt" of the diversity trainer. First, it is necessary to stop denying that discrimination and harassment, based on some ascribed or achieved characteristic(s), exists within justice organizations or between justice organizations and other groups. Second, in addition to a focus on awareness, understanding, and appreciating differences, there should be a focus on changing workplace behaviors. Third, there must be a commitment to a plan of action that, at a minimum, includes: (1) the establishment and enforcement of a zero-tolerance policy for discrimination and harassment practices, not only within the organization, but also as employees come in contact with both victims and offenders; (2) development of organization-wide behavior standards that provide specific guidelines concerning acceptable and unacceptable behaviors; and (3) the establishment of a continuing workplace relationship skills training program.

Barlow and Barlow (1994) noted that there is no "silver bullet" solution to the problem of teaching cultural diversity issues; however, they do provide a set of goals that are critically important to even the partial success of any program intended to improve the level of sensitivity of justice personnel toward minority issues. These goals include: (1) understanding the importance of power and image in maintaining a professional reputation for justice organizations; (2) understanding the contributions and life styles of the various racial, cultural, and economic groups of the served communities; (3) recognizing and dealing with biases, discrimination, and prejudices that affect both the organizations and the citizens served; (4) understanding professional behaviors of justice system employees that contribute to the development of the self-esteem of the community residents and that establish positive interpersonal relations within organizations; and (5) respecting diversity and personal rights.

Success in teaching a course of study on cultural diversity starts with the formula suggested by Barlow and Barlow (1994). There should be six clearly defined components: (1) selling the course, (2) examination of prejudices, (3) dissemination of information, (4) development of personal strategies, (5) discussion of supervisory issues, and (6) ventilation periods. The first block of instruction is intended to explain why the course is important to the officer and the police department. The second block involves definition and examination of personal prejudices. The third block involves dissemination of information on the current state of police–minority relations and includes a historical-to-present view of the relations. The fourth block involves the development of personal strategies directed at increased understanding of cultural diversity. The fifth block is directed at supervisory and management issues. The final block involves a ventilation period in which the officers can respond either to the material presented during the course or to the course itself.

Although there is no such thing as a cookbook for the delivery of a course on cultural diversity or cultural sensitivity to justice professionals, it is possible to synthesize the works of Hennessy, Barlow and Barlow, Work, and Gould. By synthesizing these works, it becomes possible to categorize the necessary parts of training into three areas: (1) Those components necessary for any type of cultural diversity training, such as avoiding accusatory language; (2) those components that are specifically about communication and adult learning, such as allowing the students to bring their life experiences into the classroom; and (3) those components specific to justice system personnel, such as discussing the image of power that the police bring to any meeting with members of the community. In general terms, these components emphasize the need in cultural diversity training for awareness, understanding, and appreciation of individual and group differences, rather than for the type of approach suggested by Hemphill and Haines (1997), which focuses on behavior changes on the part of practitioners resulting in part from the development and enforcement of rules (punishment). Hemphill and Haines' (1997) approach is discussed in greater detail in the following section.

General Components of Cultural Diversity Training

One of the first steps that should be a part of any course of study on cultural diversity or cultural sensitivity training is to assist the participants in examination and consideration of how their perceptions about other cultures and people were developed and how this affects their own behavior (Work, 1989). This can be done by asking the participants to assess their own ancestry and/or by an examination of how stereotyping works to create perceptions of both individuals and groups. Before getting too far into a discussion of cultural diversity or the effect of stereotyping, it would be helpful to remember that the very discussion of cultural differences may cause some people to be offended; thus, a discussion concerning the rules of conduct in the class, such as mutual respect, is important.

Another key to teaching cultural diversity is a recognition that learning about individuals and groups cannot take place when the participants refuse to discuss or acknowledge both differences and similarities among cultures. Usually it is best to start a discussion along the lines of those things that the various participants (regardless of whether present) have in common. A discussion of common interests, shared goals, and shared means often helps a class to learn to discuss issues in a less heated manner.

Virtually every writer on the topic of cultural diversity training has commented that administrators and managers must make a long-term commitment to offering courses on cultural diversity. In particular, line personnel often become frustrated with one-shot training, which is viewed as punishment by the officers; thus, little is actually accomplished in terms of changing behavior (Gould, 1996a; Hennessy, 1994).

The instructor and administrators/managers must be aware that success in changing either an attitude or a behavior comes in only small increments, and that actual change occurs over long periods with repeated reinforcement; thus, the need for repeated training that continually reinforces previous periods of training. It is important to remember that simply getting participants, particularly those in the justice system, to think about some of the issues presented in a cultural diversity class should be considered a significant success.

The instructor must work with managers to ensure that their subordinates will be held responsible for their actions (Gould, 1996a; Hennessy, 1994; Hemphill and Haines, 1997). Organizational policy regarding bias and prejudice must be clear and enforceable, and must be vigorously enforced and supported throughout the agency (Hennessy, 1994).

One tactic that has proved to be successful is to conduct classes that include a cross-section of all ranks within the agency (Gould, 1996b). This allows for the discussion of problems and potential solutions while many levels of participants are present.

Communication/Learning Training

To be successful in understanding the nuances of cultural diversity, justice system personnel must be afforded the opportunity to understand the dynamics of cross-cultural communication. Thus, there is a need to develop an awareness of communicative, analytical, and interpretive skills that aid in maintaining communications with both the current and changing populations. The process of understanding how to communicate with other cultures often begins with an understanding of how our behavior is perceived by other people. Thus, it is important that some time be spent on discussing the ways in which our presentation of self can facilitate or inhibit our communication with others. To facilitate this discussion, instructors must pay particular attention to helping course participants achieve an understanding of how both large and small behaviors can positively or negatively effect outcomes (see Chapter 18 by Nielsen).

The instructor should facilitate discussion on the need to understand the difference between intentions and behavior. Police, probation/parole, and correctional officers have all been immersed in the idea that their jobs are dangerous. There is nothing false in this position; however, it is important to note that within different cultures the same behaviors may take on different meanings; thus, when the officer behaves in a manner intended to protect him/herself, that behavior may elicit misunderstandings in others. The officers are not expected to change their behavior, but should be trained to understand and sometimes expect negative responses.

A brief review of Mehrahian's (1987) work on nonverbal communication would be of value to the cultural diversity class. Mehrahian (1987) suggests that body language sends about 55% of a message, that tone of voice sends about 38% of a message, and that actual words send only about 7% of a message. The instructor could use videos and other tools to provide examples of how this works.

At all times it must be remembered that the students in a cultural diversity education class are adults. Adults communicate ideas and learn much differently than do children, teenagers, or even young adults who have not had much life experience. A review of Arnold and McClure (1994) provides many of the keys to the principles of adult learning, some examples of which are provided here:

■ The trainer must be willing to challenge the participants' tendency to think in ways that may cause hard feelings.

■ The use of small groups and work exercises often facilitates the flow of ideas. Discussion between group participants is an important part of the learning phase.

■ Life experiences are an important part of the adult learning process; thus, it is important to use these experiences to the advantage of the learning process.

■ Do not set the instructor up as the "expert." The instructor should be a facilitator of communication and a communicator of knowledge.

■ Adult students tend to learn best when the subject matter is kept focused. In the case of teaching police officers, for example, the instructor should focus on how additional information might provide insights and knowledge into different cultures, which in turn could make their jobs easier.

It is not uncommon for justice system personnel to see cultural, ethnic, religious, or gender structures with which they come into contact as being dysfunctional because of differences in the manner of communication among cultures and among individuals within the culture. For example, many police officers are at a loss to understand the extended family structure commonly found among some of the racial and ethnic groups with which they come into contact. To help officers understand the importance of other cultures' extended family structures, it might be of value to discuss how the officers feel when they hear that another officer has been injured or killed.

Criminal Justice–Specific Training

In developing tactics that are specific to justice personnel, it is necessary to understand who they are and, to some extent, how they have been socialized. In other words, it is necessary to be sensitive to the social and psychological characteristics of the audience.

For the most part, justice system personnel are businesslike and, if forced to choose between tact and truthfulness, they usually choose truthfulness. Likewise, justice system personnel are usually not convinced by anything other than reasoning based on solid facts. In view of this, when teaching cultural awareness or gender issues it is important to remember that the information must be presented in a factual, rational, concrete, and practical manner for it to be considered for discussion. In other words, justice system personnel need to be informed in a pragmatic, logical, and objective manner of the importance of learning about other cultures (Hennessy, 1992).

The instructor must take into consideration that justice system personnel make decisions in vastly different ways than do other groups. This means that the police, for example, tend to view a situation in a much different light than do the media, the community, or even other justice system personnel (Hennessy, 1992). It is important that the instructor have as much information as possible on the way in which police differ from other groups, thus increasing the likelihood that the police will see the instructor as being legitimate.

The instructor must be aware of the fact that justice system personnel, particularly police officers, frequently feel that they are alone as the primary protectors of justice and that the other components of the justice system are working at cross-purposes with the police (Walker, 1992). The instructor must encourage students to have the courage to speak out against the derogatory comments and discriminatory actions made by other members of the justice system that bring discredit to the criminal justice system.

The instructor must be aware that asking justice system personnel to examine and possibly change closely held beliefs and prejudices will mostly likely result in an emotionally negative situation. Thus, the venue must allow for venting of emotion and frustration (Gould, 1996a).

Because of the manner in which many police officers tend to think, it is important to note that change in a community is continual. This means that information on cultural diversity must be provided on a continual basis (Hennessy, 1994). It is of equal importance that the officers understand that the specifics they learn today may be of little value some years from now, but that the concepts of cultural sensitivity instruction are applicable far into the future (Gould, 1996b).

Even a cursory review of either the plan of attack favored by Barlow and Barlow (1993, 1994) or by Gould (1996a), as compared to that favored by Hemphill and Haines (1997), suggests much overlap and certainly some complementary components. Adopting pertinent parts advocated by both groups increases the likelihood of a successful implementation of a multipronged approach.

Although the focus has thus far been on the police, it should be remembered that only through court orders have prisoners been allowed to practice in a limited way some of their religious beliefs; that, until recently, women probation officers were rarely allowed to work on cases other than those of juveniles or other women; and that women and minorities could not attend many law schools and, therefore, could not be judges. Criminal justice agencies have systematically discriminated against women and minorities in employment, assignments, promotions, and social acceptance. Many white males have not, and do not, consider women and minorities to be their equals in terms of either capabilities or competencies (Roberg and Kuykendall, 1997). These attitudes are based on myths that can only be debunked through education and training. The remaining vestiges of these attitudes can now only be attributed to the control of power that is so closely associated with membership in the justice system.

Although there is no single solution to discriminatory, harassing, insensitive, and/or uncivil behavior; training or education of the type described in this chapter will advance the efforts of justice agencies to become more sensitive to these issues, thus reducing their cost to justice agencies in terms of time and resources. As mentioned in the introduction, not addressing the issue will continue to cost justice agencies in terms of litigation, loss of status in the community, loss of employee productivity, and loss of diversity, leading to continued insensitivity on the part of the organization. The multipronged approach described here increases the likelihood of successfully addressing the needs of the diverse group of service providers, victims, and offenders. Ignoring the totality of concerns outlined in this chapter and favoring one set of solutions over another will certainly reduce the likelihood of success. Cultural diversity trainers/educators must emphasize awareness, understanding, and appreciation of individual and group differences, particularly of the participants, while paying attention to the more tactical solutions of stopping the denial that discrimination and harassment exist and developing a plan of action that promotes a focus on changing behavior and a commitment to the development of a zero-tolerance policy. The policy must include the development and "training to" of standards of acceptable and unacceptable behavior and relationship skills training.

Although much of this chapter focuses on training as opposed to education, it should be remembered that it is important for future justice system administrators, such as students taking this course, to be constantly and consistently exposed to the concepts discussed in this chapter. The type of insensitivity, hatred, and misunderstanding of others that leads to a lack of tolerance for cultural diversity is intergenerationally transmitted during the socialization of new justice system personnel by older justice system personnel. To break this cycle, the problem of insensitivity to differences must be brought to light and discussed in the college classroom as well as in justice system training sessions. In addition, the information contained in this chapter should forewarn and, thus, prepare students for some of the problems they will face as potential justice system personnel.

References

Arnold, W. E. and McClure, L. (1994). *Communication training and development*. Prospect Heights, IL: Waveland Press.

Barlow, D. and Barlow, M. (1993). Cultural diversity training in criminal justice: A progressive or conservative reform? *Social Justice, 20* 3–4.

————. (1994). Cultural sensitivity rediscovered: Developing training strategies for police officers. *Justice Professional, 9*, 2.

Balch, R. W. (1992). The police personality: Fact or fiction? *The Journal of Criminal Law, 63(1)*, 106–119.

Carpenter, B. N. and Raza, S. M. (1987). Personality characteristics of police applicants: Comparisons across subgroups and with other populations. *Journal of Police Science and Administration, 15*(1), 10–17.

Evans, B. J., Coman, C. J., and Stanley, R. O. (1992). The police personality: Type A behavior and trait anxiety. *Journal of Criminal Justice, 20*, 420–441.

Goldstein, H. (1990). *Problem-oriented policing*. New York: McGraw-Hill.

Gould, L. A. (1996a). Can old dogs be taught new tricks? Teaching cultural diversity to police officers. *Police Studies, 19*, 122–147.

————. (1996b). The effect of policing on the psychological characteristics of women police officers. Paper presented at the Annual Meeting of the Western Social Science Association, Reno, NV.

Gould, L. and Funk, S. (1994). In search of the police personality: First report on the findings of a longitudinal study. Paper presented at the Annual Meeting of the American Society of Criminology Meeting, Miami, FL.

Harring, S. L. (1983). *Policing a class society: The experience of American cities, 1865–1915*. New Brunswick, NJ: Rutgers University Press.

Hemphill, H. and Haines, R. (1997). *Discrimination, harassment, and the failure of diversity training.* Westport, CT: Quorum Books.

Hennessy, S. (1994). Cultural sensitivity training. In J. E. Hendricks and B. Byers (Eds.), *Multicultural perspectives in criminal justice and criminology,* pp. 234–267. Springfield, IL: Charles Thomas.

Hennessy, S. M. (1992). *Thinking cop–feeling cop: A study in police personalities.* Scottsdale, AZ: Leadership Press.

Kroes, W. H. (1985). *Society's victim—The policeman—An analysis of job stress in policing,* 2nd ed. New York.

Langworthy, R. H. (1987). Police cynicism: What we know from the Niederhoffer scale. *Journal of Criminal Justice, 15,* 17–35.

Martin, S. E. and Jurik, N. C. (1996). *Doing justice, doing gender: Women in law and criminal justice occupations.* Thousand Oaks, CA: Sage.

Mehrahian, A. (1987). Communication without words. In B. Weaver (Ed.) *Readings in cross-cultural communication,* 2nd ed., pp. 142–184. Lexington, MA: Ginn Press.

Miller, L. and Braswell, M. (1983). *Human relations and police work.* Prospect Heights, IL: Waveland Press.

Moore, M. H. (1992). Problem-solving and community policing. In M. Tonry and N. Morris (Eds.), *Modern policing,* pp. 57–87. Chicago: The University of Chicago Press.

More, H. W. and Unsinger (1987). *Police managerial use of psychology and psychologists.* Springfield, IL: Thomas Pub.

Niederhoffer, A. (1967). *Behind the shield: The police in urban society.* Garden City, NY: Doubleday & Sons.

Regoli, R. M., Crank, J., Culbertson, R., and Poole, E. D. (1989). Police cynicism, job satisfaction, and work relations among police chiefs: An assessment of department size. *Sociological Focus, 22(3),* 161–172.

Regoli, R. M., Crank, J., Culbertson, R., and Poole, E. D. (1987). Police professionalism and cynicism reconsidered: An assessment of measurement issues. *Justice Quarterly, 4(2),* 257–75.

Regoli, R. M. and Poole, E. D. (1979). Measurement of police cynicism: A factor scaling approach. *Journal of Criminal Justice, 7,* 37–51.

Roberg, R. and Kuykendall, J. (1997). *Police management,* 2nd ed. Los Angeles: Roxbury Pub.

Roberg, R. and Kuykendall, J. (1990). *Police organization and management: Behavior, theory and process.* Pacific Grove, CA: Brooks/Cole.

Skolnick, J. and Fyfe, J. (1993). *Above the law: Police and the excessive use of force.* New York: The Free Press.

Skolnick, J. (1966). *Justice without trial.* New York: Wiley.

Smith, D., Visher, C., and Davidson, L. (1984). Equity and discretionary justice: The influence of race on police arrest decisions. *Journal of Criminal Law and Criminology, 75,* 234–249.

Spitzer, S. (1981). The political economy of policing. In D. F. Greenberg (Ed.), *Crime and capitalism: Readings in Marxist criminology,* pp. 127–178. Palo Alto, CA: Mayfield Publishing Co.

Terry, W. C. (1981). Police stress: The empirical evidence. *Journal of Police Science and Administration, 9(1),* 61–73.

U.S. Commission on Civil Rights (1990). *Who is guarding the guardians?* Washington, DC: U.S. Government Printing Office.

Violanti, J. M. and Marshall, J. R. (1983). The police stress process. *Journal of Police Science and Administration, 11(4),* 389–394.

Walker, S. (1992). *Popular justice: A history of American criminal justice.* New York: Oxford University Press.

Wirth, L. (1945). *The problem of minority groups.* In R. Linton (Ed.), *The science of man in the world crisis,* pp. 23–54. New York: Columbia University Press.

Wright, R. D., Christie, D. G., Burrows, G. D., Coghlan, J. P., and Milte, K. L. (1980). *Occupational health in the police force.* Unpublished manuscript, University of Melbourne.

Work, J. W. (1989). *Toward affirmative action and racial/ethnic pluralism.* Arlington, VA: Belvedere Press.

18 Talking Through Our Differences

Intercultural and Interpersonal Communication

MARIANNE O. NIELSEN

On the whole, criminal justice system members are members of privileged groups. On the average, they are white, male, physically abled, and middle class. Their clients usually are not. This lack of commonality means that intercultural and interpersonal communication skills take on a special significance in providing justice services. Police officers, for example, are the gatekeepers to the criminal justice system. It is "an accepted fact" for most officers that citizens will be uncomfortable communicating with them (Womack and Finley, 1986:145). Many citizens see the police as representatives of the dominant society and as authority figures who have the power to determine their security, peace of mind, freedom, and even their chances of dying. This power is not limited to the police. Lawyers, prosecutors, judges, correctional officers, and parole and probation supervisors make decisions daily that can have the same impact.

Criminal justice system personnel, like ordinary citizens, often feel uncertainty and anxiety in communicating with strangers. The power they wield, however, gives criminal justice system members an added responsibility in dealing with their own negative reactions. They have the responsibility of ensuring that they have the skills to learn about the motivations and behavior of the people whose lives they affect, even more so when these people are members of relatively powerless groups. Equally important, criminal justice members must communicate with enough competence that this understanding becomes a two-way street.

This chapter, or indeed any book on intercultural and interpersonal communication, cannot provide "the" answer on how to handle all intercultural interactions effectively and appropriately[1]; it does, however, provide useful information

---

[1]It should be noted that although this chapter discusses the aggregate level characteristics of some groups, there is a great deal of individual variation within each group. It should also be noted that most of the work in intercultural and interpersonal communication has been done from a Eurocentric point of view (Martin, 1993).

about the knowledge and skills needed to do so, and the issues that can arise in communication. It also discusses the importance of communication competence for criminal justice organizations.

Improving intercultural and interpersonal communication is a vital strategy for learning more about other groups. There are two kinds of intercultural communication training: culture-general and culture-specific (Hammer, 1989). Culture-specific training focuses on communication competence in just one culture, as when an American Drug Enforcement Agency officer learns about Colombian culture. In contrast, this chapter focuses on the development of culture-general skills—that is, skills that can be generalized to intercultural interactions, regardless of the culture (Hammer, 1989:248). Although most of the discussion is on intercultural communication, the majority of the skills described here are equally applicable to interpersonal communication with members of other groups (see Milhouse, 1993).

Communication Competence in Criminal Justice

Communication is a process that occurs between two or more individuals who construct the reality of the interaction as they go long. They attach meanings to messages they transmit to others and that others transmit to them (Gudykunst, 1994). Competent communication is about developing a shared reality: It is the negotiation of "mutual meanings, rules, and outcomes that are 'positive'" (Gudykunst and Nishida, 1989:36). According to Gudykunst (1994:25), "communication is effective to the extent that we are able to minimize misunderstandings."

Communication, however, is seldom perfect. Both partners in the interaction bring in their individual personalities, life experiences, and social and cultural roles. This means that they may misinterpret the meaning of the other's communication (Gudykunst, 1994). Most people are unaware of, are uncomfortable with, or are unable to discuss the dynamics and implications of cultural differences with others. This can lead to tension and conflicts as people interpret others' words and behaviors incorrectly, make mistakes in their own words and behavior, become frustrated, make negative judgments about the other person, and cut off the interaction. They may end up avoiding situations of intercultural communication in the future because of emotional upset (Cushner and Brislin, 1996:7). In the case of criminal justice members, they may even choose to become more aggressive in their interactions (Gundersen and Hopper, 1984:133).

The more desirable alternative is to develop the knowledge and skills to operate effectively and appropriately in intercultural and interpersonal interactions; that is, to become "competent communicators."

Rewards of Competent Communication

Competent communication has many rewards. Competent communicators learn about someone else's cultural concepts and gain insight into a world very different from their own. For example, the Cree Indians, one of the largest indigenous groups in Canada, have no word for or concept of "guilt." What does this suggest about their view of crime? What might be the repercussions of this when they appear as an accused in court? Nor do the Cree have gender pronouns. What might be the impact of this linguistic difference if a Cree is asked to give testimony about the identity of an offender?

Second, competent communicators gain a new perspective on their own culture. For example, if the Japanese have many words for rice in their language because of its centrality to their diet, what does this say about all the words Americans have for guns? Why do Americans have gender pronouns when the Cree do not? Do Americans have more status and prestige distinctions based on gender than other cultures? If so, does this affect how women are treated in the criminal justice system?

Third, competent communicators are more likely to make decisions that take into account the perspectives of all parties to the interaction. Actions taken by a police officer, for example, in handling a domestic violence dispute are more likely to calm the situation than inflame it if the police officer has some knowledge of the culturally defined domestic roles of the spouses, their attitude toward authority figures, and their normal tone of verbal and nonverbal communication.

Womack and Finley (1986) believe that good communication has a number of other benefits to the criminal justice system, including better relations with the community; improvements in the work unit and in the whole organization as more competent communication skills start to decrease misunderstandings, tensions, and conflicts among coworkers from different backgrounds; and increased self-esteem among criminal justice members as they become better able to handle intercultural interactions.

Critical Knowledge about Communication

In order for criminal justice personnel to achieve intercultural communication competence, it is important to have knowledge about certain key influences on communication, including the impact of diversity on communication, the power of nonverbal communication, and the importance of the situational context.

The Impact of Diversity on Communication

There are many kinds of diversity that can influence communication. In this section we look at just three: culture, power and status, and gender. These three are among the most important for criminal justice personnel, but it should be recognized that other kinds of diversity influence communication, including race, education, physical abilities, and age.

Culture.   Cultural groups can be differentiated along a number of standard dimensions. Although a number of typologies have been developed to describe these,[2] probably the best known is the one developed by Hofstede (1997), who differentiates cultures along the dimensions of: individualism/collectivism, high and low power distance, uncertainty avoidance, and masculinity and femininity.[3] These can be summarized as follows:

> Individualistic cultures emphasize the individual's goals, while collectivistic cultures stress that group goals have precedence over individual goals. High power-distance cultures value inequality, with everyone having a "rightful place," and the hierarchy reflects existential inequality. Low power-distance cultures, in contrast, value equality. Uncertainty avoidance involves the lack of tolerance for uncertainty and ambiguity. Cultures high in uncertainty avoidance have high levels of anxiety, a great need for formal rules, and a low tolerance for groups that behave in a deviant manner. Masculinity, according to Hofstede, involves valuing things, money, assertiveness, and unequal sex roles. Cultures where people, quality of life, nurturance, and equal sex roles prevail, on the other hand, are feminine. (Gudykunst and Nishida, 1989:21–22)

Another important typology differentiates between high-context and low-context cultures (Hall, 1976). In high-context cultures, a lot of meaning is implicit and is communicated by the context and nonverbal nuances and signals. In low-context cultures, the meaning is given directly and there is little reliance on context or nonverbal signals. African American, Native American, and Latino/a cultures within the United States are relatively high context, whereas northern European–based cultures (i.e., the dominant "white" culture) are low context. In addition, police officers and most other criminal justice personnel have been trained to be very low context in their communication. Knowing where a group fits in these typologies can be a useful tool for a criminal justice practitioner trying to anticipate and prevent cultural conflict.

Power and Status Differences.   Groups who have a subordinate status have developed specialized ways of communicating based on their past interactions with members of the dominant group. Orbe (1998:16–17) presents a long list of these,

---

[2]See Gudykunst and Nishida (1989) for an overview of theoretical frameworks for intercultural communication.

[3]It should be noted that some theorists find Hofstede's use of the terms "masculine" and "feminine" sexist and stereotypical, and substitute the term "gender," which is still a questionable term (see Hecht *et al.*, 1989).

including: averting communication away from potentially dangerous topics, remaining silent when offensive statements are made, downplaying or ignoring differences, ridiculing self, confronting, educating others, imposing a psychological distance through verbal and nonverbal strategies, and avoiding communication. The strategy used depends on the perceived costs and gains of the interaction for the subordinate member (Orbe, 1998).

Individuals who travel to other regions of this country or abroad may find that they have suddenly assumed a higher or lower status than they held at home. Individuals who get a job within the criminal justice system may experience a similar instantaneous change in status. This affects how communication is carried out; there are differences in naming, respect, and nonverbal communication. An African exchange student may not have experienced black–white discrimination before coming to the United States; a Latina lawyer may be treated with more deference in court than she receives in the supermarket.

Gender.   Communication research in many different settings and populations has found that there are communication differences between men and women. Aries (1996:189) reports that these findings include: "[m]en show a greater task orientation in groups, women a greater social–emotional orientation; men emerge more often as leaders in initially leaderless groups; men interrupt more; women pay more attention to the face needs of their conversational partners; women talk more personally with their close friends." The meanings put on these differences are socially constructed. Meanings are often based in gender stereotypes so that, for example, a man's statement is interpreted as assertive, whereas the same statement from a woman is interpreted as aggressive, even "bitchy."

Women and men's verbal and nonverbal communication can be very difficult for the other to interpret. There are a wide array of variables that can influence an interaction, including the class and status of the partners, sexual orientation, age, ethnicity, and individual style. Situational factors such as the relationship between the partners, the setting, the topic, and the length of the interaction can also influence the degree to which gender differences have an impact (Aries, 1996).

According to Aries (1996:195), "gender differences cannot be understood without putting them in the context of gender inequalities in society." Women in American society are still perceived and treated by many as having lower status than men, and as discussed in the previous section on power and status, dominant–subordinate status can have a great deal of influence on communication. In addition, cultures vary in what are considered to be the proper tone of conversation, kind of touch allowed (if any), and personal distance between men and women. There are also differences in the intimacy of the topic, and expectations of response. These differences could lead to accusations of sexual harassment—for example, if one of the partners in the interaction is seen by the other as "stepping over the line" (Cushner and Brislin, 1996).

When men and women are put in the same role or have the same status, few gender differences emerge (Aries, 1996). In the criminal justice, the few communication differences that do exist have positive consequences. Female police officers and correctional officers, for example, are more willing to use reason, less likely to provoke hostilities, more likely to diffuse tensions, and more likely to mediate conflict (Martin and Jurik, 1996).

In order to deal competently with communication differences, communicators need to learn as much as possible about the cultures of the groups with which they interact. They also need to learn to recognize indicators of power differences and understand that they have evolved as the result of the history between the groups that the partners in the interaction represent. Communicators should not take such changes personally, and should keep their interactions respectful and professional. Finally, competent communicators need to recognize that job-related differences in male and female communication can be used to the advantage of the criminal justice system.

The Importance of Nonverbal Communication

According to Henderson (1994), about 70 to 80% of communication is nonverbal. Knowledge of what nonverbal communication means, although not always reliable, is an important tool for criminal justice personnel. Most nonverbal communication is spontaneous, unconscious, and subtle (Andersen, 1994:229). The manner of speaking communicates as much as the words; it just does not communicate the same thing in every culture. Characteristics that may vary across cultures and among groups include tone, placement of emphasis, volume, pitch, quality (e.g., clear versus slurring), and duration (Henderson, 1994). Following are seven key areas of nonverbal communication.

1. *Silence* makes most Americans nervous. Americans from some regions such as the northeast have been taught to finish other people's sentences for them, to interrupt, and to leap immediately into any space in a conversation. There is no intent to be impolite; it is simply a speech pattern. Many Native American and Asian peoples, however, have been taught that it is polite to wait a space after the other person has stopped talking. The length of their silence reflects how important they think the other person's words are. In a meeting between northeastern American criminal justice managers and Native American community members, we might therefore observe a significant cultural clash in communication: the Native Americans might feel that they have no room to present their concerns and that the others are imposing their point of view; and the managers might feel that the quiet Native Americans do not care or have no ideas.

2. *Gestures and movements* are among the most important aspects of nonverbal communication. There are more than 100,000 different gestures that are used around the world, and most have meanings that vary from culture to culture. A simple example is the nod that is used in the United States to signify agreement. In Greece, depending on the exact movement, a nod might actually mean "no"; in Brazil, if a man nods to a woman, it signifies seduction (Henderson, 1994).

3. *Personal space* or "zones of territory" also vary across cultures, classes, and genders. If one person invades the space of another, it causes discomfort. Some cultures prefer to stand closer than others. High contact is desirable in Latin American, African, Arab, and Southern European cultures, for example. Noncontact or low-contact groups include several Asian and Northern European cultures (Henderson, 1994).

4. *Touching* is also viewed differently by low-contact and high-contact cultures. Touching includes kissing, embracing, hugging, hand shaking, and general touch. Touching varies not only by culture but also by the gender and status of the persons in the interaction, the timing of the interaction, and the private or public location of the interaction (Henderson, 1994).

5. *Eye contact* can also vary. Cultures vary in how long people make eye contact, how intensely, when, what part of the body is looked at, and how much blinking is done (Henderson, 1994). Some cultures consider extended direct eye contact as a sign of honesty (white American); others see it as a disrespectful (many traditional Native American).

6. How much people *move* around can also vary. In some cultures, people may walk away and return to emphasize agreement (Henderson, 1994). In some cultures, individuals talking to authority figures are expected to stand still and upright; in others, there is no such expectation.

7. *Symbols* are a special category of nonverbal communication. Examples are flags, ankhs, crosses, Stars of David, badges, uniforms, road signs, jewelry, scout patches, head gear, red (pink, purple, green, yellow) ribbons, political cartoons, and thousands of others. Each group has symbols that have special meanings to its members. Some of these are easy to recognize and understand; others are not. Some are used to draw a group together (flags); others are used to divide or exclude groups (political cartoons, swastikas). In the criminal justice system, a great deal of gang identification relies, sometimes incorrectly, on colors and styles of clothing worn (see Chapter 3 by Ferrell). Police uniforms are also a symbol—to some people of assistance; to others, especially the foreign-born, of oppression and tyranny.

Competent communicators try to learn some of the nonverbal signals of cultures or co-cultures with which they interact frequently, but are very careful in using them themselves. They understand that they may not have a full appreciation of the subtleties of usage.

Situational Context

To understand each other, partners in an interaction must know something about the others' social, cultural, and personal context. Without context, "behavior is just noise" as Cushner and Brislin (1996:13) state. Each participant in an interaction operates within the context of their own life experience, motivations, culture, and group history. This means that a wide range of factors can affect an interaction, including the physical and emotional setting in which the interaction occurs—for example, in a dark park late at night or in a crowded mall; and the characteristics of the participants—for example, their numbers, attractiveness, prototypicality, personality, temperament, and mood (Giles and Franklyn-Stokes, 1989). The historical relations between the groups the participants represent can also have an influence—for example, as mentioned previously, if one group is or has been dominant and the other subordinate, such as whites and African Americans in the United States.

The participants' knowledge of the language is also an important factor. They may take for granted that they and the other person understand the meanings of words, when in fact they do not. Words and concepts can have subtly different, slightly different, or even drastically different meanings (Cushner and Brislin, 1996:289). There is a difference, for example, between a "date" with a prostitute and a "date" to the movies on Friday night; or between "snow" as in precipitation or "snow" as in heroin. The nonverbal communication that accompanies words may also completely change their meaning. For example, the word "mother" can have its meaning changed completely depending on the nonverbal communication (tone of voice, hand gesture) that accompanies it. Using slang like this can cause all kind of misunderstandings. Although a nonnative speaker in the interaction may seem to have a good knowledge of English, there is a significant chance that they are not familiar with the nuances of English words and expressions. The American English phrase "see you later," for example, has led to accusations of American insincerity, because the American does not necessarily intend to see the other later; it is simply an American ritual parting phrase (Cushner and Brislin, 1996). Similarly, an angry American English speaker's comment, "I am pissed" would be misunderstood by a Canadian English speaker. In Canada "to be pissed" is to be drunk; to be angry is "to be pissed off."

The purpose of the interaction can also affect the communication dynamic. For example, some cultures consider bargaining a normal part of shopping, or even of paying traffic tickets. Some cultures have high regard for the ability to debate; others use silence to communicate respect. Some have a great tolerance and enjoyment of small talk; some have very little use for it. Some use talk as a form of social control; others use it as a means of establishing affiliations. How to agree or disagree is an example of an important skill. In many cultures, including some Asian and some Native American cultures, it is impolite to refuse a person or turn them down. "No" is not said; instead, there are other phrases that mean "No," such as, "I'll think about it," or, "Maybe later." People familiar with the culture understand that they have been turned down; those who are not familiar might continue to make a request that has been essentially turned down, might get their feelings hurt, or might make assumptions about the dishonesty of the other (Argyle, 1982).

What each participant considers appropriate behavior or presentation of self in the situation in which the interaction occurs is also important (Henderson, 1994). These can include greetings (e.g., phrases, handshakes versus bowing or nodding), whistling, showing affection, covering the head or legs, the formality or informality of dress, removal of shoes on entering a room, how to sit "properly," how to address or touch elderly individuals, when to give gifts and what kind, how to criticize, how to give and receive compliments, and recognizing symbols of marriage (jewelry, hairstyle, clothing style).

Competent communicators try to learn what factors might affect an interaction and try not to make assumptions about the actions and words of the other person.

Critical Issues in Communication

There are many issues revolving around communication that have led and continue to lead to difficult situations for members of the criminal justice system. We look at five issues that have had, for better or worse, a great deal of impact on the criminal justice system: stereotyping, ethnocentrism, naming, humor, and translation.

Stereotyping

People cannot psychologically process all the information they receive, so that from the time they are small, they learn to place people in abstract social categories based on easily identified characteristics (Gudykunst and Gumbs, 1989). In this country, these characteristics include skin color, sex, presence or absence of disabilities, and apparent age. Stereotypes can also be based on accent, social class, and ethnicity. Stereotypes attribute certain behaviors to all members of the category, allowing for no individual variations. Positive stereotypes are formed about in-groups such as family, friends, and members of the same class or race, who are of course, all intelligent, talented, kind, and caring; negative stereotypes are formed about the out-group, who are often seen as criminal, lazy, greedy, and loud (Gudykunst and Gumbs, 1989). Categories are learned through jokes, ethnophaulisms (rude names), epithets (expressions), stories, and, of course, the mass media.

Stereotypes can prevent individuals from interacting with each other; what they think they know about each other is so negative that they are afraid of each other. Individuals might also be afraid that if they take the step to learn more, they may embarrass themselves because they say or do something "stupid." Yet, they might also find that the "real person" is, in fact, an individual just like "me," with similar family problems, career hopes, and lack of time to do everything they want to do in life. The only way to reach this understanding, however, is to see people as individuals, overcome stereotypes, and not see others as homogeneous members of some group of strangers. This requires true and meaningful communication.

Ethnocentrism

Ethnocentrism is the tendency to judge others by the standards of one's own group and form a negative opinion as a result (Hofstede, 1997). Often when individuals are faced with cultural practices different from their own, their first reaction is to complain or criticize or compare the practice unfavorably to what they are used to. Not surprisingly, such negative responses may be seen by members of the other group as insults or, at the least, disrespect. However, something is not necessarily bad because it is different. Similarly, if others criticize or seem to be acting disrespectfully about American culture, Americans may react poorly. In these situations, it is best to not assume disrespect or insult is meant (Argyle, 1982).

Naming

Meanings of names change over time and have different meanings in different regions of the country or the world. It was common in the 1950s and 1960s, for example, to refer to women as "girls," even professional women such as administrative assistants and nurses. Some older men, in particular, have a hard time understanding why this is no longer accepted practice and may sometimes evoke extreme displeasure from the targeted woman. Many people have trouble understanding that words and expressions (such as "acting like a wild Indian" about a rambunctious child) have connotations that can make them ethnic, racial, or gender slurs. Connotations are the "emotional and cognitive associations of words" (Herbst, 1997:256), and it is the connotations that are offensive, perhaps even more so than the words. These words "restrict, misrepresent, or distort how people are known" (Herbst, 1997:ix). As such, they are an element of stereotyping. How the words are spoken is also very important. The situation and the intention behind the words shape the meaning of the words as well (Herbst, 1997:xiii).

Names reveal societal and individual attitudes about specific groups. They develop in response to the changing needs of their users and the evolving needs of the society in which they are used. "In the United States the vast array of abusive ethnic words reflect the society's complexity, increasing ethnic diversity and fast-paced social change" (Herbst, 1997:255). Derogatory names advance the political interests of groups, are ideologically loaded, mark boundaries between "us" and "them," create distance between the speaker and the group spoken of, "keep people in their place," and justify discrimination in the minds of the people who are discriminating (Herbst, 1997:ix, 256). They are also used to chastise people from both the minority and the dominant society who are perceived as straying from acceptable intercultural behavior, or assimilating too far into the dominant society (Herbst, 1997:x).

Names are reflections of power relationships in society. The group named with a derogatory label does not have the power to stop the naming and may have to put up with it. The fact that members of the dominant group often do not understand the name that they use for the minority group is offensive is a sign of the social and sometimes geographic distance between members of the minority and dominant group. It symbolizes the traditional indifference of the dominant society to the concerns of minority groups (Herbst, 1997:258).

Members of named groups may use naming as a means of "talking back" to the dominant society, for example using names like "gringo" or "round eyes" for Americans perceived as members of the privileged white group. Groups who experience prejudice may also adopt the derogatory names and use them for their own purposes, such as "self-definition, solidarity, or irony" (Herbst, 1997:256, xii; Orbe, 1998:16–17). Native Americans and African Americans, especially, are fighting to maintain or revitalize their cultural identities, which means that intercultural communications with some members of these groups may have political overtones and connotations.

Humor

Humor can be used for many social purposes, including as an information-gathering tool, as a means of giving information, as a means of anxiety management, for social control, and as a means of preserving the *status quo* (Foot, 1997). The first three purposes suggest that humor can be a vital strategy for criminal justice personnel developing intercultural and interpersonal communication. It can be used as a means of diffusing tense situations, as a means of coping with the embarrassment of one of the partners in an interaction, or for gathering information. It can, however, also be a very risky tool. Humor targeting group membership, such as ethnicity, race, or gender-based jokes can lead to serious problems. These jokes are based on stereotypes and serve (perhaps unintentionally) as a means of social control and of preserving the *status quo*. Jokes reinforce the characteristics and "place" of some groups within society; that is, they reinforce prejudice. As an example, many jokes about the Irish emphasize drinking and fighting, most jokes about blondes emphasize a lack of intelligence, and most jokes about African Americans emphasize laziness and lack of intelligence. As Foot (1997:271) states, "Because the joke is a socially acceptable form, the message it conveys is extremely powerful and the recipient or target, however much offended, can hardly denounce it without standing accused of the greatest crime of all—lacking a sense of humour."

In terms of using humor, it is important to remember that a great deal of humor relies on shared cultural and linguistic experiences. It is not the words so much that are funny, but the understanding that goes with them. In other words, humor is highly culture-specific (Hofstede, 1997). It is probably best to follow the advice given by Hofstede (1997:214), who suggests, "In intercultural encounters the experienced traveller [or criminal justice practitioner] knows that jokes and irony are taboo until one is absolutely sure of the other culture's conception of what represents humor."

Translation

Translation is an intervening variable in communication between, for example, a lawyer and her client. Because translation is an active process in which the translator must make a series of decisions and judgments, it has the potential to also affect the decisions of criminal justice personnel. Cultural orientation can make direct translations meaningless, alter the meaning, or make them gain a completely different meaning. Many legal concepts cannot easily be translated into some languages. Translating the underlying ideology of concepts is even more difficult (Banks and Banks, 1991). The translator must not only translate, but must also interpret. As a result, the translation has the potential to influence the results of the interaction (Banks and Banks, 1991).

With the changing population demographics in this country, the need for translation has increased geometrically for criminal justice service providers (Banks and Banks, 1991). Sanders (1989) reports that more than 43,000 requests for translation services in 60 languages were made annually in federal courts, and that New York City courts alone needed interpreters about 250 times *a day*. Translators trained in legal terminology can be invaluable in dealing with this issue; however, there is no standard certification required by U.S. justice services (Banks and Banks, 1991). Some states have language skills tests for translators. Arizona has a federal court interpreter training institute that certifies Navajo speakers to translate in court (Wabnik, 1996).

Despite all of the issues described, the only way to learn to communicate is to learn the critical skills needed. The possible rewards in terms of cooperation and doors opened make it a worthwhile process, and there is really very little to lose. Attempting to use words and customs of the new culture is usually interpreted by members of that culture as showing respect and interest—although not always (Cushner and Brislin, 1996:291).

Critical Skills

Which skills are important and how to develop them have been the subject of many books and articles on improving intercultural and interpersonal communication (Hammer, 1989; Henderson, 1994). Gudykunst (1994) suggests that competent communicators must have the motivation, knowledge, and skills to communicate. Communicators are motivated by the fulfillment of certain needs that arise in interaction. These include a need for predictability, a need to avoid anxiety, and a need to sustain self-concept. Knowledge means knowing about the other person's group and knowing what needs to be done in order to communicate in an effective way. Gudykunst describes six skills that are particularly important. In order to reduce anxiety, communicators must have the ability to be mindful, tolerate ambiguity, and manage anxiety; in order to reduce uncertainty, communicators must be able to empathize, adapt their behavior, and make accurate predictions about and explanations for others' behavior (1994:179–194). Listening, asking questions, and conflict management are subsumed among these skills, but because of their importance to criminal justice personnel, they are discussed separately.

Being mindful means that communicators are aware of their own communication behavior and the process of communication, rather than focusing on their feelings or on the outcome. It also means being open to new information and other peoples' perspectives. *Tolerating ambiguity* means having the skill to deal successfully with situations in which a lot of the information needed for effective communication is missing. People with a low tolerance for ambiguity try to find information that supports their previous conceptions. People with a high tolerance try to gather objective information. *Managing anxiety* means being able to control bodily symptoms of anxiety as well as controlling worrying thoughts. People who are involved in an interaction with unfamiliar, "weird" people may feel uneasy, tense, and worried. They may fear that their self-concept will be damaged, that there will be negative behavioral consequences (e.g., that they will be exploited or be harmed), that the other group will evaluate them negatively, and that their in-group might evaluate them negatively. It is important to remember that a moderate amount of anxiety actually aids performance; too much or too little hinders communication.

The ability to *empathize* means trying to take the perspective of the other so that the communicator understands the other's feelings and point of view. This is not to be confused with sympathy, which is trying to imagine how *you* would feel in the same spot. The *ability to adapt* refers to being able to perceive different situational contexts and choosing the verbal and nonverbal communication strategies that are most appropriate and effective. This may include learning a new language. The ability to *make accurate predictions and explanations* for others' behavior is based in knowing that all cultures have rules of thought, feeling, and behavior, but that these vary from group to group. Effective communicators do not assume the other is using the same rules, but try to determine what rules are underlying their communications. They then use these to predict and explain the other's behavior.

Listening, according to Gudykunst (1994), is a process in which individuals take in new information, check it against what they already know, and select information that is meaningful. It is a skill that does not come naturally; it needs to be practiced. This is a particularly important skill for criminal justice personnel who must gather information and make important decisions about how to deal with people. In the dominant American culture, "active listening" is the recommended strategy. Active listening involves three skills: attending skills, which are comprised of the nonverbal body language, posture, and eye contact we maintain in interaction; following skills, which are the verbal and nonverbal ways we indicate to the person we are listening to him or her; and comprehending skills, which comprise the ways we check to make sure we are understanding the speaker—for example, by paraphrasing their words and asking questions.

Active listening may not be appropriate with all groups, however. Some cultures, as discussed in the next section, find asking questions disrespectful. Also, verbal indicators of "following" may be seen as interruptions and lead to the cessation of talk, and the "attending" skill of maintaining eye contact might be seen as a challenge.

In the American culture, *asking questions* is the simplest way of gathering information; however, within some cultures, the act of asking questions is considered rude. This can be especially problematic for criminal justice personnel with investigative roles. In some Native American cultures, asking questions, especially of Elders, is impolite and will not likely get a response. There are, however, many other ways of requesting information, for example, using a phrase such as "I wonder if . . ." or "Someone told me . . ." and pausing, thereby allowing the person time to offer the information if they wish to do so. Sometimes it is only the content of the question that is unintentionally rude. Asking questions about sacred knowledge, for example, is always questionable. Each group has topics that are not acceptable conversational topics. Most Americans are not comfortable talking to casual acquaintances about their sexual relations with their spouses, for example. Who is asking the question may also be an issue. In many Australian Aborigine cultures, there is "men's" knowledge and "women's" knowledge, and it is inappropriate for a man to share men's knowledge with a woman, no matter what her occupation, and vice versa.

Conflict management is another important skill for criminal justice personnel. Conflict is handled differently by various cultural groups. Individualistic and collectivistic cultures, for example, handle conflict differently. Members of collectivistic cultures are more likely to try to smooth over the conflict or to avoid it altogether, whereas members of individualistic cultures are likely to try to control the conflict situation and/or treat conflict as a problem to be solved (Gudykunst and Nishida, 1989). Criminal justice practitioners need to know the appropriate strategies to use with different groups, or they will add to the conflict, not manage it.

Translating Communication Competence into Organizational Success

Criminal justice organizations in the United States must provide services to a diverse population. They also employ a diverse workforce. The cultures from which their employees come influence structure, management and leadership styles, leader behavior, and organizational culture (Tayeb, 1996:101; Hofstede, 1997). Some cultural values and behaviors have more impact than others. Tayeb (1996) suggests that organizations are particularly affected by their employees' attitudes toward power, tolerance of ambiguity, individualism, collectivism, commitment, and interpersonal trust.

Issues in intercultural and interpersonal communication within organizations are the same as those between individuals. Not surprisingly, the prejudices found outside in society are also located and acted out in the workplace (Henderson, 1994). Coworkers may act in a discriminatory manner toward each other, or it may be managers who refuse to recruit, hire, or promote members of categories of difference.

There are, of course, also problems in communication. Racial groups inter-acting within the workplace, for example, may assign different meanings to ver-bal and nonverbal communications (Asante and Davis, 1989). Some occupations also have specialized argots that act as a communication code for practitioners (think, for example, of police officers using radio codes in casual conversation). These may be very difficult for new staff members to understand, especially if they come from a group that traditionally has been excluded from the occupation. There are also language usages that are exclusive to one category of individuals, leaving others out. An example is the use of sports metaphors during planning meetings. Although there are many women who are sports fans, it is mainly men who have detailed knowledge of the rules of various sports and use them in day-to-day conversation, thereby excluding anyone who does not have the same knowledge.

Organizations have three options in managing their workforce: they can ig-nore its diversity; they can recognize its diversity but not use it; or they can use its diversity as a rich resource for provision of services. Organizations that ignore or resist diversity will find two things: First, that they are denied the benefits of a fully productive diverse workforce; second, discrimination is against the law, and companies that allow discrimination not only lose offended customers and staff, but may well find themselves the targets of million dollar law suits, such as oc-curred in the early 1990s when the FBI was ordered in two separate cases to com-pensate Latino and African American agents who had been discriminated against by the Bureau (Johnston, 1995).

Organizations that actively use their workforce diversity are more competi-tive and more creative in problem solving (Tayeb, 1996). In addition, organiza-tions that recognize and work with diversity have fewer internal conflicts (Tayeb, 1996). This means that effective interpersonal and intercultural skills are valuable not only for the individuals who use them, but also for their organizations. As a result, many organizations, including criminal justice organizations, are suggest-ing and even requiring that their employees take part in initiatives that develop their communication skills.

A number of strategies can help organizations develop and make better use of the communication skills of their employees. First, management's encourage-ment or discouragement of diversity affects the behavior of everyone within the organization. If competent intercultural and interpersonal communication is to be part of the culture of any organization, it must occur with the cooperation and active participation of senior administration (Henderson, 1994).

Second, managers must learn both verbal and nonverbal communication skills. The most effective managers are those who are skilled in intercultural and interpersonal communication, and who teach by doing (Henderson, 1994). They use their skills to learn about their employees' values, motivations, communica-tion styles, attitudes, and needs (Henderson, 1994:195).

Third, intercultural and interpersonal communication initiatives must be based on the objectives and commitments of the organization. Policy must provide clear directions regarding the initiatives' objectives and how they are to be reached. Employees should be part of the planning of these initiatives. They must feel there will be personal payoffs to them for participating, such as promotions and pay raises. Every effort must be made to ensure that organizational members do not feel that the initiative will cause them to lose face (Henderson, 1994).

Fourth, policies concerning bias-free written and spoken language should be implemented. Terminology used should reflect the occupation or task, not the personal characteristics of the staff member. An example of this is referring more appropriately to "the secretary" instead of "the girl." Similarly, proper titles or proper names should be used, instead of slang names such as "honey," "fella," and "dear."

Fifth, organizations can develop programs for their employees to help them develop new skills and competencies in language proficiency, negotiation skills, and general communication competence (Tayeb, 1994). Ideally, training programs should be developed to meet the specific needs of the trainees and their organization. There is a wide range of training programs from which to choose (Cargile and Giles , 1996). According to research, one of the most effective is the "culture-general assimilator," which presents students with a series of critical incidents in which intercultural communication did not work. Students choose from a set of answers until they find the correct explanation (see Cushner and Brislin, 1996). This training method is particularly appropriate for criminal justice personnel who must provide effective services in a wide range of job scenarios every day. Hargie (1997) recommends that communication skills training is best carried out through "microtraining"—that is, carried out in small groups over short periods of time, and focusing on only one skill at a time. The needed skills are first identified, then the training stage of sensitization to the skills occurs. This is followed by a practice stage, in which students try out the skills, are often recorded on video, and then receive feedback. Evaluation of the program focuses on the impact of the students' skills on their client groups. Other training methods include lectures, role-playing, field trips, and experiential games (Cargile and Giles, 1997).

Organizations can evaluate the intercultural competence of their employees based on three very three straightforward criteria: whether the employee feels comfortable and satisfied with intercultural or interpersonal interactions; if the employee is rated as an acceptable and competent communicator by members of the different categories of difference that are dealt with; and if the employees are highly rated by a supervisor as effective in dealing with members of other groups (Argyle, 1982:62). Being able to establish meaningful interpersonal relationships with members of other groups has also been suggested as an indicator of competence.

In summary, to be effective, intercultural communication initiatives must be well planned, must occur organization-wide, must be coordinated from the top, must be on-going, and must include nonverbal communication (Henderson, 1994). In this diverse world, there is little doubt that increased competence in intercultural and interpersonal communication skills is of benefit to both individuals and organizations within the criminal justice system.

References

Andersen, P. (1994). Explaining intercultural differences in nonverbal communication. In L. A. Samovar and R. E. Porter (Eds.), *Intercultural communication: A reader,* 7th ed., pp. 229–239. Belmont, CA: Wadsworth.

Aries, E. (1996). *Men and women in interaction.* New York: Oxford University Press.

Argyle, M. (1982). Intercultural communication. In S. Bochner (Ed.), *Cultures in contact,* pp. 61–79. Oxford: Pergamon Press.

Asante, M. K. and Davis, A. (1989). Encounters in the interracial workplace. In M. K. Asante and W. B. Gudykunst (Eds.), *Handbook of international and intercultural communication,* pp. 374–391. Newbury Park, CA: Sage.

Banks, A. and Banks, S. P. (1991). Unexplored barriers: The role of translation in interpersonal communication. In S. Ting-Toomey and F. Korzenny (Eds.), *Cross-cultural interpersonal communication,* pp. 171–185. Newbury Park, CA: Sage.

Cargile, A. C. and Giles, H. (1996). Intercultural communication training: Review, critique, and a new theoretical framework. In B. R. Burleson (Ed.), *Communication yearbook 19,* pp. 385–423. Thousand Oaks, CA: Sage.

Cushner, K. and Brislin, R. W. (1996). *Intercultural interactions; A practical guide,* 2nd ed. Thousand Oaks, CA: Sage.

Foot, H. C. (1997). Humour and laughter. In O. D. W. Hargie (Ed.), *The handbook of communication skills,* 2nd ed., pp. 259–285. London: Routledge.

Giles, H. and Franklyn-Stokes, A. (1989). Communicator characteristics. In M. K. Asante and W. B. Gudykunst (Eds.), *Handbook of international and intercultural communication,* pp. 117–144. Newbury Park, CA: Sage.

Gudykunst, W. (1994). *Bridging differences,* 2nd Edition. Thousand Oaks, CA: Sage.

Gudykunst, W. B. and Gumbs, L. L. (1989). Social cognition and intergroup communication. In M. K. Asante and W. B. Gudykunst (Eds.), *Handbook of international and intercultural communication,* pp. 204–224. Newbury Park, CA: Sage.

Gudykunst, W. B. and Nishida, T. (1989). Theoretical perspectives for studying intercultural communication. In M. K. Asante and W. B. Gudykunst (Eds.), *Handbook of international and intercultural communication,* pp. 17–46. Newbury Park, CA: Sage.

Gundersen, D. F. and Hopper, R. (1984). *Communication and law enforcement.* Lanham, MD: University Press of America.

Hall, E. T. (1976). *Beyond culture.* Garden City, NY: Anchor.

Hammer, M. (1989). Intercultural communication competence. In M. K. Asante and W. B. Gudykunst (Eds.), *Handbook of international and intercultural communication,* pp. 247–260. Newbury Park, CA: Sage.

Hargie, O. D. W. (1997). Training in communication skills: Research, theory and practice. In O. D. W. Hargie (Ed.), *The handbook of communication skills,* 2nd ed., pp. 473–482. London: Routledge.

Hecht, M. L., Andersen, P. A., and Ribeau, S. A. (1989). The cultural dimensions of nonverbal communication. In M. K. Asante and W. B. Gudykunst (Eds.), *Handbook of international and intercultural communication,* pp. 163–185. Newbury Park, CA: Sage.

Herbst, P. H. (1997). *The color of words.* Yarmouth, MA: Intercultural Press.

Henderson, G. (1994). *Cultural diversity in the workplace.* Westport, CT: Quorum Books.

Hofstede, G. (1997). *Cultures and organizations.* New York: McGraw-Hill.

Johnston, D. (1995). F.B.I. hitting snag in talks about bias. *New York Times National*, September 20: C19.

Martin, J. N. (1993). Intercultural communication competence: A review. In R. L. Wiseman and J. Koester (Eds.), *Intercultural communication competence*, pp. 16–29. Thousand Oaks, CA: Sage.

Martin, S. E. and Jurik, N. C. (1996). *Doing justice, doing gender*. Thousand Oaks, CA: Sage.

Milhouse, V. (1993). The applicability of interpersonal communication competence to the intercultural communication context. In R. L. Wiseman and J. Koester (Eds.), *Intercultural communication competence*, pp. 184–203. Thousand Oaks, CA: Sage.

Orbe, M. P. (1998). *Constructing co-cultural theory*. Thousand Oaks, CA: Sage.

Sanders, A. L. (1989). *Libertad* and *Justicia* for all. *Time*, May 29: 65.

Tayeb, M. H. (1996). *The management of a multicultural workforce*. Chichester: John Wiley & Sons.

Wabnik, A. (1996). Navajo project links culture to legal realm. In M. O. Nielsen and R. A. Silverman (Eds.), *Native Americans, crime, and justice*, pp. 150–151. Boulder, CO: Westview.

Womack, M. M. and Finley, H. H. (1986). *Communication: A unique significance for law enforcement*. Springfield, IL: Charles C. Thomas.

19 Irreconcilable Differences?

Understanding the Crime Victim/Criminal Justice Worker Relationship

PHOEBE MORGAN

BARBARA PERRY

Throughout this book we explore how cultural, social, and economic structures produce varying expectations of and actions by actors within the criminal justice system. Although the actions of law enforcement officers, prosecutors, and judges are the most visible, their decisions concerning whether to act depend almost exclusively on the choices that crime victims make. Most crime workers depend on the cooperation of victims to do their jobs. In fact, without the willingness of victims to report crimes, assist investigations, or provide testimony, the criminal justice process as we know it would not exist (Gottfredson and Gottfredson, 1988). In turn, without the aid of criminal justice agents, crime victims would be forced to seek justice on their own terms. Thus, the legitimacy and effectiveness of any criminal justice organization rests on its ability to foster and sustain positive working relationships between crime victims and those whose job it is to assist them.

Despite such a requirement, in most cases relations between crime victims and crime workers are fraught with tension and discord. Few crime victims have a completely positive experience inside the criminal justice system. Often they blame the individuals who processed their cases for their disappointments and aggravations. Similarly, crime workers regularly complain that crime victims are uncooperative, manipulative, or just plain "bogus."

Observing relations between domestic violence victims and the law enforcement officers who respond to their calls for aid, Ferraro and Pope (1993) theorize that what often underlies the tensions between these two groups are the differing expectations and conflicting needs that individuals bring to the relationship. They argue that differences between victims and workers are shaped not only by discordant personality styles and disparate individual values, but also by differences in cultural backgrounds, contrasting legal roles, and organizational constraints. Knowing more about how these external pressures affect the internal workings of this relationship is the key to expanding our understanding of how interactions between crime victims and crime workers can serve to either advance and erode justice.

In the following pages, we take the highly personal relationships that exist between individual crime victims and criminal justice workers and place them within their larger cultural, legal, and organizational contexts. We begin by examining the ways in which relations between crime victims and crime workers are not only interpersonal, but intercultural as well. Next, we identify some of the key differences between the legal roles that crime victims and crime workers are required to play and discuss how those differences can foster tension between the individuals who assume them. We also examine the ways that the organizational goals of criminal justice agencies fail to meet expectations fueled by media images, public education, and social change. We conclude by proposing various strategies for managing the tensions that arise from the differences between crime victims and criminal justice workers.

When Relations Between Crime Victims and Criminal Justice Workers Are Intercultural

As we see throughout this volume, there is a disparate distribution of racial, ethnic, cultural, and gender identities across the FBI's crime index (Federal Bureau of Investigation, 1998). Analyses of these data consistently find that although young white men are at greatest risk of becoming victims of property crime, the high-risk group for personal crimes is young black males (Regoli and Hewitt, 1996). Craven's (1994) analysis of the National Victimization Survey data reports that women are five times more likely than men to be victimized by their families and loved ones. Also, while since the late 1980s violent crime has been disproportionately perpetrated on young black males, the rate of victimization among young black women is growing at a much faster rate. If this trend continues, in the third millennium, young black women will replace their male counterparts as those at greatest risk of becoming victims of assault or of murder (Sourcebook of Criminal Justice Statistics, 1997).

Although the targets of property and personal crimes tend to be young, poor, and people of color, those most likely to process their claims are not. Rates of criminal justice employment of women and people of color, for example, have not paced their rates of victimization. As the age of affirmative action appears to be coming to a close, criminal justice work continues to be the province of working-class white males (Martin and Jurik, 1996). Consequently, the claims of many crime victims are handled by criminal justice agents of a different gender and racial or ethnic background. In those cases, interactions between crime victims and crime workers are as much intercultural exchanges as they are interpersonal ones. As we have seen throughout this book, age, gender, race, ethnicity, sexuality, and religion not only create variations in social identities, but also differences in the values and practices that go with them.

Criminal Justice Workers' Responses to Minority Victims

All else being equal, defendants who are poor, unemployed, or who are members of minority racial groups are more likely to receive full prosecution than their well-to-do or white counterparts (Black, 1976). Along the same lines, reports made by women, those with brown skin, or who are gay or lesbian too often receive less vigorous prosecution than do reports made by victims who are male, heterosexual, white, or of the upper classes (McKean, 1994; U.S. Commission on Civil Rights, 1990). How does this disparity in prosecution occur?

Social psychologists note that regardless of our intentions, it is harder to connect with and sustain empathy for those who are visibly different from ourselves (Goffman, 1967). For that reason, crime workers often create emotional distance between themselves and victims who are of a different social class, gender, skin color, or sexual orientation (Kidd and Chayet, 1984). When victims appear to think in a different way or make different choices, it becomes easy to assume they are somehow less rational and therefore less deserving of legal assistance than victims whose demeanor and behavior more readily meet a crime worker's expectations (Frohmann, 1991).

Once a crime worker labels a victim as "different" from him- or herself, it becomes easier to take the next step and blame the victim for their plight (Ryan, 1976). This is especially evident in male crime workers' responses to women's reports of intimate victimization. Frohmann's (1991, 1998) studies of prosecutorial decision making, for example, finds that prosecutors regularly employ extralegal factors such as the victim's unusual dress or irrational demeanor to justify their failure to bring sexual assault charges. Along the same lines, observing interactions between lower court personnel and battered women, Merry (1990a) noticed that judges and court clerks dispensed moral lectures rather than orders of protection when the choices made and actions taken by victims did not correspond to their own personal preferences.

In sum, when relations between criminal justice workers and crime victims are intercultural, crime workers are more likely to distance themselves from the victims, blame them for their plight and, subsequently, fail to meet victim expectations of justice.

Minority Victims' Responses to Criminal Justice Workers

Given the perceived antipathy of crime workers for minority victims, it is not surprising that so many minority victims are hesitant to engage the aid of crime workers. Moreover, once they have enlisted the aid of crime workers, minority victims of crime are more likely to express hostility and resentment for the treatment they receive. Research consistently finds, for example, that relative to white respondents, people of color hold more unfavorable views toward criminal justice personnel. NBC reported that although only 14% of their white viewers distrust law enforcement, nearly 41% of the nonwhites do (NBC Special Report, 1998). More specifically, minorities rate crime workers more negatively than do whites on such dimensions as fairness, quality of service and responsiveness (Smith, Graham, and Adams, 1991; United States Commission on Civil Rights, 1992), use of force (Greene, 1996) and handling of citizen complaints (Walker, Spohn, and DeLone, 1996). Certainly, such disaffection among minorities is at least in part fostered by experiences of disparate treatment by law enforcement. More importantly, even if they have not experienced discrimination firsthand, simply the expectation of differential treatment contributes to minority victims' general reluctance to contact or cooperate with crime workers.

In addition to differences in culture, language differences also place pressure on an already strained relationship. When criminal justice workers and crime victims do not speak the same language, victims tend to avoid the criminal justice process altogether (U.S. Commission on Civil Rights, 1992). As a Latina woman explained in her native tongue: "Yes, we are very limited because we don't speak the language. If something happens to us, we cannot even ask for help" (Madriz, 1997:349). Consequently, when crime victims and criminal justice workers speak different languages, it is even harder to develop and sustain a good working relationship.

For immigrants, reticence due to language differences is compounded by a fear of abuse by authorities and of deportation. Many immigrants come to the United States to escape persecution and genocide perpetrated in the name of justice. Among this group, distrust of the intentions and motivations of criminal justice workers is especially high, making it difficult for them to trust agents of the American criminal justice system. Sadly, while a disproportionate number of undocumented workers become victims of personal and property crimes, fear of deportation also makes it difficult for them to come forward and request assistance (see Perry, Chapter 5 of this volume).

Contrasting Expectations Between Crime Victims and Criminal Justice Workers

Although cultural differences make it more difficult for criminal justice workers and crime victims to establish mutually supportive relationships, not all tensions between crime victims and criminal justice workers involve intercultural dynamics. Differing expectations about what interactions will be like as well as what victims and workers should accomplish can make the establishment of a working partnership difficult. At times, the goals of crime victims are not only different from criminal justice workers, but also in direct contrast (Conley and O'Barr, 1990).

Contrasting Definitions of Justice

Since the late 1970s, various civil rights movements have considerably heightened the expectations for justice of many crime victims (Bumiller, 1992). Increasing numbers of women, poor people, gays, lesbians, and members of minority racial groups are entering the justice system with a sense of self-worth and entitlement to justice that prior to 1965 was simply unimaginable. No longer willing to silently endure victimization, battered women, targets of hate crimes, and victims of institutionalized poverty and racialized violence are now more committed than ever to claiming their right to justice (Friedman, 1994).

In addition, the emergence of a victim's rights movement has raised even further the expectations that crime victims have, consequently increasing both the number and range of demands they place on the criminal justice system (McShane and Williams, 1992). Changes in expectations about the treatment to which victims feel they are entitled are producing a new class of crime victims who are placing increasingly higher demands on criminal justice workers. Although the victims of the 1990s are entering the criminal justice system with heightened expectations for justice, a corresponding expansion of defendant rights and increasing concern for liability has made it more difficult than ever for criminal justice authorities to realistically and consistently fulfill crime victims' demands for justice.

Unable to meet crime victims' demands for a more total justice (Friedman, 1994) while fully honoring the constitutional rights of those accused, criminal justice workers either consciously or unconsciously categorize and then rank-order claims made by "real" crime victims (i.e., helpless or innocent) and crime victims who are "bogus" (i.e., claims made by criminals or perpetrators of violence) (Frohmann, 1998). Complaints made by "real" victims receive vigorous processing, whereas the "bogus" victims are "cooled out" or ignored completely (Blumberg, 1967). Within this typology, "authentic" victims are those deemed to be innocent or especially helpful, and "bogus" victims are those who themselves violate the law or have the means to intimidate or bully others. Most of those who report crimes fail to meet the criteria for a "real" or "authentic" victim. Engagement in a criminal lifestyle puts one at significantly greater risk of victimization. An occupational hazard of working in the sex trades, for example, is a higher risk of sexual assault (Pettiway, 1996). Thus, a significant portion of those who report crimes are themselves criminals. Thus, drug addicts, sex workers, and thieves fail to meet many crime workers' criteria for authenticity. In the end, their rights to justice are denied.

In addition, for the many who are trapped inside violent families and marriages, the door to justice becomes a revolving one through which victims enter repeatedly—at times assuming the role of plaintiff and at other times the role of defendant (McShane and Williams, 1992). As with criminals, when batterers become the battered, crime workers often label their complaints as "bogus" and dismiss them. Such disparate treatment in turn engenders frustration and disappointment. With each subsequent trip through the revolving door of justice, these victims return with either greater resolve to exercise their right to see justice done, or lowered expectations for fairness and justice.

Contrasting Definitions of Service

The heightening of victims' expectations for justice has taken place in tandem with an increase in consumerism. Since World War II, consumerism has encouraged an increasing conflation of the process of criminal justice with the commercial transaction. As a result, consumer-oriented victims perceive their relationships with crime workers as analogous to those between paying customers and sales clerk or paid servant. Regardless of the facts of their case or the system's current caseload, consumeristic victims expect timely service and deferential treatment by the civil servants they encounter, and then readily complain when the service is not to their liking.

The highly sensationalized coverage of the 2-year-long prosecution of O. J. Simpson suggested to millions of television viewers that those who can most afford it are most likely to get "full service" by court personnel. Justice has a price. In reality, however, the criminal justice system operates more often as a bureaucracy than as a service-oriented business. As bureaucrats, the primary mandate of police and court personnel is not to provide "good service" but to clear caseloads quickly and efficiently. Thus, victims and their complaints are queued up and moved down the assembly line of justice (Brickey and Miller, 1975). In busy jurisdictions where caseloads are high, victims of serious crimes are fortunate to get even 1 full day in court, and victims of misdemeanors are more likely to get only about 7 minutes (Bonsignore et al., 1998). As a result, rich and poor victims alike feel that their time before the bench is too brief. Unable to get what they feel is their money's worth, those seeking to purchase justice leave the court feeling shortchanged.

Relations between crime victims and criminal justice workers are at risk of becoming dysfunctional when expectations about service conflict. Many of those who perform crime work do so because they find the call to serve especially compelling (Coles, 1993). College, law school, and academies instill idealistic values of what it means to "serve and protect" (Gould, 1997). Graduates see themselves as "human service workers" rather than commercial "dispensers of justice." As a result, criminal justice workers find the expectations of consumer-oriented victims repugnant and offensive (Merry, 1990b).

Differing Rights and Responsibilities

Unlike other working relationships, relationships between crime victims and criminal justice workers are determined not by personalities, but by statute and legal precedent. In short, the law greatly constrains what criminal justice workers and crime victims can actually accomplish together. In fact, the law purposefully allocates differing amounts and types of rights and responsibilities between victims and workers.

The Victim's Prerogative

As citizens of the state, crime victims enjoy certain prerogatives that criminal justice workers do not have. Much to the frustration of criminal justice practitioners, crime victims are under no legal obligation to press charges, produce evidence, provide testimony, or even appear in court. Fear of retaliation by those they accuse causes many women to drop charges or fail to appear in court (Ford, 1991). To avoid secondary stigmatization or victimization, minorities and the socially deviant may abandon their quest for justice before the case has been closed. As a consequence, it is a rare moment when a crime victim stays the course and participates in all phases of the criminal justice process. More often, victims exit the criminal justice process before the prosecutions of their claims are complete.

However, although crime victims can opt out of the prosecution and adjudication processes at any time, criminal justice workers cannot. No matter how frivolous a complaint may be, criminal justice workers are legally mandated to respond. As citizens of the state, crime victims have a legal right to demand protection and prosecution, and it is the duty of police, prosecutors, and court personnel to process those requests, regardless of their personal feelings regarding them. When crime victims choose to exercise their prerogative not to file charges or provide testimony, those charged with the responsibility to process the victims' claims feel betrayed and exploited.

Yet it is important to remember that for many crime victims the decision not to file charges or not appear in court is not made on a whim, but out of necessity. Most seek assistance from the criminal justice system and even become dependent on such aid because they have so little autonomy or control over abusive or violent relationships in their personal lives (Merry, 1990b). Although fear for one's life or the lives of their children compels victims of interpersonal violence to call the police, fear of retaliation often results in the dropping of charges or the refusal to testify (Ford, 1991).

Victims who do file charges find that meetings with prosecutors and court appearances can be lengthy and that postponements can extend a trial for months. Those with little job security or who do not accrue paid leaves of absence are often forced to choose between earning wages and participation in the prosecution of their own cases. Rather than relinquishing what little control they might still have over their plight, victims who are poor or working class abandon the pursuit of justice, leaving crime workers with a formidable load of open or unwinnable cases.

Criminal Justice Workers' Discretion

Victims have little power to decide who processes their claims and much less how they do so. They lack the authority to participate in most of the decisions that move their complaints through (or out of) the justice system (Erez, 1990; Erez and Tontodonato, 1990). Even in those jurisdictions that have adopted a "Victim Bill of Rights," victims have little, if any, power to determine the fate of their claims (Weed, 1995).

In contrast, criminal justice workers possess extraordinary amounts of discretionary power. How quickly a case moves down the assembly line of justice depends on the willingness and ability of crime workers to mobilize resources and activate authorities (Emerson, 1983). Thus, the whims of police officers, victim assistance volunteers, prosecutors, and even court clerks greatly affect a victim's ability to achieve justice. Without the authority to demand a different case worker or prosecutor, victims often feel helpless when their cases are placed in the hands of indifferent or prejudiced workers.

Acts of prerogative and discretion can spark accusations of exploitation. Unable to control the course or direction of their claims or their participation in the processing of them, crime victims often feel like helpless pawns in the game of justice and complain about feeling discounted, ignored, and otherwise "jerked around" (Davis and Smith, 1994). Likewise, without the authority to make victims follow through, criminal justice workers feel betrayed and let down by the very people they seek to assist. Ironically, each feels powerless to affect the cooperation of the other.

The Consequences of Conflict in the Crime Victim/ Criminal Justice Worker Relationship

Considering the cultural and structural context in which relationships between criminal justice workers and crime victims function, it is no wonder that so many of these relationships turn sour. The lived experiences of those who have actually been in or are currently in a crime victim/criminal justice worker relationship stand in stark contrast to the romantic portraits that the media, our public schools, and political figures so readily paint (Erez, 1990). In real life, relations between crime victims and those whose job it is to handle their claims are, at best, strained, and are more likely to be downright contentious. So, on an almost daily basis, at crime scenes and police stations (Stenross and Kleinman, 1989), in the offices of prosecutors (Frohmann, 1991), inside courtrooms (Merry, 1990a,b), and even at the doors of the social service agencies providing shelter and solace (Ferraro, 1983), crime victims and agents of justice commonly battle *each other* for autonomy and control (see also Ford, 1991). When relations with crime victims become difficult, criminal justice agents blame the victims they serve, calling them "assholes" (Van Maanen, 1978) and accusing them of being "overly emotional" (Stenross and Kleinman, 1989), "insincere" (Ferraro, 1983), or without "self control" or "common sense" (Merry, 1990a). With each negative interaction with a victim, criminal justice workers become increasingly cynical about the needs and motivations of those who request their aid.

Along the same lines, victims justify their dissatisfaction with entire justice system by blaming those who happened to have handled their cases for being "inept," "lazy," "petulant," "power hungry, "insensitive," or just plain "coldhearted" (Madigan and Gamble, 1989). With each disappointment, victims grow more disaffected with the criminal justice system and those who work in it. The consequences of such cynicism and disaffection are not without consequence.

The Price We Pay for Cynicism

The price the community pays for cynicism among its criminal justice workers is significant. Cynical workers too easily abandon the goal of justice and simply settle for the processing of cases. With little compassion or creativity, they move victims and their problems along a dehumanizing assembly line of justice (Brickey and Miller, 1975). Research shows that the cynicism is a formidable barrier to sensitivity training (Gould, 1997). The spillover effect is significant. Frustration with uncooperative or difficult victims is easily transferred onto others. One study, for example, reports that the families of law enforcement workers are at a significantly higher risk of domestic violence than are others (*Arizona Daily Sun*, 1998).

Perhaps more insidiously, cynicism opens the door to the abuse of authority and power. As the videotaped beating of Rodney King so vividly illustrated, pent-up frustrations from negative experiences with victims and defendants alike can become lethal. However, on a day-to-day basis, police officers, court clerks, and prosecutors abuse their discretion in much smaller ways—by harassing, intimidating, or otherwise aggravating the victims (and those who are, for whatever reason, associated with them) who have made their lives difficult.

Victims frequently report feeling violated a second time when criminal justice workers fail to take their claims seriously. Madigan and Gamble (1989:3) make the convincing argument that "women who report a rape are again raped by a system composed of well-intentioned people who are nevertheless blinded by the myths of centuries." In their zeal to file charges and close cases, investigators, prosecutors, and judges retraumatize victims when they take testimony and collect evidence without providing sufficient support or expressing empathy. Gay victims of crime also fear the courtroom experience. In Chapter 11, Perry noted the increased use of the homosexual panic defense, whereby "homosexual advance" is interpreted as a mitigating circumstance in bias-motivated assaults. We have also seen in many of the chapters in this volume, and earlier in this chapter, how minority victims of crime often derive "less justice" from the courts than do their white counterparts.

Workers at all levels of the criminal justice system engage in secondary victimization, or "derivative deviance" (Berrill and Herek, 1992). This is behavior that further stigmatizes or, in fact, revictimizes victims of crime because of their identity. Gay men and women, prostitutes, and drug dealers, for example, are often held responsible for their own victimization because of their "deviant" identities; people of color, women, and immigrants are often revictimized because of their perceived "difference." These perceptions, if held by the criminal justice workers with whom they come in contact, leave minority victims of crime vulnerable to castigation, harassment, and even violence. The King beating in Los Angeles and the alleged sodomization of Louima in New York City are extreme illustrations of broader patterns whereby people of color and poor people, in particular, bear the brunt of the frustrations of criminal justice workers. In addition, on average, 20% of gay lesbian victims of hate crime report victimization at the hands of police (Berrill and Herek, 1992; see also Comstock, 1991). Women, too, are vulnerable to sexual violence at the hands of criminal justice personnel. Sexual harassment is especially prevalent as male officers attempt to preserve the traditional masculinity of the field (Messerschmidt, 1997).

The Price We Pay for Victim Disaffection

Secondary victimization disempowers victims, who perceive themselves to be without legal redress. It instills, or in fact reinforces, distrust of the criminal justice workers, who are seen as the "enemy" rather than as advocates. Consequently, many victims exit the justice system feeling *revictimized* by their contact with the criminal system (Madigan and Gamble, 1989). Even in the absence of revictimization, dissatisfaction with either the process or the outcome engenders a sense of injustice, which in turn fosters disaffection with the entire justice system. The disaffected often lack sufficient motivation to report crimes or cooperate in either criminal investigations or prosecutions.

Given the stress and trauma that reporting a crime can entail, it is little wonder that victims of crime are reluctant to come forward; however, there is even less incentive for those who have been marginalized from power and then victimized for it by criminal justice workers. Less than 20% of hate crimes against gays and lesbians are ever reported to police (Dean, Wu, and Martin, 1992). Fear of being hassled or demeaned for being different, immigrants and people of color are also hesitant to seek aid from criminal justice authorities (U.S. Commission on Civil Rights, 1992; see also Walker *et al.*, 1996). Because they fear that they will not be taken seriously, women also tend to keep violations by husbands and lovers to themselves (Belknap, 1996; Warshaw, 1994).

In sum, the cynicism that so often infects criminal justice workers also has implications for crime victims. The frustration experienced by so many police officers, prosecutors, and judges is often played out in the context of their interactions with victims of crime. The risk is that those victims will, at best, be underserved, and at worst, be revictimized.

Reconciling Difference?

Are the differences between victims and workers truly irreconcilable? Is the crime victim/criminal justice worker relationship doomed to be one of conflict and contention? Is disaffection with and cynicism about criminal justice an inevitable by-product of such a partnership? Although the romantic portraits as painted by the media may be unrealizable and even undesirable, we can at least consider some strategies for making the relationship more empowering, if not effectual. Some of these strategies might be implemented inside the criminal justice system, and some might be more effective independent of its bureaucratic structures. The following are but a few techniques that might help to empower both crime victims and criminal justice workers.

Crime Victim Empowerment

Looking at what we have learned from our analysis, it is important for criminal justice workers to keep in mind that while in *theory* the crime victim/criminal justice worker relationship is conceptualized as a partnership between equals, in *reality*, it often is not. The individuals who step into the victim role do so because they lack the personal or social power to resolve problems and right transgressions on their own (Merry, 1990a,b). It is no accident that a disproportionate number of crime victims are women, nonwhite, and poor, as these groups are in greatest need of social and legal empowerment. Those without the means to terminate violent relationships, those without insurance to replace stolen goods, and those without access to trauma counseling seek a relationship with criminal justice workers because it is the most viable source of empowerment available to them. It is imperative, therefore, that as criminal justice workers, we seek to engage in strategies that will help, rather than harm, crime victims. What follows are but a few possible strategies that we might keep in mind.

1. *Interpreters.* Given the earlier argument that language barriers (or hearing impairments) often limit the access of non-English speakers to the criminal justice system, it is important that interpreters be available at all stages of the criminal justice process. If there is a paucity of language-trained police or court personnel, jurisdictions should contract with multiple interpreters in the area so that the problem of availability is alleviated. This should extend not only to non-English speaking interpreters, but American Sign Language experts as well.

2. *Victim advocates.* One of the factors that contributes to victim dissatisfaction is the disjuncture between expectations and experiences of the criminal justice system. The use of victim advocates would mitigate this. Advocates should be involved as early as possible in the process. They would thus be available to inform victims what to expect at every stage. Advocates would also be responsible for keeping victims informed about the ongoing status of the case, so that victims do not feel distanced from the process.

3. *Counseling.* Victims of violent crimes such as assault or sexual assault, for example, may be in particular need of counseling to assist them in coping with their victimization. This is especially true for cases in which they have experienced secondary victimization or revictimization by criminal justice workers. They may need to be reassured that they are, in fact, victims, and not offenders.

Beyond that, many victims often need assistance in coming to terms with their experiences in a way that helps to mitigate the trauma.

4. *Crisis centers.* Victim advocates or counselors might be activated through crisis centers designed to respond immediately to reported victimizations. These entities would be expected to provide a range of services, usually to specific classes of victims such as victims of hate crime, victims of domestic violence, victims of sexual assault, or victims of property offenses. The shelters would assist with all stages of the process, including reporting the crime, guiding victims through the process, and perhaps even helping to file insurance claims or orders of protection.

In the wake of the victims' rights movement, many models of intervention aimed at victims have been introduced across the nation. We offer very broad suggestions about some of the more common types of strategies employed both inside and beyond the criminal justice system.

Criminal Justice Worker Empowerment

Criminal justice workers are not to be forgotten in our efforts to enhance the worker–victim relationship. They also encounter obstacles in their efforts to engage with victims. Moreover, criminal justice workers are not immune to the emotional toll that the criminal justice process takes on those involved with it. It is important, then, that we address the needs of criminal justice workers. It is also important to recognize that all levels of the criminal justice system are subject to the types of problems identified: cynicism, distrust, or burn-out, for example. Consequently, the types of services suggested here should be available to judges, prosecutors, and police officers alike.

1. *Counseling services.* Like victims of crime, criminal justice workers often have difficulties coping with criminal justice processes. Police officers and correctional officers, for example, experience relatively high levels of emotional exhaustion and burn-out. Counseling may ameliorate these effects. Crisis counseling should also be made available to those who have experienced especially traumatic emergencies, such as a police shooting of a civilian, or the death of a colleague. We should not assume that criminal justice workers can cope with these traumas any better than civilians can cope with their victimization.

2. *Language training.* If criminal justice workers are to interact effectively with their victim counterparts, they must be able to communicate with them. Consequently, workers should be given the opportunity to learn languages that are relevant to their work. If there is a sizable population of Vietnamese immigrants in a community, for example, police officers and court workers should be rewarded for efforts to learn the appropriate dialects. This would help to minimize the frustration often experienced by both groups.

3. *Cultural awareness training.* Understanding of and sensitivity toward local communities also facilitates the process of communication and cooperation.

Criminal justice personnel should, therefore, be encouraged, if not required, to engage in periodic cultural awareness training. To do so only once at the beginning of one's career is insufficient, because communities change demographically over time. Workers should always be "in touch" with the diversity of their clientele.

4. *Problem solving/conflict resolution training.* An important element in the successful negotiation of the worker/victim relationship is the ability to render a satisfactory decision. This does not necessarily mean that someone "wins" and someone "loses" in a dispute situation. Rather, it suggests the ability to achieve some compromise whereby all parties are satisfied with the process of the decision, if not the decision itself. In an era of community policing, this particular tool is becoming more highly valued relative to traditional adversarial means of dispute resolution. Here, criminal justice workers might learn from peacemaking initiatives.

Toward an Empowering Relationship Between Crime Victims and Criminal Justice Workers

This chapter argues throughout that at the heart of the criminal justice system lies the partnership between crime victims and criminal justice workers. Consequently, to be most effective, strategies aimed toward victims and workers as separate entities should be embedded in a criminal justice system that is more attuned to the fact that the two groups are involved in a relationship. Those strategies that seek to negotiate that relationship will be paramount in our efforts to minimize conflict and dissatisfaction.

1. *Community and cultural liaisons.* One very important means of bridging the gap between criminal justice workers and crime victims is the establishment of community liaisons. These trained officers of the court, police department, or other agency are responsible for making sustained contact with the community, thereby creating a relationship that is mutually beneficial. On the one hand, it gives the community a voice; on the other hand, it helps the criminal justice agency make itself welcome in that community.

2. *Mediators.* Sometimes liaisons are not enough or do not exist in a particular area. When this is the case, and a conflict arises between the criminal justice worker and the community, mediators may play a useful interim role. For example, if the community should become alarmed about what they perceive to be as discriminatory treatment of its members, a mediator may be called in to seek some resolution. Both (or all) parties would be brought to the table and given an opportunity to voice their concerns and perceptions. The intent of this particular form of dispute resolution would be to provide a neutral process of reconciliation between the community and the criminal justice system.

3. *Citizen advisory boards.* In communities that are especially mistrustful of the operation of the criminal justice system, increasing demands are being made for the establishment of citizen advisory boards. Such bodies are assigned varying degrees of oversight with respect to the agency in question. These are most common in the field of policing; however, we are beginning to see boards that oversee sentencing practices, for example. Such bodies are intended to democratize the criminal justice system by allowing civilian input in the decision-making process. Sometimes, however, they have had the unintended effect of creating resentment on the part of the criminal justice agency in question (Miller and Hess, 1998).

4. *Community policing.* Many of the strategies listed are best employed within the context of community policing. As the label suggests, this approach to policing is explicitly concerned with forging closer links between diverse communities and the police who serve them. It is a philosophy that is finding increasing support among workers and victims alike. Implemented effectively, community policing has the potential to enhance the voice of the public—and victims in particular—while simultaneously making the work of criminal justice easier. It is itself an effort to overcome both the cynicism of the worker and the disaffection of the victim.

At the outset of this chapter, we argued that the actions of criminal justice workers are often contingent on the decisions reached by crime victims and that both are shaped by relationships between the two groups. We also argued that the crime victim/criminal justice worker relationship is fraught with tension and conflict. However, it is important to bear in mind that this tension is not generated by the personalities in question, but rather by the cultural and structural differences between these two groups. The concluding section of this chapter is intended to suggest that those tensions are not irreconcilable. We took the first step in this process of reconciliation when we recognized that problems exist. We took the second step when we suggested potential means by which the tensions could be negotiated. The next step is yours, as future or present criminal justice workers: that is, it is up to you to implement these reforms.

References

Altheide, D. (1997). The news media, the problem frame, and the production of fear. *Sociological Quarterly, 38(4)*, 647(22).

Arizona Daily Sun (1998). Police home violence a silent ill? 11 October.

Belknap, J. (1996). *The invisible woman: Gender, crime and justice.* New York: Wadsworth.

Berrill, K. and Herek, G. (1992). Primary and secondary victimization in anti-gay hate crimes: Official responses and public policy. In G. Herek and K. Berrill (Eds.), *Hate crimes: Confronting violence against lesbians and gay men*, pp. 289–305. Newbury Park, CA: Sage.

Black, D. (1976). *The behavior of law.* New York: Academic Press.

Blumberg, A. (1967). Law as a confidence game: Organizational co-optation of a profession. *Law and Society Review*, 1, 15–39.

Brickey, S. and Miller, D. (1975). Bureaucratic due process: An ethnography of a traffic court. *Social Problems*, 22, 688–697.

Bosignore, J., et al. (1998). *Before the law.* Boston: Houghton Mifflin Company.

Bumiller, K. (1992). *The civil rights society.* Baltimore: John Hopkins University Press.

Coles, R. (1993). *The call to service: A witness to idealism.* Boston: Houghton Mifflin.

Comstock, G. (1991). *Violence against lesbians and gay men.* New York: Columbia University Press.

Conley, J. and O'Barr, W. (1990). *Rules versus relationships: The ethnography of legal discourse.* Chicago: University of Chicago Press.

Craven, D. (1994). Sex differences in violent victimization. U.S. Department of Justice, Bureau of Justice Statistics online document: http://www.ojp.usdoj.gov/bjs/pub/ascii.advv.txt.

Davis, R. and Smith, B. E. (1994). Victim impact statements and victim satisfaction: An unfulfilled promise? *Journal of Criminal Justice, 22(1),* 1–12.

Dean, L., Wu, Shanyu, and Martin, J. L. (1992). Trends in violence and discrimination against lesbians and gay men. In G. Herek and K. Berrill (Eds.), *Hate crimes: Confronting violence against lesbians and gay men,* pp. 46–64. Newbury Park: Sage.

Emerson, R. and Messinger, S. (1977). The micropolitics of trouble. *Social Problems, 25,* 120–134.

Emerson, R. (1983). Holistic effects in social control decision-making. *Law and Society Review, 17(3),* 425–455.

Erez, E. (1990). Victim participation in sentencing: Rhetoric and reality. *Journal of Criminal Justice, 18,* 19–31.

Erez, E. and Tontodonato, P. (1990). The effect of victim participation in sentencing on sentence outcome. *Criminology, 28(3),* 451–475.

Federal Bureau of Investigation (1998). *The uniform crime reports.* http://www.fbi.gov/ucr/ucreports.htm.

Ferraro, K. (1995). Cops, courts and woman battering. In B. R. Price and N. Sokoloff (Eds.), *The criminal justice system and women,* pp. 262–271. New York: McGraw-Hill.

———. (1983). Negotiating trouble in a battered women's shelter. *Urban Life, 12(3),* 287–306.

Ferraro, K. and Pope, L. (1993). Irreconcilable differences: Battered women, police and the law. In N. Z. Hilton (Ed.), *The legal responses to wife assault,* pp. 96–123. Thousand Oaks, CA: Sage Publications.

Ford, D. (1991). Prosecution as a victim power resource. *Law and Society Review, 25(2),* 313–334.

Friedman, L. (1994). *Total justice.* New York: The Russell Sage Foundation.

Frohmann, L. (1991). Discrediting victims' allegations of sexual assault. *Social Problems, 38(2),* 213–226.

———. (1998). Constituting power in sexual assault cases: Prosecutorial strategies for victim management. *Social Problems,* 393–407.

Goffman, E. (1967). *Interactional ritual: Essays on face-to-face behavior.* New York: Anchor Books.

Gottfredson, M. and Gottfredson, D. (1988). The victim's decision to report a crime. In *Decision making in criminal justice,* pp. 15–45. New York: Plenum.

Gould, L. (1997). Can an old dog be taught new tricks? *Policing: An International Journal of Police Strategies and Management, 20(2),* 339–356.

Greene, H. T. (1996). Black perspectives on police brutality. In A. Sulton (Ed.), *African American perspectives on crime causation, criminal justice administration and crime prevention,* pp. 109–122. Boston: Butterworth-Heinemann.

Hudson, P. (1984). The crime victim and the criminal justice system. *Pepperdine Law Review, 11,* 23–63.

Kelly, D. (1984). Victims' perceptions of criminal justice. *Pepperdine Law Review, 11,* 15–21.

Kidd, R. and Chayet, E. (1984). Why do victims fail to report? The psychology of criminal victimization. *Journal of Social Issues, 40(01),* 39–50.

Madigan, L. and Gamble, N. (1989). *The second rape: Society's continued betrayal of the victim.* New York: Lexington Books.

Madriz, E. (1997). Images of crime and victims: A study on women's fear and social control. *Gender and Society, 11(3),* 342–356.

Mahan, S. (1996). *Crack, cocaine, crime and women.* Thousand Oaks, CA: Sage Publications.

Martin, S. and Jurik, N. (1996). *Doing gender, doing justice: Women in the law and criminal justice occupations.* Thousand Oaks, CA: Sage Publications.

McKean, J. (1994). Race, ethnicity and criminal justice. In J. Hendricks and B. Byers (Eds.), *Multicultural perspectives in criminal justice and criminology,* pp. 85–134. Springfield, IL: Charles C. Thomas.

McShane, M. and Williams, F. (1992). Radical victimology: A critique of the concept of victim in traditional victimology. *Crime and Delinquency, 38(2),* 258–271.

Merry, S. E. (1986). Everyday understandings of law in working-class America. *The American Ethnologist, 13,* 253–270.

———. (1990a). *Getting justice, getting even.* Chicago: University of Chicago Press.

———. (1990b). Law as fair, law as help. In *New directions in the study of justice, law and social control. School of justice studies,* pp. 167–186. New York: Plenum Press.

Messerschmidt, J. (1997). *Crime as structured action: Gender, race, class, and crime in the making.* Thousand Oaks, CA: Sage.

Miller, L. and Hess, K. (1998). *The police in the community: Strategies for the 21st century.* Belmont, CA: West/Wadsworth.

Morgan, P. (1999). Risking relationships: Understanding the litigation choices of sexually harassed women. *Law and Society Review, 33(1),* 201–226.

NBC Special Report (1998). Aired 18 October. "Black and blue."

Pettiway, L. (1996). *Honey, honey, miss thang: Being black, gay and on the streets.* Philadelphia: Temple University Press.

Pincus, S. and Rosen, D. (1997). Fighting back: Filing suit under the violence against women act. *Trial* (December), 20–27.

Posner, R. (1985). *The extent and causes of the caseload explosion. The federal courts: Crisis and reform.* Cambridge: Oxford University Press.

Regoli, R. and Hewitt, J. (1996). *Criminal justice.* Englewood Cliffs, NJ: Prentice-Hall.

Ryan, W. (1976). *Blaming the victim.* New York: Vintage Books.

Smith, D., Graham, N., and Adams, B. (1991). Minorities and the police: Attitudes and behavioral questions,. In M. Lynch and B. Patterson (Eds.), *Race and criminal justice,* pp. 22–35. Albany, NY: Harrow and Heston.

Sourcebook of criminal justice statistics (1997). Victimization Webpages. http://www.albany.edu/sourcebook/1995/ind/VICTIMIZATION.ind.html

Stambaugh, P. M. (1997). The power of law and the sexual harassment complaints of women. *National Women's Studies Association Journal, 9(2),* 23–42.

Stenross, B. and Kleinman, S. (1989). The highs and lows of emotional labor: Detectives' encounters with criminals and victims. *Journal of Contemporary Ethnography, 17(4),* 435–452.

U.S. Commission on Civil Rights (1992). *Civil rights issues facing Asian Americans.* Washington, DC: U.S. Government Printing Office.

———. (1990). *Intimidation and violence: Racial and religious bigotry in America.* Washington, DC: U.S. Government Printing Office.

Van Maanen, J. (1978). The asshole. In P. K. Manning and J. V. Maanen (Eds.), *Policing: A view from the street,* pp. 221–238. Santa Monica, CA: Goodyear Publishing.

Walker, S., Spohn, C., and DeLone, M. (1996). *The color of justice.* Belmont, CA: Wadsworth.

Warshaw, R. (1994). *I never called it rape.* New York: HarperCollins.

Weed, F. (1995). *Certainty of justice: Reform in the crime victim movement.* New York: Aldine De Gruyter.

Williams, M. (1995). Civil cases, criminal problems. *Trial Talk, 44(4),* 16–20.

PART FOUR

Conclusion

20 Reinvestigating Difference

BARBARA PERRY

MARIANNE O. NIELSEN

Difference matters. Each of the chapters in this book demonstrates that fact. The authors encourage readers to think about how difference is constructed and how difference is handled in the context of criminal justice. In particular, we see how the effects of difference have been and continue to be informed by privilege, power, and discrimination within the criminal justice system. However, it is not enough to identify the negative consequences of difference. Consequently, each of the authors also draws attention to the ways in which the damaging effects of difference might be ameliorated. This concluding chapter seeks to pull those threads together so that, as criminal justice practitioners, readers will be empowered to reinvestigate difference. The goal of this chapter, then, is to consider strategies by which the effects of the social construction of difference can be challenged in the interests of not only criminal justice, but also social justice.

Deconstructing and Reconstructing Difference

One of the themes that unifies the discussions in this volume is that difference is socially constructed. The mechanisms by which this is accomplished are many and varied: stereotypes, language, legislation, and differential experiences with the criminal justice system are but a few. You read, for example, how stereotyping Native Americans as "savages," or criminalizing the sexuality of gay men and lesbians, or excluding Asians from citizenship have served to maintain the stigmatized outsider identity of these diverse groups. You read how these "Others" have been defined negatively in terms of their relationship to some dominant norm—that is, how "black" is defined as inherently inferior to "white," Jewish to Christian, gay to straight. You have read how the criminal justice system has been a primary site for enacting these differences as well as acting on them by differentially enforcing the law along the lines of race, class, gender, age, ability, sexuality and religion.

However, as Wonders points out in Chapter 2 of this volume, there is reason for hope: because difference is socially constructed, it can also be socially reconstructed. In other words, as a society, we can redefine the ways in which difference "matters." We can strive for a just and democratic society in which the full spectrum of diversity addressed here is reevaluated in a positive and celebratory light.

We would do well to heed Young's (1990) advice that we embrace a positive politics of difference. This would involve much more than efforts to assimilate those who are different, or merely "tolerate" their presence. Rather, it challenges us to celebrate our differences. Of course, this requires that much of our current way of ordering the world be radically altered. It means that we must cease to define "different" as inferior and see it instead as simply not the same.

To engage in such a powerful political activity is to resist the temptation to ask everyone to conform to an artificial set of norms and expectations. It is to reclaim and value the "natural" heterogeneity of this nation rather than force a false homogeneity. It is to refuse to denigrate the culture and experiences of black people, women, or gay men, for example. It is to learn and grow from the strength and beauty that alternate cultures have to offer.

Given the historical and contemporary processes uncovered in this book, reconstructing the meaning and value associated with difference will be no easy task. It will require dramatic changes in attitudes and behavior throughout society. However, as current or potential criminal justice practitioners, you, as students, will have a crucial role to play in this transformation, because the criminal justice system has all too often been complicit in enforcing a negative politics of difference. We turn now to a consideration of concrete strategies by which criminal justice workers might lead the way in empowering those who have traditionally been weakened.

Law as a Mechanism of Empowerment

An important first step in empowering the disempowered is to question and critically evaluate the role of the legal structure in creating and perpetuating unequal relations of power. Most authors in this volume draw attention to the material and ideological means by which law has contributed to the subordination of minority groups. The law itself can effectively exclude or restrict the participation of particular groups in the ongoing activities and processes of society—just as immigration and naturalization laws have historically prevented many Asians from entry, or from attaining citizenship. Law can—by its silences—exclude groups from protections afforded others, such as in the failure to include gays or women in hate crime or civil rights legislation, for example. Law can also marginalize others: "immigration sweeps" stigmatize and victimize Latinos, in particular; legal distinctions between "crack" and white-powder cocaine incarcerate more African Americans than other groups; anti-abortion policies limit women's autonomy; social security restrictions endanger and exclude immigrants; the federal government's Indian policy marginalizes Native American populations; and the military's "Don't ask, don't tell" policy silences gays. In their own way, each of these cases serves to marginalize or subordinate the groups in question. They raise questions about the particular group's legitimacy and place in United States society; in some cases, they explicitly define their "outsider" status. In other words, law is a dramatic form of political and cultural expression that "draws the boundaries that divide us into groups, with momentous effects on our individual identities" (Karst, 1993:2). It is an integral part of the field in which difference is constructed and reaffirmed.

Consequently, if we are to democratize the criminal justice system, legislation that is unjust and discriminatory in its content or effects must be eliminated, to be replaced by legislation that promotes justice and equity. This is consistent with the fact that critical decisions about criminal justice are increasingly moved into the legislative arena (e.g., judicial oversight of corrections). This is not the place to catalog all of these legislative reforms. It is, rather, the place to encourage criminal justice workers to investigate the legislation they are asked to enforce for signs of injustice, and then act on those findings. Consider these examples: sodomy legislation criminalizes gay men in particular—lobby for its repeal; status offenses hold youth to different and unreasonable standards of behavior—lobby for the elimination of this class of offenses; domestic violence legislation trivializes the harm to female victims—lobby for reform of the legislation.

The law is not an immutable behemoth. It is vulnerable to the impact of ongoing struggles between groups. It has been used effectively in the past to extend the rights and protections afforded women, people of color, children, and disabled persons. The Americans with Disabilities Act, for example, has been crucial in enhancing the mobility and independence of those who are differently abled. The Violence Against Women Act dramatically expanded the services available to battered women. Successive civil rights acts—at the national and state levels— have been crucial to the political and economic advances of women and people of color in particular. It is not unreasonable, then, to encourage legislative reform as a means of minimizing the negative and exclusionary effects of difference.

Prejudice Reduction

The legal regulation of difference has often been grounded in broader social and cultural perceptions of difference. Across time and across the country, we have seen repeatedly how the "Other" is demonized and stigmatized, both within the criminal justice system and beyond. These processes shaped the criminalization and the victimization of those deemed both different and inferior. Stereotypes of the "promiscuous woman," for example, consistently served to enable violence against women; stereotypes of gay men as pedophiles consistently served to enable legislation criminalizing their sexuality; stereotypes of irresponsible adolescents consistently served to enable both their victimization and criminalization. In each of these illustrative cases, the stereotypes disempower those who are different because their difference is assumed to be immutable and deviant. Consequently, the key to empowerment is to eliminate the "discriminatory and/or privileging effects attached to difference" (Wonders, Chapter 2).

This is a task that will be most effective if it is attained in a broad array of contexts. Prejudice and hostility toward those who are deemed different inform every level of society. Consequently, antiprejudice initiatives will also be broadly disseminated. The most effective starting point is to reach children during their formative years, through parents and elementary and high schools. In fact, recent years have seen a dramatic growth in education-based antiprejudice programs. The most compelling of these is the Southern Poverty Law Center's *Teaching Tolerance* project. This preventative initiative assists educators in designing curricula that encourage students to recognize, understand, and value difference. It is to be hoped that such interventions break the connections between difference and intolerance, so that subsequent generations will be less vulnerable to the messages of hate propagated by the hate movement. To the extent that educational activities—in the schools and in the community—are able to deconstruct damaging and divisive stereotypes, they will continue to be effective mechanisms by which to counteract prejudice and discrimination. Although not all educators or students will be receptive to the alternative messages of tolerance, "for every school child and young adult that we can and do reach, we shall be influencing a world beyond our own" (Kleg, 1993:260).

Diversity education should not end when students graduate from high school. Rather, it is important that it be integrated into postsecondary education as well. Criminal justice curricula, for example, are beginning to adopt courses that explicitly address difference in the context of criminal justice. These courses focus on issues of cultural diversity, gender diversity, and the diversity presented by individuals in disadvantaged age categories, with physical and mental disabilities, from different religious backgrounds, and from immigrant backgrounds. With the increasing emphasis on college education as a prerequisite for entry into criminal justice employment, more and more potential workers will be exposed to such curricula. To supplement this, however, it is vital that academies and in-service training also include modules that address the differential experiences and needs of diverse populations.

The messages transmitted in our schools will have little long-term impact unless they are accompanied by subsequent repetition in society at large. Media campaigns aimed at deconstructing popular misconceptions and community organizations devoted to minimizing negative imagery are useful local initiatives. Moreover, as individuals, we also have a responsibility to recognize and eliminate prejudice within ourselves. For most of us, the learning of prejudicial (e.g., racist, sexist, ageist) ideas was an unavoidable outcome of our early socialization and learning. Whatever its source, prejudice hinders our ability to adapt to our increasingly diverse social environment. Prejudice is like a communicable disease (Skillings and Dobbins, 1991). Consider tuberculosis, for example. It is a serious disease that anyone could contract quite by accident. However, once we become aware that we have it, we are obliged to have it treated so that we do not infect others. So it is with prejudice: Once we realize we have been "infected," we are obliged to have it "treated" so that we do not pass it on and harm others. Treatment can vary from increased self-analysis of one's own perceptions to seeking out opportunities for meaningful intercultural communication, to individual counselling in extreme cases. It addition to these mechanisms, the goal of prejudice reduction should be kept in mind in the context of hiring and training practices.

Criminal Justice Employment and Training

Criminal justice agencies that are representative of the communities they serve will almost invariably be more aware of the particular problems of these communities. However, as the authors in this book indicate, minority groups are dramatically underrepresented as service providers in the criminal justice system. As the United States becomes even more diverse, it will become increasingly important for agencies to recruit those who are "different." It is these recruits who will bring with them an understanding of their clientele, as well as slightly different approaches to their jobs. Latino/a police officers, for example, will bring insights into the specificity of domestic violence among Latinos/as; women bring dialogic rather than aggressive tactics into emotional confrontations; physically challenged persons bring attention to the barriers implied by the physical environment. In other words, hiring those who are different is a way to invest in and take advantage of diversity.

There are a number of distinct advantages to employing a culturally heterogeneous workforce within criminal justice. Officers and personnel drawn from the communities they represent may play the formal or informal role of liaison between the public and the criminal justice system. They may have a better understanding and greater empathy for the people with whom they interact. The potential benefit to be derived from this bridging of the distance is a less hostile and more cooperative community. Ultimately, stronger community relations may engender greater safety for all justice workers.

There is also considerable value in members of diverse groups designing and operating their own services, such as the battered women's shelters or rape crisis centers that were first established by groups of concerned women. Similarly, Native Americans have the unique legal right to establish criminal justice organizations to provide services in their own Nations. The Navajo Nation, for example, has its own police, courts, probation services, and Peacemakers devoted to traditional justice practices. Immigrant organizations have been especially useful as advocates for newly arrived residents.

However, there are often problems associated with members of subordinated groups working within the criminal justice system. Police officers, for example, may experience "double marginality," wherein they are seen as outsiders by their predominantly white (male, straight) colleagues and as traitors by their nonwhite (female, gay) community. The distance from their fellow criminal justice practitioners may, in fact, be exacerbated by the tendency to marginalize minority officers by giving them primary responsibility for serving their own community, or serving in "culturally sensitive" roles (e.g., women in juvenile justice; people of color in communities of color).

Moreover, hiring and promoting women, or people of color, or people with disability, or anyone else within criminal justice agencies is no guarantee that those agencies will necessarily be more sensitive to cultural diversity. There are, for example, gay men who are racist, women who are sexist, and Latinos/as who are classist. Ignorance and prejudice cut across difference. Consequently, regardless of the make-up of criminal justice agencies, cultural awareness training will have a crucial role to play in sensitizing its members to the experiences, values, and needs of the communities they serve. Gould's chapter (Chapter 17) on cultural awareness training highlights the rationales and content of effective training modules. In particular, such training, whether at the point of hire or in-service, should address key cultural differences in such areas as values, communication, patterns of interaction, and the importance of family, for example.

Speaking of Difference . . .

No amount of cultural awareness training or employment of minority personnel will bridge cultural differences if problems of communication persist. Nielsen's chapter (Chapter 18) on intercultural and interpersonal communication explicitly identifies a number of potential barriers to effective communication between individuals and between groups. The most obvious obstacle is language difference. One of the prime indicators of the diversity of the United States is the fact that hundreds of languages and thousands of dialects are spoken within the nation's borders. Obviously, this can pose problems for predominantly English-speaking agents who come in contact with non-English–speaking clients. Ogawa (1999:3) tells the story of a police officer who offended a number of Latinos at an accident scene by asking them (erroneously) why no one spoke English. An African American man responded that, if the officer intended to serve the community, it was his responsibility to be bilingual. Increasingly, police departments and other criminal justice agencies are acknowledging this responsibility to serve their communities in the appropriate and relevant language.

Regions and cities across the United States—especially on the coasts—contain heavy concentrations of people whose first language is not English. Many, for example, have large Latino/a populations; some have high proportions of Native Americans; a growing number of communities host large Asian populations. With changing demographics and the increasing globalization of the economy, bi- or multilingualism will become a source of strength. Moreover, if criminal justice personnel, specifically, are to serve the needs and interests of all people, it is vital for them to provide services in languages other than English (including American

Sign Language). Hiring bilingual officers is one solution. However, this is not always possible or feasible. The alternative, then, is to have ready access to translators who help bridge the linguistic gap.

Even where language differences are absent or mitigated in some way, interpersonal and intercultural barriers to communication may still be present. Like most other professions, those in criminal justice often have a language of their own. Acronyms and numerical codes prohibit civilian comprehension. More broadly, however, even people who share a common language may use the language differently. In Canada, neither "Grits" nor "Waffles" would be eaten for breakfast, since the terms refer to political parties. These interpretive problems are often accompanied by nonverbal communication patterns. Depending on one's cultural experience, nodding one's head could mean either yes or no; silence could imply either great respect or great disrespect. Again, training in the communication patterns of local populations can minimize the misunderstandings that emerge out of these differences.

It is not only the community that benefits from such considerations. Police officers and others often voice frustration when they are unable to communicate with the people with whom they interact. This is understandable, because such barriers may make it difficult to investigate a crime, for example. Knowledge of the local language and other patterns of communication opens up the lines between criminal justice personnel and their communities. In fact, their jobs are made easier rather than more difficult when they are able to engage in a meaningful dialog with victims, witnesses, and offenders.

Community Outreach

One means by which criminal justice agencies might gain familiarity with the communication patterns, values, and needs of diverse populations is the establishment of community outreach or liaison programs. Some police departments, for example, attached outreach officers to their community policing strategies. In line with the police–community partnership philosophy, such departments created local substations and encouraged officers to become active in the communities they serve. These initiatives are intended to minimize the cultural and organizational distance between police officers and their publics. This is particularly important in immigrant communities where newcomers are often reluctant to report crime. Law enforcement agencies have sought to overcome the fear and reticence by mounting a friendly presence in such communities. They attempt to overcome language barriers by offering translation services, multilingual emergency/telephone hotlines, and community–criminal justice alliances.

Many such alliances have been formed in cities hosting large non-English speaking populations. Oakland, California's, Asian Advisory Committee on Crime (AACC) is constituted by a coalition of criminal justice officials and Asian community leaders. It has representatives from such local organizations as the Center for Southeast Asian Resettlement, the Buddhist Church of Oakland, and the Lao Iu Mien Culture Association. An innovative Boston project addresses the special fears of senior citizens through its alliance of the police department and the Department of Public Health and senior programs such as the Council of Elders and the Commission on Affairs of the Elderly. The program offers home crime prevention advice as well as strategies intended to respond to street crime. Such collaborative efforts are attempts to break the "us vs. them" mentality so common to criminal justice personnel. The initiatives seek instead to foster trusting and positive relationships between criminal justice agencies and their diverse publics.

Communities are empowered when they feel some connection to criminal justice agencies. They are also empowered when they feel they are allowed some input into the operation of those agencies. Consequently, the institutionalization of civilian review boards goes a long way toward bridging the gap between the two "sides." These are particularly effective—perhaps necessary—where there is a history of criminal justice abuse or corruption. Increasingly, community members are demanding more open and democratic oversight of investigations into police abuse, brutality, or corruption. It is hoped that such scrutiny would have the dual effects of minimizing abuse and maximizing public confidence in the investigative process. Again, the overarching goal is to strengthen the criminal justice–community relationship.

Community Organizing

Many authors in this volume also highlight the importance of communities organizing for themselves. The criminal justice system is not always willing or able to address the specific needs of the diverse communities it serves. Consequently, recent years have seen incredible growth in organizations like the National Asian and Pacific American Legal Consortium (NAPALC) and Gay and Lesbian Advocates and Defenders (GLAD). These organizations are grassroots associations dedicated to civil rights and legal advocacy for their specific communities.

Equally important are umbrella organizations dedicated to monitoring and confronting violence—especially ethnoviolence—directed at minority communities. Perhaps the most effective means of confronting hate crimes, for example, is through the maintenance and support of antiviolence projects that do battle against them—in the courts, in the media, and in public fora. Organizations like the Southern Poverty Law Center (SPLC), the Anti-Defamation League (ADL), and the Prejudice Institute perform an invaluable service for the public in their roles as monitors, litigators, and educators.

Antiviolence projects are also crucial for their activities that respond to hate groups and hate crimes directly. The Prejudice Institute, for example, supplements its research activities with direct technical assistance to communities that have been victimized and with program and policy design. The ADL has been instrumental in shaping public policy responses to hate crime and hate groups. In fact, most states have adopted legislation inspired by the ADL's model hate crime legislation.

These sorts of organizations play a critical educational role as well. Many regularly publish and distribute newsletters to members, police departments, and educational institutions. These resources highlight the threats posed by hate group activities and what can be done to dilute the threats. These regularly scheduled publications are supplemented by more specialized documents, such as the ADL's *Hate Crimes: Policies and Procedures for Law Enforcement Agencies*, Klanwatch's *Ten Ways to Fight Hate*, or the Prejudice Institute's *The Traumatic Effects of Ethnoviolence*.

Such agencies can also be important exercises in coalition building. As Wonders (Chapter 2) argues, differences are overlapping and intersecting. That is, each of us occupies multiple identities; for example, as a woman, and a Latina, and a lawyer. Consequently, each of us has an interest in bridging difference. Moreover, the groups written about in this volume have often experienced a similarity (but not sameness) of oppression. In other words, African Americans, Jews, Asians, homosexuals, the disabled, and others have all suffered various degrees of discrimination and victimization. Consequently, the interethnic alliances necessary to minimize interethnic conflicts rest on practices that empower all minority groups. In other words, such strategies must be "transformative rather than simply effective in reducing tensions or addressing particular problems" (Okazawa-Rey and Wong, 1996:35). Energies must be devoted to the identification and acknowledgment of what these communities share and what they can accomplish together.

Victim Services

Ogawa (1999:4) succinctly describes the quandary facing victims who have come in contact with the criminal justice system: "All victims of crime are susceptible to being mistreated by uncaring, misinformed or antagonistic individuals and/or an overburdened, ponderous and jaded criminal justice system. These are insensitivities or injustices that victims of every race and ethnicity have endured." Our task as criminal justicians, then, is to mitigate the negative effects of difference for not only communities, but also for individual victims of those communities. The experience of victimization is traumatic for all people; however, it can be doubly, triply so for those whose difference leaves them even more vulnerable and at the mercy of a "jaded criminal justice system." Moreover, different communities may, in fact, experience the trauma of victimization in different ways. A recent Office for Victims of Crime report (1998:157) observes that, "Different concepts of suffering and healing influence how victims experience the effects of victimization and the process of recovery. . . . Methods for reaching culturally diverse victims must include resources that are specific to their needs." Morgan and Perry (Chapter 19) explicitly address the issue of victim services. Our purpose here is not to repeat that discussion, but to highlight its significance. The criminal justice response to serving the needs of victims has been varied and broad, ranging from legislation (e.g., Federal Victim and Witness Protection Act of 1982; Victims of Crime Act of 1984) to the establishment of victims' bills of rights, such as that developed by the

International Association of Chiefs of Police in 1983. The most common and well-known approach, however, consists of the array of services known as victim–witness programs (Figure 20.1 summarizes the most common types of services offered in this context).

These services cross the boundaries of difference. They serve the general needs of victims, regardless of what "category of difference" they may occupy. However, those victimized because of their difference, or who experience victimization differently, or who have had negative experiences with the criminal justice system often require culturally sensitive services. The Violence Against Women Act acknowledges this in the context of the specificity of the victimization of women. The act is an exploitable resource for victims, offering legal redress as well as funding for programs, services, and shelters intended to confront violence against women. Hate crime legislation and antiviolence projects similarly offer protections, advocacy, and after-care for victims of ethnoviolence.

Awareness and knowledge of how crimes affect diverse communities allows criminal justice decision makers to implement services that are appropriate to localized dynamics. For example, communities experiencing high rates of victimization of the elderly may implement transportation and escort services, enact legislation criminalizing elder abuse, or create foster-grandparent programs. None of these would be an appropriate response, however, where the paramount problem is violence against gay men and lesbians. In those cases, media and educational campaigns against homophobia or the creation of a local gay and lesbian advocacy panel would be effective interventions.

The key to effective delivery of victim services is sensitivity to the needs of the victim's community. The very meaning and goals of "justice" often differ across communities. Consequently, the same Western-based philosophy of intervention does not work equally well in all communities. Consequently, service providers are encouraged to recognize and value the disparate practices and beliefs that shape cultural, religious, and other responses to victimization. Ogawa (1999:155–156) discusses an illustrative example from Albuquerque, New Mexico. The local chapter of Mothers Against Drunk Driving (MADD) conducts regular victim-impact panels. However, people from different cultures are encouraged to express themselves in very different ways. Navajo members engage in storytelling, and set up family circles intended to share responsibility for "healing." Latinas'/os' reverence for their religion is reflected in panels that integrate the rosary or other rituals. This example demonstrates how a particular program might be adapted and modified to allow for diversity.

Offender Services

Offenders share with victims disproportionate representation from disadvantaged groups—youth, the poor, and ethnic and racial minorities in particular. Many of the authors in this book demonstrate the overrepresentation of minority groups in the "official" crime statistics. Why this is the case is, of course, the focus

Emergency Aid

24-hour crisis hotline
Information on victims' rights and services
Accompaniment to hospital for rape examination
Referrals for short- and long-term counseling
Emergency restraining or protection orders
Information and assistance on recovery of stolen property
Information and assistance on document replacement
Interpreter services

Counseling and Advocacy

Crisis intervention services
Short- and long-term counseling
Access and referrals to self-help support groups
Group counseling

Investigation

Regular updates on status of investigation
Notification of suspect arrest
Basic information on the criminal justice system
Interpreter services
Protection from intimidation and harassment
Notification of pretrial release of accused

Prosecution

Orientation to the criminal justice system
Regular updates on the status of the case
Accompaniment to court
Notification of plea negotiations
Victim consultation in plea decisions
Child-care services

Sentencing

Notification of right to submit a victim impact statement
Victim impact statements
Notice of sentence

Postdisposition

Information/notification of appeal
Notification of parole hearing
Victim impact statement on parole
Notification of violation and revocation of parole/probation
Advance notification of release

FIGURE 20.1   Victim Services

*Adapted from Office of Victim Services, 1998:192–193.

of considerable debate. Is it the result of different rates of offending? Is it a result of how we have defined crime? Is it a result of disparate treatment within the criminal justice system? The answers to these questions are complex. Nonetheless, it is important to bear in mind that the offender population is diverse and, in general, disadvantaged. Thus, criminal justice service providers must also be aware of the particular problems and needs of these communities if they are to serve them appropriately.

It is beyond the scope of this chapter to provide an exhaustive overview of potential interventions that might assist offenders. What is offered is a concise discussion of a multicultural approach to offenders in the context of crime prevention and treatment, and equity in criminal justice processing of offenders.

Prevention and Treatment

In spite of the fact that minorities, and especially minority youth, are overrepresented in the criminal justice system, the vast array of crime prevention and treatment strategies have largely been devoid of a multicultural component that takes into account the social and cultural milieu in which offenders find themselves (Corley and Smitherman, 1994). One of the dangers of this is that, "attempts to offer youths of color (for example) non-delinquent activity alternatives, skill development, power enhancement and/or other delinquency prevention without knowledge of cultural specifics may further alienate diverse group members" (Corley and Smitherman, 1994:282). Successful prevention and treatment strategies will be those that are attuned to the culture and heritage of the individual in question. For example, Newark, New Jersey's, Soul-O-House Drug Abuse Program seeks to prevent and overcome drug abuse through a variety of strategies, including parent meetings, school after-care, and athletics. However, what makes it uniquely appropriate and effective is that "program participants are counseled from an African American perspective within an extended family. . . . Knowledge of one's culture and history and cultural pride are associated with positive self-concept" (Miller and Hess, 1998:549). Integrating culturally specific skills and knowledge helps to reconnect youth, in particular, to their community.

Equally important, however, is the need to (re)connect diverse communities as a means of reducing hate crime in particular. If this divisive form of violence is to be minimized, differences between groups must also be bridged. It is not enough to provide services for the victims of such hostility. The other side of the equation must also be addressed so that the pool of offenders is reduced through treatment and prevention strategies. As a condition of probation, some judges across the country have attempted to prevent secondary offending by helping the offender to see the humanity of the victims' community. This is often accomplished by requiring that the offender engage in community service with an element of the victim community: an anti-Semite might work with the ADL; a gay-basher may work with a local gay and lesbian advocacy group (Levin and McDevitt, 1993).

As a means of preventing hate crime, antiprejudice and antiviolence projects have begun to spring up across the country. Elementary and secondary schools have been the preeminent site of such interventions. The *Teaching Tolerance* project, mentioned earlier in this chapter, provides a valuable model.

Although ethnoviolence is grounded in cultural animosities, most crime finds its roots in the life conditions in which offenders find themselves. Smith (Chapter 6) explicitly addressed the ways in which poverty and the inequitable distribution of resources enhance the likelihood of criminal justice contact for African American males. The same could be said for most minority groups. Consequently, crime prevention necessitates the amelioration of those disparities. Recall Smith's suggestions: "the elimination of childhood poverty; . . . the creation and maintenance of good juvenile education and employment programs; and the provision of employment, education and training to disadvantaged and qualified young adults. These final two suggestions will help give all disadvantaged Americans, including African Americans, an equal opportunity for a decent life free of criminal justice control."

Equity in Criminal Justice Processing of Offenders

Amelioration of disparities in economic and educational opportunities will not necessarily eliminate all disparities in the criminal justice system, because differential treatment is systemic—it is embedded in the criminal justice system itself in the form of differential sentencing for "crack" and white powder cocaine, in differential applications of the death penalty, and in differential access to treatment programs, for example. If the criminal justice system is to dispense justice, then, it must be purged of systemic bias. There is no better way to make this point than to quote at length from Tonry's *Malign Neglect*, the thesis of which is that the criminal justice system should at least do no harm:

> First, think about the foreseeable effects of crime control policy decisions on members of minority groups; when policies are likely to burden members of minority groups disproportionately, reconsider the policies. Second, to guard against racial bias in sentencing and against unjustly severe penalties in general, establish systems of presumptive sentencing guidelines for ordinary cases that set maximum penalties, scaled to the severity of offenders' crimes. Third, recognize the prudence and compassion of our predecessors, and throughout the justice system reestablish presumptions that the least punitive and least restrictive appropriate punishment should be imposed in every case. Fourth, empower judges at sentencing to mitigate sentences for all defendants, irrespective of race, ethnicity, or sex, to take account of individual circumstances. Fifth, celebrate the decent instincts of our predecessors, and reinvest in corrections programs that can help offenders rebuild their lives and enhance their own and their children's

life chances. Sixth, most important of all, be honest; for as long as cynical and disingenuous appeals continue to be made by politicians to the deepest fears and basest instincts of the American people, the prospects of reducing racial disparities in the justice system will remain small. (Tonry, 1995:181)

The movement toward criminal *justice* would include utilizing community programs and treatment, especially for nonviolent offenders (Tonry, 1995). The United States has the highest incarceration rate of all Western industrialized nations, due largely to the harsh sentencing practices associated with drug offenses. The relatively long prison terms associated with these should be replaced by rehabilitation and training efforts. The emphasis would be on providing the skills and incentive necessary to escape the cycle of criminality—life skills, employment skills, financial management skills, and so on. In this way, offenders reenter or remain part of their community armed with enhanced personal resources.

As Tonry suggests, the elimination of harsh sentencing guidelines for drug offenses would have a dramatic impact on incarceration, especially for those disadvantaged by race, class, and gender. The historical consequences of drug enforcement are seen in the enduring overrepresentation of people of color and poor people in juvenile and adult correctional institutions. Prison will not make these offenders less likely to offend; prisons do not focus on educating and training inmates. The vast majority of inmates do not complete college or acquire marketable employment skills, and their years in prison are in many ways a waste of time. In addition, when they leave they carry the disadvantaged status of convicted felon. For many reasons, and on many levels, incarceration is not an effective response to crime. Alternatives that enhance offenders' community integration must be tested. For example, many Native American communities are experiencing considerable success with more traditional peacemaking initiatives. African American communities are strengthening the discipline and self-esteem of at-risk youth with Afro-centric programs. The value of such programs is that they exploit difference in positive ways, rather than constructing it as a pathology or inherent stain.

Criminal Justice/Social Justice

As the preceding discussion implied, *criminal* justice will continue to be elusive in the absence of *social* justice. In a just society, difference would not be the foundation of criminalization, marginalization, or disparate sentencing. On the contrary, difference would be the foundation of inclusion and equity in all areas of social life. This reconstruction—referred to at the outset of this chapter—will require social action both within and outside the criminal justice system. To engage in a positive politics of difference, all of those means of bridging difference discussed throughout this chapter must be embedded in social, economic, and cultural practices that empower rather than disempower diverse groups. This is a principle the

1967 President's Commission on Law Enforcement and the Administration of Justice acknowledged (but was never to realize): "crime flourishes where the conditions of life are the worst." The response, even then, was seen to be "an unremitting national effort for social justice."

Coincident with social action for reform of legislation, victim services, and criminal justice training, as criminal justice practitioners we also have a responsibility to work toward social change that mitigates the negative effects of difference. Access to adequate housing and medical care, education, full-time employment, income support, child care, and other crucial social services should be acknowledged as the inalienable rights of all rather than the privilege of a few. At bottom, "the goal should be to make sure that every child, whoever his or her parents and whatever their race or class, has a reasonable chance to live a satisfying, productive and law-abiding life" (Tonry, 1995:208). Only then can we say that this is a truly just society in which difference is not denigrated.

Recognition of social and economic rights must also be accompanied by efforts to include and integrate difference into our cultural repertoire. Culturally specific programs for victims and offenders were suggested earlier. However, the values and practices of alternate cultures have value beyond the criminal justice system. At the outset, this chapter suggests that we could learn and benefit from the strengths that other cultures might have to offer:

> Black Americans find in their traditional communities, which refer to their members as "brother" and "sister," a sense of solidarity absent from the calculating individualism of white, professional, capitalist society. Feminists find in the traditional female values of nurturing a challenge to a militarist world-view, and lesbians find in their relationships a confrontation with the assumptions of complementary gender roles in sexual relationships. From their experience of a culture tied to the land, American Indians formulate a critique of the instrumental rationality of European culture that results in pollution and environmental destruction. (Young, 1990:205)

Yes, difference matters—and it's a good thing, too!

References

Corley, C. and Smitherman, G. (1994). Juvenile justice: Multicultural issues. In J. Hendricks and B. Byers (Eds.), *Multicultural perspectives in criminal justice and criminology*, 259–290. Springfield, IL: Charles C. Thomas.

Karst, K. (1993). *Law's promise, law's expression*. New Haven, CT: Yale University Press.

Kleg, M. (1993). *Hate prejudice and violence*. Albany, NY: SUNY Press.

Levin, J. and McDevitt, J. (1993). *Hate crimes: The rising tide of bigotry and bloodshed*. New York: Plenum.

Miller, L. and Hess, K. (1998). *The police in the community: Strategies for the 21st century*. Belmont, CA: West/Wadsworth.

Office for Victims of Crime (1998). *New directions from the field: Victims rights and services for the 21st century.* Washington, DC: U.S. Department of Justice.

Ogawa, B. (1999). *Color of justice: Culturally sensitive treatment of minority crime* victims. Boston: Allyn and Bacon.

Okazawa-Rey, M. and Wong, M. (1996). Organizing in communities of color: Addressing inter-ethnic conflicts. *Social Justice, 24(1)*, 24–39.

Skillings, J. H. and Dobbins, J. E. (1991). Racism as a disease: Etiology and treatment implications. *Journal of Counseling and Development, 70*, 206–212.

Tonry, M. (1995). *Malign neglect: Race, crime and punishment in America.* New York: Oxford University Press.

Young, I. M. (1990). *Justice and the politics of difference.* Princeton, NJ: Princeton University Press.

CONTRIBUTORS

Facilitators

Marianne O. Nielsen is an Assistant Professor in the Department of Criminal Justice and the co-editor, with Robert A. Silverman, of *Native Americans, Crime and Justice* (Westview, 1996) and *Aboriginal Peoples and Canadian Criminal Justice* (Butterworths, 1992). Her work on the involvement of indigenous peoples in the criminal justice system has appeared in *Law and Anthropology*, the *Journal of Contemporary Criminal Justice*, the *Canadian Journal of Administrative Sciences*, and *Canadian Ethnic Studies*, as well as in several edited collections.

Barbara Perry is an Assistant Professor in the Department of Criminal Justice whose research interests focus on the implications of difference for social and criminal (in)justice. In particular, she has written and presented papers on the relationship between identity construction and hate crime. Her work appears in such journals as the *Journal of Social and Behavioral Sciences*, *Social Justice,* and *Crime, Law and Social Change*. She is currently completing a book-length monograph that explores hate crime as a means of "doing difference."

The Criminal Justice Collective

Dr. Alexander Alvarez earned his Ph.D. in sociology from the University of New Hampshire in 1991. His main areas of study are minorities, crime, and criminal justice; and collective and interpersonal violence. He has published on Native Americans, Latinos, and African Americans, fear of crime, and sentencing, as well as on justifiable and criminal homicide and genocide. He is currently finishing a book examining genocide from a criminological perspective and working on another book on patterns of American murder.

Cynthia Baroody-Hart is an Associate Professor in the Administration of Justice Department at San Jose State University (SJSU). She received her Ph.D. in 1990 from the State University of New York at Buffalo. Her research has included the study of art worlds in prison, inmate–artist and jailhouse–lawyer networks, as well as gender differences in social support among inmates.

Jeff Ferrell is the author of *Crimes of Style: Urban Graffiti and the Politics of Criminality* (Garland, 1993; Northeastern University Press, 1996); co-editor, with Clinton R. Sanders, of *Cultural Criminology* (Northeastern University Press, 1995); finalist for the American Society of Criminology's 1996 Michael J. Hindelang Award for Most Outstanding Contribution to Criminology; co-editor, with Mark S. Hamm, of *Ethnography at the Edge: Crime, Deviance, and Field Research* (Northeastern University Press, 1998); and co-editor, with Neil Websdale, of *Making Trouble: Cultural Constructions of Crime, Deviance, and Control* (Aldine de Gruyter, 1999). He is the recipient of the 1998 Critical Criminologist of the Year Award presented by the Critical Criminology Division of the American Society of Criminology.

Larry A. Gould is an Associate Professor of Criminal Justice whose career as a police officer spanned nearly two decades, from the early 1970s to the late 1980s. His primary research interests focus on policing, particularly issues of personality development and training. He published two papers in this area, "Can Old Dogs Be Taught New Tricks? Teaching Cultural Diversity to Police Officers" and "Does the Stereotypical Personality Reported for the Male Police Officer Fit that of the Female Police Officer?" Two of his papers have been accepted for publication in the Proceedings of the Commission on Folk Law and Legal Pluralism, "Conflicts in Spirituality of the Navajo Police Officer" and "The Dilemma of the Navajo Police Officer: Traditional versus European Based Means of Social Control."

Karla B. Hackstaff is an Assistant Professor of Sociology at Northern Arizona University. She teaches and conducts research in the areas of gender, divorce and marriage, families, feminisms, and qualitative research methods. She is interested in inequality, justice, and the politics of knowledge construction. Her work has appeared in *Feminism and Psychology* and the anthology *Families, Kinship and Domestic Politics in the United States*, and she has coauthored a chapter on "Divorce and Remarriage" with A. Skolnick. She is currently working on a book on *The Anatomy of the Divorce Culture*.

Carole Mandino is the Director of the Northern Arizona Regional Gerontology Institute and oversees the Senior Companion Program, Foster Grandparent Program, and the Retired and Senior Volunteer Program. She has been involved in providing services to seniors since 1983, and recently graduated with an Ed.D. in Educational Leadership with a focus area of Gerontological. She is also an adjunct faculty member the Department of Sociology and Social Work at Northern Arizona University.

Susanna Maxwell has been Dean of the College of Social and Behavioral Sciences at Northern Arizona University since 1993. She received her Ph.D. in Educational Psychology from the University of Texas at Austin and is a licensed psychologist and a nationally certified school psychologist. As a faculty member, her research interests are in the relationships of anxiety and attributions to academic performance in children. Since becoming dean, she has presented on topics of higher education, focusing on interdisciplinary program development, faculty accountability and productivity, nurturing and developing female and minority administrators, and preparing for tenure.

Marilyn D. McShane is Professor and Chair of the Criminal Justice Department. Her research interests include corrections and criminal justice management. She has coauthored several books in criminological theory, community corrections, and correctional management, as well as co-edited *The Encyclopedia of American Prisons*. She has also participated in a number of federally and state-funded research projects with the National Institute for Corrections, San Bernardino County Probation Department, and the California Department of Corrections, Parole Division.

Raymond J. Michalowski is a Professor of Criminal Justice whose published works span a variety of topics, including criminological theory, law and justice in Cuba, the cultural economy of crime and punishment, environmental crime, and corporate and upper-world deviance. This seemingly eclectic array of topics is part of a career-long attempt to comprehend the ways cultural and political–economic processes shape decisions to treat some harmful behaviors as crimes and some groups of people as more "criminal" than others, while leaving other behaviors and individuals who cause harm untouched by stigma of criminality.

Brian J. Smith is Assistant Professor of Justice Studies in the Department of Sociology and Anthropology at Montana State University–Bozeman. He was Visiting Assistant Professor of Criminal Justice at Northern Arizona University during 1997–1998. He received his Ph.D. in Justice Studies from Arizona State University in 1997. Ongoing research interests include the relationship between law and theories of justice, qualitative methods in the study of crime and justice, and juvenile delinquency and education. His work has appeared in *Free Inquiry in Creative Sociology*.

Phoebe Morgan is an Assistant Professor of Criminal Justice who teaches undergraduate and graduate research methods courses. Her more recent research projects include sexual harassment victimization and complaint, violence on the Internet, and discrimination in the legal profession.

Nancy Wonders is a sociologist and Associate Professor whose teaching and scholarly work focuses on issues of identity, difference, and inequality within the justice system. Her work has appeared in a variety of scholarly journals and books and includes "Determinate Sentencing: A Feminist and Postmodern Story" in *Justice Quarterly*, "Gender and Justice: Feminist Contributions to Criminology" in Gregg Barak's *Varieties of Criminology* (with Susan L. Caulfield), and "Feminist (and) Postmodern Criminology and Social Justice," which is forthcoming in a new reader by Bruce Arrigo.

About the Cover Artist

Kathleen West is a painter and Sho-do calligrapher residing in Flagstaff, Arizona. She studied art at several state colleges and received her degree from Goddard College. Her interest in Sho-do stems from her studies in Akido and Tai Chi. Ms. West has been an art therapist, educator, park ranger, and is a somatic body-worker and trauma incident reduction facilitator. She is currently a graduate student in Criminal Justice at NAU. Her graduate work focuses on restorative justice and crime victim issues.

INDEX